CLYDE RIVER AND OTHER STEAMERS

A

CLYDE RIVER AND OTHER STEAMERS

FOURTH EDITION

CHRISTIAN LESLIE DYCE DUCKWORTH

B.SC., M.I.C.E., A.M.I.N.A.

and

GRAHAM EASTON LANGMUIR

M.A., LL.B.

GLASGOW
BROWN, SON & FERGUSON, LTD.
4-10 DARNLEY STREET, G41 2SD

First Edition	–	1937
Second Edition	–	1946
Third Edition	–	1972
Supplement to		
Third Edition	–	1982
Fourth Edition	–	1990

ISBN 0 85174 421 4 (3rd edition)
ISBN 0 85174 565 2 (4th edition)

© 1990 BROWN, SON & FERGUSON, LTD., GLASGOW, G41 2SD
Printed and made in Great Britain

P.S. "GLEN ROSA", P.S. "LADY ROWENA" and P.S. "IVANHOE" at Arrochar, 1899.

Frank S. Easton

PREFACE

SINCE the publication in 1982 of the *Supplement to the Third Edition* of this book, various changes have occurred in the fleets of Clyde steamers; and as the third edition is now out of print, this would appear to be a suitable time for a completely new edition.

It has been our aim to group the various vessels into separate fleets, the order of the individual ships being determined by the date of acquisition by the particular company. In view of this, a certain amount of repetition has been unavoidable, some of the steamers having changed hands, with the result that they appear in more than one fleet. In order to preserve continuity in each group, however, such vessels have been included in each fleet, unnecessary repetition of information being as far as possible eliminated.

Only ships belonging to fleets in existence when the first edition appeared, or to fleets directly traceable as component parts of those in existence, have been included, apart from those fleets which have since commenced and a few privately-owned ships; as, otherwise, we should have been involved in recording a very large number of vessels, a complete account of which will be found in the late Captain James Williamson's *The Clyde Passenger Steamer*, published in 1904. Further information regarding the privately-owned and other steamers is contained in the late Mr. Andrew McQueen's excellent books, *Clyde River Steamers of the Last Fifty Years* and *Echoes of Old Clyde Paddle-wheels*, published in 1923 and 1924 respectively, and in Mr. Alan J. S. Paterson's *The Golden Years of the Clyde Steamers* (1899–1914) and *The Victorian Summer of the Clyde Steamers*.

The scope of this book is, in the main, on the folowing lines: First the formerly railway-owned Clyde river steamers, and those employed on Loch Lomond, are described, the history of each fleet being traced in each of Chapters I to VIII inclusive. Passing reference to the other Scottish vessels owned by the railway companies also is made, so that the development may be seen of the then recently railway-owned fleets in Scotland. In Chapters IX to XII and XV to XVII the remaining Clyde fleets of the period (including those operating the Stranraer–Larne service) are described. Chapter XIII deals with various privately-owned fleets and Chapter XIV with Loch and Canal steamers, which at one time it had been our intention to include in our previous book, *West Highland Steamers*; but for various reasons that course was not adopted. (As that volume contains an account of the MacBrayne steamers, only those operating regularly on the Clyde at and after the date of its first publication (1935) have been given full treatment in the present book). That, however, with the Chapters in this book dealing with the Caledonian steamers, covers the whole of the fleets since 1969 under the control of the Scottish Transport Group. In Chapter XV, the Clyde cross-river ferry-boats receive attention; and the two remaining Chapters cover the remaining Clyde fleets of the present time. In the Appendices will be found fleet lists giving particulars of the vessels described, so far as this information has been traceable; and a summary of the present fleets.

In the title the word "steamer" appears, as most of the Clyde vessels were of this description when the first edition was written; but readers are asked to note that it is used in its widest sense and is intended to include "motor vessel" as well, there being now very many more units of the latter category in the Clyde and loch fleets than of steam-propelled ships.

Again it has been found desirable to use the suffixes (I), (II), etc., for distinguishing vessels of the same name, and we would point out that where the numeral is placed in brackets it is not to be treated as part of the name. If on the other hand, no brackets are used, the numeral is actually part of the name of the ship.

We acknowledge assistance given to us by many people who have supplied information and who have allowed the use of their photographs for reproduction, to all whom we are most grateful; in particular Capt. J. Addison, Messrs. John Bell, Ian Brodie, Douglas Brown, J. T. A. Brown, Iain Campbell, Robert Cleary, Reg. Dean, Alastair Deayton, Richard Dell (formerly Strathclyde Regional Archivist), Alasdair Fraser, John Innes, Gerald A. Lewis, Iain C. MacArthur, Ian McCrorie, Laurence J. MacDuff, James F. McEwan, Fraser G. MacHaffie, Iain M. MacLeod, Richard Maund, Michael Moss (Glasgow University Archivist), John Nicholson, J. Craig Osborne, H. G. Owen, Alan J. S. Paterson, Stewart Redwood, Donald Robertson, John Robertson, Ian Shannon, J. Aikman Smith, James L. Stevenson, George C. Train, Harry Watson; and the late John M. Beveridge, David Campbell, A. R. Duncan, William C. Galbraith, A. Ernest Glen, Campbell L. Kerr, William Lawson, George A. Lyall, Dorothy M. Lyth, J. B. Macgeorge, Ronald B. McKim, R. B. Parr, Norman Shields, A. Cameron Somerville, George M. Stromier, Leo J. Vogt.

Our books have been criticised for containing little about the captains and crews, and not much about the passengers. For reasons of space it is not possible to deal with these fully, and we have always tried to avoid disproportionate reference to any individuals, since this would be invidious in relation to others equally worthy. It has been our aim to deal with *ships* rather than people, although we are well aware that without people the ships could not exist!

As with the other books of which the late Mr. Duckworth and I were joint authors, the revision of this edition has fallen to me alone.

GRAHAM E. LANGMUIR.

GLASGOW, *25th January, 1990.*

CONTENTS

LIST OF ILLUSTRATIONS

ABBREVIATIONS

P.S.	—	Paddle steamship
S.S.	—	Single-screw steamship
T.S.S.	—	Twin-screw steamship
Tr.S.S.	—	Triple-screw steamship
Qu.S.S.	—	Quintuple screw steamship
D.S.S.	—	Double-screw steamship
D.T.S.S.	—	Double twin-screw steamship
D.T.S.M.V.	—	Double twin-screw motor vessel
D.T.J.S.	—	Double-twin jet steamship
S.C.S.	—	Single chain steamship
D.C.S.	—	Double chain steamship
D.C.M.V.	—	Double chain motor vessel
P.M.V.	—	Paddle motor vessel
M.V.	—	Single-screw motor vessel
T.S.M.V.	—	Twin-screw motor vessel
Tr.S.M.V.	—	Triple-screw motor vessel
D.S.M.V.	—	Double-screw motor vessel
		(i.e., with propeller fore and aft)
Thw. fwd.	—	Thwart-ship propeller(s) forward
Dir. Prop(s)	—	Directional propeller(s) fore and aft
Cont.-pitch Prop(s)	—	Controllable-pitch propellers
Flex. coup.	—	Flexible couplings
Len.	—	Lengthened
L.	—	Lever engines
St.	—	Steeple engines
O.	—	Oscillating engines
D.	—	Diagonal engines
H.	—	Horizontal engines
S.	—	Simple engines (non-compound)
C.	—	Compound engines
T.	—	Triple-expansion engines
N.B.	—	New boilers
N.E.	—	New engines
D.D.	—	Direct drive
S.R.G.	—	Single reduction gearing
S.C.	—	Stroke cycle
D.A.	—	Double-acting
S.A.	—	Single-acting
Cr.	—	Crank(s)

D.E.B.	—	Double-ended boiler(s)
W.T.B.	—	Water-tube boiler(s)
H.B.	—	Haystack boiler(s)
Nav.B.	—	Navy boiler(s)
B.p.	—	Between perpendiculars
O.L.	—	Overall length
"C.C.S."	—	*Clyde and Other Coastal Steamers*
"W.H.S."	—	*West Highland Steamers*
"R.O.S."	—	*Railway and Other Steamers*
"W.C.S."	—	*West Coast Steamers*

CHAPTER 1

THE CALEDONIAN STEAM PACKET CO. LTD.
1889—1922

WHEN the Glasgow, Paisley & Greenock Railway was opened from Glasgow (Bridge Street) to Greenock (Cathcart Street) on 30th March 1841, arrangements had already been made for steamer connexions from Customhouse Quay to Clyde Coast destinations. Since they had not had co-operation from steamboat owners, they hired certain vessels, including the McKellar ships *Warrior* and *Victor* for Largs, and the Dumbarton steamers *Vale of Leven* and *Maid of Leven* for Helensburgh and Rosneath. The *Flambeau*, together with the Bute Steam Packet Company's *Isle of Bute* and *Maid of Bute* also connected with the railway to Dunoon and Rothesay, and the Lochgoil Company's *Lochgoil* took railway passengers on her daily run to Lochgoilhead (also for Inveraray by coach and ferry). The hiring of boats was expensive; and, during the first summer season it was reported that negotiations were in progress with various owners, but if it proved impracticable to obtain services in this way the Directors would recommend the Shareholders to form a company to run their own boats. It was thus that the Railway Steam Packet Company came into being, its first purchase being the *Royal Victoria* in the spring of 1842, for charter to the Railway Company for the Helensburgh route. The *Isle of Bute* and *Maid of Bute* also were purchased. When it was thought that satisfactory arrangements had been made, the *Royal Victoria* was sold, and in 1843 cheap railway fares were introduced to undercut the steamers between Greenock and Glasgow. For the expected increase in traffic two new ships were ordered, these being completed before the end of the summer season in 1844: and they gave such satisfaction that a third vessel was ordered and delivered in 1845, the three being named respectively *Pilot, Pioneer* and *Petrel*. In 1846 the Steam Packet Company disposed of its steamers to Messrs. G. & J. Burns, and an arrangement was made with them to provide connexions with the trains. In 1852-4 a further effort at steamboat-operation was made by the Caledonian Railway Company, which from 1851 had been the owners of the Glasgow, Paisley & Greenock Railway. The steamers employed included *Helensburgh, Dunoon, Gourock, Eva, Flamingo, Glasgow Citizen* and *Loch Lomond*, registered in names of Robert Little and others, partners of Morton, Little & Company. After one season this contract ended, one being then made with Mr. McIntyre, but from 1854 there were no "special" railway steamers.

The Greenock & Wemyss Bay Railway Company, whose line was opened on 15 May, 1865, also tried shipowning through its subsidiary, the Wemyss Bay Steamboat Co. Ltd. Two saloon steamers had been ordered from Messrs. Caird & Co. of Greenock, and a smaller flush-decked one from Messrs. Wingate—*Largs*— which was launched in September, 1864. One of the larger ships was, before completion, sold for blockade-running in the American Civil War, and named *Hattie*; a replacement was ordered, the other original ship and this one becoming *Kyles* and *Bute*, launched respectively in October, 1864 and June, 1865. Pending their completion, various ships were chartered for the services from Wemyss Bay, including *Arran Castle*. A very ambitious programme of sailings was instituted including Ardrishaig in competition with Messrs. Hutcheson's well-established trade there, then maintained in summer by the third *Iona*. The venture was financially unsuccessful, and in January, 1866 the larger ships—*Kyles* and *Bute*—were sold for passenger sailings on the Thames, and the Ardrishaig runs were abandoned. Using the *Largs* together with the smaller *Victory* and *Argyle* purchased in May, 1865 and April, 1866 respectively, the Steamboat Company was able to maintain sailings to Millport and Rothesay. In 1869 the Company was unable to continue in business, and arrangements were made by the Railway Company for Captain J. Gillies and his son-in-law, Captain Alexander Campbell, to take over the *Largs* and *Argyle*, to which Captain Gillies added his own steamer *Venus*, the last survivor on the Clyde of the McKellar fleet. Trading as the Wemyss Bay Steamboat Company these owners had built for them in 1872 the *Lady Gertrude*, purchasing the *Lancelot* in 1874 (when *Venus* was scrapped) and chartering the *Vale of Clwyd* and *Seagull* during 1877, following the loss of *Lady Gertrude* early in the year by stranding at Toward. Two ships were built for the fleet in 1877, *Sheila*, of raised quarter-deck design being exceptionally speedy and intended for the Rothesay route, while *Adela* was a flush-decker intended to take the place of *Lady Gertrude*, whose single diagonal engine she inherited. *Sheila* left the fleet in 1882, on going over to the North British Steam Packet Company, and was succeeded at Wemyss Bay by Messrs. Seath & Steel's *Bonnie Doon*; and in July, 1884 Messrs. Hill & Company's *Arran* was acquired. New construction occurred in 1886 with the building of the steel paddle steamer *Victoria* (for which a second Wemyss Bay Steamboat Co. Ltd. was incorporated). *Argyle* was sold in 1889 to Dundee owners, and the Wemyss Bay services continued to be provided by Messrs. Gillies & Campbell till 1890, the fleet then consisting of *Lancelot, Adela, Arran* and *Victoria*, all disposed of soon after The Caledonian Steam Packet Company Limited had placed its own ships on the services from Wemyss Bay.

The funnel-colouring of the Wemyss Bay fleet was white with black top, though the *Venus* may have retained McKellar colours; and the house-flags were a broad blue pennant with white cross (of St. George's design), flown above a narrow blue pennant. It is thought that Wemyss Bay Steamboat Co. Ltd. of 1865 also used this funnel marking, and possibly the same flags.

In time both the Glasgow, Paisley & Greenock and the Greenock & Wemyss Bay Railway Companies became absorbed by the Caledonian Railway Company, which in contemplation of the opening of its extension to Gourock had made tentative enquiries with a view to having steamer connexions provided by some of the existing private owners. Not being successful in this, and having failed to obtain parliamentary powers to run ships on the Clyde, it formed a subsidiary called The Caledonian Steam Packet Company (Limited), incorporated on 8th May, 1889. The colours adopted for the steamers were:—Funnels buff; hulls dark navy blue (later black) with broad white waterline and green underbody (later Indian red); saloons (outside) pale pink with pale blue panelling; and paddle-boxes white, with very beautiful decorations in gold. The flag was a yellow pennant bearing a red lion rampant, as on the Scottish Royal Standard.

The Greenock & Ayrshire Railway from Johnstone to Greenock, Albert Harbour (afterwards Princes Pier) was opened in 1869, and from 1870 the company obtained certain steamer services by contract. Captain Stewart's *Athole* was running on the Glasgow –Rothesay route till 22nd April, 1870; then from 23rd she began to sail from Rothesay to Greenock; Greenock to Kilmun; back to Greenock; and then back to Rothesay, in connexion with the Greenock & Ayrshire Railway. It was not till 1891, however, that that Company's successors, the Glasgow & South Western Railway Company, began to own its own ships. Its colours were among the prettiest seen on the Clyde: funnels red with black top, hulls grey, and saloon and paddle-boxes white. The flag was a blue pennant, with the G. & S. W. R. emblem comprising the trident, wings and caduceus (corresponding with the three ship names *Neptune, Mercury* and *Minerva*).

On 1st January, 1923 the London, Midland & Scottish Railway Company was formed by the amalgamation of various English Companies and of the Glasgow & South Western Railway Company, the Caledonian Railway Company joining on 1st July. From the beginning of that year, however, the two fleets were treated as one, though it took a little time for the change to be seen in the adoption of uniform colourings. The funnels became dark buff with red band and black top (the colouring previously borne by the Lancashire & Yorkshire Railway Company's East Coast ships, and inherited by them from the Goole Steam Shipping Company), the ex G. & S. W. steamers being so treated by the middle of June, though the Caledonian ships did not change till July. The South Western steamers still retained their grey hulls, and had the red bands on their funnels much broader than those of their Caledonian contemporaries. In the folowing year, however, they were made all alike in respect of breadth of band and the buff became lighter in shade; and black hulls became standard. At the same time the saloons of the Caledonian ships were painted white; and in 1925 the red bands were removed altogether, leaving the funnel-colouring of buff with black top. The red lion emblem from the houseflag was added on the yellow portion of the funnel of *Glen Sannox* in 1964 and of most of the other ships from 1965.

At the end of the 1935 season the L.M.S. and Caledonian fleet was augmented by the addition of the five steamers then owned by Williamson-Buchanan Steamers Ltd. These vessels were then registered in the name of The Caledonian Steam Packet Company, Ltd., but in the following year were transferred to a new company, Williamson-Buchanan Steamers (1936) Ltd., formed on 31st March, 1936. The Williamson-Buchanan steamers retained their white funnels, but their appearance was enhanced by the addition (in the case of the paddle vessels) of two narrow yellow bands near the top of the hull, and the ventilators of all steamers became aluminium colour, with blue interiors, thus corresponding in these respects with the other Clyde steamers of the L.M.S. group. Late in 1939 the funnels of those remaining in civilian service became yellow with black top, and in 1943 the four ships remaining were again transferred to The Caledonian S.P. Co., Ltd.

In September, 1939 the ships in passenger service were painted grey all over: in December the normal funnel-colourings were restored. In 1940 saloons and funnels became "horizon yellow", with black hulls; while from 1941 to 1945 the universal grey again appeared.

In the first place the development of the original Caledonian Steam Packet fleet will be traced, followed by that of the Glasgow & South Western Railway Company, both to the end of 1922. Next will be considered the combined fleet of the Caledonian S.P. Co. and L.M. & S. Railway Company from 1923 to 1935, followed by the Williamson-Buchanan and Turbine Steamers' history, to the latter year. Thereafter will be described the vessels added from 1936 to the end of 1947, followed by those of the London & North Eastern Railway Company and under the nationalised undertaking of the British Transport Commission of which the Steam Packet Company from 1948 became a subsidiary. The Transport Act of 1968 severed the connexion between that company and the railways with effect from 1st January 1969, after an association lasting just five months less than 80 years. The act provided that the parts of the British Railways undertaking concerned with "the provision of shipping services in Scotland by The Caledonian Steam Packet Company Limited and with the provision by the board of the ferry service to and from Kyle of Lochalsh and Kyleakin" should go to the Scottish Transport Group, to which also were transferred the British Railways piers at Craigendoran, Fairlie, Gourock, Largs, Wemyss Bay and Balloch.

* * * * * *

In December, 1888 Captain Campbell's two remaining Kilmun steamers, *Meg Merrilies* and *Madge Wildfire*, were purchased by the Caledonian Company, together with the goodwill of the Glasgow–Kilmun trade. (On account of this latter acquisition, The Caledonian Steam Packet Company, Ltd. for a number of years ran a steamer from Kilmun to Glasgow, but this was discontinued about 1908). From January to the end of May, 1889 the steamers were in names of three directors of the Caledonian Railway Company as nominees, being transferred on 1st June to the ownership of the Steam Packet Company. Captain James Williamson became Manager. At the same date through services by rail and ship *via* Gourock were inaugurated, the centenary of this having been marked on 1st June, 1989.

P.S. *Meg Merrilies*.   This steamer had been built for the North British Steam Packet Company in 1883, as explained in Chapter VI and subsequently came into the fleet of Captain Robert Campbell of Kilmun. While under his ownership an accident occurred which necessitated re-boilering; and *Meg Merrilies* re-appeared in 1888 with only one funnel. At the same time a surface condenser was fitted, and a dining-saloon was made on the lower deck aft. In 1893 she was reboilered by Barclay, Curle & Co., with a haystack of higher working pressure (140 lb.) than the previous one, thus requiring a reducing valve to bring the pressure to that for which the engines were designed (50 lb.), two safety-valves with associated steampipes being then provided (one forward and one aft of the funnel), each having at the base a high casing to cover the safety-valves. In 1897–8 the machinery was compounded by A. & J. Inglis and she received the second-hand navy boilers from *Marchioness of Lorne* but it would seem that this arrangement may not have been satisfactory, for she was in April, 1898 again reboilered, this time with two Haythorn water-tube boilers, (180 lb.). Again two steampipes were required, the aft one being of smaller diameter than the other, indicating an even higher boiler pressure, the forward one remaining as before, for escaping steam of cylinder pressure (of greater volume than the high-pressure boiler steam, according to Boyle's Law). No casings were then provided, the safety-valves being below promenade-deck level. Later she was given a deck saloon forward. In 1900 she was again re-boilered, after which she had a steam-pipe only forward of the funnel.

Meg Merrilies was employed principally on the run from Gourock to the Holy Loch, which at that time did not include Kilcreggan, Cove and Blairmore—these being served by another steamer. She was sold in July, 1902 to the Leopoldina Railway Company for service in the harbour of Rio de Janeiro, and re-named *Maua*, being broken up about 1922.

P.S. *Madge Wildfire*.   The other acquisition of 1888 had been built by Messrs. S. McKnight & Co., of Ayr, for the Campbell Kilmun fleet. She was smaller than *Meg Merrilies*, and in 1891 received a new boiler and new engines, her original Hutson & Corbett single diagonal being superseded by a compound tandem single crank engine such as had been fitted into *Caledonia* in 1889. This type was most economical in working, and *Madge Wildfire* remained for quite a considerable time in the Caledonian fleet. In 1903 her bridge was placed forward of the funnel: and at the same time the fan-vents of the paddle-boxes were superseded by horizontal gratings; and she was again re-boilered.

The usual run of *Madge Wildfire* was from Gourock to Kilcreggan, Cove and Blairmore, latterly including also the Holy Loch. She was also on the Largs and Millport route for a time. Sold to A. W. Cameron, Dumbarton, 11th April, 1911 for excursion work from Glasgow, she was in March, 1913 sold to Buchanan Steamers, Ltd., being re-named *Isle of Skye*. (*See* Chapter IV).

P.S. *Caledonia* (I).   The first steamer built for The Caledonian Steam Packet Company, Ltd., was appropriately named *Caledonia*, and appeared from the yard of Messrs. John Reid & Co., then of Port Glasgow, in June, 1889 having been launched on 7th May in that year. She was the first regular Clyde steamer in which compound machinery was fitted, this consisting of two cylinders placed tandem-wise, driving one crank by means of a common piston-rod. Two navy boilers were installed, with forced draught.

In 1893 the experiment was made of fitting this steamer for the burning of oil fuel, but, though successful, the price of oil rendered its use uneconomic and she was re-converted to a coal-burner. In 1903 she was re-boilered and her bridge was placed forward of the funnel; and about 1913 a deck-house was added over the saloon companion-way.

In her early days *Caledonia* was on the Rothesay and Millport routes, but latterly she was very well known as the Holy Loch steamer, sailing from Gourock to Kilcreggan, Cove, Blairmore, Strone, Ardnadam, Kilmun, Hunter's Quay, Kirn and Dunoon— the services of *Meg Merrilies* and *Madge Wildfire* having been amalamated by that time—and a call being made (from 1908) at Princes Pier, to provide a service for the G. & S. W. Railway to the Holy Loch.

Caledonia was engaged in mine-sweeping on the English Channel, with Spithead as her base and for a time carried troops between Le Havre and Paris, along with *Isle of Arran*, her war service extending from April, 1917 till April, 1919. After reconditioning she resumed her Clyde sailings in November 1919, principally on the Holy Loch run from Prince's Pier and Gourock. Her end came at the close of 1933, her last run being celebrated with a farewell dance on board, at Kilmun. She was sold to Messrs. T. W. Ward, Ltd., and broken up at Barrow.

P.S. *Galatea.* This was a very handsome two-funnelled steamer, much larger than *Caledonia*, fitted with a compound diagonal engine of the type that, until the First War, was almost standard for Clyde steamers. It was too powerful an engine for the hull, however, on account of which *Galatea* could not be driven as she might otherwise have been; and the inability to get the maximum speed from her may have been one of the reasons for her comparatively early disposal. Sold in 1906 to Soc. Anon. di Navigazione "Tirrenia", Genoa, she was broken up at Palermo in 1913.

P.S. *Marchioness of Breadalbane.* It was from 1st May, 1890 that Wemyss Bay trains began to run into Glasgow Central station instead of terminating at Bridge Street. Captain Alexander Campbell gave notice of termination of his services at the end of April, his complaint being that he did not receive a large enough proportion of through fares and that the Gourock services were diverting much traffic from the Wemyss Bay route. The Caledonian Company had anticipated something of this nature, and had under construction, by Messrs. John Reid & Co., two steamers, practically sister-ships of *Caledonia*, the only difference being that in the new vessels the bridge was placed forward of the funnel, whereas the older one originally had hers between the paddle-boxes. The first of these new vessels was *Marchioness of Breadalbane*, launched on 15th April, 1890, which along with her sister-ship enabled the services from Wemyss Bay to be continued without interruption. After having been engaged in mine-sweeping, first at Troon and later on the English Channel with Portsmouth as her base, she re-appeared on the Clyde in June, 1919 and till October in that year had black paddle-boxes. Until 1933 she was generally stationed at Wemyss Bay, and was usually on the Millport run. With the disposal of *Caledonia* at the end of that year, however, she was transferred to Gourock for the Holy Loch run, and this she performed for about one year. Like *Caledonia* she was an all-the-year-round boat, and so these steamers' long service is particularly creditable.

Sold to Clyde shipbreakers in 1935, she was re-sold by them to Redcliffe Shipping Co. Ltd., Hull, for excursion work from Yarmouth, Lowestoft and Newcastle. In April, 1937 she was sold to German shipbreakers.

P.S. *Marchioness of Bute*. This was the sister-ship of the foregoing and she also operated principally from Wemyss Bay. It is understood that great difficulty was experienced in distinguishing between the two, though experts were able to do this by studying the spacing of the ventilators and rake of the funnel—which in the case of *Marchioness of Bute* was more nearly perpendicular, particularly in her later years on the Clyde. Following the agreement between the Caledonian and Glasgow & South Western Railway Companies in 1908 to avoid wasteful competition, *Marchioness of Bute* became redundant and was sold in July to D. & J. Nicol for excursions on the River and Firth of Tay. Stationed at Portsmouth for mine-sweeping during the war, she became a hospital carrier and visited Archangel. Thereafter she was laid up at Inverkeithing, and broken up in 1923.

P.S. *Duchess of Hamilton* (I). It was in 1890 also that one of the best known of the Caledonian steamers was built—the first *Duchess of Hamilton*—which was placed on the Ardrossan–Arran run in connexion with the newly opened Lanarkshire & Ayrshire Railway, a concern closely associated with and worked by the Caledonian Railway Company. As explained in Chapter II, it was the competition of this splendid steamer that led to the building of the first *Glen Sannox*, and as a result the Arran ports enjoyed a wonderfully fine service for some time, until the rival owners came to a working arrangement.

Duchess of Hamilton was the first Clyde steamer to have the promenade-deck extended to the bow, this being a feature of most of those subsequently built. Her first-class saloon, which extended the full width of the ship, was magnificently furnished, and in the words of the late Mr. McQueen, "The symmetry and balance of her whole design rendered her a joy to look upon". Two-cylinder compound diagonal machinery was fitted by her builders' associate, Denny & Co. of Dumbarton.

Superseded on the Arran run by *Duchess of Argyll* in 1906, *Duchess of Hamilton* was then re-boilered by Clyde S. B. & E. Co., Ltd., Port Glasgow, and thereafter was used for excursion work and railway connexions from Gourock, until she entered Admiralty service in February, 1915. She was employed first as a transport ship, but it was not long till she became a mine-sweeper; and it was while engaged in the latter capacity in the North Sea that she was sunk through striking a mine off Harwich on 29th November, 1915.

P.S. *Marchioness of Lorne* (I). To take the place of *Duchess of Hamilton* on the Arran run in winter, and for various services during the summer, the first *Marchioness of Lorne* was launched by Messrs. Russell & Co., Port Glasgow, on 25th April, 1891. She was very much like the previous *Marchionesses*, but had her promenade-deck carried forward to the bow. The machinery was of an unusual type, being triple expansion, with four cylinders and two cranks. One H.P. and the I.P. cylinder worked one piston-rod and crank, while the other H.P. cylinder and the L.P. drove the second crank. Steam was supplied by two navy type boilers.

After returning from mine-sweeping work on the Eastern Mediterranean, with Malta (and for a time, Port Said) as her base, *Marchioness of Lorne* lay in Bowling Harbour for a few years, gradually becoming more and more rusty: being not worth re-conditioning, she was sold towards the end of 1923 and was broken up at Dumbarton in December of that year. She was the first Clyde steamer to have a deckhouse over the saloon companion-way.

P.S. *Duchess of Rothesay*. The first Caledonian steamer to be built at Clydebank was *Duchess of Rothesay*, which was launched on 20th April, 1895 from Messrs. J. & G. Thomson's yard. Rather like *Duchess of Hamilton* in design she was, however, smaller, but of even more beautiful appearance. She entered service first as an additional steamer on the Ardrossan–Arran route for a short period at the end of May, 1895 thereafter on the Rothesay station from Gourock or Wemyss Bay. After *Ivanhoe* had entered the Caledonian fleet, *Duchess of Rothesay* took her place and sailed from Gourock to Arran via Kyles of Bute, also maintaining railway connexions in the upper Firth; just before going on war service in 1915 she was sailing from Wemyss Bay to Rothesay. *Duchess of Rothesay* in pre-1914 days was known as the "cock of the walk" and carried at her masthead a small weather-cock. While mine-sweeping she towed the disabled Zeppelin L.15 into Margate; and she also assisted in the salving of no fewer than 15 ships. During the latter part of the First War she was named *Duke of Rothesay*. She swept up more than 500 mines, and though she came through the ordeal of war service unscathed, she was rather unfortunate just before being reconditioned. While moored at Merklands Wharf she sank on 1st June, 1919 on account of some carelessness, but was raised on 28th July in that year and resumed her place in the fleet in 1920. She was then employed principally on the run from Greenock and Gourock to Rothesay and the Kyles of Bute; also certain days during 1939 on her old route to Arran *via* the Kyles.

The machinery of this steamer was of the orthodox compound diagonal type, with two cylinders and two cranks, taking steam from a double-ended boiler, and at the end of 1935 she attained a speed of about 17½ knots on trial, a very creditable performance after 40 years' service, since her original trial speed was 17·77 knots.

In October, 1939 she entered a second period of war service, as a mine-sweeper, first on the Clyde, then, early in 1940, at Dover. After being laid up for a time at Portsmouth, she was re-commissioned and took the place of *Waverley* in the 12th Flotilla. From April, 1942, she was an accommodation ship at Brightlingsea, and in October, 1945 was beached there, prior to being sold on 9th August, 1946 to N. V. Machinehandel en Scheepslooperij "De Koophandel", Nieuw Lekkerkland, Holland, for scrapping.

P.S. *Ivanhoe*.   Built for the Frith of Clyde S. P. Co. Ltd., in 1880, this ship was run by them as a "teetotal boat", no alcoholic liquor being sold on board. She became very well known on the Arran *via* Kyles of Bute run, on which she remained for about 14 years. In February, 1894 she was chartered for service on the Manchester Ship Canal; but, as passenger traffic on the canal did not prove remunerative, she returned to the Clyde and in May, 1897 was taken over by The Caledonian Steam Packet Company, Ltd.

She was a fine two-funnelled steamer, with two-cylindered single crank diagonal oscillating engines, and was used by the Steam Packet Company on the "Round the Lochs", etc., run from Gourock, as well as to Rothesay, Kyles of Bute, etc.

In the spring of 1911 *Ivanhoe* was sold to a private company with a name very like that of her first owners—the Firth of Clyde Steam Packet Company, Ltd.—and she then had white funnels, later with narrow black rims. In 1914 (*via* David MacBrayne Ltd.) she came into the fleet of Turbine Steamers, Ltd. and then had white funnels with normal black tops. In this condition she performed the Lochgoil passenger service (See Chapter IV).

As she was not requisitioned for war work, *Ivanhoe* was a useful boat on the Firth, and sailed for the The Caledonian Steam Packet Company, Ltd. from 1915 on charter, having yellow funnels but retaining her black paddle-boxes. Her route at first was from Wemyss Bay to Rothesay, etc., but about 1919 she was stationed at

Gourock for the Holy Loch and Dunoon run. She did not sail again for her owners, but was scrapped at Dumbarton.

P.S. *Duchess of Montrose* (I).

Another product of the Clydebank yard appeared in 1902, this being the first *Duchess of Montrose*. She was similar to *Duchess of Rothesay*, though smaller, and was fitted with triple expansion 4-cylinder two-crank engines, like those of the *Marchioness of Lorne*. Her trial speed was 16·1 knots. When new, *Duchess of Montrose* was stationed at Ayr for excursions, but at a later date was engaged in general railway runs. She was requisitioned for trooping, and after a period of this was mine-sweeping off the Belgian coast in preparation for a British naval raid, when she was lost through striking a mine off Gravelines, on 18th March, 1917. While in the Admiralty service she was known as H.M.S. *Montrose*.

P.S. *Duchess of Fife*.

Duchess of Fife was a quasi sister-ship to *Duchess of Montrose* and was the first steamer built for Clyde service by The Fairfield Shipbuilding & Engineering Co., Ltd., Govan. She also had 4-cylinder triple expansion two-crank machinery, and was one of the most successful steamers on the river. On trial on 5th June, 1903, a speed of 17·55 knots was attained, though the contract speed was a mean of 16 knots on two runs from Cloch to Cumbrae, and altogether *Duchess of Fife* proved herself a most useful boat. She was in commission all the year round.

During the First World War as H.M.S. *Duchess*, she was employed as a mine-sweeper, based for a time at Grimsby and later at Dover. In the Second World War (under her own name) she again became a mine-sweeper, and made four trips to Dunkirk. In 1941 she was stationed at Port Edgar on the Forth as a training ship for mine-sweeping personnel. She survived to return to the Clyde in 1945 and, after very extensive reconditioning by Messrs. Lamont at Port Glasgow, she resumed her normal sailings in the summer of 1946. Her first route was that to the Holy Loch, but she was later engaged in sailings from Princes Pier and Gourock to Kyles of Bute, etc., and also on the Millport station. Rendered redundant on the commissioning of the car ferries and "Maids", she was laid up in Albert Harbour, Greenock, after her last sailing on 6th June, 1953, and sold on 12th September, arriving at Port Glasgow on 15th to be broken up by Smith & Houston, Ltd.

Tr.S.S. *Duchess of Argyll*.

The first turbine steamer for the Caledonian Company appeared in 1906, and was placed on the Arran run from Ardrossan. Her trial speed was 21·65 knots, which placed her among the fastest of the Clyde steamers. Originally open forward like the Caledonian paddle vessels, she was in March, 1910 plated, with port-holes instead of square windows, for use on the Stranraer run on which she deputised from time to time, notably in 1910 and 1911. (She had been laid up in 1908 following the agreement between the two railway companies to have only one Ardrossan–Arran steamer).

Her war service was as a transport from 11th February, 1915 to 27th April, 1919; and during that period she made 655 trips, covering a total nautical mileage of 71,624. She went to the rescue of the transport *Archangel*, which had been in collision with a destroyer; and on another occasion she succeeded in towing the transport steamer *Queen-Empress* (of the Williamson fleet) into Boulogne after the latter had been in collision with an escorting destroyer.

On her return to the Clyde, *Duchess of Argyll* was placed, in 1919, on the Arran run *via* Kyles of Bute, and became extremely popular on this route, on which she remained till 1935. In 1936 she was transferred to the Inveraray station in connexion with the Loch Eck tour on Mondays, Wednesdays and Fridays. (This tour was then restricted to four days per week, the service to Inveraray on Thursdays being provided by *Duchess of Montrose*). On Tuesdays, Thursdays and Saturdays *Duchess of Argyll* sailed to Campbeltown from Gourock *via* Dunoon and Fairlie, calling at Wemyss Bay on return, and so took the places of both *King George V and Queen Alexandra*, formerly on the Inveraray and Campbeltown runs respectively.

In the Second World War *Duchess of Argyll* remained on the Clyde, at first on passenger service between Gourock and Dunoon, etc., and latterly as a tender to troopships at Greenock and Gourock. Thereafter she was on the principal services to the Kyles of Bute from Princes Pier and Gourock till sold on 25th February, 1952 to the Admiralty for use for experimental purposes with the Underwater Detection Establishment at Portland. Without funnels or mast she was, however, still recognisable. She was withdrawn at Easter, 1969, and the following October was sold, being towed in January, 1970 to Newhaven for scrap.

*   *   *   *   *   *

As will be observed from the above, all the Caledonian Clyde steamers remaining in 1915 went on war service. With a view to keeping up certain sailings (though considerably reduced), various steamers were chartered from other owners, among them being *Ivanhoe*, already mentioned. In addition *Iona, Chevalier* and *Fusilier* were chartered from David MacBrayne, Ltd., and *Benmore* from Messrs. John Williamson & Co. These chartered steamers (except *Chevalier*) were given the usual Caledonian buff funnels, but *Iona* did not retain them for long, reverting to her better-known MacBrayne colours in a short time. During the coal strike of 1919 some Caledonian steamers sailed from Broomielaw, Glasgow to take the place of trains; and some services were given by MacBrayne's *Cygnet*, chartered by Clyde Cargo Steamers Ltd.

No new steamers were built for The Caledonian Steam Packet Co., Ltd. until after it had passed under L.M.S. control, though it was increased in 1922 by the acquisition of one steamer on Loch Awe and three on Loch Tay.

S.S. *Countess of Breadalbane* (I).   This single-screw steamer was built at Paisley in 1882 for service on Loch Awe, and as mentioned in Chapter XIV, was taken over from the Lochawe Hotel Co., Ltd. by The Caledonian Steam Packet Co., Ltd. in 1922. Superseded by the motor vessel of the same name in 1936, she was broken up near Loch Awe pier.

LOCH TAY STEAMBOAT COMPANY, LTD.

It was in 1922, also, that the Loch Tay steamers were taken over by the Caledonian Company. This concern dated from 1882, the Earl of Breadalbane of that time having been responsible for its formation and for the institution of steamer services on Loch Tay, with two steamers then built. The passenger steamers' funnels were buff with black top, while black was the original colour of those of the cargo vessels.

The pattern of sailings on Loch Tay was very similar to that on Loch Awe, with through tour passengers from a pier at each end of the loch, and intermediate calling points. The piers were, from east to west, Kenmore, Fearnan, Ardtalnaig, Ardeonaig, Lawers and Killin; and at one time the loch boasted two fine passenger vessels, two cargo steamers with more limited passenger accommodation and a small puffer—a total of five, where now there is none.

S.S. *Lady of the Lake*.   This was one of the original Loch Tay steamers, built of iron, and rather like the first *Countess of Breadalbane*. On 20th May, 1921 it was announced that the services on the loch would be suspended. The steamers, however, passed into the Caledonian fleet in 1922. After the improvement of road services the *Lady of the Lake* was withdrawn in 1929, and broken up at Kenmore.

S.S. *Sybilla*.   The other Loch Tay steamer of 1882 was *Sybilla*, which was intended principally for cargo carrying, though she conveyed some passengers in addition. Smaller than *Lady of the Lake*, she was built of oak grown on the Breadalbane estates and had a derrick on the mast. Her machinery was placed aft of amidships, and near the stern there was a small cabin. Like the other ship, she passed to the Caledonian Company in 1922 and was broken up at Kenmore in 1929.

S.S. *Magpie*.   This was a small cargo steamer of the "puffer" type, built of wood, also in 1882, and was sunk during a storm.

S.S. *Carlotta*.   Like *Sybilla, Carlotta* was built of wood, and was launched at Acharn by Mrs. Sinclair of Kenmore on 19th June, 1883, having been designed by G. L. Watson. The ship was taken over by The Caledonian Steam Packet Co., Ltd., in 1922. She was shortly afterwards, however, scrapped, as road transport on Lochtayside had made it unnecessary to have so many vessels on the loch. She was at times used by the Marquis of Breadalbane as a yacht.

T.S.S. *Queen of the Lake*.   Latterly this was the only steamer remaining on Loch Tay. She was built by Ailsa Shipbuilding Co., Ltd., at Troon and transported in sections by rail to Killin. There the sections were loaded on to a barge, which was towed by *Sybilla* to Kenmore, near which (àt Dalerb) the steamer was re-assembled and launched on 19th June, 1907, running her trials on 13th August.

Queen of the Lake was a beautiful little vessel, her fittings being of the same high standard as those of the Clyde steamers; and she was capable of a speed of 8 knots, which was sufficient for the requirements of the loch traffic.

The propellers of *Queen of the Lake* were four-bladed; and, as she was a vessel of very shallow draught, a large quantity of water was churned up as she proceeded. The machinery consisted of two sets of two-cylindered compound engines.

Two double trips were made each day in summer, and in addition evening cruises were run from Kenmore in connexion with buses from Struan, Pitlochry, Blair Atholl, Aberfeldy, etc. The steamer was also frequently chartered for evening excursions by private parties from various districts in Perthshire. From the commencement of the Second World War in 1939, *Queen of the Lake* was hauled out of the water, on the slip at Kenmore (where she also spent her winters). She was sold on 17th May, 1950, to J. A. A. White, North Queensferry, and broken up where she lay.

CHAPTER II

GLASGOW & SOUTH WESTERN RAILWAY COMPANY
1891-1922

ON deciding to run its own steamers, and having obtained the necessary parliamentary powers to do so, this Company purchased from Captain Alexander Williamson (Senior) his four steamers in the autumn of 1891 and commenced to operate its own services from Greenock, Princes Pier (of which the main part afterwards became the Container Terminal).

P.S. *Sultan.* Of these original South Western steamers the oldest and smallest was *Sultan,* which, built in 1861 for the Kilmun trade, had spent the whole of her life (except the first season) in the fleet of Captain Williamson, being employed by him in the Rothesay and Kyles of Bute service. She was a handy little flush-decked steamer, but with the coming of the larger and newer vessels she became superflous, and was the first of the original boats to be disposed of by the Railway Company, who sold her to Captain John Williamson, late in 1891. (*See* Chapter IV).

P.S. *Sultana.* Like *Sultan, Sultana* had been all her days in the Kyles of Bute trade before becoming the property of the Railway Company, for whom she ran principally to the Holy Loch.

Slightly larger than *Sultan,* she had no equals in the matter of manoeuvring at piers, and Mr. McQueen tells us that she holds the record for the run from Princes Pier to Rothesay, with the usual stops, the time taken being 57 minutes from pier to pier. Of the flush-decked type, she had a powerful single diagonal engine, and was one of the most successful steamers of her day. By the time of her joining the railway fleet a short saloon had been added on the after deck and a new boiler, fitted in 1886, was re-tubed in 1892. She was sold in March, 1897 to Captain John Williamson. (*See* Chapter IV).

P.S. *Marquis of Bute.* The third steamer purchased from Captain Williamson was *Marquis of Bute*, which had been built by Messrs. Barclay, Curle & Co. in 1868 for Messrs. A. & T. McLean; she had been acquired by Captain Williamson in 1889. She remained with the Railway Company for a number of years, and

15

was employed largely on the Fairlie-Millport service. Somewhat similar in design to *Sultana,* she also had a good turn of speed having attained 16·33 knots on trial; and like her, too, had received a small deck saloon before coming under the Railway Company's flag. Sold in May, 1904 to Captain John Williamson, she was sent to Belfast Lough on charter for two seasons. In 1904 she was registered at Newry under the name J. Gordon, and was sold by him in February, 1907, to David Monk, Preston, being withdrawn from registration in December that year and broken up in 1908.

P.S. *Viceroy*. Originally of raised quarter-deck design, *Viceroy* was converted into a saloon steamer shortly before she entered the fleet of the Glasgow & South Western Company. At the same time she was lengthened from 194 to 208 feet, being cut in two places, a new boiler and surface condenser having been fitted in 1888. She remained with the Company for 16 years. Sold to Mersey Trading Co., Ltd. in June, 1907, and re-named *Rhos Colwyn*, she was broken up in 1911.

P.S. *Chancellor*. In addition to the four Williamson steamers purchased in 1891, two other steamers were acquired in that year by the Glasgow & South Western Railway Company. Of these, *Chancellor*, bought from the Lochgoil & Lochlong Steamboat Company Ltd., was retained by her new owners in the service in which she was already employed, *videlicet* that to Arrochar, but operating from Princes Pier.

In the year following her acquisition by the Railway Company, *Chancellor* received a new boiler and engines, the latter being of the compound diagonal pattern, supplied by Messrs. Blackwood & Gordon, Port Glasgow, in place of her original non-compound double diagonal machinery. She was lighted by acetylene gas.

She was sold in April 1901, to La Herculina Ferrolana, Ferrol, Spain, and renamed *Commercio,* being after a number of years converted into a barge.

P.S. *Scotia*. This steamer was owned by Captain Buchanan, and employed by him in the Ardrossan-Arran service, in connexion with the G. & S. W. Railway. In 1891 the Railway Company took over the working of the service, and purchased *Scotia*. She did not remain long with her new owners, however, as the magnificent *Glen Sannox* was built to take her place in the year following her acquisition.

Sold to Edwards, Robertson & Co., Cardiff, in April, 1893, and passing in 1899 to P. & A. Campbell, Ltd., Bristol, she was sold by them to Societa Industriale e Commerciale Italiana, Naples, and renamed *Principessa Mafalda* (later *Epomeo*), being sunk by mine in the Gulf of Sorrento about 1914.

P.S. *Neptune*. To compete with the Caledonian Steam Packet Company's Gourock steamers, two new vessels were built for service from Princes Pier for the Glasgow & South Western Railway Company in 1892 by Messrs. Napier, Shanks & Bell, whose yard was then at Yoker, on the site now occupied by Rothesay Dock. These were *Neptune* and *Mercury,* and as built they were identical. They were larger and faster than their Caledonian competitors, and so secured for their owners some share in the coast traffic.

The first of the new steamers to appear was *Neptune,* which was launched on 10th March, 1892, and was commissioned at the beginning of April in that year. Her first service was from Ardrossan to Arran, in succession to *Scotia.* She was soon, however, relieved of that duty by *Glen Sannox* and then joined her sister ship, on the Rothesay and Kyles of Bute run from Princes Pier. With the advent of the later steamers, however, she began to be used for excursion work; and among other popular day trips was one to Stranraer, one day per week during summer. For this service plating was introduced on the forward paddle-wings, and later the forward end of her fore-saloon was plated and port-holes provided, instead of the original square windows, so that latterly she had certain features by which she could be distinguished from *Mercury.*

Both steamers were fitted with funnels of increased diameter, *Neptune* for 1913, and her sister in 1914; and at the same times deck-houses were erected over the saloon companion-ways, the steerage entrances also being covered.

Neptune became a mine-sweeper with her base at Dover, and was named *Nepaulin.* Unfortunately she was blown up on 20th April, 1917 while engaged in Admiralty service.

P.S. *Glen Sannox* (I). To provide a suitable competitor for the Caledonian Company's *Duchess of Hamilton* on the Ardrossan-Arran service, *Glen Sannox* was built by Messrs. J. & G. Thomson of Clydebank. One of the most beautiful of Clyde steamers, she was slightly faster than her rival (her trial speed being 19·23 knots), and so she regained for the Glasgow & South Western Railway Company some of the traffic it had lost on the appearance of *Duchess of Hamilton.* She was, however, very expensive to run, and that was probably the principal reason for her comparatively early withdrawal.

Glen Sannox spent practically the whole of her life on the Ardrossan-Arran run, on which she first appeared in May, 1892, and was off it only for a few odd seasons in pre-war days when it was the turn of The Caledonian Steam Packet Company, Ltd., to provide the steamer for this service, under the arrangement which had been made in 1908 between the companies. She was absent also during the First War when taken over by the Admiralty for trooping between Southampton and Havre, but not for long, being shortly returned as unsuitable. She was transferred to the London Midland & Scottish Railway Company in 1923, and two years later was sold to Smith & Co., and broken up at Port Glasgow.

The magnificent model of the *Glen Sannox* formerly at Kelvingrove is again on public display, now in the new Transport Museum in part of the Kelvin Hall building. This model shows the promenade deck extended to the stern, and companion-way deckhouses fore and aft; but, so far as is known, the ship never had these features.

P.S. *Mercury* (I). The third steamer of 1892 was *Mercury*, sister ship of *Neptune*, and she took her place in the fleet towards the end of May, having been launched on 18th April. She attained a speed of 18·44 knots on trial, and was employed principally on the Kyles of Bute run while owned by the Glasgow & South Western Company.

During the First World War *Mercury* was requisitioned for minesweeping, and was stationed at Harwich. Off the East Coast of England she had her stern blown off by a mine, but was fortunately able to keep afloat; and, after being repaired, was at sea again only for one day when she struck another mine and this time lost her bow. She was again repaired, and after re-conditioning rejoined the Glasgow and South Western fleet in 1920. With the rest of the vessels of this fleet then remaining she was transferred in 1923 to the L. M. & S. Railway Company, and sailed for them on various runs from Greenock, Gourock and Weymss Bay till the end of 1933, when she was withdrawn and sold in December to T. W. Ward, Ltd. and broken up at Barrow. Her place in the fleet was then taken by a new paddle-steamer of the same name.

P.S. *Minerva*. We have now to record another pair of sisterships, *Minerva* and *Glen Rosa*, which appeared in 1893. These were smaller than the earlier pair, and of a slightly heavier build than the average Clyde steamer, being intended for winter work on the Arran run in addition to summer service elsewhere on the Clyde estuary.

Minerva and *Glen Rosa* were of somewhat unusual design, having a short forecastle formed by a deck on the level of the mainrail, a feature that has not been repeated in any later Clyde steamer. It is of interest to note, however, that a third steamer of the same design was built at the same time for the Belfast & County Down Railway Company, originally named *Slieve Donard*, but better known later in the fleet of P. & A. Campbell, Ltd. as *Albion*. It was this ship that was really the sister of *Glen Rosa, Minerva* differing from the other two in having her fore-saloon flared forward, while the others had theirs perpendicular.

Originally fitted with a double-ended Scotch boiler, *Minerva* was given a Navy-type in 1902 and then had her funnel placed farther forward than previously, and at the same time got a small galley chimney on the starboard paddle-wing, retaining this for a few seasons.

As Admiralty Patrol Paddler *Minerva II* she was stationed at Malta: she is said to have been at the Gallipoli landings and to have sailed between Salonika and Mudros in 1916. She was paid off at Constantinople in June, 1920. Sold by the British Government to Turkish owners, she is not further traceable, though remaining in Lloyd's Register till 1929.

P.S. *Glen Rosa* This steamer spent most of her time in summer on the run from Fairlie to Rothesay via Millport and Kilchattan Bay, though in her early days she sailed from Greenock to Ayr, and did excursion work from the latter port. In winter and spring she relieved the regular steamer on the Ardrossan-Arran run, making calls on the first and last runs of the day at Millport (Keppel) and Fairlie.

The First War service of *Glen Rosa* consisted of mine-sweeping on Belfast Lough, and while thus employed her name was changed to *Glencross*, to prevent confusion with P. & A. Campbell's *Glen Rosa*. She was with the Navy from May, 1917 to April, 1919.

In 1926 *Glen Rosa* was re-boilered, and at the same time the bridge was placed forward of the funnel, the companion-ways fore and aft being enclosed in deckhouses and re-positioned fore and aft instead of athwartships. This work was carried out by James Lamont & Co.

In 1938 she was transferred to The Caledonian S.P. Co., Ltd., and the following year was laid up in Albert Harbour, Greenock. She was sold in August, 1939 to Arnott, Young & Co. (Shipbreakers) Ltd., and broken up at Dalmuir.

P.S. *Jupiter* (I).   This ship was launched from the Clydebank yard on 21st March, 1896 and ran her trials on 16th June, a mean speed of 18·18 knots being recorded.   She was larger and more powerful than her predecessors, and had the promenade deck carried forward to the bow as was done in the case of *Glen Sannox*. In pre-war days she sailed from Princes Pier to Arran via Kyles of Bute, giving an extra service from Arran to Ardrossan and back in addition, and was a most popular steamer.

During World War I she was engaged in mine-sweeping in the Dover area under the name *Jupiter II*. She was re-conditioned in 1920; and thereafter sailed from Greenock to Ayr, and later on various excursions, going on certain days of the week "Round the Lochs", others to Ayr, and others to Kyles of Bute. From 1934 she was stationed at Weymss Bay for the Millport run.

She was sold to T. W. Ward, Ltd., Sheffield, in December, 1935, to be broken up at Barrow.

P.S. *Juno* (I).   Mystery surrounded the building of this steamer until from the publication of Mr. Alan Paterson's *Golden Years of the Clyde Steamers*, it became clear that she had been ordered from the Clydebank yard for an associate of the Victoria Steamboat Association of London for service on the Thames Estuary to Margate and Continental ports, the reasons for her building being more fully described by Mr. E. C. B. Thornton in "Sea Breezes". The owners were unable to pay the price; the ship was offered to the G. & S. W. Railway Company and accepted on 28th June, 1898. She was considerably larger than any other steamer in the South Western fleet except *Glen Sannox*. On 5th July, 1898 she was on trial and attained a mean speed of 19·26 knots.

Her station was Ayr, and she was extremely popular as an excursion steamer running from that port. Her war service began earlier than that of any of the other Clyde steamers, and she was also one of the first to return. She was requisitioned in January, 1915; and as H.M.S. *Junior* was at first stationed in the Firth of Clyde, minesweeping between Ardrossan and Troon. Later she was transferred to the Firth of Forth, and based at Granton.

Juno re-appeared on the Clyde in 1919, sailing from Princes Pier to Rothesay, etc., but in the following year returned to Ayr and resumed her old duties, which she performed till the end of the 1931 season. It was then decided that her place should be taken by a new turbine steamer. She was, accordingly, sold in the spring of the following year and broken up at Alloa. Great regret was expressed at the passing of so fine a steamer.

P.S. *Mars*.   To take the place of *Chancellor* in the South Western fleet, *Mars* was built by Messrs. John Brown & Co., Ltd. (who had by that time taken over the Clydebank yard) and was launched on 14th March, 1902. She was about the same size as *Glen Rosa* and *Minerva*, but was decked to the bow like *Jupiter* and *Juno*. Requisitioned on 22nd September, 1916 for war service, as she was run down by a destroyer on 18th November, 1918, while mine sweeping during the night, in the approach to Harwich Harbour. She settled down on a sandbank, but during salvage efforts she broke in two and became a total loss. While in the Admiralty service she was known as H.M.S. *Marsa*.

P.S. *Troon*.   In 1902 the Glasgow & South Western Railway Company, Ltd. took over Troon Harbour, with the tugs *Portland* and *Titchfield*. These were withdrawn and their places taken by one new paddle tug, appropriately named *Troon*. She passed to the London, Midland & Scottish Railway Company, Ltd. in 1923 and in 1930 was sold to Middlesbrough Towage Company, in 1934 to Wm. Lamey, New Ferry, Cheshire; and in June, 1948 to V. E. Sellars, Rock Ferry, for scrapping.

P.S. *Vulcan*.   The successor of *Marquis of Bute* on the Fairlie-Millport run was *Vulcan*, purchased in 1904, from Captain John Williamson, then named *Britannia*. She remained with the Glasgow and South Western Railway Company for about four years, being sold in April, 1908 to Captain John Williamson, who restored her original name, *Kylemore* (See Chapter IV).

Tr.S.S. *Atalanta*.   The first and only turbine steamer in the Glasgow & South Western fleet appeared from John Brown & Company's yard in 1906. *Atalanta* was neither so large nor so fast as the other Clyde turbine steamers, but was quite a useful vessel, being employed on various routes. She was most usually on that from Ardrossan to Arran till the spring of 1936, when she was transferred to the Wemyss Bay-Millport station. Her turbines are said to have been made experimentally, as a model for those to be fitted into the Cunard liner *Lusitania*, alongside which *Atalanta* was built.

Her service in the First War (under the name *Atalanta II*) consisted first of trooping, and later of mine-sweeping in the Harwich area, where she was partnered with the Liverpool and North Wales steamer *St. Seiriol*. She was also for a time the leader of a flotilla comprising *Mars* and *Mercury*, and the Blackpool steamer *Queen of the North*.

Sold in March, 1937 to Blackpool S.N. Co., Ltd., for service from Blackpool and Morecambe, she was employed as a boom defence ship in 1940-5, then laid up at Methil and scrapped.

P.S. *Ayr*.   This was a tug similar to *Troon*, and was taken over by the Glasgow & South Western Railway Company from the Ayr Harbour Commissioners in 1920, being employed at Ayr. She was sold to Broomhill Steamship Co. Ltd., Newcastle, in 1930.

T.S.S. *Kyle.* This was a bucket-dredger, which was owned originally by the Ayr Harbour Commissioners. She had two funnels placed athwartships, and was stationed at Ayr.

*   *   *   *   *   *

These two vessels, taken over from the Ayr Harbour Commissioners, were the last added to the fleet of the Glasgow & South Western Railway Company, though late in 1916 (to take the place of *Minerva*), the Buchanan steamer *Isle of Cumbrae* was chartered to help with the services from Princes Pier. The funnel of this steamer was painted in South Western colours, though otherwise she was unaltered. MacBrayne's *Gael* and *Glencoe* were also chartered at different times during First World War for the Arran run in winter; and the latter also appeared at Greenock occasionally, as also did *Lord of the Isles*. All were returned to their owners at the close of the war.

CHAPTER III

LONDON MIDLAND & SCOTTISH RAILWAY CO. AND THE CALEDONIAN STEAM PACKET CO. LTD., 1923–1935

ON 1st January, 1923 the London Midland & Scottish Railway Company was formed, its Scottish Fleet consisting at that date of the former Glasgow & South Western Railway steamers *Glen Sannox* (I), *Mercury* (I), *Glen Rosa, Jupiter* (I), *Juno* (I) and *Atalanta*; the tugs *Troon* and *Ayr* and the dredger *Kyle*. The steamers owned by The Caledonian Steam Packet Co. Ltd., were *Caledonia* (I), *Marchioness of Breadalbane, Duchess of Rothesay, Duchess of Fife, Duchess of Argyll, Countess of Breadalbane* (I), *Lady of the Lake, Sybilla, Carlotta* and *Queen of the Lake. In addition, there was Marchioness of Lorne* (I), which, however, was not in commission. There were also two Caledonian Railway dredgers, *Forth* and *Caledonian*, stationed at Grangemouth.

It was not until 1925 that any steamers were added to the combined railway fleet, and in that year a replacement occurred. It should be noted that most of the steamers acquired after the amalgamation have been owned by The Caledonian Steam Packet Co. Ltd., since that concern has wider running powers than had the Railway Company, and now all are owned by it under its present name, Caledonian MacBrayne Ltd.

Tr.S.S. *Glen Sannox* (II). Virtually a sister ship to *Duchess of Argyll* of 1906, this ship (originally intended to be named *Duchess of Atholl*) was built to take the place of the famous paddle *Glen Sannox* on the Ardrossan–Arran station and was given that name. She attained a trial speed of 20¾ knots. Being intended for a particular run, she was originally owned by the Railway Company, just as her predecessor had been, but in the spring of 1936 she was transferred to The Caledonian Steam Packet Co. Ltd., to enable her to call at Campbeltown in connexion with a new service then introduced. She thereafter sailed (in summer only and except on Saturdays) from Ardrossan to Whiting Bay, then proceeded by the South end of Arran to Campbeltown, from which place bus tours to Machrihanish and Southend (Kintyre) were run in connexion. She was more or less constantly on the Arran run, during the second war years from Fairlie, but thereafter again from

23

Ardrossan. Latterly her after promenade deck was strengthened for the transport of motorcars. Laid up at the end of the 1953 season, she was sold on 16th July, 1954 to Van Heyghen Frères, Ghent, for scrapping.

Tr.S.S. *Duchess of Montrose* (II). As an additional cruising steamer *Duchess of Montrose* joined the fleet of The Caledonian Steam Packet Co. Ltd., in 1930. She followed *King George V* in having an enclosed promenade deck and was splendidly fitted throughout. She was the first Clyde steamer arranged for one class only. She became most popular, and her excursions Round the Lochs, Round Arran and Ailsa Craig and to Stranraer were well patronised. The last-named, however, was not resumed in 1936, and instead she thereafter sailed on Thursdays to Inveraray, in connexion with the Loch Eck Tour. Between 1939 and 1946 she maintained the Wemyss Bay–Rothesay service, and in 1946 was on the Arran *via* Kyles run, the cruises being later restored in a somewhat restricted form.

When new, *Duchess of Montrose* had two masts, the mainmast being very short, only about half the height of the foremast. In 1934, however, she was fitted with a new mainmast of full height, this giving her a more symmetrical appearance, and making her almost indistinguishable from her sister-ship. *Duchess of Hamilton.*

Duchess of Montrose was propelled by three direct-acting turbines, driving three propellers. Both hull and machinery were constructed by Wm. Denny & Bros. Ltd. of Dumbarton. Originally coal-fired, she was converted to burn oil in the spring of 1956. Radar was fitted in 1960.

She left Greenock on 19th August, 1965 to be broken up in Belgium.

Tr.S.S. *Duchess of Hamilton* (II). An almost exact copy of *Duchess of Montrose, Duchess of Hamilton* was, however, built by Messrs. Harland & Wolff, Ltd., at their Govan yard, the machinery being made by them in Belfast. She had a full-sized mainmast from the outset, but was otherwise practically identical with *Duchess of Montrose*. Like her, she was a "one class only" ship; and like her also, she was converted to oil-firing in the spring of 1956, radar being installed in time for the 1960 season.

Built to take the place of *Juno* on the Ayr excursions, *Duchess of Hamilton* proved herself a very successful steamer, and in pre-second war days was a favourite with excursionists from the Ayrshire ports of Ayr, Troon and Ardrossan. She was owned by The Caledonian Steam Packet Co. Ltd., and so could make certain calls, e.g. at Campbeltown and Inveraray, which were prohibited to *Juno*.

Duchess of Hamilton was on Government service, from the autumn of 1939 being allocated to the Stranraer–Larne section for troop transport. She was released in 1946, and, after refitting at D. & W. Henderson's, returned to her owners' Clyde services, principally on the Campbeltown run, in succession to *Duchess of Argyll*, but now reduced to four days per week. The other days were occupied by cruises to Ayr on Fridays and on Tuesdays to Inveraray. For the 1969 season her masts were shortened for the Kingston Bridge, but she did not in fact proceed above it after that. At the end of the 1970 season she was withdrawn and laid up at Greenock as an economy measure: she was sold in the following year to Messrs. Joseph Sims and Leonard Melling for conversion to a floating restaurant, (to be moored near Kingston Bridge), planning permission for which was granted in February, 1972 but subject to various conditions, to comply with the fire regulations, etc. A start had been made in enclosing the after promenade deck; but the purchasers came to the conclusion that the venture was too much for individuals, and the ship was sold to the Reo Stakis Organisation. One of the requirements was a permanent gangway which would adjust to the tidal level, requiring considerable expense; and another difficulty was that the ship would have been rated as a building, and the whole project was found to be uneconomic. The steamer was accordingly towed to Troon in April, 1974 and scrapped there.

P.S. *Mercury* (II). In 1934 two paddle steamers of an entirely new design were added to the fleet, one being built by the Fairfield Company and the other by Messrs. Denny. The Fairfield product was *Mercury*, built to take the place of the old steamer of the same name, and was employed in the Kyles of Bute trade from Greenock and Gourock. Like her predecessor she was owned by the Railway Company, but was transferred to the Steam Packet Company in December, 1937.

In these new steamers various unusual features were introduced, not the least striking being that their paddle-boxes were enclosed in order to give the ships the appearance of turbine vessels. The part of the paddle-box protruding above the promenade deck was square, and in that below were two small grills instead of the customary vents. In addition, these steamers had each two masts, and a large elliptical funnel, the bridge being unusually high and overhanging the sides of the vessel. Altogether they had a most surprising appearance from the point of view of anyone who had known the old-type Clyde steamer.

Triple expansion diagonal machinery was fitted, steam being supplied by one boiler. As in the case of the later turbine steamers, the dining-salon was situated on the main deck, giving passengers an opportunity of viewing the scenery while having meals.

Damaged by mine on 25th December, 1940 she sank off The Smalls while in tow between Milford Haven and the Irish Coast.

P.S. *Caledonia* (II). The other steamer built in 1934 was *Caledonia*, which was launched from the Dumbarton yard on 1st February in that year. She was similar to *Mercury* in many respects but was not an exact sister-ship, her funnel being more obviously elliptical, and being placed farther aft. She was fitted with Denny patent 7-float paddlewheels, but these were later superseded by wheels of the conventional 8-float type. The situation of her ventilators, and the style and spacing of her saloon windows, also, were different. She attained a speed of 17·27 knots on trial.

Owned by The Caledonian Steam Packet Co. Ltd., *Caledonia* took the name of the first vessel built for that company, which had been withdrawn in 1933. She was used for various services, among them being that from Wemyss Bay to Rothesay and Kyles of Bute, and also for general excursion work from Gourock, Greenock, Largs, Wemyss Bay, Rothesay, etc. In 1936 she was placed on the Arran run *via* Kyles of Bute, in succession to *Duchess of Argyll.*

Towards the end of 1939 *Caledonia* was commissioned as a mine-sweeper, as H.M.S. *Goatfell.* Like *Mercury* she relieved channel steamers for Dunkirk. She was latterly a patrol vessel, and had enemy aircraft to her credit. She was released in 1945, and, after reconditioning by her builders, took her place in the Wemyss Bay–Rothesay service in 1946, being thereafter on various runs from Gourock or Wemyss Bay, and, from 1954 to 1964 she was based at Ayr, in succession to *Marchioness of Graham*, also assisting the latter on the Arran sailings at peak periods. In the winter of 1954-5 she was given a new oil-fired navy boiler, at Troon. From 1965 she was stationed at Craigendoran in succession to *Jeanie Deans*, for the Round Bute, Kyles of Bute, etc., sailings, serving also on occasion from Glasgow, Bridge Wharf. In 1969 she was chartered by David MacBrayne Ltd. for the Tarbert mail service for ten days in April, and again was on it for a few days at the beginning of October, but for her owners the C.S.P. Co., who had taken over the Lochfyne service from the first of that month. It was a very long time since this part of the Royal Route had been operated by a paddle steamer, and it was a fitting end to her active career. Early in 1970 she was sold to W. H. Arnott, Young & Co., Ltd., Dalmuir, by whom she was re-named *Old Caledonia*, being later re-sold to Bass Charington Ltd. and moored near Waterloo Bridge on the Thames, as a floating restaurant. Unfortunately she was so badly damaged by fire on 27th April, 1980 that she was scrapped at, Grays, Essex.

P.S. *Marchioness of Lorne* (II). To take the place of *Marchioness of Breadalbane* on the Holy Loch run, the second *Marchioness of Lorne* was built by The Fairfield Shipbuilding & Engineering Co. Ltd. in 1935. Rather like the new *Caledonia* and *Mercury* in general appearance she was, however, of a neater design (apart from an absurdly squat funnel) and was a most suitable vessel for the run on which she was employed. Her service speed was not quite 12 knots. Her machinery was of the triple expansion three-crank type, and was fitted with Fairfield patent valves. Like her predecessor she was owned by The Caledonian Steam Packet Co. Ltd. For a season employed on the Millport station, she was sold on 17th February, 1955 to British Iron & Steel Corporation (Salvage) Ltd. and broken up by Smith & Houston Ltd. at Port Glasgow.

T.S.M.V. *Wee Cumbrae*. In 1935 a new ferry service was instituted between Largs and Millport to supplement the existing steamboat runs and to eliminate a competitor. For this a small motor-vessel, capable of accommodating 60 passengers, was built by Messrs. Denny, and fitted with two Gleniffer Diesel engines. Originally she had no accommodation for passengers on deck, but in 1936 a rail was erected round the top of the saloons, and seats were provided. During the Second World War she was employed as tender to the examination services at Rothesay, returning thereafter to her Clyde passenger duties, and being engaged between Gourock and Dunoon from 1947 in exchange for the *Leven*. She was sold in March, 1953 to Marine Craft Constructors Ltd., Dumbarton, re-engined and sent (by ship) to Brunei, North Borneo.

The competitor above mentioned was *Cramond Brig* referred to on page 180.

CHAPTER IV

WILLIAMSON-BUCHANAN STEAMERS LTD.
TURBINE STEAMERS LTD.

IN association with David MacBrayne Ltd. the L. M. & S. Railway company took over the remaining members of these fleets, the five Williamson-Buchanan steamers going to The Caledonian Steam Packet Co. Ltd. on 3rd October, 1935 and the two from Turbine Steamers Ltd. to David MacBrayne Ltd.

Formed in 1919 by the amalgamation of Buchanan Steamers Ltd. with John Williamson & Company, Williamson-Buchanan Steamers Ltd. had the former as its older constituent.

BUCHANAN STEAMERS, LTD.

The combination of ownership of Williamson and Buchanan dated back to 1853, when Captain Buchanan (Senior) and Captain Alexander Williamson (Senior) were the two principal owners of the steamer *Eagle*. In 1862, however, Captain Williamson withdrew, and started in business for himself, with the result that the two well-known Clyde fleets of Buchanan and Williamson came into being.

Captain Buchanan was succeeded by his sons, and the concern became a limited company under the title of Buchanan Steamers, Ltd. in 1905.

The *Eagle*, in common with some ex members of the Castle Steam Packet Company's fleet, had black funnels with white bands, which colouring was retained and perpetuated by both the Buchanan and Williamson fleets, the latter till 1898 and the former until the amalgamation in 1919, after which all the Williamson-Buchanan steamers had the white funnels with black tops adopted for the Williamson fleet in 1898. The Buchanan paddle-boxes were originally black, but in 1912 became white.

P.S. *Eagle* (I). The first *Eagle* was built in 1852, and was owned for one season by her builders, Messrs. Denny. She was engined by Messrs. McNab & Clark, Greenock, the machinery being of the oscillating type. A model of this steamer in the Glasgow Museum of Transport shows her with two bell-mouthed funnels aft of the paddle-boxes, the latter being decorated each with a large golden eagle and having no vents. Reboilered in 1860, *Eagle* subsequently ran with one funnel only, this being of ordinary shape. Her registered owners in 1853 were William Buchanan, John Cook and Alexander Williamson, co-partners under the firm of Eagle Steamer Company. She was sold in January, 1862 for blockade running, and after several successful runs, was captured in 1864 by the Federals.

P.S. *Cardiff Castle*. One of the former Burns Clyde steamers, *Cardiff Castle*, built for the Glasgow Castles Steam Packet Company in 1844, spent a short time in the Buchanan fleet. She was sold to Alexander Watson in 1861.

P.S. *Petrel*. This had been one of the three steamers acquired by the Railway Steam Packet Company for railway connexion services from Greenock in 1845. She had for a time two funnels abaft the paddles, and was somewhat similar to *Eagle* (I). Sold about 1861 to A. Watson and Henry Sharp, she became notorious on the Clyde as a "Sabbath breaker", and was scrapped in 1886.

P.S. *Eagle* (II). On the departure of the first *Eagle* a new steamer of the same name was laid down for Captain Buchanan by Charles Connell & Co., but this one also was sold for blockade-running and did not sail on the Clyde. This caused a third steamer to be built, but as the second was not ever known on the Clyde, this third vessel is commonly referred to as the second *Eagle*; and we also have so designated her.

Eagle of 1864 was built by the same builders and was a comfortable boat, though by no means beautiful, particularly in her original condition. Of the raised quarter-deck type, she had two haystack boilers and two funnels forward of the paddle-boxes, and is said to have had a fair turn of speed. Her machinery was found to be too powerful for her hull, and after two seasons she was lengthened by 30 feet; but even this did not cure the trouble, for in 1876 her original double diagonal simple machinery was removed and a single diagonal engine fitted. For this one boiler sufficed, and so she re-appeared with one funnel only. The alterations seem to have been successful, and it is understood that she was not only more economical but also was faster. In 1887 she was further improved by having a deck saloon placed on the top of her already raised quarter-deck, the result being to give her a curious top-heavy appearance. This new saloon had alleyways round it, and gave her considerably increased accommodation.

Most of the life of *Eagle* was spent on the Glasgow-Rothesay run, but from 1887 her sailings were extended to Arran till she was succeeded in this by *Isle of Arran* in 1892. She then reverted to the Rothesay route till 1894. A relic of this steamer afterwards to be found in the saloon of *Eagle III* was a panel which once formed part of the decoration of the saloon of the older *Eagle*.

She was sold to Ship Canal Passenger Steamer Co. (1893) Ltd., for service on Manchester Ship Canal, and sold at Liverpool 1899, presumably for scrapping.

*   *   *   *   *   *

The Arran service, originally operated from the island by sailing vessels to Saltcoats or Ardrossan, was provided by the paddle steamer *Hero* from 1836, followed by the first *Isle of Arran* in 1838 and the *Earl of Arran* in 1860, the latter being superseded by *The Lady Mary* in 1868 and the *Heather Bell* in 1872. From 1874 the service was maintained by Captain William Buchanan.

P.S. *Rothesay Castle*.   Built by Henderson, Colbourn & Co., of Renfrew in 1865, *Rothesay Castle*, sixth and, so far, last of the name on the Clyde, was flushed-decked, fitted with a steeple engine, and had two funnels placed fore and aft of the paddle-boxes. She had been on the Rothesay run for a number of years before being placed on the Ardrossan–Arran service, when this was taken over by Captain William Buchanan in January, 1874. On this she remained till superseded by *Brodick Castle* in 1878. She re-appeared on it during the winter of 1878-9 and was sold in May, 1879 for service at Bordeaux, being renamed *Gironde-Garonne*. A new steamer of this name was built in 1880, but the fate of the old one is not known.

P.S. *Brodick Castle*.   Readers will recollect that the original double diagonal engine of the second *Eagle* was removed from that steamer in 1876. For this engine a new hull was built by Messrs. H. McIntyre & Co., of Paisley, this ship, *Brodick Castle,* being placed on the Ardrossan–Arran service in succession to *Rothesay Castle* during the summer of 1878. After the departure of the latter, *Brodick Castle* sailed on this run both summer and winter till the end of the 1886 season.

Brodick Castle was a steamer of unusual appearance, having two funnels forward, a deck-saloon with alleyways aft, and poop-deck and forecastle. A photograph (by G. W. Wilson of Aberdeen), shows her without any mast, but this was a temporary state of affairs.

Sold to Bournemouth, Swanage & Poole Steam Packet Co. Ltd., and subsequently to Messrs. Cosens & Co., Weymouth, she was sold in 1910 for cattle carrying in Argentina and re-named *Ceca Nova*, but was sunk while in tow off Portland.

P.S. *Elaine*. On the retiral of Captain Stewart from steam-boat-owning in 1879, his remaining steamer, *Elaine* was sold to Captain Buchanan. This steamer, like all the others with names associated with King Arthur, had been built for Graham Brymner & Co., and after a short spell with Captain McIntyre had entered the Stewart fleet on 2nd February, 1874. She was owned by Donald Stewart and Robert Napier Stewart with a mortgage to their father, Duncan Stewart. (The latter died in December, 1877).

Of raised quarter-deck design, and with one funnel, *Elaine* was a pretty little steamer. Originally her paddle boxes were very low, but while she was in Captain Buchanan's fleet they were increased in size. The raised quarter-deck saloon of this steamer was fitted with square windows as in the case of several of her contemporaries.

For Captain Buchanan, *Elaine* sailed from Glasgow to Rothesay and later from Glasgow to Garelochhead: at the end of the 1899 season she was withdrawn from service, and was broken up at Bowling.

P.S. *Scotia*. Built by Messrs. H. McIntyre & Co., Paisley, *Scotia* was launched in the spring of 1880 and took her name from a sailing vessel owned by Captain Buchanan. She maintained the Glasgow–Rothesay sailings, on which she remained till she succeeded *Guinevere* on the Glasgow–Arran service in 1885. Two years later *Scotia* was placed on the Ardrossan–Arran run in succession to *Brodick Castle*, and in the interval a forecastle deck was added.

Scotia had two funnels, a deck-saloon aft, and was fitted with double steeple engines, the only machinery of this type ever provided for a Clyde steamer, and the last of the steeple design made on the Clyde. An alteration was made to the engines in 1885, this presumably consisting of the fitting of a surface condenser.

Sold to the Glasgow & South Western Railway Co. in 1891, her subsequent history will be found in Chapter II.

*   *   *   *   *   *

Early in 1885 Captain William Buchanan took over the seven steamers then owned by Messrs. Keith & Campbell, which operated from Glasgow tó Helensburgh, to the Gareloch ports, to Arran and to Kilmun.

P.S. *Balmoral*. (I). The oldest of the Keith & Campbell steamers was *Balmoral*, which had been built in 1842 for the Largs and Millport run from Glasgow, as *Lady Brisbane*. She had a slanting stem and square stern, the funnel being aft, and she was fitted with a steeple engine. She passed into the Keith fleet in 1870, and remained on the Gareloch route for Captain Buchanan.

Sold for use as a coal-hulk at Newry, she survived there for many years.

P.S. *Hero*.   *Hero* was built by Messrs. T. Wingate & Co. in 1858, and had had a varied career before entering the fleet of Mr. Hugh Keith about 1875. In 1878 she sailed to Arran, and later was employed on the Glasgow–Gareloch route; but after her transference to the Buchanan fleet she became a spare boat, being used on the different services as required and being frequently chartered for Sunday School trips, etc.

Sold in 1886 to River Tay Steamboat Co. Ltd., Dundee and in April, 1889 to Mr. Orr, Glasgow, she passed in 1890 to Mr. D. MacBrayne. After relieving *Iona* on the Ardrishaig route during 1890, she was re-named *Mountaineer* (II) and operated mainly from Oban, till scrapped after the 1909 season.

P.S. *Guinevere*.   This was a two-funnelled steamer of raised quarter-deck design, fitted with oscillating engines, and originally owned by Messrs. Graham Brymner & Co. She had been in the hands of various owners before being purchased by Mr. Keith in 1876.

Guinevere was employed on the Arran service from Glasgow, and remained on this run for Captain Buchanan till succeeded by *Scotia* in 1885. She was then transferred to the Broomielaw–Rothesay run, and maintained this till she left the Clyde on her sale to Turkish buyers in 1892. She was lost in the Bay of Biscay.

P.S. *Shandon*.   Originally *Chancellor* (II) of the Loch Lomond Steamboat Company, this steamer at that time had no mast, but received one about the time she entered the Keith & Campbell fleet, which she did at the beginning of the 1881 season.

For Captain Buchanan, *Shandon* sailed to Garelochhead or to Rothesay. On the spring holiday of 1891 the experiment was made of running this steamer, along with *Guinevere* and *Vivid*, from Paisley. This never became a regular service, but has been done from time to time. In recent years both the *Countess of Breadalbane* and *Maid of Argyll* have sailed from Paisley, on charter to the Clyde River Steamer Club.

Sold to Ship Canal Passenger Steamer Co. (1893) Ltd., Manchester, *Shandon* was re-named *Daniel Adamson*. Subsequently she returned to the Clyde for a short time about 1896, but was thereafter broken up.

P.S. *Vesta*.   The steamers *Vesta, Vivid* and *Benmore*, which had been the property of Captain Robert Campbell of Kilmun, had entered the Keith & Campbell fleet on the amalgamation of 1871, retaining the all-white funnel much later borne by the ships of P. & A. Campbell Ltd. of Bristol and Cardiff. Originally one of the McKellar fleet sailing to Largs and Millport, *Vesta* was a small steamer with funnel aft, and remained on the Kilmun run for her new owners until destroyed by fire at Ardnadam on 2nd March, 1886.

P.S. *Vivid*.   This vessel had been built for Captain Campbell's Kilmun trade in 1864 and was a popular steamer on this route.

She had the distinction of possessing the last steeple engine in any steamer in regular service on the Clyde, apart from the temporary use of the *Glencoe* during the First World War. Latterly a short deck-saloon (later extended) was added on the after deck. In 1902 she was broken up in the Pudzeoch at Renfrew.

P.S. *Benmore*.   This steamer was built for the Kilmun trade in 1876, and was a product of the Rutherglen yard of Messrs. T. B. Seath & Co. She stranded on the weir when being brought down the Clyde, and remained there for a time in danger of breaking her back, but ultimately got off all right and joined the Campbell fleet. Though she was purchased by Captain Buchanan in February, 1885, her funnel-colouring was not altered until 1886, and she remained on the Kilmun run during the 1885 season, being opposed by Captain Campbell with *Meg Merrilies*, which he had just acquired. Although the Buchanan fare was 9d. return, and that of the Campbell steamer was 1s., Captain Campbell was so well known that he was given much public support, and *Benmore* retired from the Kilmun route at the end of the season.

She was then placed on the Rothesay run, wearing Buchanan colours, and in the following year appeared with two funnels forward of the paddle-boxes. This arrangement was not successful, however, and she again became a single-funnelled steamer.

After the 1891 season she was sold to Captain John Williamson. (*See* later in this Chapter).

P.S. *Isle of Arran* (II).   To take the place of *Eagle* (II) on the Glasgow–Arran service, *Isle of Arran* was built by Messrs. T. B. Seath & Co., and launched on the afternoon of Saturday, 14th May, 1892 being named by Mrs. William Buchanan. She was on the Arran route for a few years, and then her owners abandoned the run, and placed her in the Broomielaw–Rothesay service. She was a comfortable boat, and instituted the afternoon excursions from

Rothesay to Loch Striven, Round Cumbrae and to the Kyles of Bute, which became so popular in connexion with the 11 a.m. sailing from Glasgow. She was the second of the name on the Clyde.

Isle of Arran was the last steamer to sail from the Broomielaw before going on war service, and in the summer of 1916 made a daily trip to the Gareloch. In the following year she was requisitioned for mine-sweeping, and was at first stationed on the Firth of Clyde. Lat.r she was attached to the Portsmouth Division, and for a time was engaged in transporting troops from Rouen and Havre to Paris.

She returned to the Clyde in 1920, and during re-conditioning her bridge was placed forward of the funnel and a small upper deck was added above the saloon companionway in place of the large awning-deck (or floating raft) which she carried in pre-war days. She became a Williamson-Buchanan steamer, and sailed from Glasgow until succeeded in 1933 by *Queen Mary,* her last run on the Clyde being on the spring holiday (Easter Monday) of that year.

Acquired by the General Steam Navigation Co. Ltd. for service on the Thames, she was sold in October, 1936 to Messrs. T. W. Ward, Ltd. for scrapping.

P.S. *Isle of Bute.* To take place of the second *Eagle* (which, as explained previously, returned to the Rothesay route in 1892) on her departure from the Clyde, Captain Buchanan purchased from the North British Steam Packet Company their steamer *Guy Mannering,* ex *Sheila,* and re-named her *Isle of Bute.* She became well known on the Rothesay run, on which she remained till sold in July, 1912 to Samuel Cordingley, Morecambe. Driven against a pier there, she was sold in October, 1913 to T. W. Ward, Ltd., to be broken up.

P.S. *Isle of Cumbrae* (I). Another former North British steamer found her way into the Buchanan fleet in June, 1904. This was *Duchess of York*, originally the famous *Jeanie Deans* (I), and with her new owners she received her third and last name, *Isle of Cumbrae.* She took the place of *Vivid*, and remained on the Rothesay run till the First World War. Even after the erection of the boom between Dunoon and the Cloch she continued to sail from Glasgow to Dunoon, but late in 1916 she was chartered by the Glasgow & South Western Railway Company for service from Princes Pier. On this she remained more or less consistently till the end of the 1919 season, and though she passed to the ownership of Williamson-Buchanan Steamers, Ltd., she did not sail for them, being laid up at Greenock for a time and afterwards scrapped at Dumbarton.

P.S. *Eagle III*. The last *Eagle* was built by Messrs. Napier & Miller (under a sub-contract from A. & J. Inglis, Ltd.) for the fleet of Buchanan Steamers, Ltd., and was launched on 14th April 1910. The numeral was part of her name.

The machinery of *Eagle III* was single diagonal, the last of that type built for a Clyde steamer, and her boiler was of the haystack pattern. Her trial speed was 16½ knots.

In her first year she was rather unstable, but alterations were made which enabled her to sail successfully on the Clyde, and also to take part in mine-sweeping operations during both wars. It was in 1916 that she was first requisitioned, and her headquarters were then at Grimsby. Later her base was Harwich, and on several occasions she made trips to the Dutch coast, assisting food convoys on their way to England. On her return to the Clyde in 1920 she was re-conditioned, and her bridge was moved forward, the place of the floating raft awning aft being taken by a small upper deck over the saloon companion-way, as in the case of *Isle of Arran*.

For Williamson-Buchanan Steamers, Ltd. *Eagle III* normally sailed on the 11 o'clock run to Rothesay, with the usual excursions, till succeeded in this by *King Edward* in 1933. She thereafter was generally on the 9-30 a.m. sailing to Rothesay, till this was discontinued at the end of 1935. In 1936 she sailed to Lochgoilhead from Glasgow, and was used on other services as required. She entered the Caledonian fleet on 3rd October, 1935 and was transferred to Williamson-Buchanan Steamers (1936) Ltd. on the 16th June, 1936 returning to Caledonian ownership on 4th March, 1943.

In October, 1939, she was requisitioned for the second time, and left Ardrossan in January, 1940 (with a yellow and black-topped funnel), for the south. After conversion, she was commissioned as H.M.S. *Oriole*, taking part in mine-sweeping in the North Sea, and assisting at the evacuation of Dunkirk, where she was beached for 12 hours. After her return she was laid up in the Holy Loch till sold and towed to Smith & Houston's yard, Port Glasgow, on 17th August, 1946 for scrapping.

P.S. *Isle of Skye*. An additional steamer was purchased for the Buchanan fleet in March 1913. This was *Isle of Skye*, which had previously been *Madge Wildfire*, to which reference will be found in Chapters I and XIII. She was intended to have been named *Isle of Sanda*, but on account of similarity of this name to that of another vessel it was not used.

Isle of Skye was in the fleet about three years only, when she was taken over by the Admiralty for use as a tender at Invergordon from which she also did some mine-sweeping in the Pentland Firth. In March, 1919 she returned to the Clyde, and was the first steamer to sail from Glasgow to the coast ports after the war. She remained in the Williamson-Buchanan fleet till the spring of 1927, when she was sold to Grangemouth & Forth Towing Co. Ltd., for excursion and tender service on the Firth of Forth, being re-named *Fair Maid*. From December 1940, she was managed by the Caledonian S. P. Co. Ltd. for Ministry of War Transport, as a tender and de-contamination vessel on the Clyde, and also performed a few passenger runs, in particular from Craigendoran to Dunoon, etc., for one week in the spring of 1944, and one day on the Holy Loch service from Gourock. She was broken up at Troon in December, 1945.

JOHN WILLIAMSON
JOHN WILLIAMSON & CO., } **1892–1919**
TURBINE STEAMERS, LTD. 1901–1912

As mentioned in connexion with the Buchanan fleet, Captain Alexander Williamson (Senior) was one of the owners of the steamer *Eagle*. In 1862, however, he began steamboat-owning by himself, with the steamer *Sultan*, built in the previous year. This vessel was followed by *Sultana* in 1868, and *Viceroy* in 1875. In 1889 Captain Williamson undertook the management of the steamer *Marquis of Bute* on behalf of Captain McLean's creditors, and all four steamers were sold in 1891 to the Glasgow & South Western Railway Company as already mentioned.

Captain John Williamson commenced steamboat-owning in 1892; and in 1901 there was formed the Turbine Steamer Syndicate for the purpose of running *King Edward*, Turbine Steamers Ltd., being incorporated in 1902. This company developed the Campbeltown and Inveraray traffic, and its two remaining steamers passed to David MacBrayne, Ltd. in October 1935.

The funnels of the Williamson steamers were black with white band till 1st June 1898 when white with black top was adopted. This colouring also was used by Turbine Steamers, Ltd., and also from 1919 for the combined fleet of Williamson-Buchanan Steamers, Ltd. It continued to be borne by the steamers of Williamson-Buchanan Steamers (1936) Ltd., in spite of the railway ownership of that concern until the end of 1939; and the old Williamson "Turkish" fleet house-flag—a blue pennant with yellow crescent and star—was still officially the house-flag of these steamers until their transfer in 1943 to The Caledonian Steam Packet Co. Ltd., whose colours and flag they used thenceforth.

P.S. *Benmore*.   Captain John Williamson's first steamer was *Benmore*, which he purchased from Captain Buchanan in October, 1891. As she was used principally as a cargo boat, the handsome scroll-work was removed from her hull and paddle-boxes about 1898.

During the First World War *Benmore* was chartered by the Caledonian Steam Packet Co. Ltd., as already recorded, and towards the end of 1920 returned to the Williamson-Buchanan fleet. She was, on 11th November, 1920, badly damaged by fire while laid up for the winter at Greenock, where she remained till October, 1923 when the filling in of the West Harbour necessitated her being moved. She was then towed to Dumbarton and scrapped. Her name continued to appear in Lloyd's Register for a number of years after she had ceased to exist.

P.S. *Ardmore*.   This was *Sultan*, which came back to Williamson ownership late in 1892, after about a year under the Glasgow & South Western Railway flag. She did not, however, remain long on the Clyde after that, being sold in 1894 to Mr. D. MacBrayne and re-named *Gairlochy*. After 25 years service on the Caledonian Canal she was burnt at Fort Augustus on 24th December, 1919. Her keel can still be seen there at low water and was observed being passed by the new *Loch Striven* coming through the canal on her delivery voyage on the 14th June 1986.

P.S. *Glenmore*.   The first steamer actually built for Captain John Williamson was *Glenmore*, which was launched from the yard of Messrs. Russell on 9th April, 1895. She had the promenade deck carried to the bow, the forward and after parts being plated and the intermediate part forward being open at the sides. She was a useful type of steamer, not fast, with one boiler of locomotive type and compound diagonal machinery. She was sold in the summer of 1896 to Balandin, Kitmanoff, Vestrotine & Co., Yenisiesk, Siberia and in the following year was named *Oryol*.

P.S. *Sultana*.   Another former Williamson steamer which had been in the service of the South Western Railway Company returned to Williamson ownership in 1897. This was *Sultana*, which remained till sold in July 1899 to the Lochfyne & Glasgow S.P. Co., Ltd. *See* Chapter XI.

P.S. *Strathmore*.   This was one of two sister ships, similar to

Glenmore, but plated entirely forward. She was launched on 11th March, 1897 and was intended for the Rothesay and Kyles of Bute trade, in which she remained for most of the time she was on the Clyde, though she spent a short time on the Fairlie–Campbeltown route before the advent of *King Edward.*

Sold to the Admiralty in March 1908 for service as a tender, she was re-named *Harlequin,* and was used as a mine-sweeper during the First War, stationed at Swansea. Thereafter she was on Medway ferry service till stranded in 1943. Her wreck was sold in March and she was broken up in 1945.

P.S. *Kylemore.* This was the sister-ship of *Strathmore.* Though launched on 28th April, 1897 as *Kylemore* for the same owner, she was, before completion, purchased by the Hastings, St. Leonards-on-Sea and Eastbourne Steamboat Company, Ltd., who renamed her *Britannia.* In 1904 she returned to Captain John Williamson, but almost immediately became *Vulcan* of the Glasgow & South Western fleet, as mentioned in Chapter II, in April 1908, taking her place in the Williamson fleet as *Kylemore,* in succession to *Strathmore* in the Glasgow–Rothesay trade, and having in pre-war days *Benmore* as her escort. She sailed for one season to Inveraray in the early part of the First World War, but was shortly afterwards requisitioned for mine-sweeping in the English Channel, in which she was occupied from 1915 till 1919. She was stationed first at Dunkirk, and latterly at Harwich.

After being reconditioned at Ardrossan, with her bridge forward, she broke from her moorings on 8th January, 1920 and went aground, but was refloated a few days later. She resumed her Clyde sailings, being employed principally on the 8-15 a.m. run from Rothesay to Glasgow, leaving at 1-30 p.m. on return: she was thus able to do a certain amount of evening cruising from Rothesay. She was also occasionally on the Glasgow–Lochgoil run.

Along with the other remaining Williamson-Buchanan steamers, *Kylemore* passed into the fleet of the Caledonian Steam Packet Co. on 3rd October, 1935. Her first service with her new owners was from Wemyss Bay to Millport and Rothesay, towards the end of that year, but at the beginning of the 1936 season she returned to her old station. She was owned from 16th June, 1936 by Williamson-Buchanan Steamers (1936) Ltd. In December, 1939 she again became a minesweeper, and later a net-layer. She was sunk by bombing off Harwich on 21st August, 1940.

P.S. *Athole.* This steamer, already mentioned as having been among the first to sail from Princes Pier, was purchased in 1898 by Captain John Williamson from the Bute Steam Packet Co. Ltd., who had acquired her on Captain McLean's retiral. There is no evidence that *Athole* ever ran as a Williamson steamer, as she was soon scrapped, her register being closed on 12th November, 1897.

S.S. *Alert*. Built at Paisley for the fish-buying trade of John Smith and Andrew Ritchie, this small steamer was purchased early in 1900 by Captain John Williamson, who placed her on the Glasgow/Rothesay luggage and cargo trade. After her departure her place was for a short time taken by the chartered puffer *Stormlight,* but this did not last long, as the advent of *King Edward* rendered one of the other steamers available for this service. Sold in June, 1901 for service at Flensburg, she was re-named *Skirner.*

Qu.S.S/Tr.S.S. *King Edward*. We have now to record an epoch-making vessel of the first order, *King Edward,* the world's first passenger steamer propelled by turbines. This system of propulsion had, in 1894, been fitted experimentally into *Turbinia,* a small yacht, which is said to have attained the remarkable speed of 34 knots. Nothing like that was attempted with *King Edward,* but her original mean trial speed of 20·483 knots placed her ahead of any of the paddle-boats in this respect. In dimensions she was identical with the first *Duchess of Hamilton,* but her appearance was very different. Though latterly a triple-screw steamer, *King Edward* until 1905 had two propellers on each of her outer shafts, making five screws in all.

King Edward was owned originally by the Turbine Steamer Syndicate, afterwards by Turbine Steamers Ltd., and was placed on the Fairlie–Campbeltown run in succession to *Strathmore.* She was an immediate success, and her owners in the year following her appearance decided to extend their operations and include Inveraray as an objective for excursions. *King Edward* was, accordingly, transferred to that run when the first *Queen Alexandra* appeared in 1902, sailing from Fairlie by the south and west of Bute and returning via the Kyles. She continued to call at Ardishaig till 1908.

King Edward was taken over by the Admiralty in February, 1915, and for four years was used as a troopship sailing to and from the Channel Islands, Havre, Rouen, Cherbourg, Southampton, Dieppe, Dover, Folkestone, Calais and Boulogne. Later she was engaged as an ambulance transport in the White Sea; and, when returning to the Clyde, encountered such a storm that she narrowly escaped being wrecked.

After being reconditioned she was restored in June, 1920 to her original run to Campbeltown, but from Greenock, Gourock and Weymss Bay as well as Fairlie. On this she remained, except for occasional spells sailing to Inveraray, till the appearance of *King*

George V in 1926. At the beginning of the following season *King Edward* was transferred to the ownership of Williamson-Buchanan Steamers, Ltd., and placed on the 10 o'clock run from Glasgow to Rothesay, with excursions to Arran, etc., included. She was succeeded in this by *Queen Mary* in 1933, and was then put on the 11 o'clock run with its well-known excursions above mentioned as having been introduced by *Isle of Arran*.

King Edward was taken over by The Caledonian Steam Packet Co. Ltd., in 1935, and passed to Williamson-Buchanan Steamers (1936) Ltd. on 16th June, 1936. In December, 1939 she received yellow and black-topped funnels and on 4th March, 1943 was transferred again to The Caledonian S.P. Co. Ltd. During the Second World War she performed tender services on the Clyde, and resumed passenger sailings in the spring of 1946, after being overhauled by Scott's S.B. & E.Co.Ltd., Greenock. On 1st June, 1946 she re-inaugurated the 11 a.m. sailing from Glasgow to Rothesay and Kyles of Bute. After a reported sale to Belgian owners she was sold on 6th June, 1952, for scrapping, and allocated to West of Scotland Shipbreaking Co. Ltd., Troon, where she arrived on 10th June, 1952. One of her turbines went to the Kelvingrove Museum, Glasgow.

Qu.S.S./Tr.S.S. *Queen Alexandra* (I).   About 20 feet longer than *King Edward*, and at least one knot faster, this ship, like her, had five propellers originally, and was owned by Turbine Steamers, Ltd., from the outset.

She had an upper-deck amidships, and this was so much appreciated by passengers that *King Edward* was subsequently fitted similarly. The upper or shade-deck has, in fact, become a feature of all Clyde turbine steamers, as well as of some of the paddle vessels.

Queen Alexandra was launched on 8th April, 1902 and ran her trials on 28th May, attaining a speed of 21·63 knots. After an experimental run from Fairlie to Oban, where she remained about a week, she took up the Campbeltown run at the beginning of that season. On it she remained till September, 1911 when a fire occurred on board while she was at Greenock. She was sold to the Canadian Pacific Railway Company for service at Vancouver, and re-named *Princess Patricia*. In January, 1937 she was sold to Capitol Iron & Metals Co. Ltd., Victoria, B.C., for scrapping.

Tr.S.S. *Queen Alexandra* (II). This steamer was built by Messrs. Denny to take the place of the previous vessel of the same name, and was almost identical with her in design and dimensions. She was launched on 9th April, 1912 and was placed on the

Campbeltown run, on which she remained till requisitioned for transport work. In this she was engaged from 7th February, 1915 till 10th May, 1919. While in the Admiralty service she rammed and sank a German submarine, and her skipper, Captain Angus Keith, received the O.B.E. and Distinguished Service Cross in recognition.

After being re-conditioned, *Queen Alexandra* resumed her sailings on the Firth, being usually on the Inveraray run till restored to the Campbeltown route in 1927. In 1932 her upper deck was enclosed to form an observation lounge as on the later steamers, and her accommodation was accordingly considerably improved, though the alteration rather spoiled her appearance, being out of harmony with her design.

She was sold to David MacBrayne, Ltd., on 3rd October, 1935, and renamed *Saint Columba*. *See* Chapter IX.

P.S. *Queen-Empress*. An extra steamer was built for the fleet of John Williamson & Company in 1912, and launched on 20th April in that year. This was *Queen-Empress,* a product of the yard of Messrs. Murdoch & Murray, Port Glasgow, and an improved version of the *Kylemore*. She was fitted with compound diagonal engines, and was quite an acquisition to the up-river fleet.

Her First World War service consisted in transporting troops from Southampton to various French ports, and later she was engaged in mine-sweeping, stationed on the Tyne. Finally she was used as an ambulance transport in the White Sea, and nearly had to be abandoned after running aground. She was successfully refloated, however, and resumed her Clyde sailings in 1920, running excursions from the various coast towns. A year or two later she made Glasgow her headquarters, sailing to Rothesay or Lochgoilhead, and continued thus till the end of 1935, in September each year relieving the turbine steamer on the Campbeltown run.

On 3rd October, 1935, *Queen-Empress* became a member of the Caledonian fleet, being transferred on 16th June, 1936 to Williamson-Buchanan Steamers (1936) Ltd. Thereafter she was used mainly on railway connexion services from Greenock, Gourock and Wemyss Bay, and from March, 1938 had her funnel painted yellow with black top.

In October, 1939 she went to Ardrossan for conversion for a second spell of naval work, and left in January, 1940 for Portsmouth. She was flagship of the 12th Flotilla, which included *Oriole (Eagle III), Duchess of Rothesay, Duchess of Fife, Waverley* and *Marmion*. During her war service *Queen-Empress* brought down two enemy aircraft. From 1943 she was again owned by The Caledonian S.P. Co. Ltd. On return from war service she was found to be not worth re-conditioning and was sold on 9th August, 1946 to N.V. Machinehandel en Scheepslooperij "De Koophandel", Nieuw Lekkerkland, Holland, for scrapping.

*   *   *   *   *   *

It was in April, 1912 that the fleet of Turbine Steamers, Ltd., was augmented by the purchase, in association with David MacBrayne, Ltd., of the two remaining Clyde steamers of the Lochgoil and Inveraray Steamboat Co. Ltd.—*Edinburgh Castle* and *Lord of the Isles,* both thenceforth registered in the name of Turbine Steamers, Ltd., though the steward's department of the latter was operated by David MacBrayne Ltd., that of the former being provided by contact.

It was often stated that David MacBrayne Ltd. were part-owners of the *Lord of the Isles*; but the position was that they acquired shares in Turbine Steamers Ltd., who became the registered owners of the two ships taken over from the Lochgoil & Inveraray Company.

LOCHGOIL & INVERARAY STEAMBOAT CO. LTD.

Though dating only from its incorporation on 6th May, 1909 this company, nevertheless, succeeded two much older concerns, *videlicet*:—

LOCHGOIL & LOCHLONG STEAMBOAT COMPANY

Formed by Contract of Co-partnership, this Company commenced trading on 9th February, 1825. From 1814 there had been regular service by sailing wherries between Lochgoilhead and Glasgow, the steamer *Oscar* being placed on the station in 1818 and passing to the above Company, which caused two other boats, the *St. Catherine* and *St. George* to be built and fitted out for the Lochgoil route. The *Defiance,* afterwards named *Highland Lad,* also was on this run, but whether on charter to the Company or in opposition is not certain. About this period much traffic for Inveraray went via Lochgoilhead, thence by coach to St. Catherine's and ferryboat across Loch Fyne.

In "The Highlands and Islands, A Nineteenth Century Tour", by J. E. Bowman, the Author describes the "fine steam vessel the *St. Catherine* waiting for passengers at the very head of Loch Long", to which he had walked from Tarbet when doing the Loch Lomond and Loch Long circular tour.

The original partners, whose position was confirmed at the Annual Meeting on 9th March, 1827, were Mungo Nutter Campbell of St. Catherine's, Chairman and Convener; Donald Campbell, Merchant in Glasgow; John Neilson, Engineer there; Peter Graham, Master of the steamboat *St. George*; Lachlan MacLachlan, Andrew Ranken, Archibald Campbell of Drumsynie, along with John Gordon, then deceased. The Trustees appointed were the said Archibald Campbell, Mungo Nutter Campbell, Peter Graham, Andrew Ranken and Arthur Forbes, Writer, Glasgow.

Of the above-mentioned steamers *Oscar* remained till wrecked at Roseneath Point in 1831; *Highland Lad* till broken up in 1827; *St. George* till 1829; and *St. Catherine* till about 1835, when a new steamer named *Lochgoil* was built, succeeded in 1841 by a second ship of the same name, which was joined in 1842 by a consort, *Lochlong,* the first iron steamer on the Firth of Clyde services. The latter was in 1847 registered in names of Peter Graham, Andrew Ranken, Arthur Forbes and Mungo Nutter Campbell as surviving Trustees for the Company; and in that year her name was changed to *Helvellyn* on her being chartered to the Furness Railway Company who bought her outright in December, 1848. (They employed her on the Barrow–Fleetwood station).

The place of *Lochlong* was taken in 1847 by *Breadalbane,* followed in 1851 by *Ardentinny*. The former was sold to Sydney owners in 1857, and the latter in the following year to owners in Londonderry. A third *Lochgoil* joined the fleet in 1853, leaving the Clyde in 1870 for the same destination as *Ardentinny,* and being re-named *Lough Foyle*. As such she returned to the Clyde and after a spell in Sunday-breaking work she was purchased by David MacBrayne, becoming the first *Lochness* and surviving till 1912 on the mail run between Inverness and Fort Augustus. The Lochgoil Company in 1859 took delivery of the second *Lochlong*, a ship in advance of her time in having a straight stem and her funnel forward of the paddle-boxes, and the prototype of many other flush-decked steamers built for the Clyde in the ensuing years. Her place on the Lochgoil station was taken by *Mail* and *Express* (of Messrs. Campbell of Kilmun) in 1864, when *Lochlong* was sold to owners in Copenhagen.

The next addition was *Carrick Castle*, a flushed-decked steamer, which after 11 years went to the Firth of Forth, and later to the Bristol Channel, where she became in succession *Lady Margaret* and *Lord Tredegar*. She had as a consort on the Lochgoil route *Windsor Castle* from 1875, originally flush-decked, but soon fitted with a narrow saloon aft and latterly also with a full-breadth saloon forward. *Carrick Castle* and *Windsor Castle* of this fleet were the first in Clyde service to have the bridge forward of the funnel, raised to the level of the rail.

P.S. *Edinburgh Castle.* This was the last steamer built for the Company, and dated from 1879. She was well known for her exceptionally large paddle-boxes, so high that the bridge was on a lower level than their tops; and with her narrow saloon aft and no fore saloon she was not so well proportioned as the average Clyde steamer of her time. She is believed to have been the last steamer to call at Partick Wharf, which was closed on 24th November, 1906. She passed to the Lochgoil & Inveraray Company in 1909, and to Turbine Steamers, Ltd., in 1912, with whom, however, she remained for two seasons only, being sold in November, 1913 for scrapping. After her withdrawal, Messrs. MacBrayne's *Chevalier* was put on the passenger run to Lochgoil, but in 1914 this again reverted to Turbine Steamers, Ltd., who used their newly-acquired *Ivanhoe.* From 1915 the mail service was maintained by Messrs. MacBrayne, mainly with the motor-vessel *Comet* (*see* Chapter IX).

*　　*　　*　　*　　*　　*

In 1885 the Lochgoil Company took over from Lochlomond Steamboat Company the third *Chancellor* (dating from 1880) together with the goodwill of the Arrochar trade, this ship being retained till sold in the autumn of 1891 to the Glasgow & South Western Railway Company (*see* Chapter II). The Company's Contract of Co-partnership was amended at a General Meeting at Glasgow on 20th August, 1889 the capital being increased to £7,920. The Trustees then appointed were William Maclean, Writer, Glasgow, John Carmichael, Accountant and Insurance Broker, there, William Smith, Schoolmaster, Lochgoilhead, and Malcolm Turner Clark, Shipping Agent, Glasgow, the Secretary and Manager of the Company, and very well known for his connexion with Lochgoil and Inveraray steamers. A Company was incorporated on 19th December, 1895 with the name of the old co-partnership but with "Limited" added, and the nominal capital then became £14,520. The Directors were Donald McArthur, Duncan C. McArthur, John Carmichael, Andrew Kennedy, William Barr, Master Mariner, William Smith, Malcolm Turner Clark, William Maclean, Charles James MacLean, William Robertson, William G. Kennedy and Andrew McDonald. In June, 1908 resolutions were adopted making the company a private one. On 6th January, 1909 it was resolved, as the Company by reason of its liabilities could not continue business, that it be wound up voluntarily.

(ii) THE GLASGOW & INVERARAY STEAMBOAT COMPANY

Incorporated on 24th July, 1877 under the Companies Act, 1862 as an unlimited company, certain of the subscribers being also shareholders in the Lochgoil and Lochlong Steamboat Company, and Malcolm Turner Clark being Secretary and Manager, this Company was registered as unlimited under the Companies Acts, 1862 and 1867 on 9th October, 1890 and as a Company limited by shares under the Acts 1862 to 1890, on 9th October, 1890. In 1908 it was declared a private company, and on 6th January, 1909 it was resolved that it would be wound up. The main purpose of the Company was to develop a new route to the Highlands with a daily summer passenger service from Glasgow to Inveraray and return, and with the Loch Eck Tour in connexion, thus reviving a service inaugurated by David Napier.

For the Inveraray service there was built in 1877 a very fine saloon steamer, *Lord of the Isles*, one of several products of the yard of D. & W. Henderson, fitted with their diagonal oscillating machinery. A point of interest in connexion with these engines was that with only one crank practically the same degree of flexibility in manoeuvring was obtained as if the normal design of two cranks had been adopted. This was achieved by locating one cylinder abaft and the other forward of the crankshaft, and inclining them so that results equivalent to a pair of cranks at 90° were obtained, without the additional expense. The arrangement was, however, not so compact in the fore and aft direction. Steam was supplied by two haystack boilers (one forward and one aft of the engines), the resultant two-funnelled design being very pleasing and symmetrical. She surpassed the third *Iona* in appointments, and was the direct cause of the building of the *Columba* for Messrs. Hutcheson's established mail run to Ardrishaig which in turn caused the owners of *Lord of the Isles* to have certain improvements carried out in time for the 1879 season, including the lengthening of the fore saloon almost to the mast. Like so many others of the Clyde and West Highland steamers and motorships, she also had her funnels lengthened by approximately the depth of the black tops.

After 14 seasons on the Clyde, *Lord of the Isles* was sold for service on the Thames, where she was acclaimed as a great advance on her predecessors in the excursion business. She introduced the Lochgoil funnel colours—red, with two white bands divided by a narrower black one, and black top—to London, where they were adopted by the Victoria Steamboat Association, of which her owners formed part, and which colours were subsequently borne by the well-known *Koh-i-Noor, Royal Sovereign* and *La Marguerite*.

The appearance of *Lord of the Isles* when on the Thames was ruined by the fitting of telescopic funnels, and a rather clumsy full-breadth saloon aft. Later she was named *Jupiter,* returning still later to the Clyde under the flag of A. Dawson Reid and named *Lady of the Isles*. After not very successful attempts in the excursion trade from Glasgow, she was laid up, and scrapped in 1904.

*   *   *   *   *   *

As above mentioned, in the early days of steam navigation a considerable volume of traffic for Inveraray went via Lochgoil, the journey being made by steamer to Lochgoilhead, coach to St. Catherines and ferry to Inveraray. The ferry rights were vested from early times in the Provost, Magistrates and Town Councillors of the Burgh of Inveraray. The paddle-steamer *Thalia* was stationed on Loch Fyne, and sailed in connexion with David Napier's services to the Highlands *via* Loch Lomond, Holy Loch and Loch Eck. In August, 1827, *Thalia* was advertised to sail from Inveraray every morning at 7-30 o'clock with passengers for Glasgow via Cairndow and Loch Lomond; and for Strachur every morning at 10 o'clock, with passengers for Glasgow via Loch Eck and Holy Loch. The Loch Lomond steamer mentioned in this advertisement is *Euphrosyne;* and, though the Loch Eck steamer is not specifically named, it was probably *Aglaia* which was built about 1820, and was the first iron passsenger steamer in the world. This vessel was designed by David Napier, who also ran a steam coach in connexion, later withdrawn on account of alleged damage to the road, and superseded by horse-drawn vehicles. About 1828 *Aglaia* was succeeded by another small paddle-steamer, but for some reason or other the coach and steamer were withdrawn, and it was many years before the Loch Eck steamer service was revived.

On the ferry run *Argyle* from 1849 operated from Strachur; and from 1865 another steamer, *Fairy*, owned by the Inveraray Ferry & Coach Co. Ltd., managed by Walter Malcolm, Inveraray, ran from St. Catherine's. By 1870 she had passed to the Inveraray & St. Catherine's Ferry Co. Ltd., who then ran a new coach in addition to the existing one, *Fairy* doing six crossings a day. She was succeeded in 1893 by the second *Fairy*; but from about 1913 only a motor-boat was on the run, and even this no longer operates. The first and second *Fairy* must have been among the smallest paddle-steamers ever built, and such vessels could not have failed to impress and attract anyone who saw them, probably more even than a large liner would have done.

The through service *via* Loch Eck was in 1878 revived by the

Glasgow & Inveraray Steamboat Company. The first *Lord of the Isles* had been placed on the Glasgow-Inveraray station in the previous year, and Messrs. D. Hutcheson & Co. replied to this invasion of part of their territory by having *Columba* built: it was in order to meet this challenge that the Glasgow & Inveraray Company decided to open an alternative route to the Highlands by resuscitating the tour instituted so long before by David Napier, and for the Loch Eck sailings they had built, on the loch-side, by Messrs. T. B. Seath & Co. of Rutherglen, a steamer intended to be named *Lady of the Lake* but launched on 28th February, 1878 as *Fairy Queen*. At the end of 1879 she was badly burnt and in 1880 there appeared on the loch a steamer of the same name described in some reports as 'new' but apparently the original vessel lengthened and improved since after registration in 1882 she was always shown as 'built 1878'.

The overland portion of the tour was made by means of horse-drawn coaches, instead of the steam propelled vehicles devised by David Napier; and Dunoon became the starting-point instead of Kilmun, though the latter was a possible alternative in the early days of the tour.

Passengers travelling via Kilmun went in the steamer *Vivid*, in connexion with the 7-20 train from Bridge Street Station, while it was also possible to reach Dunoon by *Guinevere*, in connexion with the 9-5 train from St. Enoch. In the former case the tourists proceeded by coach to Inverchapel, at the foot of Loch Eck, and then by steamer to the head—the journey thence to Strachur being completed by another coach. At Strachur passengers joined *Lord of the Isles* on her way to Inveraray, where an hour ashore was allowed, after which they rejoined the steamer to return to Glasgow or Greenock. Those who went *via* Dunoon were in time for *Fairy Queen* on her second run of the day, and reached Srachur in time for the *Lord of the Isles* on her homeward run. The coachmen wore scarlet coats and grey top-hats, while at intervals the guard blew a long trumpet, the whole making a splendid sight.

In 1909 Lochgoil & Inveraray Steamboat Co. Ltd. was formed to take over the assets of Lochgoil & Lochlong Steamboat Co. Ltd., and Glasgow & Inveraray Steamboat Co. Ltd. (both in liquidation), which included the steamers *Edinburgh Castle, Lord of the Isles* and *Fairy Queen,* together with the coaches used for the Loch Eck tour. The two Clyde steamers passed in 1912 to Turbine Steamers, Ltd., but *Fairy Queen* remained the property of the Lochgoil & Inveraray Steamboat Co. Ltd. An effort was made to revive the loch sailings in 1919 but in the 1920s the steamer was scrapped. The company thereafter owned no steamers, but the names *Fairy Queen* and *Lord of the Isles* were borne by two of its motor coaches, till it was dissolved in 1936.

P.S. *Lord of the Isles*. (II). To take the place of the first *Lord of the Isles* a new vessel bearing the same name was launched by Messrs. D. & W. Henderson & Company in 1891. Like her predecessor, she had a diagonal oscillating engine, and was similar in design though somewhat larger and had her deck-saloons the full width of the hull.

Some years after she was built her promenade deck was extended to the bow, thus giving increased accommodation.

Lord of the Isles was always a popular and well-known boat, and was most successful while on the Inveraray station until the opposition of Turbine Steamers Ltd. became too strong for her, and she was taken over by that company.

By her new owners, *Lord of the Isles* was used principally for excursions from Glasgow round the Island of Bute, etc., but in 1928, when *Iona* was required at Oban, she was put on the Lochgoilhead and Arrochar run from Glasgow in succession to that steamer, being then advertised by Messrs. MacBrayne. She was also for a short time in the spring of that year on their Greenock–Ardishaig mail service.

At the end of 1928, *Lord of the Isles* was considered too costly to run, and went to Smith & Co., shipbreakers, at Port Glasgow. Many regretted her passing, as she had been a fine ship in her day.

Neither of the Lochgoil and Inveraray steamers, as a result of their entering the Turbine fleet, lost their distinctive funnel-colouring, which became extinct only on the passing of *Lord of the Isles*. She was also the last Clyde steamer to have polished copper steampipes, and these she retained to the end.

TURBINE STEAMERS LTD. 1912-1935
WILLIAMSON-BUCHANAN STEAMERS LTD. 1919-1935

P.S. *Ivanhoe*. It was in June, 1914 that this well-known steamer found her way into the fleet of Turbine Steamers, Ltd., after being purchased by David MacBrayne Ltd. from the Firth of Clyde S.P. Co., Ltd. Reference has already been made to this vessel as she was owned for a considerable time by The Caledonian Steam Packet Co. Ltd., and was also chartered by them during the First World War.

While in the service of Turbine Steamers, Ltd., *Ivanhoe* had her funnels painted their standard colours of white with black top, but on being chartered by the Caledonian Company her funnels were again painted yellow. On returning to her owners in 1920 she did not resume sailing but was sold in September of that year, and broken up at Dumbarton.

T.S.S. *King George V.* Just as the pioneer merchant vessel propelled by turbine machinery was a product of Denny's Dumbarton yard, so the first passenger steamer fitted with high-pressure steam turbines—*King George V*—also was built there, and for the company which had owned *King Edward* for very many years.

Originally fitted with two Yarrow water-tube boilers working at a pressure of 550 lb. and a steam temperature of 750° Fahrenheit, the steamer was unique. The port set of machinery, consisting of four ahead turbines, worked on the principle of quadruple expansion. The starboard set worked triple expansion ahead, the first turbine on this side receiving its steam from the extra high-pressure one on the port side. Both sets operated identically when the ship was reversed, two astern turbines being incorporated in each set. The original boilers were removed in 1929, Babcock & Wilcox boilers being then installed. At the same time navy-tops were fitted to the funnels. Again in 1935 it was decided to make a change, and the steamer then received one ordinary double-ended Scotch boiler, working at 200-lb. pressure. When this last change was made the extra high-pressure turbine was taken out of the ship, and both sets were then similar and worked triple expansion ahead, each high-pressure turbine receiving boiler steam. New funnels of greater diameter than the old, and without navy-tops, were fitted at the same time. The turbines were of Parsons design and were supplied, along with the single reduction gearing, from that firm's establishment at Wallsend.

It was late in the 1926 season before *King George V* took her place in the Turbine fleet, and at the beginning of the following season *King Edward* was relegated to the up-river traffic. *King George V* was thereafter employed on either the Campbeltown or Inveraray service, more often on the latter, with the Loch Eck Tour in connexion (by coach between Dunoon and Strachur).

Though similar in general appearance to the previous turbine steamers, *King George V* nevertheless embodied many improvements. She was the first Clyde steamer to have part of the promenade deck enclosed and also had her dining-saloon situated on the main deck aft instead of on the lower deck as had been the usual practice previously. She was sold to David MacBrayne, Ltd., on 3rd October, 1935. *See* Chapter IX.

Tr.S.S. *Queen Mary/Queen Mary II/Queen Mary.* Another fine turbine steamer—*Queen Mary*—was built by Messrs. Denny in

1933, for the Williamson-Buchanan fleet. No steamer of this standard had been built for the up-river service for years, and she was splendidly patronised. Her usual run from Glasgow was at 10 a.m. to Dunoon and Rothesay, with non-landing excursions to Arran, Skipness, etc. On Saturdays she left Glasgow at 1-45 for Dunoon, Rothesay and a cruise to Kyles of Bute.

In the spring of 1935 the name of this steamer was changed to *Queen Mary II* at the request of the owners of the Cunard-White Star liner *Queen Mary*. A portrait of Her Majesty Queen Mary was presented by the latter company to Williamson-Buchanan Steamers, Ltd. and was in the forward lounge of the ship till transferred in 1971 to the new dining saloon mentioned below.

Queen Mary II was rather like *King George V* in many ways, but had solid bulwarks instead of an open rail at the bow, and the first-class accommodation was forward, an innovation so far as Clyde steamers were concerned. (She was latterly a one-class ship).

The machinery was of the ordinary direct-acting type, three turbines being fitted, and three propellers. Steam was supplied by a Scotch boiler, and she was capable of 18 knots. In the spring of 1957 she was re-boilered with a Yarrow water-tube oil-fired boiler, and re-appeared with only one funnel. As it was well proportioned, she remained a handsome ship, and many thought her appearance had been improved, though it is difficult to resist the preference for two funnels.

In October, 1935, she passed to Caledonian ownership, then through the changes shared by the other Williamson-Buchanan vessels. Her funnels became yellow with black tops in December, 1939 and during the war she went through the usual changes to all grey; and to black hull with horizon yellow funnels and superstructure. During the period 1939-1946 she was almost continuously on the Gourock–Dunoon run, reverting to the 10 a.m. service from Glasgow, from 1st June, 1946.

In 1953 she was given a mainmast, to conform with lighting regulations. Radar was installed in 1960. In time for the 1969 season her masts were shortened for the Kingston Bridge, as also were those of *Duchess of Hamilton, Caledonia* and *Waverley*. After the withdrawal of regular sailings from Glasgow at the end of the 1969 season she was based at Gourock, performing sailings to Dunoon, Rothesay, Kyles of Bute, etc., and excursions, including a few Saturday afternoon trips round Ailsa Craig; and from 1971 she became successor to *Duchess of Hamilton* on the Campbeltown run, having had a considerable refit in the Spring, including the refurnishing of the deck lounge, the conversion of the dining saloon on the main deck forward into a modern cafeteria, the removal of the bar from the lower deck to the main deck aft (known as the

"Firth Lounge") and the creation of a new dining saloon in the traditional position of bygone years, on the lower deck but forward, then named the "Queen's Restaurant".

The ship celebrated her fortieth birthday on Saturday, 5th May, 1973, by which time she was wearing the colours of Caledonian MacBrayne, Ltd. Her original name was restored at a ceremony on board on 6th May, 1976, the need for the numeral having gone with the demise of the Cunarder. She continued on excursions and charter sailings, including one on 4th September that year on the former Royal Route to Tarbert and Ardrishaig. She gave additional sailings to Brodick at peak holiday periods, supplementing the *Caledonia* there, and also on the Wemyss Bay–Rothesay route on Saturdays. Her Glasgow berth was latterly at Anderston Quay. At the end of the 1977 season she was withdrawn and laid up in East India Harbour, Greenock, being subsequently sold to the City of Glasgow District Council to become a floating museum, but this idea was abandoned on account of the cutting of public expenditure. She was put on the market, being sold in 1980 to Euroyachts, Ltd. for yet another floating restaurant venture. Apart from a few days in drydock for underwater preservation, she remained in East India Harbour. In January, 1981, she was sold for similar use on the Thames, and left Greenock under tow on 29th January. After various proposals she was reported in 1986 to have beeen sold to Bass Charrington to become the successor to *Old Caledonia* at the Thames Embankment. In July 1988 she was towed from Chatham and, after negotiating the bridges, appeared at her berth, being opened by Toby Restaurants for trading, in 1989. She again has two funnels, initially white with black tops, but later embellished with maroon bands.

CHAPTER V

THE CALEDONIAN STEAM PACKET CO. LTD. (Contd.)
1936–1947

T.S.S. *Marchioness of Graham.* Launched on 6th March, 1936 at the Fairfield yard, this was a modernised *Atalanta*, though with many features in common with the paddle-vessels then recently added to the L.M.S. and Caledonian fleets, having one elliptical funnel, two masts and cruiser stern, and of very pleasing apppearance. The promenade deck was nearly the full length, and on it were observation lounges, fore and aft, above which were two separate upper decks. As on most of the other then recent Clyde steamers, the first-class dining-saloon was on the main deck (aft), a lounge being provided on this deck forward for the use of both first- and third-class passengers. On the lower deck forward was the third-class dining-saloon, while on this level aft were situated officers' quarters, a smoke-room and a tea-room, all with separate entrances from the main deck, on account of the intervening bulkheads. Immediately aft of the funnel on the promenade deck was a large clear space for the accommodation of motor-cars, in which there was then developing a considerable traffic to and from the Island of Arran.

She was fitted with four turbines driving twin screws through single-reduction gearing. Steam was supplied by a Scotch boiler, and she remained coal-fired throughout her Clyde career.

Primarily intended for the Ardrossan–Arran service, she was, however, used for excursion work from Gourock or Glasgow as required, and also as part of her service provided evening cruises from Ardrossan. During the Second World War she operated principally from Fairlie to Millport and Brodick and sometimes from Wemyss Bay to Innellan and Rothesay. In July, 1946 she began to be used for excursions to Kyles of Bute, etc., and from 1947 was based at Ayr, also giving runs between Ardrossan and Arran at peak periods, and from 1954 succeeding *Glen Sannox* on the Arran station. By 1957 she was the only coal-fired steamer remaining in the Clyde fleet, and was used on excursions mainly from Largs, reviving the up-river sailings to Glasgow, in abeyance since 1939. At the end of the 1958 season she was withdrawn and sold to the Diapoulis Line, Piraeus, for service among the Greek islands. In Greece she was converted to Diesel propulsion, and her superstructure was entirely remodelled so that in appearance she became unrecognisable. She was named in succession *Hellas, Nea Hellas, Galaxias* and *El Greco* and had several changes of ownership. In 1970 she was laid up at Ambelaki, near Piraeus and was broken up at Perama during 1975.

T.S.M.V. *Countess of Breadalbane* (II). To take the place of the steamer of the same name, the twin screw motor-vessel *Countess of Breadalbane* was built for the The Caledonian Steam Packet Co. Ltd. by Messrs. William Denny & Bros., Ltd., Dumbarton, for service on Loch Awe. She was erected in the builders' yard, then dismantled and transported in sections by rail to Loch Awe, where the hull was reassembled. She was launched in May, 1936 rather earlier than was originally intended, as it was feared that the level of the loch might fall and so be unsuitable for the launch. The naming ceremony was performed by the youngest apprentice who had taken part in her construction.

Forward on the lower deck there was a lounge, immediately aft of which was the dining-saloon, and the remaining space on this level was occupied by the machinery. On the promenade deck, which is the full length of the ship, were deck-houses originally containing—at the forward end—an observation lounge with large windows, from which passengers had a good view of the scenery. *Countess of Breadalbane* had a cruiser stern, and one mast; and her design had several features in common with that of the then recent Clyde steamers belonging to the same owners, though, of course, everything was on a much smaller scale. In design she was similar to T.S.M.V. *Teal*, built in the same year for service on Lake Windermere, but much smaller.

The machinery consisted of two sets of six-cylinder Gleniffer high-speed Diesels, driving the twin screws through reduction gearing. As the exhaust is through the hull on the water level, no funnel was necessary; and this was unfortunate from the aesthetic point of view, but in her later days on Loch Lomond (*See* Chapter XIV) the absence has been made good. In the place where one would normally expect to find a funnel there was a small galley chimney, originally painted yellow. This was removed when calor-gas was installed for heating and cooking.

On trial a speed of 10·5 knots was recorded. With a gross tonnage of 106, *Countess of Breadalbane* was the first Loch Awe vessel to attain the dignity of a place in Lloyd's Register and was also the first motor passenger ship on the loch. The hull was painted white, and green below, with a blue water-line, and so did not conform to the standard colour-scheme of the other vessels of The Caledonian Steam Packet Co. Ltd. One run per day in each direction was made (in summer only), leaving Lochawe Pier at 11.40 a.m.; and the return from Ford was at 3 p.m., calls being made at Taychreggan and Port Sonachan. Connexion was made at Lochawe in both directions with northbound and southbound trains. In addition, evening cruises were run on certain evenings during the summer season. During the second war she was laid up on the slip near Lochawe Station, resuming service in summer each year from 1948 to 1951. On account of insufficient traffic she was withdrawn, and in April, 1952 was taken by road from Loch Awe *via* Dalmally to Inveraray, where she was launched into Loch Fyne. After an overhaul by her builders (during which her rectangular hull windows were plated over and port holes substituted) she joined the Clyde fleet in which she proved most useful, first on various "feeder" services, such as Largs–Rothesay to connect with the larger cruise steamers; Friday evenings from Rothesay to Tighnabruaich, with the first inward run therefrom on Saturdays; Largs–Millport; and the late afternoon run from Craigendoran to Rothesay. After being re-engined in the spring of 1956 (with her speed increased to 12 knots) she was able to perform this run with ease. When she came to the Clyde her white hull was painted black, becoming white again later, then monastral blue, and then again black. She was on the Holy Loch run from Gourock from 1967 till its cessation in May, 1971, continuing there for Mr. Roy Ritchie (*See* Chapters XIII and XIV).

T.S.M.V. *Arran Mail.* To provide additional facilities for the transport of mails, cargo and motor-cars between Ardrossan and Arran, this vessel was built for The Caledonian S.P. Co. Ltd., by Messrs. Denny; and her trials were run on 15th July, 1936. She was permitted to carry 10 passengers. Of coaster type with straight stem and cruiser stern, *Arran Mail* was propelled by two sets of six-cylinder Gleniffer high-speed Diesels, with three-to-one reduction gearing, and giving a service speed of about 10 knots. Additional equipment included a two-cylinder Gleniffer high-speed Diesel engine driving an electric generator, air compressor and bilge pump.

Forward of the machinery space there was a hold with one large hatchway, served by a 2¼-ton steel derrick carried on the mast. Near the stern was a deckhouse containing a small saloon, captain's cabin, galley, etc.; and in the whaleback forecastle was accommodation for the engineer, mate and two seamen. Electric light was used throughout.

The deck machinery, all electric, consisted of a windlass and two winches, the latter for operating the derrick—one of them being arranged to take mechanical slewing gear. Hand steering-gear was installed on the navigating bridge, controlling a balanced spade-type rudder.

Arran Mail left Ardrossan at 6.45 a.m. with mails, newspapers and cargo, and so relieved the regular passenger steamers of much of the traffic that formerly inconvenienced them and made timekeeping difficult. This new service was much appreciated by the people of Arran, who received the mails and newspapers much earlier than the first arrival of *Glen Sannox* at 11.5. *Arran Mail* reached Brodick shortly after 8 a.m. and so letters were able to be delivered and answered, and replies despatched the same day from the island.

The war service of *Arran Mail* consisted of acting as tender to merchant ships at Gourock. From November, 1949 cargo for Brodick and Millport, conveyed by rail to Ardrossan, increased beyond the capacity of *Arran Mail*, which was superseded by the *Arran*, displaced from the Glasgow cargo services. *Arran Mail* was then laid up at Greenock and in the summer of 1950 performed some luggage runs between Fairlie and Millport. In December, 1951 she was sold to Mrs. F. M. D. Houillon, Ruislip, and, in September, 1954 to Mr. Geo. A. Bassadone, Gibraltar, passing about three months later to Serra Bros., there, by whom she was re-named *Saint Ernest*. As such she was acquired by Allen Shipping Ltd., Alderney, and foundered at sea in January, 1962 unfortunately with the loss of her crew.

P.S. *Jupiter* (II).   In September, 1936, two paddle steamers were ordered from The Fairfield Shipbuilding & Engineering Co. Ltd., each to be fitted with one double-ended cylindrical return-tube boiler and with two funnels forward of the paddle-boxes. The first to be launched, on 9th April, 1937, was named *Jupiter*. Of the same length as *Mercury* and *Caledonia*, and with similar paddle-boxes, they were, however, of very much more pleasing design, and with their two funnnels and two masts were quite fine looking ships.

Stowage space for motor-cars was provided between the funnels, and on the shade-deck forward was a large steel house containing accommodation for the captain. The third-class lounge on the main deck forward was panelled in red serayah wood, the deck being laid with rubber tiling. On the main deck aft were the first-class lounge and tea-room, and a dining saloon and bar were to be found on the lower deck forward, the first-class smoke-room being on the lower deck aft. Mechanical ventilation was employed.

The propelling machinery consisted of triple expansion diagonal engines somewhat similar to those of *Mercury*, with the exception of the valves and valve gear, the former being of Andrews & Cameron cam-operated type and the latter a development of the Bremme single eccentric gear.

Auxiliaries included steam windlasses and capstans; steam steering-gear, operated by telemotor from the bridge or by hand from the quarter-deck; two feed-pumps, one air-pump and a feed-heater supplied by Messrs. G. & J. Weir, Ltd., one circulating pump by Messrs. Drysdale & Co. Ltd., Glasgow, one fresh-water pump by Worthington-Simpson Ltd., London, and two fans by Messrs. James Howden & Co. Ltd., Glasgow, who also supplied spark-arresters in the funnels.

After three seasons in the Clyde passenger services, *Jupiter* was requisitioned, converted for mine-sweeping and commissioned as H.M.S. *Scawfell*. She was part of the 11th Mine-sweeping Flotilla, based first at Milford Haven and later at Dover. Later as an escort ship, she made some trips to Holland, and also operated between the Tyne and Humber. Converted to an A.A. Defence ship, she formed part of the Thames Defence Flotilla, and took part in the Normandy landings on D-day plus 1. Three enemy 'planes were brought down.

Scawfell returned to the Clyde safely after the war, and was re-conditioned by Messrs. D. & W. Henderson & Co. Ltd., at Meadowside. With her own name of *Jupiter* restored, she was the first Clyde steamer that had been on war service to resume normal sailings on the Firth, which she did in February, 1946 on the Holy Loch route. She was, thereafter, on the Gourock and Wemyss Bay to Rothesay runs. Converted to oil burning in the winter of 1956-57 she cruised from Glasgow to Lochgoilhead on Sunday afternoons, and the rest of the week was on various railway services; but she was not entirely successful, and was laid up in Albert Harbour, Greenock. Sold in May, 1960 to a Belfast buyer, she was afterwards re-sold to Hammond Lane Foundry Co. Ltd., Dublin, for scrap, and left Greenock in tow on 5th April, 1961.

P.S. *Juno* (II). The sister-ship to *Jupiter* was appropriately named *Juno*, and was launched on 25th May, 1937. They were indistinguishable in appearance, the only differences being in internal furnishings. The panelling of the saloons in the case of *Juno* consisted of figured Quebec birch with light mahogany framings.

When requisitioned for mine-sweeping, *Juno* became H.M.S. *Helvellyn*, and had a career similar to that of *Jupiter* until she met her end during one of the London blitzes, when she was bombed and sunk in the Thames on 19th March, 1941.

T.S.M.V. *Ashton*. In order to give visitors to the Empire Exhibition, held at Bellahouston, an opportunity of viewing the River Clyde and its shipyards, etc., The Caledonian S.P. Co. Ltd.

decided in 1938 to run two small motor-vessels from Glasgow (Bridge Wharf, South Side) to Dalmuir. The first of these was named *Ashton*, and was launched from Messrs. Denny's yard on 11th May, 1938. In 1939, also, the sailings were maintained. During the war the two vessels were employed as tenders on the Clyde; and in 1946 they instituted a summer hourly service between Dunoon and Gourock to supplement the normal steamer sailings, giving certain runs also to Kilcreggan and Blairmore. An interesting and unusual charter sail was performed by *Ashton* on 12th October, 1962 on the Forth and Clyde Canal (*See* Chapter XIV). After withdrawal from the Millport station she was sold in 1965 to Mr. Roy Ritchie, Gourock, for ferry services to Helensburgh and Kilcreggan, being chartered back on occasion by the C.S.P. Company for the Rothesay–Tighnabruaich week-end service. In 1968 she was re-named *Gourockian*, and as such while on charter to the Clyde River Steamer Club called at Port Bannantyne pier in August, 1969 the first occasion for many years of a call there by any member of the Clyde fleet, and also the last.

T.S.M.V. Leven. The sister-ship of the foregoing was named *Leven*, reviving a name of very old standing on the Clyde, though not previously associated with the Railway or Williamson-Buchanan fleets. Both vessels had white hulls during their first season, but in 1939 the hulls became black, with standard Caledonian white water-line. In the spring of 1939 *Leven* did some sailing between Gourock and Kilcreggan; and, like *Ashton*, was employed during the war as a tender at Gourock. Like her, also, she went on to the Dunoon–Gourock station, the "Clutha" cruises in Glasgow Harbour not having been resumed after their cessation in 1939. In 1947 she changed places with *Wee Cumbrae* on the Largs–Millport ferry run, to which later her sister also was transferred. In 1965 *Leven* was sold to Thomas Jack & Co. (Shipping) Ltd., Larne, passing shortly afterwards to South Western Steam Navigation Co. Ltd., by whom she was re-named *Pride of the Bay*, and registered at Brixham. From 1986 she has been at Jersey.

*   *   *   *   *   *

The dredger *Carrick* was built in 1938 as a successor to *Kyle* at Ayr, being owned by the L.M.S.R. Company till transferred to the Docks, etc., Executive.

The Kyle of Lochalsh to Kyleakin ferry service, previously operated by lessees, was taken into the L.M.S. Railway Company's own control on 1st January, 1945 on the expiry of the lease to David MacBrayne Ltd. Up to the time of the extension of the

Highland Railway from Strome Ferry to Kyle in 1897, the County Councils of Inverness and Ross and Cromarty owned and operated the sailing or rowing craft employed on that route, but from 1897 the railway company took over the boats and leased them to various private individuals from time to time. The first motor launch (un-named) came on to the ferry service in 1914 and towed cattle and cars flats as required. She was succeeded in 1916 by another un-named motor boat from Oban and then by the *Kyle*, which passed to Messrs. MacBrayne in 1938.

M.V. *Skye*.   This launch, similar to *Kyle*, was acquired in 1922, remaining till sold in 1951 to a Gourock owner.

M.V. *Kyleakin* (I).   This ferry, built in 1930, was the first at Kyle to be fitted with the ingenious turntable device which had already proved its worth at Ballachulish, and later was developed to carry considerable loads—a great improvement on transporting vehicles on planks placed athwartships.

M.V. *Moil*.   Six years later a further turntable ferry was added, taking her name from the ruined castle near Kyleakin in Skye.

M.V. *Cuillin*.   The first steel ferryboat for this station was built by Messrs. Denny in 1942. All these were superseded in the 1950s by other turntable boats with greater capacity for vehicles and with covered passenger accommodation.

CHAPTER VI

NORTH BRITISH RAILWAY COMPANY
LONDON & NORTH EASTERN RAILWAY COMPANY

THE fleet of the London & North Eastern Railway Company in Scotland may be said to have had its origin in those of the Edinburgh, Perth & Dundee Railway Company, on the Forth, and of the original North British Railway Company, operating from Silloth. The former came into the North British Railway Company in 1862; and the Glasgow, Dumbarton & Helensburgh Railway Company, whose line had been opened in 1858, having been absorbed by the Edinburgh & Glasgow Railway Company in August, 1862 passed to North British ownership with the E. & G. R. on 31st July, 1865. It was thus that the North British Railway Company obtained an outlet to the Clyde coast, and in the following year a service was inaugurated, the steamers sailing from Helensburgh until the opening of Craigendoran Pier in May, 1882, when this became their headquarters.

The North British Clyde and Solway steamers were registered in the names of certain Directors of the Company, and were nominally owned by the North British Steam Packet Company till 1902 in the case of those on the Clyde and till 1919 on the Solway, at which respective dates the North British Railway Company resumed direct ownership of the steamers. It was on the absorption of the North British Railway Company on 1st January, 1923, that the steamers then owned by it were transferred to the London & North Eastern Railway Company.

The use of the name *Waverley* for two of the North British Silloth steamers connecting with the Waverley Route was followed by the adoption of names associated with Sir Walter Scott's novels for most ships in fleets associated with the N.B.R.

From 1866 to 1883 the Clyde and Silloth steamers of the North British S.P. Company were distinguished by red funnels with black tops, cream paddle-boxes and saloons, and black hulls. In 1883, however, the following colours were adopted, viz—Funnel red with a white band and black top; paddle-boxes and hull black; and saloons panelled in brown and cream outside. In 1936 the colour for the hulls and paddle-boxes was changed to grey, the saloons and deck-houses being painted white; but in 1946 the 1883 colour-scheme was restored, with modifications in the matter of panelling.

59

The Forth ferries had black funnels till about 1903, when Clyde funnel colours were adopted, but white paddle-boxes were retained.

P.S. *Meg Merrilies* (I).   This and *Dandie Dinmont* (I) were almost twin sister-ships, built by Messrs. A. & J. Inglis for the North British Steam Packet Company in 1866. The original idea of the Directors of the railway company was to run steamers from Helensburgh to Kyles of Bute and Ardrishaig *via* Rothesay; but, as this venture proved unprofitable, the boats were withdrawn during their first season. They were then laid up for a time and were advertised for sale in April, 1867. After spending some time laid up in Bowling Harbour, the *Meg Merrilies* was sold for service at Constantinople, being re-named *Nusetteyah* and later *Nuzhetie*, and being taken out of service about 1913.

A fine model of this steamer may be seen in the Transport Museum, Glasgow, and from it one may have a good idea of the old North British colours.

P.S. *Dandie Dinmont* (I).   The sister-ship of the foregoing had an inauspicious start in June, 1866 with machinery failures on two successive days, following which *Petrel* was chartered for a few days. After withdrawal from the Ardrishaig station and a period laid up, *Dandie Dinmont* sailed in 1868-69 between Granton and Burntisland, also for a time between Tayport and Broughty Ferry, then in 1869 re-appeared on the Clyde, her route being restricted to Dunoon and the Holy Loch. In this service she remained more or less constantly until the appearance of *Diana Vernon* in 1885, and after a short time as spare boat she was sold to Southsea, Ventor, Sandown & Shanklin Steamboat Co. Ltd., being wrecked about 1901.

P.S. *Carham*.   A short steamer, with funnel aft of the paddle-boxes, *Carham* spent her first years in the North British Company's services from Silloth to Dumfries and Annan (*See* "R.O.S."), coming to the Clyde in 1869. She then received a small detached saloon aft, and the mainmast was removed. Her route was from Helensburgh to the Gareloch ports, with certain runs to Dunoon in winter when *Dandie Dinmont* was not in commission.

She was sold in September, 1872 to the Dingwall & Skye Railway (later Highland Railway) Company for service from Strome Ferry to Portree, etc., and subsequently sold to Bournemouth Steam Packet Company, still later to Ramsgate Steamship Company, by whom she was re-named *Queen of Thanet*. In 1889 she was registered in the name of R. & D. Jones, Liverpool, and shortly afterwards was broken up.

P.S. *Gareloch*.   Built to take the place of *Carham*, this appropriately-named steamer was well known on the Gareloch run for many years, first from Helensburgh and later from Craigendoran.

Gareloch was a small, raised quarter-deck ship, and was fitted with two-cylindered oscillating machinery. She remained on the service for which she was built until superseded by *Lady Clare*, when she was transferred to the railway company's associated Galloway Saloon Steam Packet Company, Leith, being re-named *Wemyss Castle*. She was broken up in 1906.

P.S. *Sheila / Guy Mannering*.   In 1882, on the opening of Craigendoran Pier, the North British Railway Company again extended its operations to Rothesay, and for this service purchased from Messrs. Gillies & Campbell, the Wemyss Bay owners, their steamer *Sheila*. In the year following her acquisition she was re-named *Guy Mannering*, and it was as such that she became well known on the Craigendoran route.

Built for the Wemyss Bay–Rothesay service in 1877, *Sheila* was reputed to be very fast, and had many races with *Sultana*, then running in connexion with the G. & S.W. Railway from Greenock. As *Guy Mannering* she still maintained her reputation for speed, and was a useful boat to the North British Company. Her machinery was of the single diagonal type, and this produced the motion characteristic of such machinery when the vessel was sailing.

Guy Mannering was originally of the raised quarter-deck type, but early in 1892 was fitted with a deck saloon aft, the raised quarter-deck being largely cut away. In addition, a small detached fore saloon was installed, later connected to form part of the promenade deck. In 1894 she was sold to Wm. Buchanan and re-named *Isle of Bute*. (*See* Chapter IV).

P.S. *Meg Merrilies* (II).   In the year following the purchase of *Sheila* there was built for the North British Steam Packet Company the steamer *Meg Merrilies*, second of the name. Like the first she was two-funnelled, but the vessel under description had both funnels forward of the paddle-boxes. She had double diagonal simple engines, and a deck saloon aft, with promenade deck extending to the stern, the open space below being described as a "smoke-room".

The speed of *Meg Merrilies* did not come up to that required by the contract and she was, accordingly, returned to her builders as unsuitable, after one season. After being chartered for service on

Belfast Lough for the 1884 season, she was sold to Captain Robert Campbell of Kilmun. (*See* Chapter IV).

P.S. *Jeanie Deans* (I).   To take the place of *Meg Merrilies*, which had been returned to them as mentioned above, Messrs. Barclay, Curle & Co. produced in 1884 one of the most successful steamers ever built for Clyde service—the first *Jeanie Deans*. She promptly established herself as a very fast boat, and quite surpassed *Guy Mannering* in the matter of speed, attaining 17½ knots on trial.

Originally similar to *Guy Mannering* in design of hull and machinery, she was fitted with deck-saloons fore and aft in 1894, and thenceforth lost much of her speed. Just two years later she was sold out of the North British fleet, but re-appeared for a very short time on charter about 1919 as *Isle of Cumbrae* on the Gareloch run, relieving *Lucy Ashton*. She then again had a North British funnel, but retained her white paddle-boxes.

Sold to Derry & Moville S.P. Co. Ltd., Londonderry, she returned to the Clyde and was re-named *Duchess of York*, being thereafter employed on excursion work. She was, in 1904, purchased by Buchanan Steamers Ltd. and re-named *Isle of Cumbrae*. (*See* Chapter IV).

P.S. *Diana Vernon*.   *Diana Vernon* was another product of Barclay, Curle & Company's yard, and was a small saloon steamer particularly noted for the ease with which she could take piers. As she was of light draught she had originally no passenger accommodation above the fore-saloon, the promenade deck being railed off just forward of the funnel. Her trial speed was 15·86 knots.

Though used principally for the Holy Loch and Gareloch routes, *Diana Vernon* occasionally appeared on the other North British runs as required.

Sold to Lee, Ltd., Brighton, and re-named *Worthing Belle*, she was subsequently sold to J. Reid, Hove, and in March, 1914 to Administration de Navires á Vapeur Ottomane, being then re-named *Touzla* and used for ferry service on the Bosphorus. Though not shown in *Lloyd's Register* after 1920, she is thought to have been in service in 1926 and afterwards to have been broken up.

P.S. *Lucy Ashton*.   *Lucy Ashton* was the only North British steamer built by Messrs. T. B. Seath & Co. of Rutherglen, and she appeared in 1888. Not unlike *Diana Vernon*, though slightly larger, she was placed on the Holy Loch run, calling at Kilcreggan, Blairmore, Strone, Hunter's Quay, Ardnadam and Kilmun. Later she was transferred to the Gareloch route, operating from Craigendoran to Helensburgh, Row, Rosneath, Clynder, Shandon, Rahane Ferry, Mambeg and Garelochhead and became closely identified with it. She was not engaged in war service in either war, and so remained on the Clyde even when most of her contemporaries had departed.

In 1902 the original engine of *Lucy Ashton*—a single diagonal, made by Messrs. Hutson & Corbett—was removed, and its place taken by a compound diagonal set fitted by Messrs. A. & J. Inglis, Ltd. A few years later her saloons were remodelled, so that she was then bought thoroughly up-to-date.

With the cutting down of the Craigendoran services, which occurred in the 1939 season, *Lucy Ashton* became spare and later performed certain runs to Dunoon; and, after the outbreak of the Second World War and the departure of all other L.N.E.R. Clyde ships, she carried on the whole service from Craigendoran, calling at Helensburgh, Kilcreggan, Gourock (instead of Princes Pier), Kirn and Dunoon. This she did for six and a half years without being off for more than a day for overhaul, except on one occasion, when *Fair Maid* relieved her for about a week, in the spring of 1944. During this period of six and a half years, various improvements were made in *Lucy Ashton* while she still sailed, including the refurnishing of the saloon and fitting of a tea-room aft, in place of the small one previously on the starboard side of the saloon entrance, and the erection of a wheel-house on the bridge. From July, 1945 her sailings were extended to Innellan and Rothesay.

Sold to Metal Industries, Ltd., and towed from Bowling to Faslane on 10th December, 1949 by tugs *Metinda II* and *Flying Falcon*,she was not yet finished, as her superstructure was removed and the hull used for resistance tests by the British Ship-Building Research Association, for which she was fitted with jet air propulsion (to avoid disturbance of the water). About two years later the hull was finally scrapped.

* * * * * *

In October, 1888 the four Loch Lomond steamers, *Prince of Wales, Prince Consort, The Queen* and *Empress* were taken over by the North British Steam Packet Company, but as these are dealt with in Chapter VII they are not described specifically here.

P.S. *Lady Rowena.* In 1891 was added to the North British fleet the steamer *Lady Rowena*, for the Arrochar service in connexion with the Loch Lomond Tour. She was launched by

Messrs. S. McKnight & Co. of Ayr, on 31st May, 1891 and like the other North British steamers of her time was fitted with a single diagonal engine.

The fore-saloon of this steamer was carried forward of the mast, thus making a large dining-saloon, in accordance with the tradition of the Arrochar and Loch Lomond steamers such as *Chancellor, The Queen, Empress*, etc., and the later members of that fleet, including the *Maid of the Loch*. There was no accommodation below the main deck level aft.

On reduction in services in 1903 *Lady Rowena* became spare. After three months on charter to the Lochgoil Company, she was sold to Societa di Navigazione a Vapore della Penisola Sorrentina, Naples. In July, 1908 she was purchased by R. R. Collard, Newhaven, and returned to the Clyde in September, 1911, being then owned by A. W. Cameron of Dumbarton, who had bought her on 20th August, 1911, and who used her for excursions on the Clyde, except from April to July, 1912 when she was on Belfast Lough on charter to Wilson & Reid (*See* Chapter XIII). After war service as tender to the fleet at Rosyth and naval hospital carrier on the Forth, she was in April, 1919 sold to Goole & Hull S.P. Co. Ltd., and later registered in the name of W. K. David, Swansea, being ultimately sold in November, 1922 for breaking up.

P.S. *Lady Clare*.   The successor of *Gareloch* was *Lady Clare*, a steamer similar to *Lucy Ashton*, but slightly smaller. Built by Messrs. J. McArthur & Co. of Paisley, she had a single diagonal engine fitted by Hutson & Corbett, and was employed on the Gareloch or on the Greenock–Craigendoran ferry service from 1895, when the latter was taken over from Captain Buchanan. These were two distinct runs until her departure in 1906, when she was sold to Moville Steamship Co. Ltd., for service on Loch Foyle. Stationed at Belfast for mine-sweeping during the war, she was broken up at Dumbarton in 1928. The after part of her hull, with saloon, was taken to Balloch to be converted into a house-boat on the River Leven, but was not so used.

P.S. *Redgauntlet*.   To take the place of *Guy Mannering* on the Rothesay route from Craigendoran, *Redgauntlet* was built by Messrs. Barclay, Curle & Company and launched on 4th April, 1895. She was larger than any steamer previously built for the Company but similar in design to the others, though having large square windows in the saloons. Like the other N.B. steamers, she had single diagonal machinery, and had a good turn of speed. After the appearance of *Kenilworth*, *Redgauntlet* was used for excursion work, for which she was fitted with a dining-saloon on the lower deck aft. She played a large part in the development of cruises from Craigendoran.

On the agreement among the railway companies for reduction in services she was the member of the N.B.R. fleet selected for disposal. She was transferred to the Galloway Saloon Steam Packet Company (then a subsidiary of the North British Railway Company), in May, 1909 to sail on the Firth of Forth; and, after war service as a mine-sweeper at Grimsby, was sold to the Admiralty in July, 1917 and in April, 1919 to Cie. de Navires Olivier, Paris. Thereafter she was registered at Oran till 1934, when her name disappeared from Lloyd's Register.

P.S. *Dandie Dinmont* (II). The second *Dandie Dinmont* was built by Messrs. A. & J. Inglis, and was intended principally for the Dunoon and Holy Loch routes. Originally of a length of 195·2 feet she was in 1912 lengthened to 209 feet, and then received a new funnel much taller than the old one. In 1918 she was given a navy-top, then soon afterwards another new funnel, of greater diameter than the last, appparently intended for a navy-top which did not materialise, the result being that her black top was left much shorter than that of the other steamers, and by this she could be identified. Apart from small differences like this there was a marked standardisation of design in the North British steamers of the late nineteenth century, which persisted until about the First World War period, when some of them were altered.

Dandie Dinmont, not being engaged in war service, remained on the Clyde, sailing from Craigendoran to Dunoon, etc. She passed under the control of the L. & N.E. Railway Company in 1923, and after the reappearance of *Marmion* in 1926 was laid up in Bowling Harbour for two seasons until transferred in May, 1928 to the Great Central Section of the L. & N.E. Railway Company for ferry service between Hull and New Holland, for which she was re-named *Frodingham*. She was sold in January, 1936, to be broken up at Ghent.

P.S. *Talisman* (I). The first *Talisman* was originally similar to *Redgauntlet*, and was launched on 30th March, 1896. She was placed on the Rothesay route in succession to *Jeanie Deans*.

During the war she was employed along with *Kenilworth* in mine-sweeping, first from Troon and later from Portsmouth, under the name *Talla*. Both vessels were used for experimental work at Bournemouth in connexion with mine-laying and both returned to the Clyde on 26th February, 1919.

After her return from war service, *Talisman* underwent certain alterations. The fore-saloon, which previously had had alleyways round it, was extended to the full width of the hull; and the bridge was placed forward of the funnel. *Talisman* was returned to her owners on 10th October, 1919, and remained on the Rothesay (and later Kyles of Bute run) until the end of the 1934 season, her place being taken in the following year by a new vessel of the same name. She was then broken up at Barrow.

P.S. *Kenilworth*. This was the sister-ship of the old *Talisman*, and was constructed by the same builders two years later, being launched on 22nd February, 1898. Her trials were run on 30th June, 1898, and a speed of 18·6 knots was attained at 50 revolutions per minute, this being one-fifth knot faster than the speed of *Talisman*.

She was employed on the Rothesay route, and returned to this in 1919 after a period of war service, during which she was associated with *Talisman* as above mentioned.

In 1915 similar alterations were carried out on *Kenilworth* to those mentioned in connexion with *Talisman*. *Kenilworth* was broken up by her builders, A. & J. Inglis, Ltd., at Pointhouse, in the spring of 1938.

P.S. *Waverley* (III). *Waverley*, third of the name in the North British fleet (the previous two having operated from Silloth), was larger than any previous North British Clyde boat, and unlike the others was fitted with compound diagonal machinery. She was launched on 29th May, 1899 and in her early days gave excursions from Craigendoran to Ayr, Lochranza, Carradale, Campbeltown, etc. These runs, however, were discontinued on the transference of the steamers from the North British Steam Packet Company to the Railway Company in 1902.

In November, 1915 *Waverley* was taken over by the Admiralty, and was stationed in the first place at Sheerness, for mine-sweeping. In August, 1916 she was transferred to Harwich, returning in the following year to Sheerness. Later she was based successively at Grimsby, Weymouth, Harwich, Lowestoft, Grimsby and Bournmouth, finishing her war career at West Hinden on the Belgian coast.

Originally the fore-saloon of *Waverley* extended just beyond the mast; but for service during the First World War, the promenade deck was carried forward to the bow with plated topsides, and during reconditioning her bridge was placed forward of the funnel. A further alteration was made in 1933, when small "observation lounges" were added on the promenade deck, forward of the bridge deck-house and abaft the saloon companionway.

Waverley attained a speed of 19·73 knots on trial, and in

pre-war days was regarded as very fast. The alterations, however, affected her trim, and she was no longer capable of her trial speed, but remained moderately fast. She was one of the most popular steamers that have ever been in the North British or London & North Eastern fleet and after the First War was on the Arrochar run in connexion with the Loch Lomond Tour, fitting in trips to Rothesay, morning and evening.

Laid up during 1939, *Waverley* came out of Bowling Harbour in September of that year to assist in the evacuation of children from Glasgow, etc., to Clyde Coast resorts. She then returned to Bowling, from which she proceeded on 27th September to Messrs. Inglis' yard for conversion for mine-sweeping. Commissioned for the second time as H.M.S. *Waverley*, she was in the 12th Mine-sweeping Flotilla, based at Harwich. On 29th May, 1940 she was at Dunkirk, and in spite of enemy bombing and machine-gun fire, succeeded in getting away with a large number of troops on board. With her guns she fought the bombers for about two hours. The steering-gear became damaged, so that she could not zig-zag, and she was eventually hit by a bomb near the engine-room, about four o'clock in the afternoon. Just before this she had brought down one of the bombers. The ship sank in a few minutes, but fortunately many of the soldiers and crew were rescued as was her master Captain Cameron, who took part in the Dunkirk 40th anniversary memorial service on the present *Waverley*.

P.S. *Marmion*. Launched on Saturday, 5th May, 1906 *Marmion* ran her trials on the Gareloch on Tuesday, 12th June. Thereafter, with a large party of guests, she cruised to Loch Long and Loch Goil, and Kyles of Bute. She was designed for winter as well as summer work, and commenced her duties on the Lochgoilhead and Arrochar run on 18th June, 1906 with the usual Rothesay run in connexion with the 4.10 p.m. train from Queen Street. Like *Waverley*, she had a large fore-saloon carried forward of the mast, and was compound engined. She had, however, her bridge forward of the funnel from the outset. The machinery had the unusual feature of a piston valve on the H.P. cylinder and Cameron & Allen slide valve on the L.P.

Her war service was from April, 1915 to April, 1919 and consisted of mine-sweeping. She was attached to the Dover Patrol, and was named *Marmion II*.

For this work the promenade deck was extended to the bow, and this arrangement was retained on her return to the Clyde in 1920. It appears, however, that it did not suit her build, as after only one season's sailing she was withdrawn and laid up in Bowling Harbour. She was again altered in 1923, the fore-saloon being cut away just forward of the bridge; and after another spell in Bowling Harbour, she came out in 1926 in place of *Dandie Dinmont*, which then went into Bowling as already mentioned. Thereafter *Marmion* was regularly employed on the Clyde, having been in commission all the year round up to the spring of 1935, though she was then superseded in the winter service by the new *Talisman*.

In 1932 *Marmion* was re-boilered and given an extensive overhaul, being fitted with a lounge and tea-room instead of the ordinary saloon. *Waverley* was similarly treated in the following year.

In September, 1939 *Marmion* was maintaining the services from Craigendoran to Clynder, Greenock and Dunoon, when she was requisitioned and taken to Messrs. Inglis' slip on 27th September. Her promenade deck was again extended to the bow, and again she became a mine-sweeper. She was in the 12th Mine-sweeping Flotilla in the Harwich Area, and made three trips to Dunkirk. She was sunk by air attack in Harwich Harbour on the night of 8th/9th April, 1941. Though raised, she was found unfit for further service and was scrapped.

P.S. *Fair Maid*. Though built for the N.B.R. Company by Messrs. A. & J. Inglis, Ltd., from whose yard she was launched on 23rd December, 1915, this ship was requisitioned for mine-sweeping before completion, and left the Clyde on 13th March, 1916 never to return. She was more or less a sister-ship to *Waverley* (as altered) and of similar dimensions. She was sunk by a mine near Cross Sands Buoy on 6th November, 1916.

No further steamers were added to the North British Clyde fleet until after it had passed to the London & North Eastern Railway Company in 1923. At that time six of the Clyde steamers remained, and of the Forth and Silloth vessels two and one respectively, there being also a small tug at Dundee and the dredger *Almond* at Bo'ness. Being outwith the scope of this book, the Forth and Solway steamers have been omitted, but will be found in "R.O.S.", Second edition.

LONDON & NORTH EASTERN RAILWAY COMPANY (SCOTTISH AREA)

P.S. *Jeanie Deans* (II). The second *Jeanie Deans* was built by The Fairfield Shipbuilding & Engineering Co. Ltd., at Govan, and was very much larger than any previous steamer operating from Craigendoran, having a gross tonnage of 635 and a length between perpendiculars of 250·5 feet. Her name revived that of one of the most successful steamers of the North British fleet, and she became very popular. She was among the fastest of the Clyde paddle steamers of the 1930s, having attained a speed of about 18·5 knots on trial when new.

Jeanie Deans had triple expansion three-crank engines, the first of this type built for Clyde service, and steam was supplied by one double-ended boiler. Two funnels were provided, both forward of the paddle-boxes, and the steam pipes were enclosed within the funnels. Originally the funnels were very short, (as on *Meg Merrilies* of 1883), but after one season's running she reappeared with the forward funnel lengthened by 9 feet, and the after one by 6 feet, the result being rather unpleasing in appearance, though beneficial for avoiding smoke and ashes. At the same time an observation lounge was erected on the promenade-deck forward of the bridge deckhouse, thus giving increased shelter for passengers in inclement weather.

Requisitioned for mine-sweeping in October, 1939 she was at first flagship of the Flotilla based at Irvine, being later in the 11th Mine-sweeping Flotilla at Milford Haven. She was damaged by bombing in the Thames in March, 1941 but survived as an escort ship and A.A. vessel to return to the Clyde in June, 1945. She was extensively re-conditioned by Messrs. Inglis, and fitted with two equal-height elliptical funnels, deck shelters fore and aft, with boat-decks and the four boats erected thereon, on Welin "crescent" davits. She also received a mainmast and was much improved in every way. Her accommodation was of a high standard, the dining-saloon being then on the main deck aft, and the lounge on the same deck forward. The promenade deck was extended to the stern, the galley being situated there. She was converted to oil-firing in the winter of 1956-7. Radar was fitted in 1960.

The placing of lifeboats on an upper deck forward of the funnels is a feature introduced on the North British Railway associate's *Roslin Castle* of 1906 on the Forth.

After a season out of service, *Jeanie Deans* was sold to a group of London enthusiasts for whom she was partially overhauled at Port Glasgow, leaving Greenock in November, 1965 for the Thames, with the lower part of her funnels painted red, giving a temporary funnel colouring of red with yellow band and black top. Later the band was changed to white, thus restoring the N.B.R./ L.N.E.R. colours. She was registered as *Queen of the South* in name of the Coastal Steam Packet Co. Limited and at the end of May, 1966 commenced sailing from Tower Pier, but not for long. After frequent failures she was towed on 23rd August to Chatham and laid up. It was thought this might be her end; but next season large sums of money were spent on her for fitting a bow rudder, fore-and-aft navigation lights, and protecting nets to prevent driftwood from damaging the paddle-floats. When she should have sailed on her inaugural cruise on 8th June, 1967 with a large invited party, she was not able to raise sufficient steam to leave Tower Pier, and was towed out to buoys. The catering was excellent, but there was no sail that day! After a few unsuccessful attempts she was laid up; and early on 27th December, 1967 she was towed away from the river front at Erith, to be broken up at Antwerp.

P.M.V. _Talisman_ (II). This was a vessel of an entirely new type, built by A. & J. Inglis, Ltd. for the L. & N.E.R. Company. She was the first direct-acting Diesel-electric paddle vessel in the world, and the largest Diesel-propelled paddle boat.

The four Diesel engines of _Talisman_ drove direct current generators at 600 revolutions per minute, and current was supplied to a double-armature motor situated on the paddle shaft, which was driven at a speed of 50 revolutions per minute. One most interesting and unique feature was that passengers so inclined could study the electrical instrument board adjacent to the main motor room from which the revolutions, amperes and horse-power developed could be observed.

Externally _Talisman_ was not very unlike an orthodox Clyde steamer, and had paddle-boxes of standard North British design, which, together with a large funnel (slightly elliptical) and promenade-deck the full length of the ship, gave her quite a good appearance. She had a cruiser stern, and very little flare forward. Originally, she had bulwarks at the forward portion of the promenade deck, initially black, but changed to cream in time for the winter of 1935-36.

The first-class accommodation of _Talisman_ was forward, and she was the first paddle vessel on the Clyde to be so arranged. latterly she was one-class only.

The outstanding feature of _Talisman_ was economy of working. For 100 miles' sailing she used only 1·47 tons of liquid fuel, as compared with 11½ tons of coal burnt by her predecessor for a similar run. (The first _Talisman_, it should be remembered, was a steamer of the same length, but of 160 tons less displacement).

The second _Talisman_ was capable of a speed of 17 knots, and for slower speeds could run on three engines instead of four, and even with only two engines running she could maintain a speed of 14 knots. It is only just, however, to note that certain disadvantages are associated with Diesel machinery, among them being a considerable amount of vibration and noise, and, in earlier times, lack of reliability.

Talisman was employed on the principal runs from Craigendoran to Rothesay and the Kyles of Bute, and was used in winter as well as in summer. She was fitted out in 1940 as a Bofors gun vessel, under the name of H.M.S. *Aristocrat*, and did good work as an A.A. ship on the Thames. She was in the Dieppe raid and acted as a protection ship for transports prior to the North Africa invasion. Later she was H.Q. ship at the construction of the Mulberry Harbour. She was damaged by gunfire, but survived to escort the first convoy to Antwerp, and returned to the Clyde in February, 1946. She was re-conditioned by her builders and received one pair of boats on the boat-deck forward of the funnel, and was given a mainmast. The bulwarks forward gave place to the more usual open rails.

In June, 1953 she was laid up, on account of the condition of her machinery; but, as *Marchioness of Lorne* proved too slow for the Millport run, *Talisman* was re-engined in time to take her place there for the 1954 season, remaining till the end of the 1966 season. During 1967 she was broken up by W. H. Arnott, Young & Co. Ltd. at Dalmuir.

P.S. *Waverley* (IV).   On 2nd October, 1946, a notable ship was launched by Messrs. Inglis for the L. & N.E.R. Clyde services, bearing the popular name *Waverley*. Her length is about the same as that of her 1899 namesake, but she has about four feet more beam; and the propelling machinery is triple expansion, made by Messrs. Rankin & Blackmore, taking steam from a double-ended boiler, intended to be oil-fired but originally coal-fired. Externally there is a strong resemblance to *Jeanie Deans* (as altered), with two elliptical funnels forward, two masts, boats on upper decks, etc., and it is most pleasing to record that again the tradional North British type of paddle-boxes forms a feature of the design. With accommodation for about 1,350 passengers, the ship was a great acquisition to the Craigendoran fleet, and was the first step towards making good the war losses suffered by the Clyde passenger fleet. She entered service early in the 1947 season, and was at first on the Arrochar station, being later on the Rothesay and Kyles of Bute or Round Bute run. For the 1947 season she carried L.N.E.R. colours, being repainted (along with *Lucy Ashton, Jeanie Deans* and *Talisman*) in B.R. colours in time for the 1948 summer season. During the winter of 1956-7 she was converted to burn oil. From 1958 she succeeded *Marchioness of Graham* on the up-river excursions from Largs, Rothesay and Dunoon to Glasgow, once each week (later discontinued). Radar was fitted in 1960. After transfer to C.S.P. Co. she was given white paddle-boxes. With these restored to black in 1972, the last paddle steamer on the Firth continued cruising, mainly to Kyles of Bute (Arrochar and

Craigendoran Piers being both closed), until the end of the 1973 season, when she was laid up in James Watt Dock, Greenock; then in 1974 she was sold for a nominal sum to the Paddle Steamer Preservation Society, who transferred her to Waverley Steam Navigation Co., Ltd. (*See* Chapter XVII).

* * * * * *

Jeanie Deans, Talisman and *Waverley* were transferred from the British Transport Commission to The Caledonian Steam Packet Co. Ltd. on 5th November, 1951.

CHAPTER VII

LOCH LOMOND STEAMERS

STEAM naviagtion on Loch Lomond dates from 1817, when David Napier (cousin of Robert Napier) placed on it the steamer *Marion*.

There was a steadily increasing demand for swift transport of passengers from Balloch to the north end of the Loch. One must remember that many of the steamers gave vital transport services—swift, reliable and far more comfortable than the equivalent journey by horse-drawn coach over the primitive tracks which then served for roads in many parts of Scotland.

In 1825 The Lochlomond Steam Boat Company was formed to compete with Mr. Napier's steamers, while in 1845 a further opposition company with the imposing title of "New Lochlomond Steam Boat Company" came into existence. Before it commenced operations on the loch, however, an arrangement was made whereby it was amalgamated with the firm of Napier & McMurrich (Mr. Napier had assumed a partner by this time); and this combined company, under the title of Lochlomond Steam Boat Company survived till 31st October, 1888 when its assets were taken over by the North British Steam Packet Company.

A further change of ownership occurred on 1st October, 1896 when the four steamers then on the loch, together with the railway line (and stations thereon) from Dumbarton East Junction to Balloch Pier were transferred from North British ownership to the Dumbarton & Balloch Joint Line Committee, which represented the interests of the North British, Lanarkshire & Dumbartonshire and Caledonian Railway Companies. In 1909 the Lanarkshire & Dumbartonshire Company was taken over by the Caledonian, and so from that time ceased to be represented separately on the Committee. In 1923, as a result of the grouping, the places of the Caledonian & North British Companies were taken by the London Midland & Scottish and London & North Eastern Railway Companies respectively, and in 1933 the Dumbarton & Balloch line and steamers were transferred, with all other joint lines and property in Scotland, to the control of Group Committee No. 4 of the two companies passing in 1948 to the British Transport Commission.

The colours of the Lochlomond Steam Boat Company's steamers were:—hulls grey, funnels black with white hoops (and in

73

some cases red with black top). After the North British Steam Packet Company had assumed control in 1888 the funnels were painted in the usual North British colours, red with white band and black top, the grey hulls being retained.

The Joint Committee removed the white bands from the funnels, but retained grey as the colour for the hulls, the saloons and paddle-boxes also being grey, with pink panelling. The water-line was red, and the whole gave a most pleasing effect. With this colour scheme *Princess May* and *Prince Edward* were among the most beautiful of the smaller paddle steamers, and with the wonderful scenery of the loch made a perfect picture. On nationalisation in 1948 they were given buff funnels with black tops, black hulls and paddle-boxes, and white saloons with cream panelling. Later the hull and the boxes of *Prince Edward* became white, to match those of the *Maid of the Loch*.

P.S. *Marion*.   This little wooden paddle steamer was built in 1816 for service on the Clyde, and had the distinction of having sailed farther up that river than any other steamer before or since, *viz*. to the Clyde Iron Works, Dalmarnock. She had a gross tonnage of 57, and a side-lever engine of 20 h.p., her length being 60 feet and her beam 13 feet.

In 1817 *Marion* was taken up the Leven, to spend most of her remaining days on Loch Lomond. At that time the loch was approached by sailing from Glasgow to Dumbarton and driving to Balloch; the steamer started in the River Leven, passengers being conveyed to her from the shore at Balloch by means of scows. She may for a time have been on Loch Fyne as *Thalia*, one of David Napier's "Three Graces", the others being *Euphrosyne* next mentioned and *Aglaia* on Loch Eck (*See* Chapter IV), all running connecting tours. After being sold in 1832 the *Marion* stranded, when being taken down the Leven.

P.S. *Euphrosyne*.   To meet the growing demands Mr. Napier had the Clyde steamer *Post Boy* transferred to the Loch in 1832 to take the place of *Marion*; and, under the name *Euphrosyne*, she proved most popular with the travelling public. The traffic was increasing rapidly; and, in spite of opposition and great reductions in fares, Mr. Napier's business prospered so much that, after six years' service on the loch, *Euphrosyne* was deemed no longer adequate and was then sold.

P.S. *Balloch*.   In July, 1835 this steamer, previously named *Robert Napier*, was placed on the Loch, believed to be by Mr. McMurrich, of the Lady of the Lake Company. Arrangements were made to avoid competition; and he became a partner with David Napier. *Balloch* was on the afternoon run, *Euphrosyne* remaining on the morning run. There must have been insufficient traffic for the two; for, in January, 1836 The Lochlomond Steamboat Company advertised that they wished to dispose of either *Balloch* or *Euphrosyne*. The former, then a comparatively new boat, was sold to the Dumbarton Steamboat Company and re-named *Dumbuck*.

P.S. *Lochlomond*. This was the first iron steamer on the Loch, commencing in August, 1836, and the last built for David Napier's Loch Lomond service. She was transferred to the new company formed in 1845 as above mentioned, but did not long remain, being sold on 7th March, 1846 to Mr. William Ainslie of Glasgow and Fort William, by whom she was re-named *Glencoe*, afterwards entering the Burns (later Hutcheson) fleet as *Curlew*. (*See "W.H.S."*).

P.S. *The Lady of the Lake*. In January, 1825 the first Lochlomond Steamboat Company was formed, with a view to capturing some of the trade which was then being enjoyed by Mr. Napier. It is evident that difficulty was experienced in raising the necessary funds, as we read that on 14th January, 1825 a meeting of the members of the company was held "to endeavour to get more subscribers". On the 21st of the same month the necessary backing seems to have been forthcoming, as it was then decided to build a steamer; and Mr. William Denny of Dumbarton undertook to provide the hull for £638, payable in three instalments, the contract for this being signed on 25th January, 1825. Mr. Robert Napier was entrusted with furnishing the machinery for £1,000.

The steamer was launched on 8th April, 1825 and was named *The Lady of the Lake*. She commenced to ply on the loch, and severe competition began. So cheaply, in fact, did her owners offer to carry passengers, that by the end of the 1827 season they were in serious financial difficulties, and the company had to be dissolved. A new company was, however, formed in March, 1828 its title being similar to that of the defunct concern, viz. "The Lochlomond Steam Boat Company". The directors came to the conclusion that one of the reasons for the failure of the previous company was that the Dumbarton Steamboat Company (on whom The Loch Lomond steamship owners depended for the conveyance of passengers from Glasgow), were unable to carry passengers for *The Lady of the Lake* on account of their previous agreements with Mr. Napier; and the same applied to the innkeepers of Dumbarton, who ran the coaches between that town and Balloch, and who sold the tickets for the Loch Lomond sailings. It was, accordingly, resolved to overcome this difficulty by having a boat of their own between Glasgow and Dumbarton, and so The Lochlomond Steam Boat Company chartered from Dr. Stevenson of Glasgow the steamer *Bangor Castle*. In addition, they acquired a coach, and ran it in connexion with the steamers between Dumbarton and Balloch. These enterprises, however, do not appear to have done much good; and on 9th December, 1828 the new company was dissolved, their steamer being sold on 5th March, 1829 to John McMurrich for the Glasgow–Dumbarton trade, and in June, to David Napier for his Kilmun trade. She was broken up in November, 1834.

*   *   *   *   *   *

About 1838, Mr. Napier was again faced with the problem of competition, this time from Mr. Lewis McLellan (one of the partners of the opposition company before its dissolution) and Mr. Thomas Barclay who placed on Loch Lomond the paddle steamer *Queen of Scots*. This vessel had previously been on the excursion trade from the Broomielaw to Arrochar and is known to have given Sunday sailings on that run, for the Communion services at Arrochar. In June, 1842 it was announced that she had ceased to ply on Loch Lomond; and the following year she was operating from Ayr to Girvan and Campbeltown. She was broken up before 1852.

P.S. *Waterwitch*.   In 1845 the newly formed New Lochlomond Steamboat Company took over from the bankrupt business of McBrayne & McIntyre a steamer for service on the loch; but before she actually sailed, negotiations had been entered into with a view to effecting an amalgamation of the two concerns and so eliminating unnecessary and wasteful competition. The upshot of these negotiations was that at a meeting of the new company on 25th April, 1845, it was decided to amalgamate with the established concern; and this took effect from the 30th of the same month. Under the agreement for amalgamation, the name was changed to Lochlomond Steam Boat Company, and the first steamers owned by the new company were *Waterwitch*, which had just been acquired by the opposition concern, and *Lochlomond*, already mentioned as having been built for David Napier in 1836. The new company also took over from the New Lochlomond Steam Boat Company a contract with William Denny for the building of a steamer which they had intended to run on Loch Katrine, further reference to which will be found in Chapter XIV; and the new company operated in close association with the Dumbarton United Steamboat Company.

Waterwitch was an iron paddle steamer, and in the *Glasgow Herald* of 1848 we find her advertised to sail from a pier in the River Leven at Balloch to Inverarnan in Glen Falloch, with calls at Balmaha, Luss, Rowardennan, Tarbet, Inversnaid and Ardlui. Piers at these places were built in the '40s (with the exception of Balmaha, which was not constructed till 1850 and Luss, opened in June, 1851): previously it had been necessary to board the steamers by means of ferries.

In 1847 a canal had been made from the head of the loch to Inverarnan Inn, Glen Falloch, and there a turning basin was provided. The steamers conveyed goods and passengers thither, and from it started the coaches for Fort William and Killin. At Inverarnan was also erected a small slipway for the repair and overhaul of the steamers; but with the silting up of the canal this was abandoned, and from the mid 1870s the service extended only to Ardlui. All the early calling places remained in use, except Luss, closed from 1952 till 1980; Ardlui, closed since 1963; and Tarbet temporarily closed in the early 1980's, re-opened in 1984.

In a fleet-list in a minute of a meeting of the company held in 1848 reference is made to the "steamer" *Waterwitch* and also to the "lighter" *Waterwitch* (apparently on Loch Katrine). The same list includes the scow *Ann.* The hull of the steamer *Waterwitch* was taken over by A. Denny & Bro. in part payment of *Queen Victoria*, her engines and boiler being transferred to the latter.

P.S. *Marchioness of Breadalbane.* With the departure of *Lochlomond* in 1846 a replacement became necessary, and Messrs. Denny Bros. of Dumbarton, got the order. When the steamer appeared, however, she did not conform to the specification, being of too great draught and in one or two other respects. Sold to the P. & O. on behalf of the Pasha of Egypt, she sailed from Greenock on 1st October, 1846 for Southampton, leaving about two weeks later for Egypt.

P.S. *Prince Albert.* To take the place of the unsuitable *Marchioness of Breadalbane*, a new steamer was ordered from Messrs. Denny Bros. This was *Prince Albert*, which was built in 1850 and was the pioneer of the style of nomenclature which became standard on the loch.

Understood to have been sold to Dumbarton Steamboat Co., she sailed on the Clyde in 1862 and next year was sold to Liverpool owners for Eastham Ferry service and re-named *Richmond*, being broken up about 1873.

*   *   *   *   *   *

In 1850 Mr. David Napier sold his shares in the company to Messrs. G. & J. Burns, and thus ended his connexion with the Loch Lomond steamer services. On taking over these shares, the transferees became bound not to compete with the Lochlomond Steam Boat Company; but, in spite of this, they suggested running their steamer *Pilot* on the loch temporarily, during the withdrawal of *Waterwitch* for overhaul and re-boilering. The company pointed out to them that this would be a breach of their obligations, but they insisted upon it and *Pilot* was taken up the River Leven. She did not remain long on the loch, however, as she struck a rock, subsequently known as the Pilot Rock, off Rowardennan and sank. She was later raised; and, after a short time on the Clyde again, was sold to Dublin owners.

It was in 1850, also, that the first railway communication between Loch Lomond and the outside world came into use, Balloch Pier being opened in June. The Caledonian and Dumbartonshire Junction Railway was opened in that year from Bowling to Balloch, and threafter the steamers ran in connexion with the trains. Messrs. G. & J. Burns held a controlling interest in the Railway Company, and as above explained also acquired some shares in the Lochlomond Company. It was they who provided the Glasgow–Bowling service in conjunction with the Loch Lomond tours, by means of *inter alia* the steamer *Plover*. They sold their interest in the Lochlomond Steam Boat Company in 1851 (when they also disposed of their Clyde and West Highland trade to Messrs. David Hutcheson & Co.), and thereafter concentrated their attention on the Glasgow–Liverpool and Glasgow–Belfast services, and on those of the Cunard Line.

P.S. *Queen Victoria*.   It was found in 1852 that the hull of *Waterwitch* was in rather a bad state; but she had received a new boiler and her machinery had been overhauled in 1850. It was, accordingly, resolved to built a new hull for her engines, and this was duly done in only four weeks. Christened *Queen Victoria* by Miss Mary Bell and launched on 26th May the new steamer lay in the Leven till 1st July, when it was considered the water was of sufficient depth and she was towed up to Balloch Bridge to get her engines on board. She was superseded in 1866 by *Princess of Wales* and according to her register was sold in 1868 to a foreigner who named her *Swallow* and almost immediately she passed to Captain James Swallow of Whitby, who used her for excursions in the area of The Wash. Later as *Swallow* she was on the Wallasey ferry service on the Mersey and by 1882 was owned by Thos. Seed, Liverpool.

P.S. *Prince of Wales*.   On 1st May, 1858 the through railway route from Glasgow to Helensburgh was opened by the Glasgow, Dumbarton and Helensburgh Railway Company. As a result, Balloch and Loch Lomond received through rail communication with Glasgow, though they had already direct communication with the East Coast by means of the Forth and Clyde Junction Railway, which had been opened from Balloch to Stirling in 1856. To meet the expected expansion in traffic, *Prince of Wales* was ordered from Laurence Hill & Co., of Port Glasgow. As built in 1858 she was a flush-decked paddle steamer; but in 1864 deck saloons were added fore and aft, having alleyways round them in the fashion of the time. She had a simple double diagonal engine, the cylinders being placed forward of the paddle-shaft. Her funnel was aft.

In September, 1860 *Prince of Wales* struck a rock near the east side of Inchmurran and had to be beached. Fortunately the accident was unattended by serious injury to anyone, but the hull of the steamer was damaged and she was, accordingly, taken down the Leven to be repaired on Messrs. Scott, McGill & Duncan's slip at Bowling. *Prince of Wales* had a long life on Loch Lomond, and passed first to the North British Steam Packet Company in 1888, and in 1896 to the D. & B. Jt. Line Committee.

In 1901 she was sold for use as a coal hulk at Newry, and remained in *Lloyd's Register* for many years.

P.S. *Prince Consort.* To take the place of *Prince Albert, Prince Consort* was built by Caird & Co. of Greenock, in 1862. She was of somewhat unusual design for a British steamer, having the sponsons carried from stem to stern, giving an unusually roomy deck. Deck saloons were fitted the full width of the hull (alleyways being formed by the sponsons), and the funnel was placed forward of the paddle-boxes as in modern practice. The steering-wheel was placed forward of the funnel, though the steamer had no bridge. Like *Prince of Wales, Prince Consort* passed to the N.B.S.P. Co. when they took over the control of the Loch Lomond services in 1888, and to the Dumbarton and Balloch Joint Line Committee in 1896. She was scrapped about 1900.

P.S. *Chancellor* (II). About 1864 the directors of the Loch-lomond Steam Boat Company became somewhat concerned about the neglect of the Arrochar service (which meant so much to them on account of the circular tour that was provided), and accordingly they set about improving matters by ordering a steamer themselves. This vessel perpetuated the name traditionally associated with the Arrochar route on which the Dumbarton Steamboat Co. placed the *Dumbarton* in June/July, 1830, the *Leven* in 1834 and the first *Chancellor* in 1853. This and the 1864 steamer operated from the Broomielaw, and the later one from Helensburgh in connexion with the North British Railway.

To work the Arrochar trade a subsidiary concern was formed, known as the Loch Long Steam Boat Company. It was, however, amalgamated with the Loch Lomond Company in 1867, the advertisements thereafter bearing the designation "Loch Long & Loch Lomond Steam Boat Company", though no change had been officially made in the title of the parent company. *Chancellor* has been included here on account of her ownership, even although she did not sail on Loch Lomond.

The new steamer appeared in 1864, and was similar in design to *Prince Consort*, above described. She remained on the Arrochar station till sold to Keith & Campbell, Glasgow, on 18th April, 1881 for their Gareloch service, and re-named *Shandon*, being later owned by W. Buchanan. (*See* Chapter IV).

P.S. *Princess of Wales.* Built in 1866 as successor to *Queen Victoria*, this steamer's main deck aft protruded two feet beyond the hull, with an elegant deck saloon above, having alleyways three feet wide. Above the saloon was a promenade deck 85′ × 15′. After fifteen years' service in summer and winter on the loch she was sold to Matthew Brydie, Alloa, on 26th October, 1881 for service on the Forth; she was later sailing on the Tay (for which her deck saloon was removed), being re-named *Albion* and later *Shamrock*. She was for a short time on the Tyne. In August, 1908 she was reported to have been in collision with *Marchioness of Bute* on the Tay, and in 1911 was registered in name of the Foreland Steamboat Co. Ltd.

P.S. *Chancellor* (III). For the Arrochar service a new steamer was laid down in 1880, and like her predecessor is included here for reasons of ownership only.

Chancellor (III) was the last steamer built for Clyde service with alleyways round the saloon. She had simple double diagonal engines (like those of all the Loch Lomond steamers from *Waterwitch* to *Princess May*), fitted by M. Paul, of Dumbarton, who received the contract for the whole ship, but who had the hull built by Messrs. Chambers & Company.

She remained the property of the Loch Lomond Company till 1885, when she was sold, along with the goodwill of the Arrochar trade, to the Lochgoil and Lochlong Steamboat Company. She was sold in 1891 to Glasgow & South Western Railway Company. (*see* Chapters II and IV).

P.S. *The Queen.* Like *Prince Consort*, *The Queen* came from the yard of Messrs. Caird & Co. of Greenock. She was however, of normal design and had alleyways round the saloons; one funnel forward; one mast; and the bridge between the paddle-boxes. Built in 1883, she may be regarded as the fore-runner of the later standard type of Loch Lomond steamer; and like the others of her time, she had double diagonal simple machinery. During her ownership by the Loch Lomond Company she seems to have had a red funnel with black top, receiving the North British white band when taken over by the N.B.S.P. Company. The winter of 1894-5 was exceptionally cold, and early in the latter year the Loch was frozen over so that people were able to walk from Luss to Balmaha; and, to feed the thousands who flocked to the Loch to skate, or simply to look, the laid-up steamers were opened up as restaurants.

The Queen was sold in April, 1911 and is understood to have been broken up.

P.S. *Empress.* This was the last steamer ordered by the Loch Lomond Company, and was on the stocks at Yoker when her owners were taken over by the N.B.S.P. Company; they acquired four steamers in all, viz. *Prince of Wales, Prince Consort, The Queen* and *Empress.* The last-named was launched on 14th November, 1888, and ran trials on the Gareloch in December, but did not reach the loch till January, 1890 having spent the intervening period stuck in the Leven.

She and *The Queen* maintained the principal services till the advent of *Prince George* and *Princess May* in 1899, being threafter relegated to extra runs, reliefs, charters, etc. *Empress* was the only Loch Lomond steamer to be requisitioned by the Admiralty, her period with them being from 3rd to 12th February, 1919. She did not sail after 1925, but lay in the bay at Balloch till sold in 1933 and broken up alongside the pier there.

P.S. *Prince George.* The joint Committee had not been long in existence when it was decided to improve the loch services by having two new steamers built. A dispute arose as to the type to be constructed, and ultimately the matter was submitted to arbitration. The North British Company considered it advisable to build steamers of a limited size and with non-compound machinery (this being, in fact, in line with its policy in the design of Clyde steamers), while the Caledonian Company favoured the building of larger ships and taking them to Balloch in sections, there to be assembled and to have compound machinery. The arbiter ultimately decided in favour of the North British view, with the result that the two steamers were the same length as *The Queen* and *Empress,* and were fitted with similar non-compound two-crank double diagonal machinery, which appears an anachronism in ships built at so late a date.

The steamers under consideration were *Prince George* and

Princess May, and they were similar in design to their immediate predecessors, apart from having the deck saloons the full width of the hull. They came from the yard of Messrs. A. & J. Inglis, Pointhouse, and were exact sister-ships.

Prince George was launched on 11th October, 1898 and reached the Loch on 10th December. She was regularly employed in the Balloch–Ardlui service in summer. Her mast was removed in 1936.

Prince George was broken up at Balloch in 1942, after having served for some time as an accommodation ship for war-time evacuees from the Clydebank blitz.

P.S. *Princess May*. Like the foregoing, this steamer took up the Loch Lomond sailings in the summer of 1899, having been launched on the previous 17th October, and reached the Loch on 12th November. She was generally used as an extra steamer on Saturdays and Sundays, or as a relief boat when one of the others was off for overhaul. Latterly, however, she and *Prince Edward* undertook all the Loch sailings between them. *Princess May* passed to British Railways and was succeeded in 1953 by *Maid of the Loch*, being then broken up on the slip at Balloch.

P.S. *Prince Edward*. Though launched in 1911, it was not until July, 1912 that this ship appeared on the Loch, as she missed the tide for getting up the Leven the previous year and was too large to make the attempt at any other season. One of the earlier steamers had had a similar experience, when it was found that her saloons were too high to pass under the bridge at Bonhill. The problem was overcome in a practical way by giving the local children a day off school, so that they might be put on board; and the vessel, thus loaded, passed under the bridge and safely up the river to the Loch!

Prince Edward, though larger, was similar in design to her immediate predecessors, but at last the long tradition of non-compound machinery was broken, though she continued the use of a haystack boiler, but of higher pressure. Her designed speed was 15 knots. She continued in service after the advent of the *Maid of the Loch*, but by that time there was insufficient traffic for two steamers. She was broken up on the slip at Balloch in 1955.

In the inter-war period there seemed to be a shortage of masts among the Loch Lomond steamers. When there were four steamers, there were three with masts; when there were three, only two had masts! *Prince Edward* was the first to be without one, but *Prince George* and *Princess May* each suffered this indignity; then *Maid of the Loch* came out with two masts!

P.S. *Princess Patricia*. In August, 1914 two other sister-ships

1.   **P.S. "MEG MERRILIES" c. 1898.**

2.   **P.S. "CALEDONIA" (I) in 1923-4.**

3.   P.S. "GALATEA" at mooring in Rothesay Bay, c. 1899.

4.   P.S. "MARCHIONESS OF BREADALBANE"
          approaching Wemyss Bay, c. 1899.

5.　　　P.S. "DUCHESS OF HAMILTON" approaching Largs, c. 1899.

Frank S. Easton

6.　　　P.S. "DUCHESS OF ROTHESAY" off Corrie, pre-1914.

David Campbell

7.   P.S. "DUCHESS OF FIFE"

8.   Tr.S.S. "DUCHESS OF ARGYLL" off Corrie, 1919.

9.   P.S. "BENMORE" (C.S.P. Co. charter) at Kilcreggan, 8/1919.

10.   T.S.S. "QUEEN OF THE LAKE"
approaching Ardtalnaig, Loch Tay, 5/7/1932.

11.   P.S. "MARQUIS OF BUTE" off Keppel.

James McClure

12.   P.S. "CHANCELLOR" approaching Kirn.

per John Bell

13.   P.S. "GLEN SANNOX" (I) leaving Brodick.

David Campbell

14.   P.S. "MERCURY" (I) off Kirn.

per John Bell

15. P.S. "JUPITER" (I) arriving at Rothesay, c. 1925.

16. P.S. "JUNO" (I) in Rothesay Bay, c. 1899.

17.   P.S. "MARS" off Greenock.

J. B. Macgeorge Collection

18.   Tr.S.S. "ATALANTA" off Dunoon, in 1924.

J. B. Macgeorge Collection

19.   P.S. "ISLE OF CUMBRAE" (I) (G.&S.W.R. charter) c. 1919.

20.   Tr.S.S. "GLEN SANNOX" (II) arriving at Rothesay, 21/8/38.

21.   P.S. "BRODICK CASTLE" near Whiting Bay.

per John Bell

22.   P.S. "SCOTIA" near Keppel.

per John Bell

23.   P.S. "ISLE OF ARRAN" (II) approaching Rothesay, c. 1899.

Frank S. Easton

24.   P.S. "EAGLE III" approaching Dunoon, 1920-35.

J. B. Macgeorge Collection

25.   P.S. "ISLE OF SKYE" leaving Rothesay, 1925.

per John Bell

26.   Tr.S.S. "KING EDWARD" approaching Dunoon.

J. B. Macgeorge Collection

27.   P.S. "QUEEN EMPRESS"

J. B. Macgeorge Collection

28.   P.S. "LORD OF THE ISLES" (II) approaching Rothesay.

Stromier/Vogt Collection

29.   Ts.S.S. "KING GEORGE V" off Rothesay, 6/5/35.
      (Silver Jubilee Day)   *J. B. Macgeorge*

30.   Tr.S.S. "QUEEN MARY" on trials off Wemyss Bay, 1933.
            J. B. Macgeorge Collection

31.   T.S.M.V. "WEE CUMBRAE" off Keppel.

Stromier/Vogt Collection

32.   T.S.M.V. "ARRAN MAIL" arriving at Ardrossan, 5/9/36.

G.E.L.

33.   P.S. "MEG MERRILIES" (I) at Ardrishaig, 1866.

34.   P.S. "GARELOCH" approaching Shandon.

35.   P.S. "GUY MANNERING" in Rothesay Bay.

36.   P.S. "JEANIE DEANS" (I) leaving Dunoon.

37.   P.S. "DIANA VERNON" off Kilcreggan.

Rev. Wm. C. Galbraith's Collection

38.   P.S. "LUCY ASHTON" backing out from Craigendoran, 25/3/1948.

G.E.L.

39.   P.S. "REDGAUNTLET" and P.S. "NEPTUNE" at Rothesay.

40.   P.S. "DANDIE DINMONT" (II) leaving Dunoon.

41.   P.S. "MARMION" off Craigmore in 1920.

Rev. Wm. C. Galbraith's Collection

42.   P.S. "FAIR MAID" (as minesweeper)
on trials on the Gareloch, 2/1916.

C.L.D.D. Collection

43.   P.M.V. "TALISMAN" (II) in winter 1935-6.

Rev. Wm. C. Galbraith's Collection

44.   P.S. "WAVERLEY" (IV) backing out from Lochgoilhead, 22/7/47.

G.E.L.

45.   P.S. "PRINCE OF WALES" leaving Luss.
        (in Loch Lomond Company colours)

46.   P.S. "PRINCE CONSORT" leaving Luss.
        (in N.B.S.P. Co. colours)   *Stromier/Vogt Collection*

47.   P.S. "PRINCESS OF WALES" at Luss.

G. W. Wilson Collection, by courtesy of Aberdeen University

48.   P.S. "EMPRESS" (in D.&B.Jt.Rlys. colours).

per John Bell

49.   P.S. "PRINCESS MAY" (in B.R. colours) leaving Tarbet, 31/5/49

50.   P.S. "PRINCESS PATRICIA" arriving at Balloch.

51. P.S. "COLUMBA" (I) and P.S. "IONA" (III) at Ardrishaig.

52. P.S. "COLUMBA" (I) and S.S. "DAVAAR" off Gourock, c. 1935.

53.   S.S. "BUTE 4" arriving at Dunoon, 4/8/26.

54.   S.S. "ARDYNE" in Kyles of Bute, 9/1935.

55.   S.S. "KINLOCH" off Greenock.

56.   S.S. "DALRIADA" off Gourock, 25/9/37.

57.   P.S. "CULZEAN CASTLE" approaching Fairlie.

J. B. Macgeorge Collection

58.   S.S. "FAIRY QUEEN" off Inverchapel, Loch Eck.

Stromier/Vogt Collection

59.   S.S. "CALEDONIA" off Port Sonachan, Loch Awe.

Rev. Wm. C. Galbraith's Collection

60.   S.S. "SIR WALTER SCOTT" at Trossachs Pier
        and S.S. "ROB ROY" (II) in background.

Rev. Wm. C. Galbraith's Collection

61. T.S.M.V. "DARTHULA II" at Achnacloich Pier, Loch Etive, 8/1946.

62.   S.S. "GIPSY QUEEN" on Forth and Clyde Canal.

63.   D.S.M.V. "FERRY NO. 8" (I) leaving Govan West for Meadowside, with "FERRY NO. 4" (II) in background, 29/2/32.   *G.E.L.*

64.   D.C.S. ex "GOVAN FERRY NO. 3" and D.C.S. "RENFREW" (I) at Renfrew, 16/11/35.

G.E.L.

found their way to the loch, but they were not new, having been built for the London County Council in 1905. These were *Shakespeare* and *Earl Godwin*, which became respectively *Princess Patricia* and *Queen Mary*, both during 1915.

The subject under consideration was built by Messrs. Thornycroft, and was used principally for excursions round the islands from Balloch, and for evening cruises in connexion with evening rail excursions from Glasgow. She had compound diagonal machinery, with cylinders forward of the paddle shaft, and boiler aft. On occasion *Princess Patricia* was used for the Balloch–Ardlui run in late autumn and winter, when the traffic was not sufficiently great to warrant the running of one of the larger steamers. She was sold in May, 1938 and broken up at Balloch the following year.

P.S. *Queen Mary*. As mentionmed above, the other London County Council boat became *Queen Mary*, and it is perhaps fortunate that she had ceased to exist before 1934, as otherwise she might have had to become *Queen Mary III* on the anology of what happened to the Williamson–Buchanan turbine steamer! There is no evidence that the Loch Lomond *Queen Mary* ever carried passengers on the loch, as she was badly damaged by fire quite soon after her arrival there. Her funnel was transferred to *Princess Patricia*, and she lay in the bay at Balloch in semi-derelict condition till scrapped about 1929.

The steamer service on Loch Lomond is now maintained in summer only and by private owners (*See* Chapter XIV). An all the year round daily service was kept up until the first war, after which it was restricted to three days per week in winter, being discontinued entirely in winter from 1933.

CHAPTER VIII

BRITISH RAILWAYS, SCOTTISH REGION, 1948-1968
and
THE CALEDONIAN STEAM PACKET COMPANY, LTD.
from 1948

ON the nationalisation of railways the L.M. & S.R. (controlling The Caledonian S.P. Co. Ltd.) and the L. & N.E.R. became part of British Railways under the British Transport Commission on 1st January, 1948 managed by the Railway Executive (Scottish Region). The Caledonian fleet carried on as before, while that of the L. & N.E.R., though operated along with the Caledonian, and wearing their funnel colours, was not affected till the transfer to the C.S.P. Co. on 5th November, 1951 of its three then remaining steamers. The Kyle of Lochalsh ferryboats and Loch Lomond steamers remained in the ownership of the British Transport Commission till transferred in May 1957 to The Caledonian S.P. Company Ltd. From 1952 the title Clyde Shipping Services was used as a trade name to cover the Railway and Caledonian Steamers, and those of the Clyde & Campbeltown Shipping Co. Ltd. The Railway Executive ceased at the end of September, 1953 and the British Railways Board assumed direct control. By 1955 greater regional freedom was permitted.

British Railways adopted as a funnel colouring buff with black top (already used by an overwhelming majority of their constituents and subsidiaries, including the C.S.P. Co., Ltd.), and a flag based on that of the L. & N.E.R. Co., consisting of a dark blue ground with white St. Andrew's cross edged in red, and on a circle in the middle the "lion and wheel" emblem. This was used on the ex L.N.E.R. Clyde steamers, and for a time, from April, 1949 on the Caledonian steamers; but these later (between 1952 and 1954) reverted to the use of their own yellow pennant with red lion rampant, which also was adopted for the ex L.N.E.R. ships, Skye ferryboats and Loch Lomond steamer from the dates of respective transfers.

The red lion emblem (from the Caledonian houseflag) was introduced to the funnel of the *Caledonian Princess* when new, and to the *Glen Sannox* in 1964, spreading to most of the other members of the fleet by 1965, by which time there had been adopted the British Railways standard colours of "monastral" blue hull, grey rails, ventilators, davits and masts (in the case of those made of

84

metal, the wooden ones remaining varnished). Black hulls and silver-painted ventilators and rails were restored, commencing with *Bute* in October, 1960, but reverting to grey from May, 1974. (The insides of cowl ventilators have remained blue throughout). Buff took the place of grey for the metal masts from 1974.

M.V. *Coruisk* (I). To provide covered accommodation for passengers on the Kyle-Kyleakin crossing, this totally enclosed passenger launch was acquired by the Railway Executive in 1950. She had no vehicle space, and lasted only until the advent of ferries having both this and passenger shelters.

T.S.M.V. *Lochalsh* (I)/*Lochalsh II* (I). A further turntable ferry was added to the Kyle fleet in June, 1951 similar in design to her predecessors and capable of carrying two motor-cars, or one lorry, on her turntable, or alternatively up to 100 passengers. Her change of name occurred early in 1957, to make way for a new boat of the original name. She was laid up at Kyleakin and late in March, 1958, was transferred to the British Waterways Division and converted to a crane barge for use on the Caledonian Canal.

T.S.M.V. *Portree* (I)/*Portree II*. In time for Easter, 1952 this turntable ferry was introduced at Kyle, on completion of an extension to the jetty there. Larger than her predecessors, she could carry four motor-cars on her turntable and about 100 passengers. There was a small deck shelter aft, giving much greater comfort for travellers on foot. Her name was changed in April, 1965 in preparation for the advent of a new *Portree*. After being laid up for a time at Kyleakin and at Greenock, she left the Clyde accompanied by the tug *Cultra* for Belfast, and was later sold to the United Kingdom Atomic Energy Authority; and, after conversion at Lowestoft in 1967 to bow loading, she took up private service between Orford and Orford Ness, continuing her Glasgow registration, but owned by the Secretary of State from 1974.

P.S. *Maid of the Loch*. After long discussions the Railway Executive in July, 1950 ordered from A. & J. Inglis Ltd. a new steamer for service on Loch Lomond. Considerably larger than her predecessors there, she was assembled first in the Pointhouse yard, then sent in sections by rail to Balloch and re-assembled on the slip there. From the main deck upwards she is constructed of aluminium, to reduce weight, and keep her draught to a minimum. She followed the other Loch steamers in certain features of design, such as having curved companionways on the sponsons leading down to the main deck, these being in this instance used not only for the forward entrances, but also for those aft, leading to the main saloon, and having their rails decorated with attractive heraldic shields. In accordance with Loch Lomond tradition, she had her dining saloon on the main deck forward, allowing passengers good views even during meals. She has deck shelters as on the later Clyde paddle steamers, with an upper deck above; and her paddle-boxes are of standard Loch Lomond design with horizontal slots, but having a most attractive Celtic decoration originally in silver paint, the name being in red on a blue blackground. On her bow she had the British Railways lion and wheel emblem. The hull is white, with green waterline, as on the other British Railways inland water ships, and the funnel, originally buff with black top, became plain buff shortly before her launch on 5th March, 1953. Her naming ceremony did not take place till 22nd May, and her inaugural sailing was on 25th May. Though in many respects an anachronism, she was welcomed by steamer enthusiasts and others for her beauty and excellent passenger accommodation. Her machinery is compound diagonal, rather like that installed by the same makers in *Kylemore* in 1897; and, like her, she takes steam from a navy boiler, but with three furnaces, having two oil burners to each, and with a working pressure of 120 lb. per sq. in. Her paddle-wheels have each eight floats, of American elm, thus following the N.B.R./L.N.E.R. practice of wooden floats. Her contract speed was 14 knots.

It is possible that this vessel would not have been designed as a paddle steamer, but for the shallow approaches to Luss Pier, which, however, was closed before she entered service: it was not till 1980 that she was able to call there. At first the *Maid of the Loch* had as consort the *Prince Edward* of 1911; the *Princess May* was almost immediately taken on to the slip at Balloch and scrapped. For some years the services on the Loch incurred heavy losses, and the question of their continuance arose from time to time. A very considerable publicity drive was made for the 1965 season, including the appointment of a hostess with the title "Maid of the Loch". These efforts continued, and traffic materially improved, but only for a time.

Owned from May, 1957 by The C.S.P. Co., Ltd., *Maid of the Loch* was from 1969 transferred (on paper) to Walter Alexander & Sons (Midland) Ltd., the bus operators, and like the C.S.P. Co., a subsidiary of the Scottish Transport Group. This move, stated to be for administrative convenience and for "obscure legal and financial reasons", it was hoped, would provide sufficient resources to keep the service going, and produce some benefit from association with bus operators who have a large tourist traffic in Central Scotland, and who provide a considerable volume of trade for the *Sir Walter Scott* on Loch Katrine.

During the 1975 season the ship had a funnel of Caledonian-MacBrayne red with black top, but without the lion emblem, reverting to buff next season. Withdrawn at the end of the 1981 season, she was sold in March, 1982 to a partnership of Ind Coope Alloa Brewery Co., Ltd. and Verigen Ltd., a Loch Lomond marina company (*see* Chapter XIV).

*   *   *   *   *   *

In February, 1951 Lord Hurcombe, then Chairman of the British Transport Commission, announced a £1,000,000 plan to modernise Clyde steamer services. This involved the building of four passenger ships for shuttle ferry services, each carrying about 500 passengers and with a speed of 15 knots and three general purpose ships to carry 500 passengers and cargo, livestock and motor vehicles, to be fitted with electric lifts and ramps to enable vehicles to be driven on or off at any state of the tide, and with a speed of 16 knots. (A proposal in 1939 for a Gourock-Dunoon car ferry had been abandoned on account of the war). Severe losses were being sustained in operating the existing coal-fired fleet, and much study had been given to securing more economical working.

Orders for the seven ships were placed with Clyde yards, and announced on 8th June, 1951. At New Year, 1952 efforts were made to reduce losses by closing Kirn, Largs, Hunter's Quay, Strone and Kilmun Piers; but in view of protests arrangements were made by 8th January, 1952 to bring into use again Kirn and Largs; to retain Hunter's Quay as an emergency port of call; to have Rothesay's early morning boat restored; and to have the *Countess of Breadalbane* brought from Loch Awe for the Kilcreggan services. Mr. L. E. Marr was appointed by the Railway Executive as manager of the Clyde Shipping Services.

In December, 1952 it was announced that the shuttle ferry plan had been dropped, and the four new passenger ships would be used on conventional routes; but that *Duchess of Argyll* and *King Edward*, already withdrawn, would be followed by *Duchess of Fife* and *Talisman*. The latter in fact remained for many years more.

The design of the new passenger vessels was released in December, 1952 and their names in the following month. It became apparent that they would be useful and economical passenger carriers, smaller than any (other than the small craft *Wee Cumbrae, Ashton* and *Leven*) since the Greenock & Helensburgh Company's quartette of 1866 (built also initially for shuttle ferry services); and they had several features not seen in new Clyde vessels for many years, e.g. the promenade deck not continued to the bow; lifeboats placed low at the stern, as on *Diana Vernon* of 1885; short alleyways round the rear portion of the saloon (containing the galley; no bridge above promenade deck level (though there is a landing platform above the ticket office and wheelhouse). As originally designed they were to have been without funnels, and to have had the machinery aft, with a very large saloon occupying most of the main deck; but they were modified to have the machinery amidships, and the galley aft. They also were to have been single-masted, but were given two masts to carry lights as required by the then new regulations. All were fitted with Radar, as also were the three car-carrying vessels. They had speeds of 15–15½ knots, and their twin screws and rudders made them even more easily manoeuvred than paddle steamers.

T.S.M.V. *Maid of Ashton.* The first of the new ships was launched by Yarrow & Co. Ltd., Scotstoun on 17th February, 1953 and was the first ship to be built by them for Clyde service. With accommodation for 627 passengers on a Steam IV certificate, she was associated initially with the Holy Loch route from Gourock and Craigendoran, was employed also on the various railway connexion runs as required. In April, 1957 she conveyed H.R.H. Princess Margaret on a short cruise down the Clyde from Bridge Wharf, Glasgow. In 1971 she was laid up, for economy. The first of the four "Maids" was also the first to leave the fleet, being sold in January, 1973 to the Yardarm Club of London. Later she was moored as club premises near the *Old Caledonia*, under the name *Hispaniola II*, later without the numeral. Her promenade deck was extended to the bow and the funnel removed: by 1978, however, she had a new funnel. It was interesting to see two former members of the Clyde fleet together, even though both static: unfortunately the *Old Caledonia* is no longer there, having been towed away for scrapping after a serious fire on Sunday, 27th April, 1980, but *Queen Mary* is now in her place.

T.S.M.V. *Maid of Argyll.* This was the first of the two built at Pointhouse, from which had come so many of the North British and L.N.E.R. ships. She entered the water on 4th March and became based at Craigendoran, performing the Dunoon and Rothesay services and also on Saturdays the Arrochar section of the Loch Lomond circular tour; and she alternated with the other *Maids* on various services. Exceptional runs included a charter by the Clyde River Steamer Club from Paisley to Dunoon and Loch Striven on 17th September, 1966; and in the spring of 1970 the Tarbert mail service, for which she received the locked mail-room partitions and shelter from her sister next mentioned. Donning the new livery in 1973, this vessel continued on Clyde services, mainly from Wemyss Bay, and with calls at Ardyne during the period of oil-rig construction there. On 1st March, 1974 her sale was reported. She was prepared at the Port Glasgow yard of James Lamont & Co., Ltd. for the long voyage to Piraeus, leaving on 6th April, named *City of Piraeus*. Her new operators—Cyclades Tourist Cruising Company—altered her considerably, extending the landing-platform to form an upper deck, with new funnel (and mast combined) above; and the boats were raised to the level of the promenade deck, which was extended to the stern. Internally she was refitted in a luxurious manner; she was employed on day excursions from Piraeus (Zea) to Hydra, Poros and Aegina for one season, then was superseded by the even more luxuriously-fitted *City of Hydra,* previously the *Claymore* of 1955.

T.S.M.V. *Maid of Skelmorlie.* The other Inglis product was launched on 2nd April, and was identical with *Maid of Argyll*. Both originally had their destination boards on the landing platform, but these were later moved to the promenade deck as on *Maid of Ashton*. On the installation of a bar, *Maid of Skelmorlie* had her passsenger accommodation reduced from 627 to 625, though *Maid of Ashton* did not. *Maid of Skelmorlie* had been associated mainly with Weymss Bay, Rothesay, Largs and Millport, though interchanging with the others and in 1953 providing the Tighnabruaich connexions with Rothesay; also sometimes performing the Arrochar sailings on Saturdays, and taking the Wemyss Bay–Innellan runs. In September, 1969 she was given small mail-rooms forward of the saloon, and had a temporary shelter above the galley for parcels and luggage, to make her more suitable for the winter service to Kyles of Bute and Tarbert, Loch Fyne, to which she was transferred next month following its having been taken over by the C.S.P. Co. Ltd. from David MacBrayne Ltd. on 1st October, 1969. Sold in April, 1973 to Panamanian interests, this member of the fleet left Gourock, named *Ala*. She was subsequently registered as owned by Felice Giuffe in 1977-8, and converted to a small car ferry, with stern-loading ramp and part of the after saloon and galley removed to make a flush car deck. In this condition she has been engaged in sailing to the Isle of Capri.

T.S.M.V. *Maid of Cumbrae.* The fourth *Maid* was built by Ardrossan Dockyard Ltd. (their first for the Clyde passenger fleet) and was launched on 13th May, 1953. She had minor differences from the others, such as the position of the galley chimney, and the name on the dark portion of the hull at the bow. This was the only *Maid* to suffer major change while still on the Clyde. On account of urgency to obtain an additional end-loading vehicle carrier, she was sent to Barclay Curle's Elderslie Dockyard, where her galley and after saloon were, in March, 1972, cut away, clearing the main deck from the stern to a point just abaft the funnel, giving capacity for 15 cars and with both stern- and side-loading. A 13-ft. turntable was installed; and all passenger accommodation was crammed into the forward portion of the ship. She had a "capuchon" added to the funnel, and became a useful addition to the vehicle-carrying fleet. She was occasionally chartered, and on 30th April, 1977, became the only *Maid* to have visited Inveraray, on a charter to the Clyde River Steamer Club, with Loch Eck Tour in connexion. After a spell in James Watt Dock, she was sold and named *Hanseatic*, but later was registered in name of Navigazione Alto Tireno S.p.A. under the Italian flag as *Noce di Cocco*, afterwards changed to *Capri Express*, employed from Sorrento to Capri and Naples.

T.S.M.V. *Arran* (V).   The first of the "general purpose" ships was launched at Messrs. Denny's yard at Dumbarton on 22nd September, 1953 and revived a name well known in the Clyde & Campbeltown fleet and its predecessors. (It had originally been intended that these ships also would have *Maid* names, but that idea was abandoned). The *Arran* represented a most interesting development, in being designed for the carriage of vehicles on the main deck, which they reached by an electrically-driven lift. Samson posts of goal-post type were provided, with derricks intended to lift containers and to take vehicles off in emergency; but in practice these were seldom used and were removed from all three of the general purpose vessels in the winter of 1958-9, tripod mainmasts being substituted. The changes permitted the prom-enade deck aft to be used for vehicles and increased the capacity from 26 cars of average size to 34. Passenger accommodation included a lounge with bus-type seats, and a tea-room on the promenade deck level while a smoke-room and bar were provided on the lower deck forward. British Polar engines gave a speed of about 15½ knots, slightly lower than that originally indicated.

Entering service on the Gourock-Dunoon station on 4th January, 1954 *Arran* from that time alternated with her two sisters on the Wemyss Bay–Rothesay and Fairlie–Brodick runs and also on the thrice-weekly car and cargo run from Wemyss Bay to Millport. She was transferred to David MacBrayne Ltd. in November 1962 for the West Loch Tarbert–Islay run, which she took up in the following January, after an extensive overhaul, being then transferred back to her original owners, and chartered to David MacBrayne, Ltd. Continuing on the West Loch Tarbert–Islay, Gigha and Jura run, the *Arran*, early in 1974, went to Barclay Curle's for treatment similar to that given to the *Maid of Cumbrae*, involving also removal of the lift and side-loading ramps. In this condition she returned to the Islay route, end-loading ramps having been installed at West Loch Tarbert and at Port Ellen (the MacBrayne service to Port Askaig being at that time suspended). This continued till the advent of the *Pioneer* in 1974, after which the *Arran* was mainly employed on the Clyde, performing relief runs on Ardrossan–Brodick and Gourock–Dunoon–Kilcreggan–and doing some of the gas tanker runs from Gourock to Rothesay. (A side ramp was restored). She acted also as relief in the West Highlands, including Mallaig–Kyle–Portree and Mallaig–Small Isles, Oban––Craignure and the special runs from Coll and Tiree, calling off Mingary for Tobermory Highland Games. She was sold to the same owners who purchased her two sisters, but this fell through and she remained in East India Harbour after her withdrawal in 1979. She was subsequently sold for use as a floating restaurant in Dublin, but in 1986 it was reported she had gone for scrap.

T.S.M.V. *Broadford* (I)/*Broadford II*. A further Skye ferryboat similar to *Portree* was obtained from Messrs. Denny in time to enter service early in 1954. Re-named in 1967, she was sold next year to Orwell & Harwich Navigation Co. Ltd. and resold to Marine Transport Services Ltd., Cobh, going south by the Crinan Canal, calling at Campbeltown.

T.S.M.V. *Cowal* (II). The other two general purpose ships were built at Troon; and of these the first was launched on 20th January, 1954. She differed from *Arran* in having space for two gangways. She was the first Clyde vessel to be fitted with Radar, this subsequently being installed in most of the other members of the fleet. In 1970 she opened a new route from Fairlie to Brodick and Tarbert, with morning and evening runs to Millport. The Fairlie–Brodick–Tarbert service ceased on the introduction of the vehicle ferry (summer only) between Lochranza and Claonaig in 1972. Thereafter the *Cowal* was employed on various Clyde routes, usually Wemyss Bay–Rothesay, and including calls at Ardyne until work ceased there. The withdrawal of services to Ardyne rendered *Cowal* redundant, and by July, 1977 she had retired to East India Harbour, in the following March being transferred to James Watt Dock. She was sold to Greek interests and ultimately left Greenock on 15th May, 1979, in tow of the tug *Creta Salvor,* previously the *Wrestler* of Steel & Bennie, Ltd./Cory Ship Towage (Clyde), Ltd. The tow parted south west of Ushant, and the *Cowal* was taken into Brest by a French tug, ultimately reaching Piraeus. Although re-named *Med Star*, she did not sail for her new owners, and was scrapped in 1984.

T.S.M.V. *Bute* (VI).   The last of the three general purpose vessels
was launched at Troon on 28th September, 1954 and in December
entered service on the Wemyss Bay–Rothesay station, being
subsequently engaged on the other vehicle ferry routes on interchange
with *Arran* and *Cowal*; and all three at different times relieved *Glen
Sannox* on the Brodick run. On Sunday, 5th October, 1954 Gourock
sailings were diverted temporarily to Princes Pier, and *Bute* was one of
the vessels so employed. She also on occasion called at Craigendoran.
She was the sixth *Bute* in the fleets of the railways or their
predecessors, including the Wemyss Bay steamer of 1865. Continuing
in similar employment to that of the *Cowal*, the *Bute* was altered in
1975 by having the gear raised to enable the lift to reach the higher level
of the pier at Armadale, between which and Mallaig she provided the
vehicle service in that and subsequent summers, re-appearing on
Clyde reliefs during parts of the winter. She relieved *Loch Arkaig* on
the Small Isles–Mallaig–Kyle run (for which a ferry door was cut in
her ramp), also visiting Portree and performing cattle runs from Iona
to Oban and relieving on the Mull Ferry from Oban to Craignure.
Laid up in James Watt Dock, she was sold to the same owners as
Cowal—Thetouris Shipping. In April, 1980, she was arrested for
non-payment of ship-keeping and watch duties; but ultimately this
was withdrawn: and, named *Med Sun* and flying the Greek flag, she set
sail on 17th June, 1980 for Piraeus. She was broken up about 1985.

T.S.M.V. *Lochalsh* (II)/*Lochalsh II* (II)/*Scalpay* (II).   In 1956 it
was announced that a further turntable ferryboat capable of carrying
six cars and one hundred passengers was to be built at Troon in
succession to the previous boat of the same name, which could carry
only two cars and 12 passengers. The new vessel had covered
accommodation, as on the *Portree* and *Broadford*. The first renaming
occurred in September, 1970, in preparation for the advent of the third
Lochalsh.. After use as relief at Scalpay, this vessel was transferred to
David MacBrayne, Ltd. and re-named *Scalpay*, for regular service
there. In this she continued till succeeded by the *Kilbrannan* in 1977,
after which she was spare, relieving for a time at Corran–Ardgour on
charter. In November, 1979, she was sold to Ardmaleish Boatbuilding
Company, Bute; and, after being laid up in Rothesay Harbour, left in
tow on 5th June, 1980 for Ardrossan, where she was employed as a
barge alongside a contractor's dredger engaged in deepening the berth
used by the *Pointer*. She subsequently returned to Rothesay and after
dredging at Ayr became a work barge at Troon, without engines.

T.S.M.V. *Glen Sannox* (III).   In April, 1955 an announcement
was made of an impending order for a large vehicle-carrying ship for
the Ardrossan or Fairlie to Brodick station. During that summer a

vehicle service to Arran was provided on certain Saturdays by one of the smaller vessels, *Arran, Cowal* or *Bute*. The order for the new ship was in due course placed with the Ailsa Company; and she was launched at Troon on 30th April, 1957 bearing an illustrious name associated from 1892 with the Arran service. In design she was a much enlarged and improved version of *Arran, Cowal* and *Bute*, with much more spacious lounges, and a saloon set out to the extent of half as a dining-saloon, and to the extent of the other half as a tea-room. The lift was in this case hydraulic, and somewhat slow in operation (though capable of taking a greater load than the electric lifts of the three smaller vessels), as a result of which loading and unloading took a considerable time, and when traffic was heavy she tended to run late in spite of her speed—she attained 18 knots on trial. Instead of derricks she had a crane, which was seldom used. Until 1970 she was almost exclusively associated with the station for which she was built, apart from occasional special runs to Rothesay or Keppel, and charters by the Clyde River Steamer Club from Brodick round Arran or round Bute.

Glen Sannox was the first passsenger ship to be equipped with inflatable liferafts in place of buoyant apparatus and lifeboats, there being only two of the latter. Radar was installed from the outset. She was in 1964 the first member of the C.S.P. Clyde fleet to have the red lion emblem on her funnel (introduced at Stranraer by *Caledonian Princess*); and in 1965 was the first to be given the new colour scheme of "monastral" blue hull, retaining at first the white band at main-deck level, though this was soon removed.

Modifications made in 1970 included removal of all superstructure aft, and the fitting of a stern ramp (the lift being retained). In this condition she was employed mainly on the Dunoon route, and later on the Wemyss Bay–Rothesay run, using the stern ramp at Weymss Bay and the side ramps at Rothesay from May, 1977. Calls at Ardyne took place until no longer required. She was engaged on the Oban–Craignure run from time to time, including calls at Colonsay and, exceptionally, at Gigha in February, 1979. In the autumn of 1976 it had been indicated that she might be refitted to perform the dual role of vehicle ferry and cruise-ship, and so succeed *Queen Mary*. The *Glen Sannox* had already done a limited amount of cruise and charter work, her first being round Arran with the Clyde River Steamer Club in May, 1968; and she was used for school cruises from Anderston Quay. Early in 1977, she was sent to Hall Russell's yard at Aberdeen to be re-engined with German Diesels, returning to the Dunoon or Rothesay route. In the summer of 1978, she took over the cruises from the *Queen Mary*, with white lines round the hull and café tables under sunshades (or umbrellas!), a mobile bar on the car-deck, and moveable companionways to that deck from the one above. In 1980, regular sailings from Glasgow were abandoned and instead on Saturdays she supplemented the Wemyss Bay–Rothesay sailings, with extra runs on certain Fridays from Ardrossan to Brodick and back to Gourock. In winter she is normally on the Mull Ferry from Oban to Craignure, but in January–February, 1981, also relieved on the Islay services from Kennacraig. In summer she is normally spare, but used where extra capacity is required *e.g.* between Wemyss Bay and Rothesay on Cowal Games Day, to relieve another ship to supplement the Gourock–Dunoon runs. Sold for use in the Red Sea, she left the Clyde on 9th August, 1989, named *Knooz*, registered in Panama.

T.S.M.V. *Kyleakin* (II)/*Kyleakin II/Largs*. The last of the turntable type ferryboats for service to Skye to be built was similar to *Lochalsh* (II) and came from the Troon yard, entering service in July, 1960. These are the largest of the turntable-type ferries, subsequent vessels being fitted with ramps only. Superseded at Kyle of Lochalsh by the larger ferries, this vessel was sent to Troon for conversion to bow-loading (as in the case of *Coruisk*), and in April, 1972, under the name *Largs*, took up the Cumbrae Slip service, for which she was latterly stand-by vessel. Her new name revived that of the Wemyss Bay Railway steamer of 1864, and also could be associated with a steamboat of 1822 on the Glasgow–Largs–Millport route. She was sold to Ardmaleish Boatbuilding Company, Bute, who in turn sold her for service in South Yemen. When being unloaded at Mukalla from a Dutch freighter, the leading crane failed to hold and she crashed into the water, but fortunately without much damage.

                    *   *   *   *   *   *

During the 1965 and 1966 seasons the weekend evening runs to Tighnabruaich were maintained by chartering the small m.v. *Maid of Bute* from Messrs. Knox of Rothesay, but this service was not continued in the 1967 season.

T.S.M.V. *Portree* (II) A side-loading vehicle ferry of new design, capable of carrying nine cars, but with no covered passenger accommodation, was built at Port Glasgow in 1965. She differed from all the others in having her wheelhouse close to the bow. In 1970, however, this was removed, and a new bridge erected near the stern, as on the other ferries of this type; and she was converted to bow-loading by the installation of a hydraulic ramp and the removal of the side ramps and deck turntable. In this condition she was transferred from Kyle of Lochalsh to the service of Bute Ferry

Co. Ltd. between Rhubodach and Colintraive. Having also on occasion relieved on that between Largs and Cumbrae Slip. She was sold in November, 1986 to Mr. Hooper of Sandbank on being superseded by the end-loading drive-through vessels of the "Loch" class.

T.S.M.V. *Broadford* (II).   Similar in layout of her car deck, this boat differed from the foregoing in having from the outset her bridge in the traditional position aft. She entered service in 1967, and later had a small space under the bridge enclosed for covered passenger accommodation. In 1971 she joined her sister at Rhubodach, similarly converted, and like her was superseded in 1986, when sold to the same purchaser, both being used as tenders to American Naval ships. In January, 1988 she was sold to Divemex Ltd. of Powys and re-named *Boreford*.

M.V. *Rose/Keppel.* It has not often occurred that a vessel from other parts has come to the Clyde for passenger service; but the Tilbury Ferry *Rose* sailed round the North of Scotland and, after modifications at Greenock, entered service between Largs and Millport on 12th June 1967, being later renamed as above. With Voith-Schneider propulsion she is easily manoeuvrable, but her speed does not rise to normal Clyde standards. She has a combined funnel and mast, originally yellow with black top, but without the lion emblem, but latterly in normal Cal-Mac colours. Apart from a weekly call at Rothesay, she did not deviate much from her normal route. In the summer of 1980, on charter to the Clyde River Steamer Club, she became the first Caledonian MacBrayne vessel to call at Ormidale Pier.

The Largs–Millport (Old Pier) summer service was withdrawn in May 1986, since which time the *Keppel* has been engaged in reviving cruising on the Clyde. Based at Largs, she has visited Millport, Rothesay, Tighnabruaich, Dunoon, Helensburgh, Carrick Castle, etc. and in the 1988 season Renfrew and the Garden Festival.

*   *   *   *   *   *

On 1st January, 1969 The Caledonian Steam Packet Co. Ltd. became a wholly-owned subsidiary of the Scottish Transport Group, in terms of the Transport Act of the previous year.

The following month it was announced that two new car ferries (side-loading) would be built for Clyde services; but a certain amount of controversy arose over the advisability of perpetuating a type which had caused delays in loading and unloading, and was rapidly coming to be regarded as obsolete in view of the successful end-loading vessels in use on many routes in Britain and elsewhere.

In August, 1969 the company reported having acquired the share capital of Arran Piers Limited, a private company previously in the hands of the family of the late Duke and Duchess of Montrose, and in control of all piers and harbours on Arran. This acquisition prepared the way for the conversion by the Scottish Transport Group of the piers for end-loading ferry vessels, and a start was made almost at once with a survey for this purpose at Brodick. Later the same month, Mr. P. M. Thomas, Chairman of the S.T.G., stated that the ultra-modern Swedish 50-car drive-through ship *Stena Baltica* had been purchased, and was expected to be operating by Easter, 1970 on the Ardrossan–Brodick run. Arrangements were put in hand for an end-loading berth at Ardrossan, to the south-west of Winton Pier.

Other developments mentioned by the Chairman at the same time were the purchase of a Hovercraft—probably a Hovermarine Mk. 2—to carry up to 60 passengers at speeds of up to 40 knots; the temporary transfer to the Clyde of one of the MacBrayne large car ferries, during the conversion of the *Glen Sannox* to stern-loading; the transfer to the Clyde, for an initial period, of the drive-through ferry vessel being built for David MacBrayne Limited, originally intended for West Loch Tarbert–Islay (subsequently named *Iona*) (see later in this Chapter); also the building of a large vehicle-carrying vessel, probably of roll-on, roll-off type, and the construction of two 28-car ferries for the Kyle of Lochalsh–Kyleakin station. Not long afterwards it was announced that the hovercraft project had fallen through, but later it was restored to the programme.

T.S.M.V. *Coruisk* (II). In July, 1969 a fifth ferryboat was added to the Kyle of Lochalsh fleet, similar to her immediate predecessor *Broadford*, but with covered passenger shelter as on *Lochalsh* and *Kyleakin*. The administration of the Skye ferries was reported to be transferred in 1969 to the Highland Omnibus Co. Ltd., Inverness, also a member of the S.T.G., with a local manager at Kyleakin; but this did not result in any operational change, and the Caledonian Company continued to own the ships.

This Skye ferry was taken to Troon in September, 1971 and converted to bow-loading, to carry six cars and 70 passengers on the new route between Largs and the Tattie Pier, Cumbrae (soon re-named Cumbrae Slip). This she inaugurated on 11th March, 1972, Fairlie Pier being then closed. She was sometimes relieved or assisted by *Portree* or *Broadford, Largs* or *Kilbrannan*, etc., and herself relieved on other routes, including Iona–Fionnphort, Colintraive–Rhubodach and her original run, Kyle–Kyleakin. The

Coruisk was sold in September 1986 to Euroyachts Ltd. and in the next year to a Penzance owner.

T.S.M.V. *Stena Baltica/Caledonia* (III). This was the first end-loading vehicle ferry in the C.S.P. fleet and as such marked a radical change in the design of the Clyde steamer. Though her speed was only 14 knots, it was expected that with her much faster loading and unloading of cars, this ship should be able to keep time on a schedule similar to that of *Glen Sannox*, and give an additional sailing in each direction in summer, which would to a certain extent compensate for her much lower passenger capacity, though doubts were expressed regarding her adequacy for day return passengers. She had belonged to the Stena Line of Gothenburg, one of whose other ships—*Stena Nordica*—had already become known on the Stranraer-Larne run. *Stena Baltica* arrived at Greenock on Sunday, 11th January, 1970 having had her funnels already painted yellow with black top, and having been already registered at Glasgow. She was taken in hand by Scott-Lithgow Limited for overhaul; and, with a black hull and Caledonian boot-topping, she received the name *Caledonia* in April. She was not ready by Easter, but neither were the end-loading berths at Brodick or Ardrossan: and she entered service on 29th May, 1970 by this time in full Caledonian livery, including red lions on the funnels and bow. On the same day *Iona* made her appearance on the Gourock-Dunoon station and next day *Cowal* inaugurated the Fairlie-Brodick-Tarbert car ferry route.

Displaced from the regular Arran sailings in 1974, this former Swedish car-ferry found new employment on the Oban-Craignure route in summer, changing places with the *Clansman*, which became the regular Arran summer vessel. On 29th October, 1983 she performed a charter sailing from Brodick to Tarbert and back, for the Clyde River Steamer Club.

Withdrawn at the end of the 1987 season, she was sold and was taken to Dundee for conversion to a floating restaurant. After about a year this had not been carried out; and she was re-sold to Libera Navigazione Laura to sail between Naples and Ischia, named *Haidi*.

HM2-011. A Hovermarine HM-2 (Mark II), of rigid side-wall type (described as "silent"), capable of carrying 62 passengers at 35 knots, was purchased by the Scottish Transport Group for operation by The Caledonian Steam Packet Co. Ltd., and made an inaugural run on Saturday, 6th June, 1970 from Gourock to Largs, thereafter operating successfully from Gourock to Dunoon,

Rothesay, Largs and Millport, with intermittent cruises Round Cumbrae and to Rothesay Bay. The experimental use of this hovercraft lasted during two seasons after which she disappeared from the Clyde scene, having been sold to the American parent company of Hover Marine, Southampton.

T.S.M.V. *Kyleakin* (III).   The first of the large Kyle ferries was already under construction at Newport, Monmouthshire, when the above announcement was made, and it subseqently became clear that these were to be end-loading vessels, 116 feet in length, and with covered passenger accommodation at one side only, in the manner of the *Rosehaugh* at Kessock, Inverness. The new ship was due to enter service in June, 1970 but was considerably delayed, not appearing at Kyle till August, and then having trouble with her hydraulic ramps and cooling system. After these were cured she settled down to provide a much improved service.

T.S.M.V. *Lochalsh* (III).   The second Kyle ferry, due to join the fleet in August, 1970 was long delayed. She entered service in 1971 and traffic queues were eliminated. The two large ferries have not deviated from the route for which they were built. They are normally overhauled at Stornoway. Their design was the prototype for that of the smaller *Isle of Cumbrae*, and from it also has developed that of the "Loch" class drive-through ferries.

BUTE FERRY COMPANY LIMITED

On Hogmanay, 1969 came the announcement by radio news that The Caledonian Steam Packet Co. Ltd. had taken over the control of the above Company, which worked the Colintraive–Rhubodach ferry. Great credit was given to the Bute Ferry Co. Ltd. for its development of a vehicle ferry service across the Kyles of Bute, commencing on 13th July, 1950 in a small way with an ex-landing-craft operating from the beach, on which were laid metal nets to assist the vehicles in running over the stones. Later small concrete jetties were built at each terminal. The route constituted the revival of an ancient ferry which had been in use before the days of steam, and had developed to a certain extent for passengers and light goods, especially after the closing of Colintraive Pier. Plans for jetties and boats had been prepared in 1939, but the coming of the war prevented their fruition, though a 10-foot-wide road was constructed from Port Bannatyne to Rhubodach. From 1945 onwards the County Council renewed their efforts to have a vehicle ferry put into operation, but, though the matter was approved in principle, no funds were available, and it was in the spring of 1950 that the Bute Ferry Co. Ltd., without any subsidy, took the matter in hand. Part of the delay had been due to local opposition to the building of a road which might spoil the amenity of the Kyles, the opposition including the then Marquis of Bute, whose son, having succeeded him, became a Director and Chairman of the Company along with Councillor A. B. Fisher, whose father had been strongly in favour of the project. The official opening was one week after the service had commenced, and was performed by the Marchioness of Bute. The boat was afterwards named *Eilean Mor,* later *Eilean Mhor,* after the largest of the islands at the Narrows. As a spare boat a slightly smaller landing-craft was acquired, afterwards named *Eilean Fraoich.* The company had also various craft with auxiliary motors, for delivery of newspapers, etc., to Bute in the late 1940s, and a further landing-craft, *Eilean Fraoich II,* was acquired in 1957.

The first boat specifically built for the Rhubodach vehicular ferry was an interesting craft, being the first vessel constructed of plywood to receive a Ministry of Transport certificate. She was somewhat like a small version of one of the Clyde chain ferries such as *Erskine,* being loaded from either end by ramps, and with the machinery at one side, and two exhaust pipes in place of funnels. She could carry up to 75 passengers and eight cars or two 15-ton lorries, and was propelled by twin screws at each end. She entered service on 25th May, 1963, and was officially named *Eilean Buidhe,* though facetiously nicknamed the *Maid of Plywood*! She was taken out of service shortly afterwards, and was returned to her builders—Dickie's of Tarbert—for extensive modifications, including the installation of jet propulsion, somewhat on the lines of the Clyde Navigation Trust Ferries Nos. 1 and 2 of 1865 (see Chapter XV). The jet units drew water in and forced it out again; and, being placed diagonally opposite each other at bow and stern, the craft could be steered on a swivel system. Her gross tonnage was 32.

During the absence of the *Eilean Buidhe* there was acquired another landing-craft, which received the name *Eilean Dhu;* and the turntable ferry *Dhuirnish* was bought from J. & A. Gardner & Co. Ltd. following the closure of the Bonawe Ferry. The turntable was removed and she was converted to bow-loading, her method of operation being then similar to that of the landing-craft. Both of these boats sank during the winter of 1968-9, but were duly raised.

With the near completion of road improvements in Glendaruel, traffic had increased to such an extent that vessels with larger capacity were required, and the The Caledonian S.P. Co. Ltd. supplied the immediate need by transferring one of the Kyle of

Lochalsh ferries to the Kyles of Bute. From June, 1970 the *Portree*, then capable of carrying 11 small cars or two large commerical vehicles, operated on the Rhubodach–Colintraive ferry and in 1971 was joined by *Broadford*. These have been superseded late in 1986 by a "Loch" class ferry.

*   *   *   *   *   *

In July, 1971 The Caledonian S.P. Co. installed a v.h.f. radio telephone system linking their head office at Gourock with the pier offices at Dunoon, Wemyss Bay, Rothesay, Largs, Fairlie, Millport and Brodick, and with all the members of the Clyde fleet then in service, so as to keep in close contact with the ships and reduce delays due to bad weather, heavy traffic or other circumstances.

CHAPTER IX

CLYDE STEAMERS OF DAVID MACBRAYNE, LIMITED

AS the history of the MacBrayne fleet has been covered in our book, *West Highland Steamers*, we shall not repeat in here, but may mention that it was in 1851 that Messrs. D. Hutcheson & Company took over the working of the West Highland steamers, which passed to the ownership of Mr. David MacBrayne in 1879. In 1905 the concern became a limited company, and in 1928 was reconstructed under the title of David MacBrayne (1928) Ltd., being thenceforth controlled jointly by the London Midland & Scottish Railway Company and Coast Lines, Ltd. The former name of David MacBrayne Ltd. was restored in 1934.

The 50 per cent holding of the L.M. & S. Railway Company passed to the British Transport Commission on 1st January, 1948 and the Scottish Transport Group on 1st January 1969. The other 50 per cent, held by Coast Lines Ltd. was purchased by the S.T.G. in 1969, so that David MacBrayne Ltd. became a wholly owned subsidiary of that statutory body.

In the following chapter are included only the MacBrayne steamers which have actually operated on the Clyde during and since 1935, the history of the others being conveniently traceable as indicated above.

P.S. *Iona* (III). As is well known, the third *Iona* was built to take the place of the previous steamer of the same name, which had been sold for blockade-running. Launched on 10th May, 1864, she inherited the deck-saloons and certain other fittings from that vessel, and was, at the time of her withdrawal, the only example of a pleasure steamer of the mid-Victorian period sailing on the Clyde.

The original horizontal boilers of *Iona* were removed in 1891, and two "haystacks" were then installed. The latter did duty for the remainder of the ship's career. The machinery consisted of two simple oscillating cylinders, a surface condenser having been fitted by Messrs. Hutson & Corbett in 1891.

The Clyde sailings of *Iona* were latterly somewhat restricted compared with those of her earlier days, as she appeared only for a short time in spring and autumn on the Ardrishaig run, being stationed at Oban in summer, and laid up at Greenock in winter.

Sold to Arnott, Young & Co. (Shipbreakers) Ltd., Dalmuir,

Iona left Greenock in tow on 27th February, and was broken up in March, 1936, alongside *Columba*.

P.S. *Columba* (I).   Dating from 1878, this was the finest and most famous steamer that ever sailed on the Clyde and we suggest that she was perhaps the most noteworthy vessel of her class in the world. She was admired by thousands of passengers from all parts who travelled in her on the first stage in the Royal Route to the Highlands.

She was built of steel, the use of which for shipbuilding was then in its infancy, and was the longest steamer that had so far sailed in regular Clyde service. (It is interesting to note that the distinction of being the longest steamer engaged in service on the Clyde belonged also to her successor, *Saint Columba*.)

The machinery of *Columba,* like that of *Iona,* was of the two-cylinder oscillating type, non-compound, steam being supplied originally by four navy-type boilers, but latterly by two large haystack boilers working at a pressure of 50 lbs. per square inch, fitted in 1900. Her engines thereafter ran at 40 revolutions per minute instead of 36 as previously, and her speed was increased from the original 18 knots to over 19½.

With her two large funnels painted in the well-known Mac-Brayne colours, curved slanting stem and square stern, she was a stately looking craft, making a sight never to be forgotten when seen amid the beautiful scenery of the Clyde coast.

It is worthy of mention that with the passing of *Iona* and *Columba* there were no Clyde steamers left of the once common type with two funnels, one forward and one aft of the paddle-boxes, an arrangement which made such a symmetrical and well-balanced outline as was to be found in vessels like the three *Ionas, Columba* (I), *Lord of the Isles* (I) and (II), *Galatea, Ivanhoe* and *Glen Sannox* (I). The only two-funnelled paddle steamer then left on the Clyde was *Jeanie Deans*, which had both funnels forward; and in this the new *Jupiter, Juno* and *Waverley*, resembled her, the last-named being now the only example.

The withdrawal of *Iona* and *Columba* caused great regret wherever these steamers were known, and the interest taken in them is shown by the very large prices paid for souvenirs sold publicly by the shipbreakers.

Though they had both attained a considerable age as things are reckoned in the world of maritime affairs, *Iona* and *Columba* seemed endowed with almost perpetual youth in some respects, reappearing as they did year after year in all the glory of their new paint. Of course their accommodation, particularly with respect to the protection of passengers from inclement weather, was far behind that of then current standards, and it appears to have been due largely to this shortcoming, coupled with their relatively high fuel consumption, that they were finally withdrawn. Their speed, however, was maintained, but it must be remembered that there is often a large margin between what a ship can do and what her service normally requires. It is understood that both ships remained perfectly sound to the end.

One could scarcely imagine the Clyde bereft of these two celebrities, and it was hard to believe that *Iona* and *Columba* would never be seen again.

There was, however, one consolation, and that was in the knowledge that neither ship suffered the fate of relegation to new owners and inferior duties. Instead, both retired gracefully at the end of long and meritorious careers on their owners' then most important services. *Columba* was sold to Arnott, Young & Co. (Shipbreakers), Ltd., Dalmuir, and left Greenock in tow on 27th February, being broken up in March 1936, alongside *Iona*.

T.S.M.V. *Comet* (III). This little motor vessel was engaged continuously as the "Lochgoil Mail Steamer" from her appearance on the Clyde about 1915 with the exception of a short period in 1919, when she sailed between Ardrishaig and Inveraray in connexion with *Columba,* calling at Otterferry, Crarae and Strachur. She made her last run from Lochgoilhead on 1st October, 1946, and thus terminated one of the oldest regular passenger services in the world. Motor buses were substituted by Messrs. MacBrayne, running from Carrick Castle to Lochgoilhead and Arrochar, where connexion was made with the trains on the West Highland Railway and with other service buses.

P.S. *Mountaineer* (III). The small paddle steamer *Mountaineer,* which was built by Messrs. A. & J. Inglis Ltd., in 1910, seldom appeared on the Clyde, being used principally for excursions from Oban. She sometimes, however, relieved *Comet* on the Lochgoil run.

An unusual feature of the design of the *Mountaineer* (as built) was the boarding round the promenade deck instead of the usual open rails. This solid surface was, however, inclined to catch the wind and added to the tenderness of the vessel. Latterly open rails were substituted.

The machinery of *Mountaineer* consisted of a neat set of compound diagonal engines, steam being supplied by a haystack boiler. She was broken up at Port Glasgow in 1938.

T.S.M.V. *Lochfyne*. This was the first Diesel-electric vessel built for service in Britain, and became quite a favourite at Oban in summer, and on the Greenock or Gourock-Ardrishaig service in winter. A full description of her accommodation and machinery will be found in "W.H.S."

During most of the war period she was on the Ardrishaig run, from Wemyss Bay instead of Gourock, because of the boom at the Cloch, and wearing wartime colours of dark grey hull and upperworks and black funnels. From 1947 to 1958 she spent her summers as consort to *King George V* at Oban and in winter she relieved *Saint Columba* on the Gourock to Loch Fyne service, then restricted to Tarbert. When the *Saint Columba* was withdrawn at the end of the 1958 season. *Lochfyne* was transferred full-time to the Clyde, and ran in summer and winter until 30th September, 1969, when, bedecked with flags to mark the occasion, she took the last passenger sailing on the Firth of Clyde for David MacBrayne Limited, thus ending a connexion of over 120 years between that company or its forbears and the Ardrishaig run.

Shortly afterwards *Lochfyne* was sold to the Northern Slipway Limited, Dublin, and laid up at Faslane. After providing electric power for the shipbreaking yard at Faslane, she was drydocked at Govan with a view to static use, but was scrapped at Dalmuir where her famous predecessors *Iona* (III) and *Columba* (I) had ended their careers. She was photographed there on 1st April, 1974, the day of the launch at Leith of the third *Pioneer,* thus making a further link with early history, in that the *Lochfyne* when new in 1931 was photographed alongside the veteran *Glencoe* of 1846.

T.S.M.V. *Lochnevis*. This Diesel-electric ship, built in 1934 for the Portree mail service, carried on the Ardrishaig run for a time in 1940, hence her inclusion in our previous edition among the Clyde steamers of Messrs. David MacBrayne, Ltd. As H.M.S. *Lochnevis* she became a minelayer, and was returned to her owners in 1944. She performed on the Gourock–Tarbert or Ardrishaig service regularly as a relief to *Lochfyne,* till the substitution of a Caledonian *Maid* class ship in the autumn of 1969. She was then sold to Dutch owners, and was broken up at Wormer, Holland, in May, 1974.

Tr.S.S. *Saint Columba*. At the end of the 1935 season the assets and goodwill of Williamson-Buchanan Steamers, Ltd. and Turbine Steamers, Ltd were acquired by the L.M. & S. Railway Company in association with David MacBrayne Ltd. Of the steamers owned by the two Williamson concerns, Messrs. MacBrayne received two, one being *Queen Alexandra,* of which the previous history will be found in Chapter IV. At the date of the transfer she was laid up for the winter in the Albert Harbour at Greenock, but even so her white funnels were forthwith painted red.

She did not, however, sail for her new owners in this condition; for, when she emerged from the yard of Messrs. James Lamont & Co. Ltd., in May, 1936 she was scarcely recognisable, the upper deck having been extended aft, and a third funnel and second mast added. Her name had been changed to *Saint Columba,* her owners desiring, no doubt, to perpetuate in some measure the name of her illustrious predecessor, but wisely refraining from copying it exactly.

The new funnels, which were elliptical, were shorter than the original ones and were slightly "stepped".

It is noteworthy that until 1935 there had been no turbine ships in the MacBrayne fleet; but the two vessels acquired in that year were both propelled by this type of machinery, the one under review being fitted with triple screws and three direct-drive steam turbines.

Saint Columba was employed on the Glasgow–Ardrishaig run, which had always been regarded as the most important of the MacBrayne summer services. Like her predecessor, she left Bridge Wharf at 7-11 a.m. each day (except Sundays), making calls at the usual ports.

She was in 1937 converted for burning oil fuel, and was the second steamer in the MacBrayne fleet so fitted, the first being *Lochness* of 1929.

From 1939 to 1946 *Saint Columba* was an accommodation ship in East India harbour, Greenock, for Boom Defence personnel. She was re-conditioned in 1947 and returned to the Ardrishaig route in that summer. In time for the 1952 season, her mainmast was lengthened, so that the new masthead light would be in such a position as to comply with the new regulations. She went aground at Ettrick Bay, Bute in August, 1953, but was little damaged. After the 1958 season her end came, when she was sold to British Iron & Steel Corporation, and was towed to Port Glasgow on 23rd December to be broken up, during the following year. After her withdrawal, her place on the Ardrishaig station was taken by *Lochfyne* for most of the year, the smaller ship being by this time adequate for the traffic, even in summer. This route, previously regarded as the most important of the MacBrayne "Swift Steamer" services, had its capacity successively reduced by the substitution of first *Lochfyne,* then *Lochnevis* for quite a large part of the year, and finally by a "Maid" class ship of the C.S.P. Co. Ltd. from the autumn of 1969, till it was superseded on 30th May, 1970 by (*a*) an all-the-year round car ferry service from Fairlie via Brodick to Tarbert only (soon abandoned), and (*b*) a summer excursion run on certain days of the week from Gourock or Largs, by *Waverley* or a "Maid" class vessel, now confined to a weekly call by the former during her Clyde summer season (*See* Chapter XVII).

T.S.S. *King George V*.   The other turbine steamer taken over in 1935 was this fine ship which had been built for Turbine Steamers Ltd. in 1926 (See Chapter IV). On entering the MacBrayne fleet *King George V* was repainted in their colours, and in 1936 appeared on the Oban–Staffa–Iona service with six lifeboats instead of her previous four—the two extra lifeboats were inherited from *Columba* and had previously done duty on *Scout*. She was converted to burn oil fuel, in 1938. In the Second War *King George V* was employed as a tender on the Firth of Clyde; she also acted as a troop transport at Dunkirk, making six trips in all in May, 1940. In recognition of their services on these occasions her master, Captain MacLean and her chief engineer, Mr. W. Macgregor, were each awarded the D.S.O., and her bo'sun, Mr. Mackinnon, the D.S.M. She returned to the Clyde and served as a tender when Dominion and later American troops were being landed at Gourock; and she carried Mr. Winston Churchill to his battleship when on his way across the Atlantic.

During the winter of 1950-1 *King George V* was converted by her builders to burn oil fuel, which resulted in an increase over her recent speed. In 1952 she received a mainmast, in preparation for the regulations regarding masthead lights about to be brought into force.

On acquiring inflatable dinghies in the spring of 1959, her lifeboats were again reduced to four, these being the new boats supplied to *Saint Columba* in 1947, and she lost the historic pair. It was agreed in March, 1959 to instal a buffet for coffee and sandwiches, and in January, 1960 to have a cafeteria. In time for the 1962 season her dining saloon was extended forward, the galley being transferred to the stern (with a tall chimney above), and the lavatories to the forward end of the boiler casing. The after ends of the deck shelter were enclosed, bringing G.T. up to 985. She was engaged on the Oban–Staffa–Iona run in summer (without the call at Staffa after 1968), and appeared on Clyde services from time to time, notably on the Gourock–Tarbert–Ardrishaig route in the summer of 1946, and again in the winter of 1960-1, during the absence of *Lochiel,* when *Lochfyne* was required for the Islay service (temporarily operated from Oban), and on C.S.P. charter in spring, 1971. This was the prelude to the use of this favourite steamer on Clyde cruises in the early parts of that season and the following, calls being made at several places to which she had not been, even in her Turbine Steamer days. Later in each of these seasons she was back on her normal run from Oban to Iona, cruising near Staffa.

In 1973 she passed to Caledonian MacBrayne Holdings Ltd., having yellow discs on the funnels, with the red lions from the *Duchess of Hamilton.*

Withdrawn at the end of the 1974 season, she spent the winter as usual in East India Harbour, Greenock and was sold at 12 noon on 3rd April, 1975 to Nationwide Transport Ltd. She was towed away from Greenock on 12th April by the tug *Mumbles,* a sad farewell to the last two-funnelled (fore and aft) MacBrayne ship—a feature of the Highland scene since the advent of the first *Mountaineer* in 1852. While undergoing conversion to a floating restaurant she was severely damaged by fire at Cardiff on 26th August, 1981, and in April, 1984 was finally dismantled opposite Penarth.

T.S.M.V. *Lochiel*(IV).   This motorship was built in 1939 for the Islay mail service, but is included here on account of having performed the Ardrishaig run for a time in the spring of each of the war years, when *Lochfyne* was off for overhaul and *Lochnevis* was absent on war service; also, during Fair Holidays periods, she supplemented *Lochfyne,* which was inadequate for the large numbers of passengers then travelling. Like *Lochnevis* she had the third-class accommodation at the starboard side, and first-class to port, but latterly became a one-class ship. She was superseded by *Arran* in January, 1970, and sold in April to Norwest Shipping Ltd., Douglas I.O.M., and renamed *Norwest Laird,* being employed on a service between Douglas and Fleetwood during that season only. She later became a floating restaurant at Bristol, resuming the name *Lochiel.*

T.S.S. *Robina*.   This small tender, previously at Belfast, was after the Second War acquired by Coast Lines Ltd., and registered at Falmouth. She was chartered to David MacBrayne Ltd. for the 1946 and 1947 seasons, spending the former at Oban on short excursions (and also on a short relieving duty from West Loch Tarbert to Islay); but in the summer of 1947 reviving the Gourock–Lochgoilhead run abandoned on the last sailing of the *Comet* at the end of the previous season. She gave a double daily service, and also during the Fleet visit that summer performed cruises round the naval ships. The service was, however, not repeated in subsequent years, and *Robina* was transferred to other owners

T.S.M.V. *Hebrides* (II).   As extra ship on the Ardrossan–Brodick station at New Year, 1973, the first of the MacBrayne large vehicle carriers of 1964 *(see W.H.S.)* was for the first time employed on Clyde passenger service. She was normally on the Uig–Lochmaddy-Tarbert Harris station. She was sold to Torbay Seaways late in 1985. As *Devoniun* she plies between Torquay and the Channel Islands.

T.S.M.V. *Clansman* (IV).   This large car ferry normally employed on the Mallaig–Armadale station, was chartered to The Caledonian S.P. Co. Ltd. in the winter and spring of 1970 for the

Gourock–Dunoon route. Her extensive passenger accommodation was much admired, but the embarkation of passengers with only one narrow gangway took considerable time. For this service she carried a yellow funnel with black top (without lions), reverting to red when she returned at the end of May to her usual run. In 1970, following new Board of Trade Regulations which exclude measurement of the car deck, her gross tonnage was reduced from 2104 to 1420·41, but even this gave her the greatest tonnage of any ship until that time employed on Clyde passenger services.

After extensive alterations at Troon, including lengthening by the insertion of about 30 feet forward of the superstructure and construction of a new bow; heightening to give space for high vehicles to drive through; and the fitting of stern and bow doors and ramps and the removal of the lift, the *Clansman* was placed on the Ullapool–Stornoway service in succession to the *Iona* in 1973; but her speed following the conversion was unsatisfactory, and she was superseded on that run by the Norwegian-built *Suilven,* though continuing to act as relief, as she had also each winter, on the Scabster–Stromness crossing of the Pentland Firth on charter to P. & O. Ferries in place of *St. Ola.* Her summer employment in her later years was on the Ardrossan–Arran station. Her speed of loading and unloading compensated for her slow performance at sea, but in stormy conditions she had difficulty in using Ardrossan and had to be diverted to Gourock.

Being succeeded on the Arran run in the spring of 1984, following a major breakdown, she was laid up for some time in James Watt Dock, Greenock, and on 14th August, 1984 was delivered to Torbay Seaways for a Torquay–Guernsey service, which however did not materialise on account of refusal of planning permission. She was accordingly re-sold to Mira Shipping Line Ltd., Malta, who had just parted with their recently-acquired *Free Enterprise III* (which they had re-named *Tamira*) to the Isle of Man S.P. Co., Ltd. (who re-named her *Mona's Isle*); and the *Clansman* took the name *Tamira* for her Malta–Gozo run. She left the U.K. in December, 1984 and before long it was reported that she had been sold to Euch Zammit & Sons Ltd., also of Malta, by whom she was re-named *Al Hussein.* In February, 1986 she was sailing in the Gulf of Akabah.

T.S.M.V. *Columba* (II). Clyde service for the bearer of this famous name has been infrequent. In 1978 and again in 1987 and 1988 she called at Largs on her cruise round the Mull of Kintyre to Oban calling at Campbeltown in 1987 and Tarbert next year; and at Christmas and New Year 1981 she was in reserve to supplement the Arran sailings, making a few runs to and from Brodick.

In the summer of 1988 it was announced that the *Columba* had been sold to Hebridean Princess Cruises P.L.C. (later changed to Leisure & Marine Holdings P.L.C.), the ship being handed over at Greenock on 14th October. After preliminary work at Rochester and conversion at Great Yarmouth, she commenced her first voyage for her new owners (trading as Hebridean Island Cruises) from Oban on 27th May, 1989 as a luxury cruise ship operating from Oban, Mallaig and Kyle of Lochalsh to various places with which she was already familiar, and spending the nights in sheltered locations such as Plockton. The project is aimed at the upper market, with fine staterooms and lounges, the Columba Restaurant perpetuating her former name, the Tiree Lounge recalling one of her ports of call; and passengers can take their cars with them as the lift and vehicle deck remain in use.

T.S.M.V. *Iona* (VII).   Intended for a passenger and vehicle service to Islay, this ship is the first of drive-through design in the MacBrayne fleet (though not the first in service on any West Highland route, which was *Sound of Jura,* built in Norway in 1969 for Western Ferries Limited). The intention had been to use the new ship from a new pier near the entrance to West Loch Tarbert, but that was abandoned on account of expense, in favour of building a new pier at Escart Bay, this in turn being delayed on account of the expenditure of public money involved. Not being suitable for use at the existing pier at West Loch Tarbert, the new *Iona* was chartered to the C.S.P. Co. Ltd. for the Gourock–Dunoon run, and their *Arran* went to David MacBrayne Ltd. for the West Loch Tarbert–Islay run. The *Iona,* seventh of the name in the MacBrayne fleet (including powered small craft), is a fine passenger and vehicle-carrying ship, though with very little open deck space for passengers, but having a very pleasent lounge, seating 101 passengers, on the boatdeck forward, with chairs upholstered initially in shades of violet and blue, the cafeteria for 97 persons being at the after end of this deck. Her car space is the height of two decks, except for the "gallery" decks at the sides and she can carry 47 large cars, or 11 30-ft. vehicles and 7 cars. She has a hydraulically-operated stern ramp and bow door and ramp; also a lift and turntable system capable of moving 27·5 tons for side-loading at piers where end-loading facilities do not exist. Below the car deck is a smoke-room and bar for 50 persons, and also crew accommodation in two-berth cabins, while the officers have single-berth cabins on the gallery decks and in the house on the navigating bridge deck. Fitted with Denny-Brown retractable stabilisers, she has also a Diesel-driven 3-ton bow-thrust controllable pitch propeller; and the main machinery, consisting of twin

Paxman engines each driving a fixed-pitch propeller through a gear, gives propeller speed of approximately 300 r.p.m., compared with the engine speed of 900 r.p.m., and a speed of 16 knots at 80 per cent continuous rating. On trials on the Skelmorlie measured mile she attained a speed of 17·51 knots. Control can be from the consoles in the engine-room, in the wheelhouse, in the bridge wings, or at the aft end of the navigation bridge deck, for astern working. Though commencing service in MacBrayne colours, she had her funnel changed to yellow with black top within a few days. After a spell on the Gourock–Dunoon run in Caledonian colours, the *Iona,* with red funnel restored, took up various West Highland services (Oban–Craignure; Mallaig–Kyle–Stornoway; Oban–Castlebay––Lochboisdale) and has also supplemented the Ardrossan–Brodick runs. For the Lochboisdale route she had cabins erected on the upper deck, the small dummy funnel was removed, and the side uptakes extended were painted as funnels. After being relieved by the *Claymore* she was placed on the Islay run for which she had originally been intended, operating from Kennacraig to Port Ellen, and (from 1980) also to Port Askaig. In 1989 she succeeded the *Pioneer* on the Mallaig–Armadale route, with extension to Barra on certain Sundays.

CHAPTER X

CALEDONIAN MACBRAYNE, LTD.

IN February, 1972 an association known as Caledonian Mac-Brayne Services was formed by The Caledonian S.P. Co., Ltd. and David MacBrayne, Ltd. to co-ordinate certain departments of the two companies, becoming the registered owners of the first and second small bow-loading ferry vessels. (Plans had also been prepared for a larger model, but in fact only the small version was built). Designed by Messrs. Burnett Corless, these were developed from the bow-loading converted *Coruisk,* but with a ramp slower in operation, to conform with Class II A requirements of a watertight seal. They are bridge-controlled; powered by twin Bergius Kelvin engines of type RS6, fresh-water cooled; with an electric start or hand start and with a Diesel-driven battery-charging unit, indepen-dent of the main engines. The one lifeboat is motor driven, to comply with II A regulations. They can carry 50 passengers and four cars (or fewer commercial vehicles) and with deck turntables these can be turned, though at many places they are normally reversed on or off.

T.S.M.V. *Kilbrannan.* The first of the type was launched without ceremony in May, 1972 for David MacBrayne, Ltd., intended for the new route between Lochranza and Claonaig, near Skipness, across the Kilbrannan Sound, taking the place of the Fairlie–Brodick–Tarbert relic of the Royal Route, inaugurated by the *Cowal.* She carried Caledonian colours initially. She opened the new route on 8th July, 1972. The route, operated in summer only, became popular, and a slightly larger ship of similar type was employed on it from 1973, after which the *Kilbrannan* was on various routes, including relieving (on charter to Western Ferries, Ltd.) between Port Askaig and Feolin (Jura) and relieving at Largs. Since 1977 she has been normally on the Scalpay station.

T.S.M.V. *Morvern.* Launched on 18th December, 1972, the sister-ship to the foregoing, destined for the Fishnish–Lochaline route (opened on 30th April, 1973 by Mrs. Spencer's *Island Queen* on charter) began on the Largs–Cumbrae Slip service, in full MacBrayne colours and flying their house-flag. Her upper deck was extended to accommodate the lifeboat. She was for a time engaged in tender duties at Ardyne and at Tarbert Loch Fyne during oil-rig construction, and later was on Oban–Lismore, Fishnish–Lochaline, etc., and now regularly on the Fionnphort–Iona run, where vehicles are limited to those of Iona residents or engaged in delivering goods to the island. When on purely passenger service, she has seats on the car-deck, these being removed when space is required for a vehicle. She was on the Colintraive–Rhubodach run in the spring of 1983.

*   *   *   *   *   *

From 1st January, 1973, The Caledonian Steam Packet Co., Ltd. was re-named as above, and was to be responsible for all major vehicle ferry operations of the Scottish Transport Group without direct Government subsidy; and the two fleets began to operate more or less as one, but with the crews remaining members of their existing different trade unions. The MacBrayne ships were transferred to this company, except eight, which remained the property of David MacBrayne, Ltd., viz. *Loch Seaforth, Lochnell, Lochdunvegan, Loch Carron, Claymore, Loch Toscaig, Scalpay,* and *Loch Arkaig.* These were to continue operating cargo, passenger and mail and minor ferry services. None of these qualified as a Clyde steamer, and all have now left the fleet. The Caledonian MacBrayne vessels' funnels became a darker red, with yellow disc bearing the red lion emblem, while the house-flag was the MacBrayne double saltire, with yellow disc bearing the red lion superimposed. This, unfortunately, had to be abandoned in 1980 on account of heraldic infringement, and the flag now reflects the funnel colours in the form of a pennant.

Arran Piers, Ltd., a Caledonian subsidiary since August, 1969, was re-named Caledonian MacBrayne Holdings, Ltd., to hold heritable property and other fixed assets: and to it many members of the combined fleet were transferred, though continuing to be operated by the parent company. Bute Ferry Co., Ltd. was renamed MacBrayne Haulage, Ltd., taking over the road haulage section of the MacBrayne organisation, whose bus services passed to other members the S.T.G. MacBrayne Haulage Ltd. was privatised in 1985 as Kildonan MacBrayne Ltd.

M.V. *Tiger*.   An addition was made in 1973 to the fleet of "red" boats at Iona, on the purchase of this one from Mr. Ritchie of Gourock.

T.S.M.V. *Bruernish*.   When *Kilbrannan* and *Morvern* were nearing completion six more similar craft were ordered from the same builders, slightly longer to carry two additional cars of average size. Names originally proposed for the six were *Bernera, Eriskay, Vatersay, Soay, Raasay,* and *Staffa,* but most of these appear to have been unavailable. Known as the "Small Island" Class, these ships have become most useful members of the fleet on the shorter ferry crossings. This vessel along with *Rhum* and *Coll* were completed in 1973. *Bruernish,* which takes her name, not from an island, but from a peninsula in Barra, is the most widely travelled, including Lismore, Fishnish, Mingary and Gigha among her calls, while all three have relieved at Kyleakin and have served Cumbrae slip from Largs.

T.S.M.V. *Rhum.* From her entry to service in April, 1974 this vessel was the regular incumbent of the Claonaig–Lochranza station (in summer only), and has operated also from Largs, both to Cumbrae and, with calor-gas, to Brodick. In October, 1980 she made two trips between Inchmarnock and Kilmichael, Bute, with sheep and tractors during a farm removal, and in November the same year relieved the *Sound of Gigha* on the Port Askaig–Feolin route; she has also relieved at Scalpay and at Raasay. On charter to the C.R.S.C. on 15th May, 1982, she became the first passenger vessel to call at Carradale since 1939. In winter 1982-3 she was on duty at Colintraive–Rhubodach. From March, 1975 till early in 1981 the *Rhum* was distinguishable from her sisters by having her funnel red to the base.

T.S.M.V. *Coll* (II). In September, 1973 the *Coll* was fitted out for the Small Isles run during the overhaul of *Loch Arkaig,* being fitted with Radar and full VHF between the mast and a post on the wheelhouse; a fire-pump was installed and a ferry-door cut on the port side of the car deck. With a mobile crane on board she proceeded through the Crinan Canal and performed Oban–Craignure for one day, with passengers only, taking up the Small Isles run from 19th November. The Portree–Raasay section was performed by *Rhum.* During a spell on Fishnish–Lochaline she released *Bruernish* for Tobermory–Mingary; and she has also done Western Ferries' Port Askaig–Feolin run on charter. During her time on the Small Isles route in April, 1979 she operated from Kyle to Canna only, while *Etive Shearwater* took the calls at Eigg, Rhum and Muck. *Coll* happened to be relieving on the Kennacraig–Gigha service when the new jetty at Tayinloan came into use, and so became the first vehicle ferry to operate on that route, from 11th November, 1980. She has also served Cumbrae.

D.S.M.V. *Jupiter* (III). Two much larger vehicle ferry vessels (in contemplation in various forms for quite a number of years) were orderd from Messrs. Lamont, intended for Gourock–Dunoon and Wemyss Bay–Rothesay, the first being launched in November, 1973 and completed in time to take up her intended run in the following spring. The designs followed that of *Arran* (as altered) in having a flush vehicle deck aft, with not only a stern-loading ramp for use at Gourock, but also side loading ramps for use at Dunoon; and there are main, saloon and upper decks forward with (in the case of *Jupiter* initially) a wheelhouse and bridge on the upper deck, afterwards altered (as in *Juno* from the outset) to have a flying-bridge above. The machinery consists of two Mirrlees-Blackstone 8-cylinder diesels driving fore and aft directional propellers, the exhausts being by two short thwart-ship funnels at the sides of the vehicle deck, and having tetrapod mainmasts joined to the funnels. A small foremast above the bridge supports the radar scanner. On the main deck level forward are a lounge, ticket-office and toilets, while on the deck above is another lounge with self-service cafeteria. The ships have great manoeuvrabililty and can spin round in their own length. When the *Juno* was completed in November, 1974 she was immediately required on the Dunoon run to give a frequent service along with *Jupiter;* and, since the departure of *Maid of Cumbrae,* the two have been the regular ships there, alternating with *Saturn* and in recent years giving Gourock–Dunoon–Wemyss Bay–Rothesay services, reliefs during overhauls having been provided by *Arran, Glen Sannox, Pioneer,* etc. In addition, one of the ships on the Dunoon route serves Kilcreggan, morning and evening. The *Jupiter* was in 1983 given necessary equipment to obtain a passenger certificate for the route from Ardrossan or Wemyss Bay to Brodick, on which route she has on occasion provided extra capacity for passengers and vehicles.

T.S.M.V. *Pioneer* (III).   For the Islay service this ship was built at Leith, reviving the name of one of the Greenock Railway Steam Packet Company's ships of 1844 (afterwards a well-known member of the Hutcheson/MacBrayne fleet) and also used for a previous Islay steamer, built in 1905. The new vessel followed the layout of the *Jupiter* and *Juno,* but with higher bulwarks for the more exposed routes. The influence of the design of oil-rig supply ships is noticeable. There are two passenger lounges, that on the upper deck having cafeteria service, and that on the main having a bar. The open vehicle deck can take 30 cars, or six 40 ft. CRVs, and 9/10 cars. The main machinery is bridge-controlled. Navigational aids include wireless telegraphy, radio telephone, V.H.F., Radar, Echo sounder and public address system. The ship has twin controllable pitch propellers (by J. W. Berg, Sweden), twin rudders, retractable fin stabilisers (Denny Brown) and a bow thruster unit (British Pleuger), the stern ramp (by Cargospeed) being hydraulically controlled; and a hydraulic crane capable of lifting

3½ tons was provided at each side, for handling cargo at conventional piers, but is now not carried. The absence of vibration is noticeable, despite her speed of 15·8 knots.

West Loch Tarbert, which had been the mainland terminal for the Islay via Loch Fyne service since 1826, ceased to be used from 25th June, 1978, on the transfer to Kennacraig. In addition to her normal routes, the *Pioneer* has relieved on the Gourock–Dunoon–Kilcreggan, Wemyss Bay–Rothesay, Ardrossan–Brodick and Oban–Craignure stations; and, when superseded as regular Islay ship, in 1979 she had a lift installed (with ferry door cut in it) to operate the Mallaig–Armadale summer service and to relieve on the Small Isles run. In November, 1980 she introduced a new service from Largs to Brodick on Friday evenings, continuing this up to Christmas each year till the advent of the *Isle of Arran*. From 1989 she has succeeded *Glen Sannox* as spare and relief vessel, her lift having been removed but the side ramps retained. She performed a special sailing to Tarbert Loch Fyne on 28th August, 1989 to commemorate the termination, twenty years before, of the Loch Fyne mail service, the link between the Clyde and West Highland routes. It was particularly fitting that this was performed by a ship with a name associated with the MacBrayne fleet and its predecessors from as far back as 1844.

T.S.M.V. *Suilven*. To improve the Stornoway–Ullapool service, a ship under construction by Moss Rosenberg Vaerft A/S, Norway was purchased and launched by Mrs. C. B. Leith under the above name (new in the fleet) taken from the very prominent mountain near Lochinver. She arrived at Gourock in August, 1974, and has not deviated from her normal route. She was the first of the fleet to have Caledonian MacBrayne on the side, this being done during her overhaul at Govan in November, 1983.

D.S.M.V. *Juno* (III). Both the Dunoon vessels have been chartered at various times and have sailed to such destinations as Tighnabruaich, Tarbert, Millport, Largs, and have cruised up Loch Long and on the Gareloch. For all these the display on the hull of "GOUROCK-DUNOON FERRY" was incongruous, and was removed from *Jupiter* in 1983, but kept by *Juno* till changed to "Caledonian MacBrayne" in 1985. Since the advent of *Saturn* a certain amount of interchanging has taken place among these three ships.

T.S.M.V. *Eigg* (II). The remaining three Burnett-Corless "Small Island" class vessels were completed at intervals between 1975 and and 1976. This, the sixth of the series, inaugurated a temporary twice-daily service between Portree and Raasay on 18th March, 1975. She has been fairly constantly on the Oban–Lismore route, apart from exceptional runs such as conveying sheep from Eigg to Glenuig, and operating between Largs and Cumbrae; also calling at Ailsa Craig for granite and at Girvan.

M.V. *Kildonan* (II).   Purchased in March, 1975 from Mr. Murdo McSween of Fort William, the *Silver Darling* ex *Falcon,* originally a demonstration launch of The Bergius Company, was re-named as above, for tender duties at Eigg. In September, 1979 she was transferred to Loch Aline for ferrying crew to the spare vessel moored in Miodar Bay, performing also passenger runs on the Lochaline–Fishnish station in May/June, 1981 during the absence of *Canna.* After a period of idleness she was sold in 1985 to Mr. James Cowie and taken to Ardmaleish on 19th April, minus her engine.

M.V. *Staffa* (VII).   About two months after the last acquisition the motor launch *Silver Spray* was bought from Wm. H. Dick Ltd., Largs for the Fionnphort–Iona ferry and for tendering at Iona, later at Eigg; and finally at Tobermory for tendering, and for the Mingary service from 11th May, 1981. For this she had a wheelhouse with small landing platform erected above the engine casing. She was succeeded in this by the *Applecross* later the same month, and thereafter did little sailing.

T.S.M.V. *Canna*.   The seventh "Small Island" class ship performed the last scheduled sailing to Portree from Raasay on 15th April, 1976, and inaugurated the new slip at Sconser the next day. She also visisted Fladda off the north east coast of Raasay, landing on the shingle beach. In March, 1983 she relieved at Largs and on 25th November, 1984 she took a digger to Eilean Shona in Loch Moidart. She however, become associated particularly with the Fishnish–Lochaline station until superseded by the *Isle of Cumbrae* and later by a "Loch" class ferry in 1986. She has twice been used experimentally in the Orkneys, and in 1988 has been based at Bunessan for supplementary duties at Iona.

T.S.M.V. Raasay.   The last of the series began her public service by taking over from the *Kilbrannan* at Largs (the latter being absent at Tarbert in connexion with oil rig matters). She ultimately took up her own service for which she was named, on Friday, 9th July, 1976, giving in addition evening cruises round the island, and to the Great Harbour at Rona. She relieved at Claonaig in May, 1978.

D.S.M.V. *Isle of Cumbrae* (II). Following the design of the two large Kyle of Lochalsh ferries, but about two-thirds of their size, this drive-through ship was built at Troon for the Cumbrae Slip service from Largs. With directional propellers fore and aft she is as manoeuvrable as *Jupiter* and *Juno,* but with a speed of only 8·7 knots, which suffices for the short crossing. Her name was chosen by competition among the schoolchildren of Millport and, in addition to being appropriate, is an interesting revival of an old Buchanan name, borne by their paddle steamer which began life as the first *Jeanie Deans* of the North British S.P. Co., and for several years in the First War operated under charter to the G. & S.W.R. as *Isle of Cumbrae,* even performing short charters to the Caledonian and North British Companies, so that the name has associations with several of the constituents of Caledonian MacBrayne. She was the first to have a Cal-Mac funnel emblem on the wheelhouse. In August, 1986 she was transferred to Fishnish–Lochaline, where her greater vehicle capacity proves useful. She reverts to Cumbrae in winter except when relieving at Kyle.

D.S.M.V. *Saturn.* The Wemyss Bay–Rothesay route did not get its new regular ship till 1978, the service being maintained principally by the *Glen Sannox* after the introduction of stern-loading at Wemyss Bay and side-loading by link-span at Rothesay. The new vessel was a product of the Ailsa yard at Troon, somewhat similar to *Jupiter* and *Juno*, but with a tripod mainmast at the rear of the upper deck, which gives her a better-balanced profile, and with the upper deck carried forward of the bridge, giving passengers a view forward. She has seldom deviated from her accustomed route, except for interchanging with her sisters on that from Gourock to Dunoon and Kilcreggan and having performed a *Columba* centenary charter in 1978 to Ardrishaig for the Clyde River Steamer Club. The choice of a G.S.W.R.-type name not previously used is noteworthy.

T.S.M.V. *Claymore* (III). Named by Lady Kirkhill, wife of the Minister of State at the Scottish Office, when launched at Leith on 31st August, 1978, this ship is a development in design from that of the same builders' *Pioneer,* but with four decks above the car deck, the top one being the navigating bridge deck, containing bridge, *Claymore* took over the Oban–Castlebay–Lochboisdale run from the *Iona* early in 1979, leaving the latter free for the Islay service. She has not deviated much from that route, apart from cattle, etc. runs to Islay and an exceptional charter from Govan to Rothesay on 7th June, 1986, which justifies her being treated as a Clyde steamer.

T.S.M.V. *Lochmor* (II).   Launched at Troon on 11th June, 1979, this ship was named by Mrs. G. S. Sinclair, wife of the General Manager of Caledonian MacBrayne Ltd., reviving the name of one of the 1930 sisters, which had been the first vessel specifically allocated to the Small Isles run when it became separated from that to the Outer Isles.

T.S.M.V. *Isle of Arran* (III).   For some time there had been an intention of building a ship to take the place of the *Clansman* and *Caledonia* on the Arran run in summer and winter respectively; and in July, 1982 it was announced that the Scottish Office had approved the construction of a new vehicle-carrying ship for that route. The following month it was stated that, subject to adjustment of details of the contract, the vessel would be built at the Port Glasgow yard of Ferguson Ailsa Ltd. Of drive-through design with short open section at the stern for out-of-gauge loads and livestock floats, the ship was launched by Miss Joanna Younger, daughter of the Secretary of State for Scotland on 2nd December, 1983. In grey undercoat paint, but with the funnels in full Caledonian MacBrayne colours, the ship looked almost like a Glasgow & South Western Railway steamer. The hull had, however, become the normal black by the time she went on trials on the Skelmorlie Mile on the following 4th April. After berthing trials next day the returned to her builders, then made inaugural sailings to Brodick on 12th and to Rothesay Bay on 13th April, entering regular service in time for Easter in place of the *Clansman,* which was out of action.

The first of a new design, the *Isle of Arran* is a drive-through vehicle-carrier of 3,296 gross tons, when new the largest in the fleet. She has accommodation for 80 cars or 10 articulated lorries, and for 800 passengers, with a crew of 16. Her passenger accommodation is good, comprising observation lounge and bar lounge, cafeteria and non-smoking lounge, and with an invalid lift from the car deck to the upper decks. Loading is by bow and stern ramps, and she is fitted with bow-thrust, twin rudders, and has computerised control and monitoring system in the engine-room, and the usual modern navigational aids, including Gyro Compass, Auto Pilot, Echo Sounder, etc. A "Marine" escape system was subsequently fitted.

In her first winter the *Isle of Arran* relieved the *Suilven* on the Stornoway run, repeating this also in her third winter. In 1985 she was given white topsides in the manner of the saloons of ships like *King George V,* etc., which improved her appearance. She seems to have given general satisfaction, although even with her more powerful bow thrust she still sometimes has to be diverted to Gourock, during adverse weather, as were the *Clansman* and *Caledonia.*

T.S.M.V. *Hebridean Isles.* After the launch of the *Isle of Arran* in December, 1983 it was announced that the Government had authorised the Scottish Transport Group to invite tenders for the building of a new drive-through vessel to take the place of the *Hebrides* on the Uig–Lochmaddy–Tarbert triangle, to carry about 500 passengers and 80 cars; and on 20th March following, it was announced that the contract had been awarded to Cochrane Shipbuilders Limited, Selby, where the launch took place— sideways into the River Ouse, with an enormous splash—on 4th July, 1985, the naming ceremony being performed by H.R.H. The Duchess of Kent, the first "Royal" launch for this fleet, famous as operators on the "Royal Route". The hull of this is similar in design to that of the *Isle of Arran,* but the internal layout differs, particularly in having a lift in addition to bow- and stern-loading, and short open vehicle deck at the stern; and the funnels are placed farther aft. Her name it will be observed means the same as that of her predecessor. So far she has not appeared on any of the Clyde routes.

D.S.M.V. *Loch Striven.* At the launch of the *Hebridean Isles* it was announced that the Company was considering the building of two 12-car ferries for the Largs–Cumbrae station, and shortly afterwards it was confirmed that the order for these had gone to R. Dunston (Hessle) Ltd., followed by an order for other two similar ferries from the same builders, the design being developed from that of the *Isle of Cumbrae,* but with covered passenger accommodation on both sides and only two vehicle lanes, to accommodate twelve cars or one articulated lorry. The passenger lounges at the sides provide covered cushioned seating accommodation, and there is open deck space above. Loading is by hinged articulated ramps at each end, operated hydraulically from the wheelhouse, or manually in emergency. Ramps of Kvaerner manufacture are fitted on *Loch Striven* and *Loch Linnhe.* On the starboard side above the promenade deck is a small wheelhouse (painted as a funnel), surmounted by a lattice mast of tubular steel inclined inwards to the centre-line. Equipment includes a deckhead-mounted Racal Decca radar, a Cooke shelf-type compass, a Sailor VHF radio telephone, and electric whistle control and a Minerva alarm panel for fire detection and extinguishing systems; also remote controls for the main engines' speeds and handwheels on a console to control the Voith-Schneider cycloidal propulsion units, which assure precise navigation with positive thrust in any direction. Power is provided by two diagonally-aligned Volvo Penta high-speed Diesels, normally running at a constant speed, each driving one propulsion unit through a Fluidrive coupling to a Norgear gearbox. Speed is about 9·25 knots.

The European Economic Community being involved in the funding of the new ships, it was appropriate that the launching ceremony of the first should be performed by Mrs. Beverley Mathijsen, wife of the Director General. This she did at Hessle on 8th May, 1986, naming the vessel as above. The revival of "Loch" names is noteworthy, these having been almost standard in the MacBrayne fleet between 1929 and 1955, some of them dating back to 1876-7.

The *Loch Striven* sailed up the east coast from Hull to Inverness, then through the Caledonian Canal, at Fort Augustus, passing the remains of the *Gairlochy*. After traversing the Canal and negotiating Neptune's Staircase at Banavie, she duly arrived on the Clyde and after a short spell in James Watt Dock took up her service between Largs and the Cumbrae Slip. She carried out trials at Rhubodach and Colintraive, and went in winter to Kyleakin as stand-by ferry.

D.S.M.V. *Loch Linnhe*. The second of the "Loch" class vessels was launched at Hessle on 22nd May, 1986, and was taken immediately to Hull for fitting out. She obtained a Class VIA certificate for 50 passengers and three crew, for Lochaline-Fishnish, Lochranza-Claonaig, Oban-Lismore and Sconser-Rassay. She made her debut on the Fishnish-Lochaline route, and changed places with the *Isle of Cumbrae* in the week-end of 2nd/4th August 1986. She inaugurated the drive-through service at Rhubodach with invited guests on 27th October, 1986 in place of the *Loch Riddon* which had been delayed by weather on her delivery voyage. She reverted to Lochaline in winter.

D.S.M.V. *Loch Riddon*. The third of these ferries is employed principally on the Colintraive-Rhubodach run, in succession to *Portree* and *Broadford*. This (and the fourth) differ from the first and second in having McGregor-Navire type ramps, with (like the others) remote or local control. She took up the Fishnish-Lochaline run relieving *Isle of Cumbrae* on 28th October, 1986 and entered service at Rhubodach-Colintraive in early November.

D.S.M.V. *Loch Ranza*. Drive-through facilities were introduced in 1987 on the Claonaig-Lochranza summer service by this appropriately-named vessel, the fourth of the "Loch" class. She has relieved on the Largs-Cumbrae route on occasion.

T.S.M.V. *Isle of Mull.* The second royal launch in the history of the fleet took place at Port Glasgow on 8th December 1988, when H.R.H. Princess Alexandra named this ship, for the Craignure and Colonsay runs from Oban. The *Isle of Mull* entered service in the following year, but so far has not operated on any of the Clyde routes. At 4,719 tons gross since her lengthening she is the largest Caledonian-MacBrayne vessel to date.

* * * * * *

After indications of impending privatisation it was announced by Mr. Malcolm Rifkind, when launching the Transport (Scotland) Bill in the House of Commons on 30th November, 1988, that the plans would provide the basis for maintaining and improving services to the Scottish public. After detailing the proposed division of the Scottish Bus Group, he stated that Caledonian MacBrayne Limited would remain under public ownership for the foreseeable future, but controlled by a new board, which he would ask to explore the possibility of transferring to the private sector the Gourock–Dunoon and Wemyss Bay–Rothesay routes, and to examine existing practices to find more efficient and cost-effective ways of continuing the present standard of service, no options in the longer term being excluded, subject to the over-riding proviso that the present quality of service to the islands be maintained.

T.S.M.V. *Lord of the Isles* (III). A further ship on the lines of *Hebridean Isles* (but with a bridge like that of *Isle of Mull*) was ordered from the Port Glasgow yard, whose owners had become Ferguson Shipbuilders Limited by the time of the launch on 7th March, 1989. Mrs. Edith Rifkind, wife of the Secretary of State for Scotland, gave the ship a name most appropriate not only for her intended services from Oban to Coll and Tiree and to Barra and South Uist, with their historical association with the title assumed by the chiefs of Clan Donald from about 1354, but also for the revival of the name in the fleet and the continuance of the "Isles" theme. The *Glasgow Herald*, reporting the launch, stated that the ship was named after a famous Clyde paddle steamer that had been broken up in 1928 only a few hundred yards from the Ferguson yard (See Chapter IV).

The *Lord of the Isles* entered service on her intended route in May, 1989.

CHAPTER XI

CLYDE & CAMPBELTOWN SHIPPING CO. LTD.
CLYDE CARGO STEAMERS, LIMITED

IN August, 1915, at the request of the Admiralty, Clyde Cargo Steamers Ltd. was formed, in order to provide a minimum service to the outlying Clyde ports, the interests represented being those of Hill & Co., David MacBrayne Ltd., John Williamson & Co., and the Minard Castle Shipping Co. Ltd. Mr. J. D. Rodger, of Messrs. Hill & Co., became the Managing Director of the new company. The cargo services formerly carried on by Messrs. Hill, and the Lochfyne services of Messrs. MacBrayne and the Minard Castle Shipping Co. Ltd., were thereafter maintained by Clyde Cargo Steamers Ltd.

On the formation of the new company each of its three steamers had the funnel painted to represent the colours of the constituent companies; thus the funnel of *Bute 4* was red with black top, representing both Messrs. Hill & Company and Messrs. MacBrayne; that of *Arran* was white with black top, representing the Williamson interest, while *Minard Castle* retained her black funnel. Black shortly afterwards became the standard colour for all the vessels of Clyde Cargo Steamers Ltd.

At midnight on 3rd/4th March, 1937, Clyde Cargo Steamers, Ltd. took over the two ships of the Campbeltown & Glasgow Steam Packet Joint Stock Co. Ltd.; and on 9th March in that year the name was changed to Clyde & Campbeltown Shipping Co. Ltd. (the majority of shares being held by MacBrayne Trust Ltd.), remaining thus till taken over by the British Transport Commission under the management of the Railway Executive in 1949. After the disposal of *Kildonan* the company was without ships, but remained in being; on 31st December, 1959 its name was changed to Caledonian Steam Packet Co. (Irish Services) Ltd., which took over the management and for a time the ownership of the Stranraer–Larne ships, being later named British Transport Ship Management (Scotland) Limited (*see* Chapter XII).

HILL & COMPANY

S.S. *Success* (II).   So far as can be discovered, this was Messrs. Hill's first steamer, succeeding a sailing-vessel of the same name. She was advertised along with the better-known *Bute* in 1881. She was sold to Wm. W. C. Smith, Glasgow, and in 1883 to Thos. R. Lee, Sunderland.

S.S. *Bute* (I).   The first *Bute* in the Hill fleet was built by Messrs. Scott & Macgill, of Bowling, in 1879, and was an iron single screw steamer, fitted with compound reciprocating machinery. After a period of about 12 years with the company, she was wrecked in 1891 while on an exceptional run from Islay to Liverpool.

P.S. *Cumbrae*.   When Fairlie Pier was opened by the Glasgow & South Western Railway Company in 1882, Messrs. Hill & Company arranged to run a passenger steamer to Millport in connexion with the trains. For this purpose they provided the steamer *Cumbrae,* which they had been operating between Glasgow and Millport for a time. Originally named *Victory* (*see* Chapter I) and later *Marquis of Lorne*, she remained on the Fairlie–Millport run until the Railway Company placed their own steamers on the station in 1892. After lying for a few years unemployed, she was sent to Newry for use as a coal-hulk in the canal there, but is not now in existence.

P.S. *Arran* (I).   To operate the sailings from Fairlie Pier, the former "Sunday breaker", *Dunoon Castle*, was purchased in 1883 and renamed *Arran*. Like *Cumbrae*, this steamer had had many owners on the Clyde, and she did not remain long with Messrs. Hill. Flush-decked and steeple-engined, *Arran* had one funnel aft of the paddle-boxes. She was sold to Messrs. Gillies & Campbell for service from Wemyss Bay, and subsequently to different owners on the Mersey, Thames and Shannon.

S.S. *Bute No. 2.*   This steamer was intended to carry both passengers and cargo and was launched in April, 1890; but with the improved passenger services, instituted by the Railway Companies about 1891, this proved unremunerative, and *Bute No. 2* was sold. It should be noted that the word "No." with the numeral formed part of her name, the reason being that the first *Bute* was still in existence when the steamer under review was built. She was sold to Carenero Railway & Navigation Co. Ltd., La Guayra, Venezuela, and renamed *Higuerote,* being subsequently sold to V. Crassus, La Guayra, and renamed *Ossun*.

S.S. *Bute* (III).   To take the place of the previous *Bute*, a new steamer bearing the name (but without any numeral) was built by Messrs. J. Fullerton & Company, of Paisley, and launched on 31st

January, 1892. She remained with Messrs. Hill & Company for about nine years and was then sold to Glasgow Steam Coasters, Ltd., and re-named *Dunard*, being subsequently sold to various other owners.

S.S. *Bute 4*.   Like her predecessor, the fourth *Bute* was built by Messrs. J. Fullerton & Company, Paisley, from whose yard her launch took place on 21st January, 1898. She was the only vessel of which we had heard in whose name an Arabic numeral was used until the naming of the Cunard liner *Queen Elizabeth 2*. (The third *Bute*, it should be noted, was still in the fleet when *Bute 4* was built).

Bute 4 was employed on the various Clyde cargo routes by Messrs. Hill & Company and latterly by Clyde Cargo Steamers, Ltd., being ultimately broken up at Ardrossan in 1935.

S.S. *Arran* (II).   A steamer was added to the Hill fleet in November, 1912, and was given the name *Arran*. This had at one time been a yacht named *Barmore*, but had been converted into a cargo vessel by an Orkney owner who purchased her in 1911. Her disposal occurred in August, 1917 on her sale to John Boyle, Fish Merchant, Glasgow.

LOCHFYNE & GLASGOW STEAM PACKET CO., LTD.

S.S. *Jura*.   This small coaster, dating from 1869, was owned by the Jura Steamboat Company, apparently predecessors of the above. She sometimes was chartered to Messrs. MacBrayne.

S.S. *Minard Castle*.   This steamer was built in 1882 for the Lochfyne & Glasgow Steam Packet Co. Ltd., for service between Glasgow and the Loch Fyne ports in opposition to Messrs. MacBrayne. Some of the merchants and farmers of Lochfyneside were interested in the Company, and refused to accept goods sent by any vessel other than *Minard Castle*. She was a very graceful little steamer with a black funnel and two tall masts, and was long known at all piers between Glasgow and Inveraray, carrying a few passengers in addition to cargo and livestock.

In February, 1913 she was taken over by Mr. R. G. Campbell, and shortly afterwards was registered as belonging to the Minard Castle Shipping Co. Ltd., which, as above mentioned, came under the control of Clyde Cargo Steamers, Ltd., in 1915, though it maintained its separate identity till 1922. She was thereafter registered in the name of Clyde Cargo Steamers, Ltd. She lasted till sent to Port Glasgow on 17th November, 1926 for scrapping.

P.S. *Sultana.* In July, 1899 the Company purchased from Captain John Williamson the paddle steamer *Sultana,* and ran her to Ardrishaig with passengers and goods, via Dunoon, Fairlie and Millport, for Skipness, Tarbert and the terminus. On Wednesdays and Fridays she started from Kingston Dock at 6-30 a.m., returning from Ardrishaig at 2-30 and proceeding to Glasgow on Tuesdays and Thursdays. It is understood that she at this time had a yellow funnel with dark blue top. After less than a year she was sold on 27th March, 1900 to M. Clavel, Cherbourg, and was broken up about 1907.

CLYDE CARGO STEAMERS, LTD. (Contd.)

S.S. *Lapwing/Cowal* (I). *Lapwing* was built for Messrs. MacBrayne in 1903; and, after service on various Hebridean routes, ran aground at Oban in 1916. Being taken over by the underwriters, she was sold by them to Clyde Cargo Steamers, Ltd., and was reconditioned and converted into a pure cargo carrier, one mast being removed and independent cranes fitted fore and aft, instead of her original derrick on the forward mast. She had only run for Clyde Cargo Steamers, Ltd., for a few weeks when she was requisitioned by the Government and placed on the mail run from Penzance to Scilly Isles. After a spell there, she was for nine months sailing from Plymouth to the Channel Islands; and in 1920 she returned to cargo work on the Clyde. About 1926 her name was changed to *Cowal,* and as such she remained in the fleet of Clyde Cargo Steamers, Ltd., till broken up at Troon in 1932.

S.S. *Jane.* This vessel had previously been a trawler, and was built by the Ardrossan Dockyard Company in 1901. She was purchased by Clyde Cargo Steamers, Ltd., with a view to developing an express service to Rothesay, but remained with them for two years only, being superseded by the third *Arran,* and sold to an Alloa owner in May, 1926.

S.S. *Lintie. Lintie* belonged originally to Messrs. Steel & Bennie, Ltd., the well-known tug owners who previously also operated cargo steamers between Glasgow and Greenock. Her machinery was aft, and she had a very short funnel which enabled her to berth above Glasgow bridge. She was taken over along with this trade and in the year following her acquisition was sold to J. Shiels, Jr., Belfast, later to a Dundee owner.

S.S. *Arran* (III). Two new steamers were built for the

Company in 1926. Of these, *Arran*, third of the name was launched on 26th January that year, and attained a speed of 11 knots on trial. She succeeded *Jane* and gave additional services to the ports on the lower reaches of the Firth. She was similar to *Bute 4*, with machinery aft; and, though usually on the Arran and Skipness service, was occasionally on the Loch Fyne run. It was while thus engaged in January, 1933, that she was wrecked on Barmore Island, Loch Fyne, near the point where the MacBrayne steamer *Chevalier* had stranded six years earlier.

S.S. *Minard*. This ship came from the yard of Scott & Sons, Bowling, really as a successor to *Minard Castle*—though the latter was not scrapped immediately. She was a useful little steamer, and might be seen at various parts of the Firth, though mostly usually on the Loch Fyne run. Her machinery was amidships, and she had one mast and two independent cranes for handling cargo. The Glasgow–Rothesay direct cargo service ceased on 1st October, 1954 on the introduction of a car ferry route via Wemyss Bay, and *Minard* was scrapped at Port Glasgow.

S.S. *Ardyne*. This additional steamer was built in 1928 to provide further cargo services to the Clyde coast ports, and was like *Minard*, though slightly shorter. A useful addition to the fleet, she was employed on the various cargo services as required; and during the period after the Second War, she was often on the Campbeltown cargo run, till discontinued after 31st October, 1949, when road transport was substituted for Campbeltown, Dunoon and Hunter's Quay, all Arran traffic being thenceforth handled *via* Brodick. *Ardyne* became spare, and relieved the other two steamers from time to time, till sold to Mr. J. Lee, Belfast, but soon afterwards was broken up at Troon in the Autumn of 1955.

S.S. *Arran* (IV)/*Kildonan* (I). To take the place of the previous *Arran*, a new steamer was immediately ordered from the Ardrossan Dockyard Ltd., and, taking the same name, was delivered to the owners in the summer of 1933. She was an up-to-date cargo carrier with a crane as well as a derrick, and like her predecessor, had the machinery aft. She latterly was on the Ardrossan–Arran–Millport cargo services, taking the place of *Arran Mail*. She was renamed as above in 1952, to make way for the new car ferry *Arran*, and was withdrawn on the appearance of the third *Glen Sannox*. Laid up in Albert Harbour in July, 1957, she was scrapped at Port Glasgow early in the following year.

CAMPBELTOWN & GLASGOW STEAM PACKET
JOINT STOCK CO. LIMITED

This Company had a very long history, having celebrated its centenary with the launch of *Dalriada* in 1926. Its vessels carried cargo, passengers and mails for about 111 years, and the company survived against all competition, of which it had its share; even against turbine opposition, which began with the appearance of *King Edward* in 1901.

The Company was formed in 1826 by some Campbeltown merchants and had it headquarters at Campbeltown. It was registered as unlimited in 1867, and as a limited company in 1883. A fuller account of its history will be found in the Centenary History of the Campbeltown & Glasgow Steam Packet Joint Stock Co. Ltd., published by the proprietors of the *Campbeltown Courier* in April 1927.

The Campbeltown steamers were well known on the Clyde, and distinguishable by their funnel-colouring of black-red-black. Their hulls were black, with a pink water-line.

P.S. *Duke of Lancaster*.   The Company's first steamer was *Duke of Lancaster*, which had been built at Liverpool in 1822, only ten years after the famous *Comet* had appeared on the Clyde. Two Campbeltown captains went to Liverpool to purchase a steamer suitable for the Campbeltown–Glasgow service, and their choice fell on *Duke of Lancaster*, a wooden paddle steamer of 91 tons net, which was purchased in 1826.

With the advent of a second steamer in 1835, *Duke of Lancaster* was given an extensive overhaul, and in 1836 instituted an extended service to Larne and Islay. From 1837 calls were made at Ayr, but in 1841 this and the Larne and Islay sailings were discontinued. She was sold on 30th May, 1845 and scrapped.

P.S. *St. Kiaran*.   This was the second steamer in the Campbeltown fleet, and the first actually built for the Company. She was a product of the Greenock yard of Messrs. R. Duncan & Company, and was constructed of wood. Her design was similar to that of *Duke of Lancaster*.

She was sold for service at Leith, and advertised from Leith to Copenhagen in 1850.

P.S. *Duke of Cornwall*.   The first iron steamer on the Campbeltown route was built by Messrs. Caird & Company in 1842. Apart from material she was practically the same as *St. Kiaran*, but seven feet longer. Though rather slow, this steamer did her work successfully until superseded by some of the later vessels. After being later laid up in Bowling Harbour, she was sold on 20th October, 1866, for breaking up.

P.S. Celt.   This was a fine iron steamer, and was long a favourite on the Campbeltown route. She had a clipper bow, one funnel (aft), two masts and large paddle-boxes, ornamented by a gilt figure of a hand holding a dirk. She was much admired when new, being a great advance on the previous steamers. She was sold in April, 1868 for use as a tug on the Hooghly at Calcutta.

P.S. Druid.   To take the place of *Duke of Cornwall* on the regular runs, a steamer similar to *Celt* was built. This was *Druid*, and she was the first of the fleet to have a straight stem and no figure-head. She was for many years the consort of *Celt*, though never so great a favourite, on account of her liability to ship water in a storm.

Sold to Mr. Robertson, Shipbuilder, Greenock (presumably in part payment for *Kintyre*), she was converted by him into a three-masted schooner. She was last heard of on 5th October, 1880, when she left Irvine with coal for Lisbon, and is believed to have foundered in the Bay of Biscay.

P.S. Gael.   Encouraged by the success of an opposition company in the running of day trips to Campbeltown, the Campbeltown Company had *Gael* built for this purpose in 1867. Her maiden voyage was made on April, 1867, and a dinner was held on board to celebrate the advent of the new ship. She is said to have attained a speed of 16 knots on this run, and from the first became extremely popular. She was long commanded by Captain Kerr, the commodore of the Campbeltown steamers.

Originally flush-decked, *Gael* was fitted with a large deck-saloon aft in 1879, this together with the lower cabin (then converted into a dining-saloon) being furnished in a splendid manner. At the same time she was re-boilered, but unfortunately the alterations carried out were not so successful as had been anticipated, the speed and coal consumption being particularly unsatisfactory. Accordingly, after only a few seasons more she was sold to Great Western Railway Company, and registered at Milford, being subsequently sold to David MacBrayne in 1891. She spent one night at Campbeltown on her way to the shipbreakers in 1924. (*See* "R.O.S." and "W.H.S.").

S.S. Kintyre.   The first screw steamer for the Campbeltown fleet was *Kintyre*, built in 1868. This was one of the prettiest steamers ever seen on the Clyde, with a beautiful clipper bow and graceful lines, a single funnel and two masts, the whole giving the appearance of a yacht rather than of a passenger and cargo carrier. She was fitted with simple reciprocating machinery, which was compounded in 1882, a new boiler being fitted in 1883. Unfortunately *Kintyre* was run down and sunk off Skelmorlie on 18th September, 1907, by the steamer *Maori*, then running trials, and no new vessel was built to take her place.

A contemporary correspondent referring to the loss of *Kintyre* in the *Campbeltown Courier* wrote:—"Who on the route did not know her? She was inimitable. Her successors were but sorry imitations of her beauty. She was looked on from Greenock to the Broomielaw as a joy for ever, and by every man along the quays she was known to be a model steamship and the finest design of a screw steamer that ever sailed the Clyde. And her like will be no more! She sat squat, yet lightly, and snug in the water like no other creation. No feeling of top-heaviness ever entered into one's calculation of her poise. By the stern, whether light or loaded, there sat *Kintyre,* with apparently the same draught, ever graceful, ever secure. Forward her beautiful cut-water, curving out to the inimitable bowsprit, put her in a class alone, and all her lines were in beauteous symmetry".

S.S. *Kinloch*.   This was another beautiful yacht-like steamer, similar to *Kintyre* but larger, and with better passenger accommodation. She was designed by Mr. Robertson (Junior), the son of the builder of *Kintyre,* and was built by Messrs. A. &. J. Inglis. Her name was the shortened form of Kinloch Kilkerran (Cinn Loch Cill Ciaran) by which Campbeltown was formerly known.

Kinloch was the first Clyde steamer to have a wheel-house, this being below the level of the bridge. It was removed shortly after she went into service, however, being blamed for the occurrence of an accident to a rowing-boat with which *Kinloch* collided. Compound machinery was fitted from the start, and a new boiler was installed in 1890. Her speed was 13·6 knots, and she remained on the Campbeltown run till superseded by *Dalriada* in 1926, when she was sold to the Channel Islands Packet Co. Ltd., for service between the Channel Isles and France, being broken up at Bo'ness in 1928.

S.S. *Davaar*.   To take the place of *Gael* in day excursions to Campbeltown, *Davaar* was built by the London & Glasgow Shipbuilding Co. Ltd., at Govan, and launched on 17th May, 1885. This steamer was similar to the foregoing but larger, and was fitted with a narrow deck-saloon aft, having alleyways outside. She also was designed by Mr. Robertson (Junior)

Originally *Davaar* had two funnels, but in 1903 she was re-boilered and reappeared with only one funnel, this being of considerably greater diameter than those previously carried. At the same time a new saloon the full width of the vessel was fitted, and it is generally agreed her appearance was enhanced, this being one of the few instances of improvement being brought about by alterations in the original design of a ship.

On occasion *Davaar* used to make special trips to Belfast from Campbeltown, and on one such excursion she ran aground on the County Down coast and was nearly wrecked. Her passengers were taken off, however, and she was refloated little the worse for her adventure.

After the loss of *Kintyre, Kinloch* and *Davaar* carried on the service alone, one leaving Glasgow and the other leaving Campbeltown each morning. This continued until the appearance of *Dalriada*, which thereafter, along with *Davaar*, maintained the service and both passed to Clyde Cargo Steamers, Ltd., in March, 1937. On 22nd April the red portion of *Davaar*'s funnel became crimson, and on 7th May the funnel became crimson from deck level with black top. Later it was painted in MacBrayne red with black top, as on the other members of the Clyde & Campbeltown Company's fleet.

On 2nd October, 1939 *Davaar* left Campbeltown on what was stated to be her last run, and was laid up in East India Harbour, Greenock. In January, 1940, however, she returned to the service when *Dalriada* was damaged in a collision. She then had a black funnel and black saloon. The passenger service came to an end on 16th March, 1940, after which she was again laid up; then in July of that year she was requisitioned and sent to Newhaven, where she was kept with steam up, ready to be sunk as a blockship. Fortunately this was not necessary, but she did not sail again, being beached near Newhaven Harbour and scrapped in July, 1943.

S.S. *Dalriada* (I).   Built by Messrs. R. Duncan & Co. Ltd., Port Glasgow and launched on 16th March, 1926, *Dalriada* broke the tradition of clipper-bowed steamers; and while she had not the yacht-like appearance of some of her predecessors, she was rather a handsome ship, though her enormous funnel tended to spoil her appearance. She had a slanting stem and two masts, and was credited with being the fastest single-screw steamer in the world. She broke the record of all the previous steamers of the Company by doing the run from Gourock to Campbeltown in less than three hours on 30th April, 1926, and could attain about 17 knots. Her machinery was triple expansion with four cylinders, fitted by Messrs. D. Rowan & Co. Ltd.

In addition to regular sailings, *Dalriada* made extra runs on Saturday afternoons in summer, so that it was possible to have an afternoon excursion to Campbeltown or Carradale and back. In early summer before these trips began she was frequently chartered for private excursions to various places on the Firth of Clyde.

The name was selected for this steamer as the result of a competition held among the school children of Campbeltown and was really most appropriate, as Campbeltown is in the ancient kingdom of Dalriada, which comprised the whole of Kintyre peninsula and certain other parts of Argyll.

Dalriada became the property of Clyde Cargo Steamers, Ltd., in March, 1937, and in May of that year was given a plain red funnel with black top. From 2nd October, 1939 she maintained the Campbeltown service alone, her funnel being painted black about the middle of that month, and her saloon a few days later. Early in January, 1940 she was in collision with a destroyer, and went to Messrs. Lamont's for repair. She was laid up in East India Harbour, Greenock, till April, 1941, then went on service as a salvage vessel on the Thames, where she was sunk on 19th June, 1942, and in June, 1946 was blown up to clear the channel.

CLYDE & CAMPBELTOWN SHIPPING CO. LTD. (Contd.)

S.S. *Marie*. In July, 1939 the company purchased from Messrs. McKinney & Rafferty the small fish-carrying steamer *Marie*, which they had had on charter from time to time. She was employed principally on the cargo runs to ports on the upper Firth, and was withdrawn in 1949. She was sold to Norwegian owners and next year was registered at Mandal as *Svinør*. In 1951 she became a motor vessel and was re-named *Sølve*, registered at Haugesund under a different owner. Her name dropped from the registers in 1951-2.

M.V. *Empire Tulip*. This vessel was chartered from the Ministry of Transport during part of 1945 and 1946 for the cargo run to Campbeltown.

*   *   *   *   *   *

Though primarily intended for cargo work, some· of the steamers owned by Clyde Cargo Steamers, Ltd., had passenger certificates, and were in fact the only steamers by which it was possible to reach such ports as Skipness and Otterferry.

The funnel colouring of this company became red with black top from February, 1937 for the *Minard, Ardyne* and *Arran,* and from May of that year for *Davaar* and *Dalriada.* From 1950 the survivors carried the buff funnel with black top of the Railway Executive and C.S.P. Company.

After being without ships for a few years, the Company had its name changed to Caledonian Steam Packet Co. (Irish Services) Ltd. and was used to manage and later to own the steamers on the Stranraer–Larne station, as mentioned in the next chapter.

CHAPTER XII

BRITISH TRANSPORT SHIP MANAGEMENT (SCOTLAND) LIMITED
SEALINK (SCOTLAND) LIMITED
SEALINK BRITISH FERRIES (STRANRAER)

THE Portpatrick Railway was opened from Castle Douglas on 11th March, 1861 to Stranraer and to Portpatrick on 28th August, 1862, express trains being introduced from 1st October, 1862 to connect with the daily sailings then commenced by *Briton* of the Glasgow & Stranraer Steam Packet Company, of which the Agent was Mr. Alexander Langlands. The railway between Carrickfergus and Larne had been opened at this time, as also was the Stranraer Harbour Branch to the newly-constructed East Pier.

There had been hopes of creating an efficient service between Donaghadee and Portpatrick, but after much delay this was finally abandoned by the railway companies.

A cross-Channel service had been established in 1662 between Portpatrick and Donaghadee, maintained by a privately-owned but subsidised Company until 1790, when the Post Office took over. The steamers *Dasher* and *Arrow* were employed as mail and passenger carriers from 1837, followed about 1840 by the Admiralty steamers *Fury* and *Spitfire*. A few sailings between Stranraer and Belfast were given by the Glasgow & Stranraer S.P. Company's P.S. *Briton*, and in 1861 a private Company was formed with a view to running a service between Stranraer and Larne, to connect with the railway on the Scottish side and the recently opened Carrickfergus and Larne Railway. This company purchased the new steamer *Briton*, built in 1862, but sold her in the following year. The service reverted to the Glasgow & Stranraer S.P. Company. In 1864 the Caledonian Railway Company entered into an agreement to work the line and in 1866, backed by the L. & N.W.R., put the 12-knot paddle steamers *Fannie* and *Alice* on the Stranraer–Belfast route. Built in 1859 and 1857 respectively, these ships had seen service as blockade-runners in the American Civil War. By an agreement made at the end of January, 1867 the L. & N.W.R. Company undertook to bear one-third of the expense of working the Portpatrick Railway and steamers. On 21st January, 1868 the *Alice*, on her voyage from Belfast, suffered serious storm damage and was at Stranraer Pier for five months under repair. The

133

certificate of *Fannie* had been allowed to expire, and the service was terminated, to the annoyance of the Portpatrick Railway Company, which had borne its share of expenses.

After much consideraton the Treasury decided not to subsidise a mail route via Portpatrick and Donaghadee. The Portpatrick Railway Company proposed that the Belfast & County Down Railway Company should assist in providing a steamer service on this route, which was declined; but the Donaghadee & Portpatrick Steam Packet Company was formed in Belfast, commencing operations in July, 1868 with the paddle steamer *Dolphin*, which, had been the first *Islay* (built in 1849), salved after being almost a total loss in 1866. A double daily service was provided, but in September this was cut to one crossing in each direction, and on 31st October it was discontinued entirely. The ship seems to have passed to the Portpatrick Short-Sea Steam-Packet Company (Limited), and on 13th August, 1869 a notice appeared "to determine as to her sale". Another ship whose name is mentioned in connexion with the Portpatrick route about this time was *Dromore*; and she was followed in 1871 by the privately-owned *Aber*, which was sunk by collision on 29th August, 1871. One or two spasmodic excursions were made between Donaghadee and Portpatrick, e.g. by the Belfast steamer *Shamrock* in May, 1871, and in June, 1873 a further attempt on the route was made by the *Avalon*, presumably the Great Eastern Railway steamer of that name, which, however, was withdrawn from 12th July.

LARNE & STRANRAER STEAMBOAT COMPANY LIMITED

The Portpatrick Railway Company by 1870 realised that a service between Portpatrick and Donaghadee without Treasury aid was a hopeless proposition, and it was resolved to use part of the Government compensation received for its failure, to institute a Stranraer–Larne service, provided the Belfast & Northern Counties Railway Company and other Irish interests contributed similarly. No contractor could be found willing to provide a ship; and the estimated cost of a new steamer was £20,000. It was believed that half of this could be raised in Belfast, and the Portpatrick Railway Company decided to contribute the other half. So the above company came into being; and it held the mail contract from 1874. The Railway Company's £10,000 Stock in this Company passed on 1st August, 1885 to the owning Companies of the Portpatrick & Wigtownshire Joint Committee (viz L. & N.W.R., M.R., C.R. and G. & S.W.R.). In 1889 the Joint Committee decided to pay off all private owners of shares in the Steamboat Company, this becoming effective on 1st January, 1890. Further reorganisation of ownership took place in 1893, when there was formed the Larne & Stranraer Steamship Joint Committee, whereby the four owning railway companies retained four-fifths of the shares, the remaining one-fifth being owned by the Belfast & Northern Counties Railway Company, the latter passing to the Midland Railway Company in 1903. The steamers thus became the sole property of the L.M. & S. Railway Company in 1923.

The Steamboat Company's funnel colours were apparently red with black top till 1890, then buff till L.M.S. days since which time they have followed the standard colouring of these owners and British Railways until the advent of *Caledonian Princess* (*see* below). The house-flag was a scarlet pennant, having in the middle a white diamond in which was the Red Hand of Ulster.

P.S. *Princess Louise* .   The Larne & Stranraer Company's first ship was this two funnelled paddle steamer, constructed at Meadowside in 1872. She inaugurated the service on 1st July that year, and was well abreast of her time: the owners were proud that the time allowed for the passage was only 2¾ hours from port to port. Due, however, to lack of boiler capacity, she was not able to maintain this schedule, and it was not till 1878 that improvements in her speed were made. She was sold in 1890 to Mr. D. MacBrayne and as *Islay* (III) was wrecked on Sheep Island, Port Ellen in 1902 (*see* "W.H.S.").

P.S. *Princess Beatrice*.   The experience gained in the earlier steamer was utilized in the designing of *Princess Beatrice*, which was built by Messrs. Harland & Wolff at Belfast. The space below decks was better arranged, and the vessel was superior in many other ways. The uptakes were directed into one funnel placed aft; otherwise she was similar in appearance to the Glasgow-built ship. The machinery, however, was double diagonal simple, later altered to compound. She was withdrawn in September, 1904 and scrapped.

PORTPATRICK & WIGTOWNSHIRE JOINT RAILWAYS

P.S. *Princess Victoria* (I).   The first *Princess Victoria* was built by Messrs. Denny, as were all the subsequent members of the Stranraer fleet as long as these builders were in existence. On trial she attained a speed of 19·77 knots, and was a most successful steamer, though sometimes inclined to be sluggish in heavy seas. She inaugurated a "Daylight" service between Larne and Stranraer from 14th July, 1890. She was withdrawn in September 1910 and broken up.

P.S. *Princess May*. This ship followed the general lines of the preceding vessel, but here again opportunity was taken to remedy the few shortcomings of the earlier steamer. *Princess May* was capable of a speed of 20 knots. Some time after she was built, the under-deck space was altered considerably and her accommodation was made more convenient for the travelling public. Taken out of service in 1912, she was laid up in Loch Ryan till 1914, when, on the outbreak of hostilities, she was purchased by the Admiralty for employment on special duties. After being laid up in the Holy Loch, she was sold in 1921 to be broken up at Garston.

Tr.S.S. *Princess Maud* (I). In 1903 the need for a steamer to take the place of *Princess Beatrice* was under consideration. The turbine had already proved itself on other routes; and, after negotiations lasting some months, Messrs. Denny were given the contract to build a steamer with that type of machinery, and capable of service in the shallow waters of Loch Ryan. The vessel was delivered in time for the summer of 1904, and was propelled by three screws, the middle one being driven by the H.P. and the others by the L.P. turbines. *Princess Maud* had two covered decks and a promenade deck, her steerage accommodation being much in advance of that on the former ships.

Early in June, 1931, *Princess Maud* ran on the rocks at Barr's Point, Islandmagee, just outside Larne. She was subsequently refloated, but was found to be beyond economical repair, so was sold in January, 1932, to Messrs. T. W. Ward, Ltd., by whom she was broken up.

Tr.S.S. *Princess Victoria* (II). Six years after the advent of the pioneer turbine steamer on the Stranraer route the second *Princess Victoria* was built, also by Messrs. Denny. She was substantially on the same lines as the earlier vessel, but had a slightly longer promenade deck and better accommodation for saloon passengers. Three Parsons' turbines were fitted, to which steam was supplied by Babcock & Wilcox water-tube boilers. Full speed was 21 knots, but 18 knots was sufficient for service requirements. This vessel was engaged in transporting troops to and from France from October, 1914 till December, 1919, after which she was restored to the Larne–Stranraer station. She was sold to Norwegian shipbreakers in March, 1934.

LONDON MIDLAND & SCOTTISH RAILWAY
(Stranraer Section)

T.S.S. *Princess Margaret*.   As a successor to *Princess Maud* (I), this very fine geared-turbine steamer was constructed by Messrs. Denny in 1931. She was considerably larger than any of her predecessors on this run, and luxuriously appointed. Third-class sleeping accommodation was provided for the first time on this service, and the first-class accommodation also was in advance of previous practice. The berths were so arranged that each formed a bed on each side of the cabin, the older type with one berth above the other having been discarded. On the completion of *Princess Victoria* (III) in 1939, *Princess Margaret* was transferred to the Heysham–Belfast run to supplement the sailings of the *Dukes*, the traffic having so increased as to warrant the employment of five steamers at weekends. When *Princess Victoria* was taken over by the Admiralty on the outbreak of war, *Princess Margaret* returned to her old route, apart from a few trips engaged as an infantry landing-craft in the Normandy landings during the Second War. In the spring of 1952 she was converted to burn oil fuel. From that time the L.M. Region's Marine Office at Euston (then designated "Irish Shipping Services") became responsible for the Stranraer services. In January, 1962 it was announced that *Princess Margaret* was to be sold and in April she left for Hong Kong where, named *Macau*, she entered service to the Portuguese territory of that name.

T.S.S. *Princess Maud* (II).   The success of the previous new ship on the Stranraer station, and the fact that *Princess Victoria* (II) was beginning to suffer from the effects of her war service during 1915–19 led to the placing on the run in the spring of 1934 of a vessel in many ways superior to *Princess Margaret*. *Princess Maud* (II)—she revived the name of a famous predecessor—had a larger part of the below deck space given over to cabin accommodation for both classes: and the fittings were even finer than those of *Princess Margaret*. The ship was of greater beam, and slighty longer, but of the same moulded depth. As a safety measure Ginnel automatic fire extinguishers were fitted, as also in the case of *Princess Margaret*. Both ships had below the bridge, at the forward end of the boat deck, an "observation lounge".

Both ships had a service speed of 21 knots, and the trip from Larne to Stranraer was made in two hours. In the reverse direction, however the time taken was 15 minutes more, for the steamer had to back out of the harbour at Stranraer and into the harbour at Larne. The reason for the latter reversal is apparently that in early days of the turbine service one of the steamers went in too fast, and removed a piece of Larne Harbour! As in the case of all the earlier vessels on the Stranraer route, *Princess Maud* (II) was coal-fired, but Erith-Roe electrical stokers were employed. From 1946 she was oil-fired. She resumed her sailing on 1st August, 1946; but from the spring of 1947 was on the Holyhead–Dun Laoghaire service, being more economical in fuel than the ex-L.N.W.R. ships *Hibernia* and *Cambria*, which were laid up from time to time on account of the coal shortage. Apart from a period on the Southampton–St. Malo station in the summer of 1951, *Princess Maud* continued there till succeeded by *Holyhead Ferry I*, and was then sold to Lefkosia Compania Naviera, S.A., Panama, and renamed *Venus*, being sold in 1969 for use as an accommodation ship at Copenhagen.

T.S.M.V. *Princess Victoria* (III).   The first British railway-owned cross-channel motor ship entered the water at Dumbarton on 21st April, 1939, when Messrs. Denny launched this exceptionally interesting vessel for the Stranraer–Larne route. Up to that time all the railway cross-channel steamers had been driven by steam reciprocating or turbine machinery; but in the case of the new ship, Sulzer Diesels were installed. *Princess Victoria* was constructed primarily to provide means of transport for motor-cars between Great Britain and Ireland, and was described as a "floating garage". In spite of this, however, she was a handsome ship, having no suggestion in her appearance of being anything but a first-class cross-channel packet. Her stern was of peculiar design, not unlike the modern whale factory-ship, to enable the cars to be run on and off directly on to the main deck, which was completely clear almost to the bow, all the passenger accommodation being situated on the promenade and upper decks. Like the other Stranraer steamers she was fitted with a bow rudder, and a supplementary bridge at the stern, for use when proceeding astern; also the customary double navigation lights, for the same purpose. A unique feature, so far as railway steamers are concerned, was the large grill ventilator on the front of the funnel at the top, as on the Cunard White Star Liner *Mauretania* (II). She was the prototype of very many other stern-loading car ferries.

Like so many of her contemporaries, *Princess Victoria* went on war service, being used principally for the transport of mechanized forces; and unfortunately this fine ship became the victim of an enemy mine off the mouth of the Humber towards the end of May, 1940, after a career of only 13 months.

T.S.M.V. *Princess Victoria* (IV).   To take the place of the previous vessel of this name an almost exact replica was produced by Messrs. Denny, entering the service in March, 1947. The differences from the former ship were mainly internal, and consisted in giving greater passenger accommodation. During 1948 the Eastern Region cargo ship *Felixstowe* was on the milk run from Larne to Cairnryan, but next year the deck of *Princess Victoria* was strengthened to take large road tank vehicles, bringing milk from Ireland. On 31st January, 1953, *Princess Victoria* foundered in a storm off the County Down coast with very tragic loss of life—one of the worst disasters in the history of British coastal shipping. This left the Stranraer fleet with a strength of one only, as *Princess Maud* was by this time permanently on the Holyhead–Dun Laoghaire service. To cope with the vehicle traffic in summer, and as reliefs in spring, *Hampton Ferry* and *Shepperton Ferry* were borrowed from the Southern Region of British Railways, at various times.

CALEDONIAN STEAM PACKET COMPANY (IRISH SERVICES) LIMITED

On 31st December, 1959 the Clyde & Campbeltown Shipping Co. Ltd., (which had passed from the control of MacBrayne Trust Ltd. to that of the Railway Executive on 1st October, 1949, and so to that of the British Transport Commission in September, 1953), was renamed as above for the purpose of carrying on the Larne–Stranraer service. From 1953 the London Midland Region had assumed responsibility for this service. From 1st December, 1960, *Princess Margaret* was chartered by the above company from British Railways Scottish Region, continuing on her usual run. The Company's name was again changed in 1968, this time to British Transport Ship Management (Scotland) Ltd., when it was again resuscitated for management purposes in preparation for the transfer of the C.S.P. Co. Ltd. to the Scottish Transport Group from 1st January, 1969.

T.S.S. *Caledonian Princess*. The successor to *Princess Victoria*, which had been discussed for so many years, at last materialised when this very fine steamer was launched from Messrs. Denny's yard at Dumbarton on 5th April, 1961, the last of a very long line of railway steamers built there. She combined the faciles of a modern passenger liner with the ability to carry cars and trailers, which were driven on and off by the stern. To seal the stern opening there was a massive watertight door, opening upwards and outwards, and held in the open position by safety latches. With a speed of $20\frac{1}{2}$ knots, she could do the crossing in $2\frac{1}{2}$ hours; and with a side thrust Voith Schneider cycloidal propeller, and twin rudders at the stern, she had very great manoeuvrability. The interior was most elegantly decorated, the murals in the cafeteria, based on Celtic themes, being noteworthy—crosses, standing stones, turf-roofed cottages, seashells and seadrift, coracles, a donkey laden with peat, and a seaward-gazing boy. This ship, owned by the above Company, introduced a new funnel marking in having the Caledonian red lion rampant on each side of the yellow portion of the funnel. This, however, gave way to the Standard B.R. funnel in 1967, following the transfer of her ownership to British Railways Board (though management remained with the C.S.P. Co. Ltd.). The ship was such a success on the run, and traffic developed to such an extent, that each summer further accommodation for vehicles required, and supplied by chartered tonnage; and this continued even after the advent of the next new ship, since *Caledonian Princess* was used for nine weeks peak-period in the summer on the Holyhead–Dun Laoghaire or Fishguard–Rosslare station. She was sold in the spring of 1984 for use as a floating restaurant on the Tyne, under the trading name *Tuxedo Princess*, being transferred in October, 1988 to Anderston Quay, Glasgow for a similar purpose.

*   *   *   *   *   *

For the extra summer services various charters occurred, first M.V. *Slieve Donard* from the London Midland Region in the 1964 season and in the following summer the *Löhengrin* of Wallenius Lines, built at Bremen in 1964, and specially designed for "drive-on, drive-off" car transportation. Both these ships carried vehicles only, and their passengers had to travel by the principal passenger steamer on the route.

T.S.M.V. *Stena Nordica*.   In January, 1966 it was announced that Caledonian S.P. Co. (I.S.) Ltd. had chartered the Swedish ship *Stena Nordica*, built in the previous year, and first used on "The Londoner" service between Tilbury and Calais. In this case the charter was a long-term one, for 18 months, to fill the gap until a new ship should be completed, but subsequently extended. The intention was that the Swedish ship should operate all the year round, along with *Caledonian Princess*, and the charter cost is understood to have been very high; but traffic was increasing to such an extent that it was considered worth this extra expense, and this was further justified later when a third ship was ordered for this route. The *Stena Nordica* was a twin-screw motorship of 262 ft. overall, with a car deck 45½ ft. broad and 13¾ ft. high. She was well appointed, with, on the boat deck, two large lounges and three bars, and on the promenade deck a restaurant with seating for 126, and a 190-seat cafeteria. The large funnel amidships was a dummy, though accommodating air-conditioning plant and an emergency generator. The exhaust from the main and auxiliary engines was carried away by inconspicuous white uptakes placed athwartships, one at each side of the ship. Though initially retaining her own funnel colouring, *Stena Nordica* was given a standard B.R. funnel in 1967. All the chartered ships have flown the Caledonian pennant while on the Stranraer–Larne station. In the spring of 1966 and 1967 the relief ship provided at Stranraer was *Holyhead Ferry I*, from British Railways Holyhead – Dun Laoghaire station, none being required thereafter till 1970, when *Baltic Ferry* was chartered from Atlantic S.N. Co. Ltd., for vehicle traffic only.

T.S.M.V. *Antrim Princess.* The placing of an order for a further ship for the Stranraer station was announced in March, 1966, this being the first ship owned by B.R. with "drive-through" facilities, having a bow lifting door as well as the conventional stern door, in which features she was similar to the chartered *Löhengrin* and *Stena Nordica*. Being owned from the outset by British Railways Board, she carried their colours, though under the management of Caledonian S.P. Co. (I.S.) Ltd., Gourock until transferred to that of British Transport Ship Management (Scotland) Ltd. in 1969. A two-class vessel of modern design, she could carry 1,200 passengers, with cabins for nearly 70, and had a capacity for 170 cars, or 50 large commercial vehicles, with axle-loads up to 11 tons.

Being required at Heysham for the Isle of Man service on account of the shortcomings of the *Mona's Isle*, the *Antrim Princess* took up the Steam Packet sailings in 1987, later becoming the sixth *Tynwald*.

T.S.M.V. *Ailsa Princess/Earl Harold.* So greatly did vehicle traffic develop on the Stranraer-Larne route that in 1969 an order was placed for a sister-ship to *Antrim Princess,* for delivery in 1971. The placing of this contract with a Venice shipyard caused some questions to be asked in Parliament, but it was soon realised that British Railways were under obligaton to run their business on a commercial basis, and the terms of this contract were more favourable than could have been obtained from any British yard, particularly with reference to date of delivery. As with many British yards, however, her builders were not able to keep to the delivery date, and it was not until July 7, 1971 she entered service, the thirteenth "Princess" on this route. She can carry 1,200 passengers and 200 cars, and has 37 sleeping cabins, with a lounge having reclining chairs for 100 passengers. The Diesel engines driving twin controllable-pitch propellers give a service speed of 20 knots. She has a bow-thrust unit, a bow rudder and twin stern rudders, giving great manoeuvrability.

After the privatisation of Sealink the *Ailsa Princess* was used on the Weymouth–Channel Islands route, for which she was re-named *Earl Harold* in 1985. She re-appeared at Stranraer as relief from time to time.

T.S.M.V. *Dalriada* (II).   On June 24, 1971 this bow-and-stern loading three-deck vessel with accommodation for 45 large commercial vehicles and 70 cars for trade delivery entered service, as successor to *Baltic Ferry*. Owned by the Stena Line of Gothenburg, she had been launched in Norway earlier that year, as *Stena Trailer*, but for her long-term charter revived a name (with both Scottish and Irish associations) previously borne by a predecessor (though the owners were then named Clyde & Campbeltown Shipping Co., Ltd.).

SEALINK (SCOTLAND) LTD.
SEALINK BRITISH FERRIES LTD.

The name first above was adopted in 1980 by the much-renamed company, British Transport Ship Management (Scotland) Ltd., which continued to manage the ships on the Stranraer–Larne route for Sealink (U.K.) Ltd., the shipping subsidiary of British Railways.

T.S.M.V. *Ulidia*.   In December 1974 so much freight traffic had been generated that the *Dalriada* could no longer cope; and her sister (bearing a Latinised name for Ulster) was placed on the route. *Dalriada* herself was superseded by the *Darnia* in 1978 and after a time on the Heysham—Belfast station was back at Stranraer for a short spell before being returned to her Swedish owners.

T.S.M.V. *Darnia*.   In January, 1978 it was announced that a ship, expected to enter service in April, was to be chartered from James Fisher & Sons, Ltd. Launched for Stena A/B of Gothenburg, as *Stena Topper*, she was built on the Danube, near Vienna, fitted out at Constanti in Romania, modified at Belfast (this including the fitting of stabilisers and a high-capacity lift between her vehicle decks, to give her better access than her existing 1-in-8 ramp). She entered service in August, 1978 as *Darnia* (after the district round Antrim, inhabited in ancient times by the Darnii), with accommodation for 92 passengers, 60 road-haulage vehicles (or an equivalent in cars or caravans) on two decks, greatly increasing the capacity on the route. Her service speed is 17½ knots. She has had additional passenger accommodation from 1981.

Chartered ships on the route have included in 1975-6 *Roro Dania*, and *Maid of Kent* and *Cambridge Ferry* both from Sealink (Eastern), *Cerdic Ferry* from Townsend-Thoresen, *Anderida* and *Iggesund* in 1977, *Stena Timer* (sister of *Darnia*) early in 1979, and *Penda* (from the Heysham–Belfast station) early in 1980.

T.S.M.V. *Galloway Princess.* In September, 1977 it was announced that an order had been placed with Harland & Wolff, Ltd., Belfast, for a very large ship for this route. Her launch took place on 24th May, 1979 without ceremony; and, after very considerable delays, she ran trials on the Arran mile and visited Larne, Stranraer and Glasgow towards the end of April, 1980, commencing service on 1st May. Of roll-on roll-off, drive-through type with twin vehicle decks and twin ramps (the first on this route), bow visor and inner bow doors, stern door, twin thwart-ship bow thrusters, bulbous bow, twin rudders, fin stabilisers, twin funnels and two self-supporting masts, she has a spacious forward lounge and bar, midships lounge and griddle, drivers' lounge and bar, with emphasis on comfort for the lorry drivers; restaurant, information bureau and tea-bar on the boat deck. There is an automatic sprinkler and fire-alarm system. Eight diesel-driven lifeboats are provided, and 12 inflatable liferafts. The propelling machinery comprises two Crossley-Pielstick 16-cylinder PC2V Mark 2 uni-directional engines, driving variable-pitch propellers, controllable from the engine-room or from the bridge, speed being 18·5 knots. The usual navigational aids and auxiliary machinery are installed. Of greater depth than any of her predecessors on the route, the new ship required the channel approaching the pier to be further dredged; and double-tier ramps were installed, to load and unload simultaneously. She is the prototype for the new generation of channel ships based at Dover. (*St. Anselm* and *St. Christopher*) and of *St. David* intended for Fishguard–Rosslare, all built at Belfast.

* * * * * *

Charters have included, in 1982, *Breizh-Isel* from Brittany Ferries and *Villandry* from French Railways; and reliefs were provided by *St. David*.

T.S.M.V. *St. David.* After sporadic employment on the Stranraer–Larne route, this sister of the *Galloway Princess* joined her there, and now they, along with *Darnia* maintain the service.

* * * * * *

With the impending privatisation of Sealink (U.K.) Ltd. the British Rail emblem was removed from the red funnels of the Stranraer ships, and those remaining were later given the new livery of white hull and superstructure with funnels navy-blue decorated with "gold braid".

A very well documented work entitled *The Short Sea Route*, by Fraser G. MacHaffie was published by T. Stephenson & Sons, Ltd., Prescot, Merseyside, in 1975, giving in much greater detail than any previous book the history of the Stranraer-Larne, Portpatrick-Donagahadee and Cairnryan-Larne routes. The last-named dates from 1973, using part of the war-time complex at Cairnryan, and its earlier years are covered in the above book. Ships later employed have included *Europic Ferry, Gaelic Ferry, Cerdic Ferry* and *Ionic Ferry* ex *Dragon*.

CHAPTER XIII

VARIOUS PRIVATE OWNERS

James Orr. The *Hero* of 1858 was owned by Mr. Orr from February, 1889 (after her sojourn on the Tay), passing to Mr. David MacBrayne in 1890 (*see* "W.H.S."). The next acquisition was the *Daniel Adamson,* ex *Shandon,* ex *Chancellor (see* Chapters IV and VII), which was brought back from the Manchester Ship Canal, and performed some sailings on the Clyde till broken up about 1895.

The Scottish Excursion Steamer Co. Ltd. The Wemyss Bay steamer *Victoria (see* Chapter I) was purchased by Mr. Morris Carswell, and the above company was incorporated on 2nd November, 1891, following an agreement made the previous month with Mr. Hugh McIntyre, Marine Surveyor in Glasgow, for the purchase by the Company of this steamer, described as "now or lately lying at Dover". She was placed on the Fairlie–Campbeltown run (with buff funnels with black tops) and would seem to have performed there for two seasons. On 17th September, 1893 the *Victoria*, lying at the Broomielaw, took fire. The fire-brigade had difficulties in obtaining water, due to interruption of supplies on account of work on the temporary bridge, and the river was too low for them to be able to pump from it; but the small ferryboats, Nos. 1 and 5, proved of great service, and after nearly two hours the fire was mastered, but not until over £3,000 worth of damage had been done. She was sold publicly the following February, being purchased again by Morris Carswell, then on 2nd May she passed to the London & East Coast Express Steamship Service Ltd. for service on the Thames, but she returned to the Clyde for them in 1897. In the following March she was sold to Mr. A. D. Reid (see below). The Excursion Company had been wound up in December, 1894.

The Glasgow, Ayrshire & Campbeltown Steamboat Co. Ltd. After the withdrawal of *Victoria* the excursion sailings to the West of Arran and Campbeltown from Fairlie lapsed for a season, then were resumed in 1895 by the above Company, (registered 1st June, 1895) which had purchased from the Bournmouth and South Coast Steam Packet Co. Ltd. their *Windsor Castle* of 1891, a fine

145

large steamer with saloon aft, and forecastle, with clipper bow and figurehead, and propelled by triple expansion diagonal engines (the first on the Clyde) driving the paddle-shaft through gearing. The Company was managed by Mr. Duncan T. Clark, a son of Mr. Malcolm T. Clark of the Lochgoil and Inveraray Companies, and provided just such a service as the G. & S.W. Railway Company desired, to Lochranza and Campbeltown, but which it had not power to operate itself. Under her new name of *Culzean Castle* the ship took up the run on 1st June, 1895, sailing from Greenock (Princes Pier), and calling at Dunoon, Largs, Fairlie and Keppel, to Lochranza, Pirnmill, Machrie Bay and Campbeltown. Special connecting excursions were run—the 'Glen Sannox' Coach Tour allowed a drive from Lochranza to Sannox and Corrie and back; connexions were available from Machrie Bay for Shiskine and Blackwaterfoot; and at Campbeltown for Machrihanish. Unfortunately the steamer had several machinery failures, due it is said, mainly to gearing. In her first season she had a buff funnel with black top, but by the next year this had become dark red with black top, and a continuous promenade deck to the bow had been built, leaving open sides forward between the fore saloon and the forecastle, in the manner of Captain John Williamson's *Glenmore*. The house-flag consisted of a white pennant bearing three red six-pointed stars.

She continued during the 1896 and 1897 seasons, then went up-river, and engaged in general excursion work. For a time she had a funnel buff with a dark red band, and also for a time a Lochgoil funnel; and her name was changed to *Carrick Castle* in 1899. The following year she was sold to the Russian Government and under several more names she finished her career as the *Tenri Maru* on the Inland Sea of Japan. Captain John Williamson had used the *Glenmore* for certain sailings to Campbeltown in 1895-6, but in 1897 made a more serious attempt at capturing this trade, with the *Strathmore*. This continued till 1900, then in 1901 the epoch-making experimental turbine steamer *King Edward* was placed on the run, a bank overdraft of her owners—The Turbine Steamer Syndicate—being guaranteed by the Glasgow & South Western Railway Company, on condition that she were placed on the Fairlie–Campbeltown route; and the steamer in fact made Princes Pier her base, so giving the Railway Company connexions by more than one route.

The sailings of *Culzean Castle* appeared in the G. & S.W. Railway public timetable, and by 1897 a circular tour was offered by rail to Ardrossan, steamer *Glen Sannox* to Brodick, coach to Machrie Bay and *Culzean Castle* to Fairlie Pier or Greenock, thence to Glasgow.

In August, 1899, *Carrick Castle* was advertised to sail to Campbeltown for Kintyre Agricultural Society Show, leaving Bridge Wharf at 8 a.m., and calling at Kirn, Dunoon, Rothesay, Tighnabruiach and Campbeltown; also musical cruises to Kirn, Dunoon, Rothesay, Keppel, thence Round Arran; to Ayr; and to Tighnabruaich and Campbeltown.

The Clyde Steamers Limited. The first of the several companies with which Mr. Andrew Dawson Reid was associated appears to have been the above, incorporated on 25th February, 1897. It acquired from the Moville Steamship Co. Ltd. the former North British steamer *Jeanie Deans* of 1884, renaming her *Duchess of York*, and giving her a most unusual colour scheme of grey hull and paddleboxes, yellow funnel with two red bands divided by a white one. In May, 1898 the Company acquired from Mr. Reid the *Victoria* (*see* above), which was advertised in Mr. Reid's own name with the heading, "Victorian Pleasure Cruising", or "New Victorian Route", to sail from Glasgow daily except Wednesdays for Skipness via Kyles of Bute, calling at intermediate piers. On Sundays she left Glasgow at 10-30 and cruised Round Bute, Inchmarnock and Cumbrae, this being shortened during August to Loch Striven Head and Kyles or to Ormidale. It was during this period that there occurred disgraceful scenes at Dunoon when the pier was closed on Sundays and passengers forced their way ashore.

The Glasgow Steamers Limited. It would seem that all was not well with the trade of the foregoing company, for on the 17th May, 1898 this company was registered, one of the subscribers being Mr. A. D. Reid. To it was transferred the *Duchess of York*. On 28th March, 1900 it was resolved that as the Company could not, by reason of its liabilities, continue in business, it be wound up; and a similar resolution was made on 24th October, 1900 with regard to The Clyde Steamers, Ltd.

Reid Limited. This Company was incorporated on 29th December, 1900, the principal subscriber being again Mr. Andrew Dawson Reid, who by agreement was to be the first Manager. The Company was kept in being till the end of 1907, after which Annual Returns were not lodged and the Company was removed from the register. The *Duchess of York*, after being laid up in 1900, was given a new boiler by Hutson & Son in 1901, and taken over by them presumably towards settlement of claims, continuing to be advertised by A. Dawson Reid, when not laid up. She sailed all through the 1902 season, on some Saturdays and most Sundays and on public holidays, being available for charter on the other days. In

1903 she was laid up, and in the next year became the *Isle of Cumbrae* in the Buchanan fleet (*see* Chapter IV).

Isles Steamship Co. Ltd.　This Company had on charter from 1903 the *Lady of the Isles* ex *Jupiter* ex *Lord of the Isles* (I), which had returned to her native river after a spell on the Thames. She was given Lochgoil funnels (thus matching the *Lord of the Isles*), as also were *Victoria* and *Duchess of York* (though for a time the dividing band in the case of the latter was red). She had also at different times a funnel which appears to have been buff with a red band divided from the black top by a buff band, and possibly also a red funnel with black band divided by a red band from the black top (as in Furness Withy colours). After being reboilered in 1901 she had a dark red funnel with black top. The house-flag was a blue pennant with white St. Andrew's cross, with an emblem superimposed.

Lady of the Isles, after two seasons, had a mishap to her boilers, thereafter spending over a year in Bowling Harbour. In March, 1905 she was advertised for sale by public roup in the Faculty Hall, Glasgow, on behalf of mortgagees, and appears shortly afterwards to have been scrapped.

A. S. Girvan.　The steamboat service from Girvan to Ailsa Craig was of comparatively late origin, dating from 1906. Prior to that time, however, Mr. Girvan, of Girvan, ran two sailing boats, named *Maggie Sinclair* and *True Vine*; and, in order to be able to tow these in calm weather he purchased the small steam yacht *Nimrod*. The sailings were afterwards maintained by Mr. A. S. Girvan, son of the originator of the service.

S.S. *Ailsa* (1) was a very neat little yacht-like steamer of 60 tons gross, built by the Ailsa Shipbuilding Co. Ltd. at Troon in 1906, and was the first steamer to carry passengers between Girvan and Ailsa Craig. Her funnel was buff, and hull black, with white water-line. She was sold in 1924 to John Watson, Cromarty, for service from Invergordon to Cromarty and Inverness, and later served in Orkney South Isles.

The successor of the foregoing vessel was constructed by the same builders, but at Ayr, and was originally named *Ailsa II.* She was soon, however, renamed *Lady Ailsa*, and as such became well known on the run from Girvan to Ailsa Craig. She was larger than the first *Ailsa*, and had a short forecastle deck. She had one funnel, and two masts, and was painted in colours similar to those of her predecessor. The propelling machinery was triple expansion made by Messrs. Hall & Company, Aberdeen, and steam was supplied by one Scotch boiler. She was sold in 1932 to Société Anonyme de Vapeurs Brestois and renamed *Camaret.*

Though much smaller than her immediate predecessor, the second *Lady Ailsa* made more frequent sailings possible by running in conjunction with *Carrick Lass*, a similar vessel. The capacity of the two was no doubt about equal to that of the former *Lady Ailsa*. Constructed of wood by Messrs. H. McLean & Sons Ltd. at Govan, the second *Lady Ailsa* had the lines of a fishing-boat and was fitted with a paraffin engine. She was lowered into the water by crane at Princes Dock, Govan, on 4th July, 1934. She carried one mast, but no funnel, and the hull was varnished teak, with white water-line.

Carrick Lass also was built by Messrs. McLean, and was owned by Mr. Greig. She was used for pleasure sailing from Girvan; and in the summer gave evening cruises to Ailsa Craig, etc., along with *Lady Ailsa*. She was sold in 1937 to General Estates Co. Ltd., Hythe, for ferry service on Southampton Water; and *Lady Ailsa* in 1955 to W. W. Hogarth, Morecambe.

The Vale of Clyde Steam Packet Co. Ltd. Registered on 13th April, 1911 as a Private Company, this was formed by Captain Alexander William Cameron, formerly a master with the Wilson Line, whose colours (green hull, red funnel with black top, white superstructure) he subsequently adopted for his Clyde steamers. The first acquisition was *Madge Wildfire*, from The Caledonian S.P. Co. Ltd., in May 1911. For that season she was not much altered, the only visible change being the addition of a black top to her buff funnel, but with the stay-ring buff as on the Southern Railway steamers. For her next season, however, she was given a dining-saloon on the lower deck aft, with two tall ventillators at the after end; and she was painted in Wilson Line colours. She did not sail another season for Captain Cameron, being sold in March, 1913, to Buchanan Steamers, Ltd., who renamed her *Isle of Skye* (*see* Chapter IV).

The *Lady Rowena* Steamship Co. Ltd. On 15th June, 1912 this company was registered, owned partly by Captain Cameron and partly by his other Company above-mentioned. It purchased the former North British steamer *Lady Rowena*, which had been bought by Captain Cameron in September, 1911, after a varied career in Italy and the South of England. She was given Wilson colours, and retained the framework for an awning over the after promenade deck: by the beginning of the 1914 season, however, she had been painted more or less as was the *Madge Wildfire* in 1911, except that her paddle-boxes were black. Both ships performed excursions form Glasgow to Dunoon, Rothesay, Millport, etc. (including Sunday sailings) and both seem to have had reasonable success, the *Lady Rowena* being one of the few passenger steamers

to continue sailing from Glasgow after the outbreak of the First
World War; but she was not left for long, being requisitioned in
1916 for minesweeping. Though she returned safely, she did not
resume sailing on the Clyde, being sold to the Goole & Hull S.P.
Co. Ltd. and subsequently to W. K. David, Swansea. Both of
Captain Cameron's Companies were wound up following meetings
held on 7th May, 1919.

T. L. Duff & Co. In 1920 this firm advertised for private
charter on the Clyde, the Anchor Line tender *Skirmisher* (on loan
from Cunard Line), followed by the *Paladin* when she returned to
Anchor Line tender service.

James Hogg. In 1919-20 a cargo service between Glasgow and
Rothesay was operated by the steam drifter *Ossifrage*, advertised as
S.S. *Argyll*. She was towed from Rothesay on 3rd September, 1924
to shipbreakers at Port Glasgow.

Neil Macnair. A similar service was provided to Loch Fyne by
the S.S. *Karrier*, which had a blue funnel with black top.

Clyde Hover Ferries, Limited. Highland Engineering, Ltd.,
the owners of Dickie's yard at Tarbert, decided to make that the
base for an experimental hovercraft service on the Clyde, proposed
ports of call being Abbotsinch, Gourock, Helensburgh, Dunoon,
Wemyss Bay, Rothesay, Largs, Millport, Tighnabruaich and
Tarbert. When first announced in February, 1965 it was intended
that the service be operated by SRN 5 Hovercraft built by Westland
Aircraft Ltd. and later it was announced that the service would start
on 1st June, on a twice-daily basis between Tarbert and Gourock,
the estimated time between these points being 40 to 45 minutes.
    The above Company, a wholly-owned subsidiary of Highland
Engineering, was formed to operate the service, and instead of the
proposed vehicle, two Westland SR.N6 were obtained, this being
an improvement in that each carried 38 passengers or three tons of
freight compared with 20 and two respectively of the SR.N5. The
SR. N6009 was delivered to Scan Hover of Oslo, while SR.N. 6010
and 6012 came to the Clyde, being sent in three sections from the
Isle of Wight to Clydebank for re-assembly. After some delay the
first craft gave a demonstration run to Finnart, Loch Long, on 18th
June, 1965, followed by the first public run on 26th June. After
further delays in delivery of the second craft, on 3rd July the first
regular service began between Largs and Millport, the novelty
attracting large number of passengers. It was announced in August
that in a fortnight's time a service would commence between

Tarbert and Gourock, and with a run arriving at Tarbert (Monday to Saturday inclusive) to connect with the MacBrayne steamer to Islay, etc., which arrived at West Loch Tarbert at 11-40 a.m. Claimed as the world's first all-the-year-round hovercraft service, it ultimately commenced early in September with a commuter service between Dunoon, Gourock and Craigendoran (landing on the beach at each of these); and on 9th September, 1965, 6012 was caught by a strong wind and hurled against Gourock Pier, being badly damaged, fortunately without injury to anyone. It was then stated that the craft would not be long out of service, and that the other hovercraft would extend its activities to the upper part of the Firth. It, however, also ran into difficulties with battery trouble at Rothesay, but this was ultimately remedied. In September, Largs Town Council banned the craft from the use of the beaches, on account of various complaints, of noise, etc., and that the Company refused to pay for the use of the beach, though it was known to have made certain payments to British Railways for the use of piers. The two craft were leased under a five-year charter agreement. The future of the services, was, however, placed in jeopardy by the decision at Largs. After various troubles—mechanical, electrical and structural—doubts began to be entertained as to whether the services would continue, but on 16th October it was announced that they would, despite a loss of more than £1,000 a week on this subsidised undertaking. The number of passengers built up over several days, only to drop for no apparent reason. The Gourock-Dunoon route had been very busy, and the Company was gratified at the numbers travelling to and from Tighnabruaich; but results to and from Craigendoran and on the Wemyss Bay–Rothesay route had been disappointing. In November the doubts again arose but apart from stoppages due to gales the service continued till about the end of the year. No more was heard of the hovercraft till July, 1966 when one of the two was at Cowes having about 100 modifications made. The other craft was available for charter, but the Company did not wish to attempt a scheduled service until they had two craft available. If they decided to resume, they stated, the second craft would go for modifications towards the end of the year. No resumption of services, however, took place; and it was not long afterwards that the operators' parent company went into liquidation.

Mac Shipping Co. Ltd. and **Wimaisia Shipping Co. Ltd.** Registered on 11th and 25th May, 1948 respectively, these companies were founded by Mr. William E. McCaig, Wholesale Fruit Merchant, Glasgow, and Deputy Chairman of the Clyde Navigation Trust, with the intention of developing passenger and cargo services on the Clyde. The first acquisition in April, 1948, was the tug/tender *Duchess of Abercorn*, dating from 1936, intended originally to be renamed *Delice*, but in fact re-named *Wimaisia*, this name being made up from the first and second letters of each of the names of the owner, his wife, his daughter and son. The ship was transferred to her name company in May, and after an inaugural cruise for the staff of Messrs. McCaig & Webb on the King's Birthday holiday, she was available for charter, taking up a regular Glasgow–Greenock–Lochranza–Campbeltown service from 1st June, leaving Glasgow (Bridge Wharf) at 8 a.m., and carrying only first-class passengers and light luggage. This service during June was to operate on Fridays, Saturdays, Sundays and Mondays only, but during July and August daily. At the same time there commenced a general cargo service, carrying also a few third-class passengers, by the former yacht *Taransay*, leaving Glasgow (Prince's Dock) daily at 12 noon, calling at Greenock, the return trip being from Campbeltown at midnight. Both services were advertised by Mac Shipping Co. Ltd., who were the owners of *Taransay*. From 21st July the *Wimaisia* operated from Ardrossan instead of from Glasgow, and from 1st August she called at Whiting Bay instead of Lochranza. It had become obvious that the ship was much too slow for a Glasgow-Campbeltown daily service. In October, 1948 she was laid up in Queen's Dock, Glasgow, till sold to Liverpool Fire Service and renamed *William Gregson*. The *Taransay* did not fare much better, but was transferred to Wimaisia Shipping Co. Ltd. in April, 1949, being sold in December, 1955 to Smith & Houston, Ltd. for breaking up at Port Glasgow. Meanwhile Mac Shipping Co. Ltd. had in October, 1948 commenced a Glasgow-Belfast cargo service with the steam coasters *Rimsdale* and *Morefield*, adding the *Isle Ornsay* the following month. A twice-weekly cargo service from Glasgow to Port Askaig commenced in December, 1948, but none of these lasted long. The Company was taken over by Angus Campbell, and then by T. J. Metcalf from 1952.

John Hall (Cruises) Limited. Formed by Mr. John Hall of Kirkcaldy, this Company operated cruises on the Forth from 1947, adding the Tay to its sphere of activities in the following year, with a converted "Fairmile" launch to which was given the name *Royal Tay Lady*, the word "Royal" being soon dropped from the name. Cruises on the Tay being by this time not in much demand, the ship was transferred next season to Belfast for cruises on the Lough there, and to Bangor, being suitably renamed *Ulster Lady*. She seems not to have had much more success there, and her next venture was on the Clyde, where she commenced on 1st June, 1950 to sail from Greenock (Princes Pier) to Rothesay, and with short cruises from the latter port. Her Agents were Clyde Marine Motoring Company, Greenock. By the middle of September she was laid up at Granton, being after some years sold to Regent Diesels, Ltd., Leeds, and broken up.

Clyde Marine Motoring Co. Ltd. This Company, founded by A. Dunlop Munro, Greenock, operated various tenders on the Clyde, and also, as mentioned above, acted as Agent for the owner of the *Ulster Lady* during 1950. In April, 1964 there was launched for the Company by Messrs. Hugh McLean & Sons, Ltd., Renfrew, the tender *Rover*, with accommodation for 120 passengers, and intended to be used for ferrying personnel and stores to and from ships at the Tail of the Bank. She was available also for chartering. An interesting development in 1969 was the acquisition of the motor vessel *The Second Snark*, which had been built by Messrs. Denny in 1936 for their own use as successor to their tender S.S. *Snark*, and which had subsequently been engaged in passenger cruising on the Forth, followed by a period of experimental work there for Messrs. Brown Bros. During Greenock Fair Holidays, from 5th to 18th July, she operated "mini cruises" from East India Harbour, Greenock, to the Docks, Shipyards and Tail of the Bank anchorage; to Carrick Castle; to Gareloch; to Cloch Lighthouse and Lunderston Bay; to Holy Loch; to Loch Long, passing Coulport and Ardentinny; and to Carraig nan Ron; and these were repeated in subsequent summers. She had been used also on charter to the C.S.P. Co. Ltd. as a relief on the Holy Loch and Dunoon runs, as also has the *Rover*. The launch *Hunter* was added to the Marine Motoring fleet in 1970. *The Second Snark* continued to be used for charters, including on occasion being so used by Caledonian MacBrayne Ltd., and by other organisations for cruises to Ormidale, Carrick Castle, Dumbarton etc. and on 2nd September, 1989 for one of the most unusual, including the first passenger landing at Kerrycroy, Bute and a call at the Marine Biological Society's new pier at Keppel.

The launch *Fencer* followed the *Hunter*, but a larger vessel was acquired to perform the contract sailings between Gourock and Kilcreggan in succession to those provided by the late Mr. W. Roy Ritchie. This was the former Southampton–Hythe ferry *Hotspur II* of 1938, which was re-named *Kenilworth*, thus reviving an old North British name. She took up her regular run from 2nd April, 1979. She is advertised in the Caledonian MacBrayne timetables as an associate. She gives cruises from Helensburgh in summer and in addition, she has occasionally been chartered, notably by the Paddle Steamer Preservation Society for Hogmanay or Christmas Cruises to Carrick Castle.

For the Garden Festival in 1988 Clyde Marine Motoring Ltd. acquired two "water-buses" of continental type, named *Sir William*

Wallace and *Robert the Bruce*, which operate from a new pontoon landing stage moored against the northwest piers of the original Central Station Bridge, entering by a gangway from the quay at the berth formerly used by MacBrayne's *Cygnet* and *Texa* on the Lochfyne cargo run, and almost on the site of the "Clutha" landing stage named "Jamaica Bridge". The water-buses gave frequent sailings to the Garden Festival, going upstream as far as the *Carrick*, and down as far as Braehead, and continuing in a limited way even during the winter. The Company's 1989 summer programme included cruises by the *Kenilworth* from Gourock, Kilcreggan and Helensburgh to the Holy Loch, and by *The Second Snark* from Greenock, Helensburgh, Kilcreggan and Dunoon to Rothesay, Largs and Millport.

Strathclyde Cruisers.   The former MacBrayne vessel *Lochnell* (see "W.H.S.") was purchased in 1987 by Mr. Jim Brown of Paisley, with the intention of restoration and operation from Paisley to the Garden Festival in 1988. After overhaul she appeared in Renfrew Harbour with an awning over almost her full length, but unfortunately was denied a passenger certificate for Paisley until a survey of the river could be carried out; and there were difficulties also in securing a berth at the Festival. She has accordingly been offered for charter and performed a few sailings to Garelochhead, landing by pontoon.

Lithgows, Ltd.   A most interesting event in 1962 was the building of a replica (full size) of Henry Bell's *Comet* of 1812, for the 150th anniversary celebrations. The machinery was a replica of the original side-lever, jet-condensing engine, taking steam from a coal-fired boiler, and driving two sets of paddles on each side, driven through spur gearing, as on the original ship. She made a ceremonial trip from Port Glasgow to Helensburgh on Saturday, 1st September, with passengers in appropriate period costume, and was later exhibited at Glasgow Bridge Wharf (S.S.). After spending some time in a shed at Port Glasgow, she was taken by road across the Erskine Bridge to Helensburgh, for the Clyde Fair International celebrations, and has since returned to her native town, in the centre of which she is a static exhibit, across the main road from the yard where the original *Comet* was built by John Wood.

GOUROCK SMALL CRAFT

Robert Ritchie.   For many years there have been motor ferry-boats from Gourock to Kilcreggan including the *Port Star*, which was owned originally in Port Glasgow, the *Kempock Lad*, *Lady Jane Ritchie* and *Westering Home*.

Walter Roy Ritchie. The motor fishing-vessel *Granny Kempock*, dating from 1941, was acquired in 1955 and placed on a ferry service between Gourock and Helensburgh, being joined in 1965 by the former C.S.P. vessel *Ashton* (*see* Chapter V), to which the name *Gourockian* was later given. She was sometimes taken by her former owners on charter, and has performed various charter cruises, including one for the Clyde River Steamer Club to Port Bannatyne on 9th August, 1969, believed to have been the last call by a Clyde passenger vessel at that pier. She was sold in 1972 to the Borough of Fleetwood for the Knott End ferry, and re-named *Wyre Lady*, being later sold for service on the Severn, which seems not to have taken place. She was soon purchased by Alan Oliver (Cruises) Ltd., who employ her on trips on the Sheffield and South Yorkshire Navigation from various bases between Rotherham and Thorne, and with occasional special cruises from Doncaster to Goole and from York to Goole.

The *Countess of Breadalbane*, which had been sold by The Caledonian S.P. Co., Ltd. to A. C. Craven, Ltd., Dublin was purchased by Mr. Ritchie in November, 1971, to re-open certain of the closed Clyde routes on which she had been previously employed; and she commenced on 1st May, 1972 sailing from Gourock to Blairmore and Kilmun, also operating the Gourock--Helensburgh ferry service (which had been maintained by Mr. Ritchie each summer since 1950), sharing duties with the *Granny Kempock*. It was a condition of the sale that the vessel be re-named; and, to provide links with her past and her present, she became *Countess of Kempock*, after a short time as *Countess*, though not registered as such. An interesting charter by the Clyde River Steamer Club took place on 8th June, 1974, when leaving Gourock, calls were made at Port Glasgow (Steamboat Quay), Greenock (Customhouse Quay), Craigendoran, Helensburgh and Kilcreggan to Blairmore, Strone, Kilmun, (past Ardnadam), Hunter's Quay, (past Kirn), Innellan and Rothesay; and on 11th September the Paddle Steamer Preservation Society took her from Helensburgh and Gourock to Strone, Innellan, Ardyne and (*via* Kilchattan Bay) to Millport. On 29th January, 1977 the Coastal Cruising Association had her for a sail up the Gareloch. She visited Carrick Castle for the Paddle Steamer Preservation Society Hogmanay Cruise at the end of 1978, in a blizzard. After Mr. Ritchie's death in 1978 his vessels passed to his widow, who sold them to Offshore Workboats, Ltd. By them *Countess of Kempock* was chartered in the summers of 1979 and 1980 to Staffa Marine, who based her at Ulva Ferry in Mull to perform cruises to Staffa and Iona along with the *Laird of Staffa* (built of fibre glass and fitted out at Sandbank). The latter was sold to Mr. Gordon Grant of Iona, who added the

Fingal of Staffa in 1988. It was most interesting to find the *Countess*, built for inland water service on Loch Awe, and such a versatile member of the Clyde passenger fleet, plying in the even more exposed waters off the west coast of Mull. In 1982 she was bought by the purchasers of the *Maid of the Loch*, and reverted to inland water sailing (*see* Chapter XIV).

The *St. Gerrans* of Falmouth appeared on the Clyde in the summer of 1988, based at Gourock and has visited Dunoon, Rothesay and Millport.

ROTHESAY SMALL CRAFT

In the 1890s an attractive little clipper-bowed paddle steamer named *Comet* operated short cruises from Rothesay to Kyles of Bute, etc. She was rather like a miniature *Fusilier*, with yellow funnel. In more recent times similar cruises have been given from a jetty in Rothesay Bay by the motor boat *May Queen*, superseded in 1938 by the *Gay Queen*, similar but with slightly more shelter, and owned by Mr. Wilson, (previously by McIver & Morris Ltd.). Their hull colouring of red with cream painted square ports was noticeable, as also was that of *Maid of Bute*, owned by Mr. John Knox. She had at different times been bright green, or bright mustard yellow, with white superstructure and buff funnel. Her base was Rothesay Harbour; and, in addition to cruises from Rothesay to the Kyles, and to Port Lamont, Loch Striven, etc., she was sometimes chartered, as for example, in 1968, when she performed for the Coastal Cruising Association the first passenger sailing on the Crinan Canal since 1929, when the *Linnet* was withdrawn. That steamer's bell was borrowed and used on the *Maid of Bute* on that occasion. The *Maid of Bute* was sold in 1973 to Murdo McSween of Fort William, and used on local cruises and charter trips and after his death passed to owners at South Queensferry, who ran trips to Inchcolm, advertising her as *Maid of the Forth*. After the 1988 season the *Gay Queen* was sold to a Poole owner.

In August, 1971 the bow-loading ferry *Dhuirnish*, previously at Rhubodach, was purchased by Mr. Robert Beattie from the Bute Ferry Co., Ltd. with the intention of opening a route between Port Bannatyne and Ardyne, the service on which began on Saturday, 21st August, 1971, but which was of very short duration. The owner had ideas of obtaining a larger boat to run between Rothesay and Largs; but, apart from charters of the *Dhuirnish* to take cattle from Inchmarnock to Bute and to convey a trench-digging machine from Millport to the mainland, she seems to have been little used and was for a time laid up in Port Bannatyne Bay.

With the construction at Ardyne of quays and associated works for the building of oil-rigs, great activity prevailed there for a few years. At first workers were taken by bus to Innellan to join ship for Wemyss Bay, but later services were provided by the Wemyss Bay–Rothesay vessels calling at Ardyne on certain runs; and the contractors Sir Robert McAlpine & Sons, Ltd. provided certain services between Ardyne and Rothesay, using the twin-screw motor-vessel *Bournemouth Queen*, ex *Coronia*, previously engaged in excursion trade in the Poole–Isle of Wight area. She appeared at Rothesay in October, 1974, and on 23rd June, 1975 was re-named *Queen of Scots*, apparently reviving a name from the Arrochar route in the 1840s, but actually called after the L.N.E.R. train. She performed a few short public cruises from Rothesay in July, 1975, but it was not till after she had ceased to transport workers from and to Ardyne that she did much public sailing. Following the run-down of the workforce at Ardyne, she was laid up there for a time, before taking up charter work as mentioned in Chapter XVII, during the absence of the *Waverley* in the summer of 1977. One of her associates in the McAlpine fleet was *Herm Trident I* (previously sailing between Guernsey and Herm), which received the name *Lord of the Isles* on 24th April, 1975, reviving a very famous name in Clyde steamer history, but, like her colleague, deriving it in fact from a railway source, the L.N.E.R. West Highland line loco-motive.

ARROCHAR SMALL CRAFT

The *Viking Saga* of Arrochar Boat-Hiring Co., Ltd. appeared on the Clyde in 1974, operating cruises to Dunoon, etc., and later was employed on charter between Tarbert and Portavadie till 31st October, 1975, during preparations for oil-rig construction (which, however, did not materialise). A later acquisition was *Maid of Arrochar*, from Roderick Cunningham (Scalpay), Ltd., previously named *Isle of Skye*, and three of the Loch Lomond vessels previously at Balloch are now operated by Arrochar Boat-Hiring Co. from Tarbet (See Chapter XIV).

DUNOON SMALL CRAFT

B.B. Shipping (Dunoon), Ltd. chartered and subsequently bought the *Queen of Scots* from McAlpines; and after two seasons cruising on the Clyde, including calls at Carrick Castle and at Prince's Dock, Glasgow, she was laid up at Blairmore Pier, the subject of claims by creditors. It is understood she was purchased for static use as a restaurant ship in England.

HELENSBURGH SMALL CRAFT

The motor vessel *Scots Guard*, built in 1963 by Timbacraft Ltd., Shandon for Guard Ferry Co., Ltd., was operated during 1964 from Helensburgh pier on cruises to Gareloch, Carrick Castle, etc., having as consort the even smaller *Irish Guard*. By the following year the former had been transferred to Lough Neagh, performing excursions from Antrim as the *Maid of Antrim*, owned by Rainey Enterprises Ltd., Larne, who had also the two ex Loch Lomond 'water-buses'. (*see* Chapter XIV). The *Jessie Ellen* from Orkney was based at Helensburgh in 1969 and the *New Roseland* from Falmouth spent two seasons there, in the 1980s for short cruises.

CHAPTER XIV

LOCH AND CANAL STEAMERS

LOCH LOMOND. In addition to the railway etc., steamers covered by Chapter VII, various steam and motor launches have been based in the Leven for pleasure cruises on the Loch.

Two fibre-glass vessels of the Dutch water-bus type named *Lomond Lass* and *Lomond Maid* were acquired by Highland Marine Charters for a new service from Balloch to Inchmurran in 1962; but they were the subject of several legal actions and after lying in the Leven and later in McAllister's yard at Dumbarton were bought by Rainey Enterprises Ltd., Larne, who renamed them *Maid of Bann* and *Maid of Coleraine*, using them for excursions on the River Bann, in association with *Maid of Antrim* ex *Scots Guard* on Loch Neagh.

Small craft operating from the River Leven at Balloch have been numerous, including those of Messrs. Blair and Messrs. Lynn and of Loch Lomond Boat Hirers (John Sweeney), the latter of which acquired in 1974 *Shandon* (previously *Irish Guard, Scots Guard* and *Balloch Castle*) and *Henry Rose II* (ex *Brixham Belle*), taking the place of *Rob Roy* and *Glen Falloch*, while *Skylark 9* remained in the fleet.

The activities of various owners were co-ordinated from 1974 by Loch Lomond Sailings Ltd. a subsidiary of Gratispool International Holdings, Ltd. Two new 87-passenger launches— *Lomond Princess* and *Lomond Duchess* (54' in length, of 39 GT.) were built, and some of the older craft were taken over and re-named, e.g. *Lomond Queen, Lomond Gael* and *Lomond Breeze*. Others were sold, such as *Glen Finlas*, which was purchased in 1977 by a boat-hirer at Clynder. *Lomond Lady* operated from Luss Pier from 1986; and *Lomond Queen* (II) (ex *Lochaber Lady* ex *Jacobite Clansman*) and *Lomond Princess* were based at Tarbet, by Arrochar Boat-hiring Co., (who had previously operated *Southern Star* there) together with *Lomond Chieftain* (previously *Jacobite Chieftain*, from Inverness), for short excursions including calls at Inveruglas (in connexion with coach tours) Ardlui, Inversnaid, Rowardennan, Luss and Inverbeg. These were joined in 1989 by *Lomond Mist* (ex *Prinses Juliana*) from Amsterdam, all then trading as "Cruise Loch Lomond".

Some of the Loch Lomond small craft make their terminus at Inchmurrin, the largest island on the Loch, which was first given a regular mail service in 1948, in common with Inchtavannach, Inchlonaig, Inchcruin and Inchfad. This service was provided by the motor-vessel *Lady Jean*, owned and skippered by Mr. Alex. J. Macfarlane of Balmaha, whose ancestors had a long association with boats on Loch Lomond. His grandfather was the owner of a gabbart named *Waterwitch*, based at Balmaha from about 1850 to 1870, engaged in taking slates from the quarries and also, once a year, taking a cargo of birchwood to Paisley for making bobbins for the cotton-thread, travelling by the rivers Leven, Clyde and Cart and using hired trace horses for the return journey up the Leven, then much-less obstructed than now. The Macfarlane fleet subsequently had motor launches named *Marion* (after the first Loch Lomond steamer), *Waterwitch* and *Margaret*, used for cruises from Balmaha in addition to the mail service.

There have been several cargo steamers on Loch Lomond, including two belonging to the owners of the Luss slate quarries and one—named *Glen Sloy*—which carried on general cargo runs; also *Mary*, engaged in carrying timber.

Non-passenger craft on the Loch have included the small tugs *Dart* and *Seiont* used for towing barges during the building of the Loch Sloy power station.

Ferry services for pedestrians are provided between Rowardennan and Inverbeg and from Inversnaid to the point opposite, the boats on the latter including *Silver Spray* and *Potter*. Inversnaid Hotel has its own service with *Arklet* (previously a tender from P. & O.'s *Sea Princess*). A service is given (by arrangement) from Inchmurrin to Midross, near Arden.

MAID OF THE LOCH LIMITED
P.S. *Maid of the Loch*.   As mentioned in Chapter VIII this paddle steamer was sold in March, 1982 to a partnership of Inde Coope Alloa Brewery Co., Ltd. and Verigen Limited, and registered in the name of the above Company, later wholly owned by the brewery company. She remained laid up at Balloch Pier, while various plans for her future were considered, the intention being to transform the ship into a leisure centre with restaurant, bars, discotheque and family rooms; and it was hoped also to offer passenger sailings at least one day a week. The closure of the bear park at Balloch delayed plans further. In February, 1985 it was announced that the plans still remained, but the owners were anxious to get everything right before proceeding. The proposal was that power would be supplied by Diesel hydraulic equipment turning the existing engines. Plans for the interior were "sumptuous". Externally the ship would remain substantially unchanged, but in a livery of black hull with white upperworks, and

a red and black funnel. (This would be much more in keeping with Loch Lomond tradition than the yacht-like livery she has carried for most of her life). The Paddle Steamer Preservation Society took an interest in the matter of preservation, and in May, 1988 it was announced that restoration work was to be carried out under the Manpower Services Commission. The ship was to be given to a trust representing local authorities and other interests, and leased back to Alloa Brewery for use as a luxury leisure complex; but please see below.

T.S.M.V. *Countess Fiona*. In order to maintain continuity of the summer passenger services on Loch Lomond the above Company purchased the *Countess of Kempock*, previously better known as the *Countess of Breadalbane* on Loch Awe, on the Clyde and at Oban, Staffa and Iona. She was lifted from the Clyde by the big crane at Finnieston, and taken in two parts (hull and superstructure separately) to Balloch, the second time in her life to have an overland journey. A temporary launching berth was made at Balloch, on which she was re-assembled. Notice of change of name was given in the *Glasgow Herald* of 21st May, 1982, registration being at Alloa. The naming ceremony was performed by the Countess of Arran, formerly Miss Fiona Colquhoun of Luss, after whom the ship is named.

The deckhouses were combined into one larger apartment, with companionways to the forward and aft lower saloons, one of which is used as a cafeteria. A dummy funnel was erected, slightly aft of amidships, and two masts, the livery being that described above as intended for *Maid of the Loch*, but from 1983 with the addition on the black portion of the funnel of the owners' "badge". In 1986 a white hoop was added between the red and the black, somewhat reminiscent of the white hoops on the David Napier funnels of early days on Loch Lomond. The *Countess Fiona* sailed in spring and autumn daily (originally except Monday) from Balloch to Inversnaid and return, giving two such sailings in the high season, and calling at Luss, Rowardennan, Tarbet (from 1984) and Inversnaid. For the 1989 season the ship was given a full-breadth deck-shelter, carpeted and well furnished, with a new funnel (red with black top) close to the wheelhouse, and two light metal masts. In the low season she sailed to the head of the loch, and called at Balmaha, reverting in high season to her former itinerary.

*　　*　　*　　*　　*　　*

In April, 1989 the owning company Maid of the Loch Ltd. was taken over by James Fisher & Sons of Barrow-in-Furness and the Sea Management Corporation of Queensland, Australia (55% and

45% respectively). It was planned to introduce a catamaran, to be named *Lady of the Loch*, and to restore the *Maid of the Loch* (with livery as indicated on the previous page).

LOCH AWE.

S.S. *Eva*.   This smaller steamer, built at Kelvindock, Maryhill, in 1861, is understood to have been the first on Loch Awe. She was advertised for sale within the Argyll Arms Hotel, Inveraray in October, 1862.

S.S. *Queen of the Lake*.   This steamer, built in 1863, passed into the ownership of Messrs. Hutcheson by the early 'seventies. She carried on their service alone till 1876, when *Lochawe* was acquired, and after withdrawal was beached some distance south of Ford Pier, where she lay derelict for many years. The remains of her keel and stem can still be seen there when the level of the loch is exceptionally low.

S.S. *Lochawe*.   This vessel made her appearance on the loch in 1876. Owned by Messrs. Hutcheson, she had a saloon amidships on the main deck, with dining saloon below; and the machinery, consisting of a pair of cylinders (simple) exhausting to atmosphere was situated aft. *Lochawe* plied originally from Ford to Pass of Brander, from which the journey to Oban was completed by horse-drawn coach; but from 1880, Lochawe Pier became the Northern terminus, and passengers travelled onwards to Oban by the Callendar & Oban Railway. There was thus a through route from the south via Ardrishaig and Ford to Oban and the north, even before the railway was opened to Oban. During the First War she was laid up, and in 1925 was scrapped.

S.S. *Kilchurn Castle*.   Mr. Thomas Cameron of Port Sonachan Hotel appears to have been the next owner of steamers on Loch Awe, of which he had three, with their headquarters at Port Sonachan. They had the somewhat unusual funnel colouring of white with a blue band and black top. The first, named as above, entered service on 21st May, 1883, and in a guide-book of the next year was shown as running in connexion with the Glen Nant tour. She was probably broken up some time after 1895.

S.S. *Sonachan*.   This was a very small steam launch, used locally at Port Sonachan.

T.S.S. *Caledonia*.   Built by Messrs. Bow, McLachlan & Company, this steamer was erected in the builder's yard at Paisley, then taken to pieces and sent by rail to Loch Awe, where she was re-assembled. Her trials were run on Saturday, 15th June, 1895.

Caledonia had a spacious promenade deck nearly the full length, and saloons fore and aft upholstered in a tasteful manner. The machinery consisted of two sets of compound surface-condensing engines, steam being supplied by one horizontal marine return-tube boiler.

In March, 1918, *Caledonia* was sold for service in Belguim, it being the intention to take her to that country and lengthen her. She was, accordingly, dismantled at Port Sonachan, and the sections were conveyed by the barge *Ben Cruachan* to Lochawe Pier, the boiler being plugged and towed behind the barge. The lengthening scheme, however, did not materialise, and she was broken up by her purchasers.

S.S. *Margery*. The cargo steamers on Loch Awe (locally known as "barges") were run by various owners from time to time. The first, named as above, was built of wood, and is thought to have been owned originally by Messrs. MacFarlane, Timber Merchants, Loch Long. She was later purchased by Mr. James West, Merchant, Loch Awe, and on his decease, was sold to Mr. Thomas Dow, carrying his funnel colouring of brown. She remained till 1901.

S.S. *Eagle*. This puffer was built in 1881 at Leith for Mr. Campbell Muir of Innistrynich. She was taken by sea to Bonawe, then by road up the Pass of Brander. Built of iron, and screw-propelled, she had one mast, provided with a derrick, and had her machinery aft. By her original owner, *Eagle* was sold to Messrs. H. & D. McCowan, Oban, who advertised her in 1902 to sail from the Railway Pier for Ford every Monday and Friday, receiving and discharging goods at all intermediate piers. In winter her southern terminus was Eredine, calls being made at New York and Portinsherrich. She was sold to Mr. Dow, passing in 1921 to Mr. David Wilson, and in 1929 to Mr. Sheriffs. Sold in 1935 for scrapping, she sank in the early part of next year, while laid up at Lochawe Pier. For some years afterwards her mast could be seen a short distance west of the Pier.

S.S. *Alder*. This was a yacht and estate boat, belonging to the owner of Ardbreaknish, often used for towing barges loaded with timber from the local sawmills.

S.S. *Ben Cruachan*/M.V. *Glenorchy*. This was the successor to *Margery*, built by Messrs. Rodger of Port Glasgow, at Loch Awe. She was owned by Mr. Dow, by whom she was sold to Mr. Wilson in 1921. She was then fitted with a motor engine in place of her original steam machinery, and was renamed *Glenorchy*. Along with *Eagle* she was transferred to Mr. Sheriffs in 1929, and was withdrawn in 1935. She was the last cargo vessel to ply for public trade on the loch.

S.S. *Countess of Breadalbane* (I). Mr. Duncan Fraser of Lochawe Hotel entered the field of steamboat ownership in 1882, with this single screw-steamer, which had saloons fore and aft, somewhat similar in general design to *Lady of the Lake* built in the same year for service on Loch Tay. In common with all other steamers on Scottish fresh water lochs, she took her boiler feed-water direct from the loch on which she sailed. The Lochawe service was suspended in 1914, and was not reinstated until 1922, when the ship was sold to The Caledonian Steam Packet Co. Ltd. (*see* Chapter I). She served that company for 14 years, and was broken up in 1936.

S.S. *Mona*. This was a wooden steam launch with a small cabin forward, and was used for short pleasure trips from Lochawe Pier to Falls of Cruachan, Pass of Brander, round the islands, etc. and for towing boats for fishing. She was owned by Mr. Duncan Fraser, and was broken up in 1900.

S.S. *Growley* (I). To take the place of *Mona*, this steam launch was purchased by Mr. Fraser about 1900. She had been built by Scott's Shipbuildibng & Engineering Co. Ltd., Greenock, and had been used by Mr. Scott for private sailings from Eredine, his loch-side residence. Later she was used by Mr. G. S. Hartley of Hayfield, by whom she was sold to Mr. Fraser for passenger traffic. Occasionally she was used for the towage of non-propelled barges, in a similar way to *Alder*, and was sold in 1936.

M.V. *Growley* (II). Built in 1936, this small motor launch came from Cockenzie and was the successor to the first vessel of the same name. It is understood that she was taken over by the Admiralty in 1939-40, and was wrecked near Inveraray.

*   *   *   *   *   *

In 1936 also there appeared a notable addition to the Loch Awe fleet, viz. the second *Countess of Breadalbane*; but as she was built for The Caledonian S.P. Co. Ltd., she is included among their steamers in Chapter V.

*   *   *   *   *   *

The cargo motor boat *Coileach Coille* was on the Loch after the Second World War, engaged in the transport of timber for the Forestry Commission; and two small motor launches, *Glen Strae* and *Glen Orchy* were used for short trips from Lochawe Hotel. After the transfer of *Countess of Breadalbane* to the Clyde, there was placed on the Loch in June, 1952 a small motor launch named *Lady of Lorn*, owned by Mr. J. H. Lynn of Dalmally, who, however, after having taken over the *Darthula II* concentrated on the Loch Etive sailings. *Lady of Lorn* then returned to the Clyde as *Kempock Lad* in the ferry fleet of Messrs. Ritchie Bros., operating between Gourock and Kilcreggan.

In 1979 a converted lifeboat made her appearance on the Loch, giving short cruises from the site of the slip previously used by the *Countess of Breadalbane*, but a much greater attempt to revive cruising on the loch was made in 1985-6. It was Mr. Harry Watson who was responsible for this, with the placing on the Loch of the motor cabin cruiser *Silver Heron*, followed in 1986 by S.S. *Lady Rowena*, owned by the Dalriada Steam Packet Co., Ltd. (Loch Awe, it should be noted, is bounded on the north east by part of the ancient Kingdom of Dalriada). On Lake Windermere named *Water Lily* from the 1920s and powered by a Gleniffer petrol/paraffin engine, the boat later had a Morris engine, and left the Lake in 1973, being from 1981 owned by Trentside Café, Gunthorpe, Nottinghamshire. Having been bought by Averil and Harry Watson in September, 1984, she was taken by road to Renfrew for restoration and conversion to steam power, with a Sisson-replica non-condensing compound engine, taking steam from a vertical fire-tube boiler made by Langley Engineering of Storrington and using wood or peat as fuel. Completed in July, 1986 she obtained a certificate for 30 passengers. Taken by road to Loch Awe, she was launched by crane, taking up passenger service from Lochawe Pier on 9th August, under the name *Lady Rowena*, chosen by her owners who had been favourably impressed by the frontispiece of this book in its earlier editions, showing the three steamers at Arrochar, the middle one being the North British Clyde steamer *Lady Rowena*. The boat is the first propelled by steam on Loch Awe for fifty years, and in addition to running short cruises for the public was used in her first season to provide a sail each week for the passengers on the "Royal Scotsman" train, conveyed by coach from Bridge of Orchy to Loch Awe Pier, then taken by coach to Oban to rejoin their train. In 1988 her sailings were extended to include calls at Port Sonachen, Taychreggan, Dalavich and Ardanaseig.

LOCH ECK.

The history of Loch Eck sailings will be found in the section on the Lochgoil & Inveraray Steamboat Co. Ltd., in Chapter IV.

LOCH KATRINE.

P.S. *Gipsy*. This small vessel, built at Stirling, was taken overland by Callander to the Trossachs in 1843. Prior to her advent a small company operated a large rowing-boat named *Waterwitch*, whose owners, fearing competition, are alleged to have scuttled the *Gipsy* in the deep water below Ben Venue. There were also small steam launches, *Spunkie* and *Kelpie*.

P.S. *Rob Roy* (I). As mentioned in Chapter VII, when the Lochlomond Steamboat Company was formed in 1845 it took over a contract which had been entered into between Mr. Wiliam Denny and the New Lochlomond Steamboat Company for the building at Dumbarton of a steamer for service on Loch Katrine. The steamer which Mr. Denny produced was named *Rob Roy*, an iron paddle vessel 70 feet in length and fitted with an engine of 15 n.h.p., made by Messrs. T. Wingate & Company. She sailed up the Leven and Loch Lomond to Inversnaid, and the intention was to drag her across to Loch Katrine in a cradle; but this proved too formidable a task, so she was dismantled, and taken over in eight sections, being re-assembled on the shore of Loch Katrine at Coalbarns in the early summer of 1846.

Before the Lochlomond Company could sail this steamer on Loch Katrine, Lord and Lady Willoughby, who were among the riparian proprietors in that region, interdicted them from running a steamer on the loch, averring that they alone had the right of navigation. In the Court of Session, however, the interdict was recalled, on condition of the formation of a new company (called at that time Loch Catrine Steamboat Company), in which half the shares were conveyed to Lord and Lady Willoughby's tenant at Trossachs Inn, the other half being retained by the Lochlomond Company. This settlement was reached on 8th April, 1847 and a joint minute was lodged in the Court of Session whereby the Duke of Montrose and Mr. Macgregor of Glengyle on the one part and Lord and Lady Willoughby on the other should recognise the agreement between the Company and the tenant of Trossachs Inn, and should grant the Company an exclusive right to navigate the loch for ten years from Whitsunday, 1847.

In "A Summer in Scotland", published in 1848, Jacob Abbot, an American, describes the steamboat "paddling away with her twelve passengers" and states:- "It was the smallest steamer I ever saw afloat. It was in fact an open boat, long and narrow, with a little engine in the centre, and seats around the sides. It is true there was a sort of canvas canopy over the seats in the stern, with windows in the sides, but there were no decks, except a partial one about the engine, where perhaps ten persons might stand".

In 1854, meetings and correspondence took place among the Company and the tenants of the inns at Trossachs, Inversnaid and Coalbarns with regard to the building of a new steamer for the loch, it being stated that the existing one was neither suitable nor safe. The Government inspector of steam vessels was asked to report on her condition: and, after due consideration, it was decided in 1855 to have a new steamer built. An idea of dismantling the old one and converting her to screw propulsion for use on Loch Tay seems to have been abandoned and instead she was sold as mentioned below.

S.S. *Rob Roy* (II). It was in 1855 that Mr. Alexander Denny received an order for a new steamer for the Loch Katrine service. This became the second *Rob Roy*, a pretty little yacht-like vessel with a clipper bow and square stern which was advertised by the Caledonian & Dumbartonshire Junction Railway Company to commence on 24th July, 1855, with coach connexion from the Loch Lomond steamers at Inversnaid. After the expiry of the ten-year period of exclusive navigation rights, differences of opinion arose among the joint proprietors of the owning company, leading to the steamer being advertised for sale, which the Lochlomond Company interdicted. In February, 1859, to avoid litigation, the Duke of Montrose offered to buy that Company's interest; and this was accepted. The *Rob Roy* then became the joint property of the tenants of the three hotels, Trossachs, Inversnaid and Stronachlachar (the last-named having taken the place of Coalbarns). The Lochlomond Company funnel colours—black with two white hoops—were used by the *Rob Roy* till at least this time, being later plain black, and finally yellow with black top.

In 1855, also, the Corporation of Glasgow obtained Parliamentary authority to raise the level of Loch Katrine and use the water therefrom for the main supply to the city. The first *Rob Roy* having been bought by the contractor for the erection of the works next to the loch, for conveying materials along the shore to the mouth of the tunnel at Calagart, was ultimately sunk, not far from the place where the *Gipsy* is thought to have been scuttled.

When Queen Victoria visited the Loch in 1859 to inaugurate the City of Glasgow's fresh water reservoir there, she travelled on the second *Rob Roy*, which became known to thousands of tourists and after 1900 was kept in reserve till scrapped about 1911.

S.S. *Sir Walter Scott*. It was not until 1900 that a new steamer was built for Loch Katrine; and, when she appeared, she bore the above name, most appropriate in view of what her namesake had done in bringing to the attention of the public the beauties of Loch Katrine and district. She is a splendid little ship, with, for her size, spacious cabins fore and aft in a somewhat similar way to those on

Queen of the Lake on Loch Tay. The machinery is triple expansion, taking steam from two horizontal boilers, and a jet condenser is fitted. During the early part of the Second War, when precautions were being taken throughout the country against possible paratroop landings, the *Sir Walter Scott* undertook patrols on the Loch, as part of the defence arrangements for Glasgow's water supply. For the remainder of the war she was camouflaged and laid up at the loch side. Originally steered from the deck, she now possesses a bridge forward of the funnel, and for some years has had a wheelhouse. Reboilering took place in 1956. when the use of oil fuel was considered, but rejected on account of possible pollution. Instead, the furnaces were fitted to burn smokeless coal, the application of this type of fuel being at the time much publicised. At the same time her large saloon windows, whose lower edges were very close to the water, were replaced by portholes.

The level of Loch Katrine has been raised twice, with consequent alteration of the piers and in the case of Stronachlachar, the building of a new pier farther south.

The original owners of the ship were Loch Katrine Steamboat Co. Ltd., of Callander, later controlled by Eglinton Hotels, Ltd., from whom the Corporation of the City of Glasgow took over the steamer, the Trossachs tea-rooms, etc., so as to have full control over the City's water supply, much of which comes from Loch Katrine. In 1969 the whole water undertaking including the steamer, passed to the Lower Clyde Water Board. Unlike many of the other inland water services, the sailings on Loch Katrine have continued to carry large numbers of passengers, largely due to the bus trips to the Trossachs; and increasing use has been made by school excursion parties. It is difficult to realise the age of *Sir Walter Scott*, and she celebrated 1971 by commencing her sailings at Easter, three weeks earlier than usual, as part of a tourist drive by the Lower Clyde Water Board, and to coincide with Sir Walter Scott's bicentenary. On the formation of Strathclyde Regional Council in May, 1975 the undertaking of the Lower Clyde Water Board passed to them, including the steamer *Sir Walter Scott* on Loch Katrine. The blue wavy line emblem of the Water Board was removed from the plain white funnel, leaving the ship looking like a member of the fleet of P. & A. Campbell.

LOCH ETIVE.

S.S. *Ben Starav*. Passenger services were initiated in 1877 by Mr. Donald Campbell of Oban with this small steamer, previously named *Morvane*, and built as a yacht for the Duke of Westminster. She was fitted out for the accommodation of 100 passengers on deck and in the cabin. On 9th July, 1877, she ran a trial trip from Oban to Loch Etive-head, and began operating from Oban; but due to difficulties with the tide at the Falls of Lora at Connel, this plan was abandoned in favour of basing the ship at Achnacloich, with a horse-drawn coach connexion from Oban. At the head of the loch passengers landed by small boats at Inveretive (there being then no pier there) and proceeded by coach to King's House, from which they could get a coach to Ballachulish for the steamer to Oban, or, in the other direction, a coach to connect with the railway at Tyndrum (it did not reach Oban till 1880). Messrs. MacBrayne provided the principal service with their *Lochiel* during 1878. The sailings by *Ben Starav* ceased in 1879.

S.S. *Glenetive*. In 1880 the passenger service was resumed with this steamer, one of the many products of Messrs. T. B. Seath & Company's Rutherglen yard and owned by Mr. James Murray of Taynuilt.

S.S. *Ossian*. Like *Glenetive*, this steamer came from the Rutherglen yard. She had a long career on Loch Etive, and became known to tourists from all over the world, doing the circular tour as above described, but from 1880 completed from Tyndrum to Oban by rail, and from 1901 being also capable of being performed by rail from Ballachulish to Connel and Oban. From just before the First World War there was a general falling off in the numbers of passengers using the tourist services, and it was found uneconomic to maintain the four-in-hand coaches and the steamer on the Loch. *Ossian* was, therefore, sold in August, 1913, to Turkish owners, and it was some time after the cessation of the war before anything was done towards the resumption of tourists sailings on the Loch. Owned initially by Mr. James Murray, *Ossian* passed to Mr. John Currie of Ballachulish, and later to Mrs. Margaret Macpherson of Corpach.

M.V. *Jano*. It was not till 1922 that passenger sailings on the Loch were resumed. Messrs. Scott and Smith, Ferrymen at Island Ferry, Taynuilt, then purchaed this comfortable and speedy motor launch from a Tighnabruaich boat-builder, for excursions from Bonawe and Achnacloich: the circular tour was revived, with a charabanc instead of a coach.

M.V. *Loch Etive Queen*. By 1923 passenger sailings on the Loch were provided by this motor launch, built at Dumbarton for Mr. Donald R. MacKay of Taynuilt. She was taken over in 1941 for Admiralty duties. Thereafter she was owned at Mallaig.

M.V. *Rena.* It would appear that the foregoing vessel was rather small for the traffic and in the following year (1924) this little ship was added to the fleet. The sailings appeared in the railway timetable, there being one advertised run in each direction, from Achnacloich to Lochetivehead, calling at Taynuilt (Bonawe Pier). Serving as a fire-boat in Glasgow Harbour during the Second World War, she was damaged by bomb splinters during the Clydeside blitz of 1941.

M.V. *Euglena.* This small motor-launch was built at Kilcreggan in 1924 and was owned by Mr. Alexander Black, Taynuilt, being employed on the Loch Etive mail run. On one occasion at the end of January, 1945, when the loch was frozen over for about nine miles from the head, the inhabitants of Glen Etive were without rations for about two weeks until some people set out with pack-horses to meet the mailboat *Euglena.*

T.S.M.V. *Darthula II.* In 1939, Mr. Black had a new motor vessel built by Messrs. Dickie at Tarbert, Loch Fyne, for the Loch Etive passenger service. She was a useful little ship, with commodious cabin (considering her size), and was designed to provided the sea link in the Oban to Lochetivehead excursion. During the Second World War she was engaged in convoy duties off the coast of Argyll, and returned in 1946 to her normal service from Achnacloich to Lochetivehead. In March, 1955, Mr. J. H. Lynn of Dalmally purchased the *Darthula II*, retaining her in the Lochetive sailings. From 1962 she belonged to Loch Etive Cruises, Ltd. (Edward T. F. Spence), Oban. From 1964 she was on the Thames, and by 1966 she was owned by R. G. (Passenger Launches) Ltd., Bexleyheath. She has since been in the Portsmouth area.

T.S.M.V. *Shearwater/Etive Shearwater.* In June, 1964 there appeared on Loch Etive a successor to *Darthula II*, at first named *Shearwater*, and almost immediately renamed as above. She was a former Fairmile launch. Owned by Loch Etive Cruises, Ltd., she was restricted in being unable to use Lochetivehead Pier, (due to lack of progress in restoring the road from Ballachulish) but she resumed during the 1966 summer season the call at Lochetivehead; though the circular tour was not revived. In 1967 she then went to Wester Ross, giving short cruises from Ullapool and later was transferred to Arisaig Marine giving excursion sailings to Eigg, Rum, Muck and Canna.

M.V. *Caterina.* This small motor yacht was acquired by Loch Etive Cruises, Ltd., in 1965, and was used at first to provide restaurant facilities at the pier at Achnacloich, those of *Etive Shearwater* being somewhat restricted. Later she did some cruising on the Loch, but did not resume in the 1966 season, being sold in April to London, later to Gibraltar owners.

M.V. *Eula.* Mr. Donald Kennedy operated this boat on the mail run in succession to Mr. Black's *Euglena* but without a passenger certificate.

M.V. *Jessie Ellen.* After a break of two years when there were no public sailings on the loch, Mr. Kennedy purchased the *Jessie Ellen*, and from 1970 she operated from Taynuilt Ferry slip (Achnacloich Pier being no longer used). She gave cruises towards the head of the loch, and down to the Falls of Lora. She also carried the mails to both sides of the Loch throughout the year. (She formerly sailed on Loch Ness). The *Jessie Ellen* migrated to Orkney.

M.V. *Anne of Etive.* This fibre-glass cabin launch was built for Mr. Kennedy on the Thames in 1976, with accommodation for 125 passengers. Her large windows are excellent for viewing the magnificent scenery of the loch.

LOCH SHIEL.

S.S. *Maud.* The first steamer on Loch Shiel appears to have been Mr. MacBrayne's *Maud*, placed there in 1893. (See "W.H.S.").

In 1899, Lord Howard of Glossop, one of the local lairds, decided to start steamer sailings. The contract for the carriage of mails between Glenfinnan and Acharacle was secured, and a steamer was ordered. In 1921 the Loch Shiel Steamboat Service Co. Ltd. was formed.

S.S. *Clanranald.* Built at Rutherglen, this steamer of one deck, with two masts, proved unsuitable, and was sold early in 1903 to Robert Kerr, Irvine. She later became a yacht named *Madge*.

She passed to various owners including Major Struthers of J. & A. Gardner, who in May 1914 gave her the name *Hinba*, from one of the Isles of the Sea. After further changes of ownership she became a total wreck on the Gold Coast in November, 1924.

S.S. (afterwards T.S.M.V.) *Clanranald II.* A new steamer was built for the Loch Shiel route in 1900, also at Rutherglen. She maintained the mail service between Glenfinnan and Acharacle (with regular intermediate calls at Polloch and Dalilea, and occasional calls at Achanellan, Gorstanvoran, Glenaladale and Scamodale, also Gasken) all the year round, except when off for overhaul. At Glenfinnan she sailed up the River Callop for a short distance and used the pier there, except when the water level was too low for this: she then used the pier on the west side of the loch, on the site of which was built the present pier. This service provided the daily (except Sundays) mail run from the West Highland Railway to the communities in the Ardnamurchan Peninsula. It should be emphasised that, in common with many of the inland loch services, the steamer provided a vital link and gave, especially in the early years, a method of travel which was smoother, speedier and more reliable than the alternative routes by the often very rough tracks which then served as roads in the West Highlands. It was for these reasons that travel by steamer was indeed attractive, both for the carriage of passengers and for the transport of goods. In 1926 *Clanranald II* was taken down the River Shiel to have new Gardner machinery fitted at Oban. She then became a twin screw motor vessel, and remained in service till 1953, after which she was beached at Acharacle, following the introduction of the MacBrayne launches, and was broken up during 1954.

S.S./M.V. *Lady of the Lake*.   This was little more than a steam launch, being an open boat with a small cabin aft, and having a speed of about eight knots. She was used only as a relief to *Clanranald II*, and for extra runs for Glenfinnan Highland Games: and when not so employed she spent her time in a boathouse at Acharacle. She reached the Loch by being transported by rail to Oban, without her boiler; the boiler was installed and she steamed up the River Shiel. During the winter of 1951-2 she sank at her moorings.

M.V. *Lochshiel* and **M.V. *Lochailort*.**   In 1951 it was announced that the Loch Shiel Steamboat Service Co. Ltd. could no longer carry on the services, and David MacBrayne, Ltd., who provided, with the backing of government subsidies, similar mail services throughout the West Highlands, agreed to take over the responsibility for the Glenfinnan–Acharacle run. For this they built two wooden motor vessels, intended to be named *Rosalind* and *Celia*, but, on account of difficulties over registration (and local protests) they were named *Lochshiel* and *Lochailort*. With improvements in road communications in the area, the traffic dwindled, and the first-named was transferred in 1962 to Iona for ferry duties. On 28th April, 1970, while on a passage from Ardrishaig to the Gareloch for a refit, her engine broke down during the hours of darkness, and she was run down and sunk by an unidentified vessel off the Holy Isle, fortunately without loss of life. With the opening of the road from Lochailort to Moidart in the summer of 1967 the Loch Shiel mail service was replaced by bus and mail van connexions, and *Lochailort* made her last run there on 30th September in that year. She was transferred to Kyle of Lochalsh in the following year for the Toscaig run, but in 1969 was condemned for further passenger work following a Board of Trade survey of her wooden hull. She was then intentionally destroyed by fire at Kyle.

M.V. *Rose Isle.* This small motor launch, (brought from Ullapool) was placed on Lochshiel in 1968 by Mr. Duncan Henderson of Newton, Acharacle, to provide a passenger service after the cessation of that operated by Messrs. MacBrayne and continuing to provide the link one day each week in the circular tour from Fort William.

M.V. *Garry.* Previously used by Messrs. MacBrayne at Fort William, Glenelg, Rodel, etc., this motor-boat became their successor to *Lochshiel*, and was sold by them to Mr. Henderson in March, 1969. By him she was used to provide some sailings on the Loch.

LOCH EARN
T.S.M.V. *Queen of Loch Earn.* Built in 1922 by Forbes Bros. of Fraserburgh for Mr. Peter Crerar, Crieff, this vessel was acquired to run pleasure cruises on Loch Earn in connexion with her owner's bus tours. She was twin-screw, the engines being two 6-cylinder Penta paraffin motors, of Swedish make. Her port of registry was Perth. Mr. Crerar's business was taken over in March, 1928 by Scottish General Omnibus Co. Ltd., whose shares in June, 1930 passed to W. Alexander & Sons, Ltd., Falkirk, and to each of them in turn went *Queen of Loch Earn* as part of the bargain, though the Scottish General Company was not finally wound up till June, 1934. The vessel was laid up in the autumn of 1936; and, as the Board of Trade would not pass her for 1937 without an extensive overhaul, she was sold to a scrap merchant, but soon was resold by him to Mr. Sholto Douglas, late R.A.F., and converted into a house-boat named *Earnhull.* The machinery was removed and its space used to make a bathroom. She was pulled out of the water opposite St. Fillans, and remained there for many years.

LOCH RANNOCH
S.S. *Gitana,* built at Loch Rannoch and described as the 'Dunalastair Estate boat', was allowed to convey passengers for pleasure sailing, under certain restrictions, during the summer months, commencing on 10th June, 1881. Unfortunately she sank at her moorings in a storm there on 6th February, 1882.

A pleasant surprise for steamer enthusiasts was the raising of the *Gitana*, after nearly 90 years at the bottom of the Loch. She was in a wonderfully-good state of preservation and was beached, then sandblasted and partially painted. It was hoped she might yet again have been seen sailing on the Loch. Her engine was overhauled at Perth Technical College. Considerable top weight was added by an enclosed upper deck. The ship was refloated and moored in a position near that at which she had previously been sunk. Unfortunately a storm arose, as had happened when she was new; but this time she was driven ashore and disintegrated: there was no hope of saving her and so ended a most interesting restoration project.

S.S. *Firefly,* owned by Captain Wentworth of Dull, and occasionally used for passengers on Loch Rannoch.

M.V. *Have a Go.* This Windermere launch appeared on the loch about 1975, operated by the owners of Kinloch Rannoch Hotel.

VARIOUS LOCHS.

We have endeavoured in this chapter to give a brief survey of the steamers on the many lochs of Scotland. Mention should be made also of the following:—

S.S. *Mabel,* on Loch Maree, which was a member of the MacBrayne fleet and as such has been detailed in "W.H.S.".

S.S. *Loch Treig,* a puffer which operated on that Loch before and during the construction of the West Highland Railway (1894).

S.S. *Cailleach,* which was launched by the wife of the local minister in 1902 at Loch Ossian, has the honour of having provided a steamer service at the greatest height above sea-level in Scotland: at 1,280 feet this is only a few feet lower than Lake Lucerne. Loch Ossian lies a short distance to the east of Corrour Station on the West Highland line and even in 1990 can be reached only by rail, there being no road. The duty of *Cailleach* was to convey the guests of Sir John Stirling Maxwell and all supplies to his shooting-lodge at the far end of the loch. For this purpose there appeared in the wages bill of the time, as well as the more usual gamekeepers, stalkers and footmen, "a steamer captain and two of a crew"! She was a small steamer with a cabin forward; and, although she was withdrawn in the early 1930s, the piers she used are still visible, as is the small slipway used for her overhauls.

S.S. *The Rifle,* placed on Loch Arkaig in the 1860s by Cameron of Lochiel and used each Thursday for a weekly supply trip up the loch to the remote settlement at the head, she was used also occasionally to tow barges loaded with timber and daily each shooting season during August and September she conveyed Lochiel's guests up the loch. It was on one of these trips that she carried Queen Victoria in 1873; and the Duke of York (later to become King George VI) travelled in her in the early 1930s. She served the loch-side settlements for over 60 years, before being withdrawn and partially broken up in 1939. She sank before this had been completed, however, and to this day her hull lies just out from the shore at the south end of the loch.

S.S. *Heron* and **S.S. *Shieldrake*,** were small steamers on Loch Ericht in the early years of this century. *Heron* was owned by the proprietor of Truimbank Hotel, Dalwhinnie, and had come from the Solent in 1910, being an ex-Admiralty pinnace. She was withdrawn about 1919. *Shieldrake* was later converted to a motor-boat, and carried on until the early 'thirties.

M.V. *Grampian Enterprise.* Placed on Loch Ericht by the Grampian Electricity Supply Co. Ltd. (now North of Scotland Hydro Electric Board), this small launch was not much employed after completion of the dam during construction of which a 30-ton hopper barge was used on the loch for carrying soil from the tunnel between Loch Garry and Loch Ericht.

M.Vs. *Silver Spray, Gobhar* and ***Chieftain.*** These motor launches (the last-named belonging to Mr. Bruce Watt of Mallaig) were for a time in the 1950s and early 1960s on Loch Morar, performing that link in the circular tour from Mallaig or Morar to Kyles Nevis. Previously a lifeboat of the P. & O. liner *Mooltan*, the *Chieftain* later passed to Messrs. MacLean & MacRae of Kyle of Lochalsh, by whom she was renamed *A'Mhaighdean Mhara*, becoming still later the property of David MacBrayne, Ltd., and named *Eigg* for ferry duties at that island. There may have been a steam launch on Loch Morar in much earlier times.

M.V. *Jacobite.* This small motor-vessel performed the mail service on Loch Ailort from Inverailort to Glenuig, but ceased on the opening of the Moidart road in 1967.

M.V. *The Macgregor.* Rather a neat-looking motor-vessel, and launched on 20th June, 1902 for service on the Lake of Menteith (Scotland's only "lake"), *The Macgregor* succeeded a small steamer (which may have been named *Mary*), and was herself taken from the lake about the First World War period. Small motor-boats operated by the Ministry of Works now take passengers from Port of Menteith to Inchmahome to visit the ruined Priory there.

A similar service to the foregoing is given by the same authority to Loch Leven Castle from Kinross on Loch Leven.

* * * ·* * *

A small unnamed steam launch operated for a time on Lanark Loch.

FORTH AND CLYDE CANAL.

The Forth and Clyde Canal is older than many people would think, having been opened as long ago as 28th July, 1790, and is of particular interest to students of nautical history, for it was there that the first practical steamboat in this country—*Charlotte Dundas*—sailed, in 1803.

Originally owned by a private company, the canal became the property of the Caledonian Railway Company in 1867, and so in 1923 was vested in the London, Midland & Scottish Railway Company, and from 1948 in the British Transport Commission and so to the British Waterways Board. The Forth & Clyde Canal Company ran track-boats on it, the later ones being constructed of iron. An old print shows one of these boats as a longish barge, with saloon amidships, having large square windows along the sides.

Connexion was effected near Falkirk with traffic from Edinburgh, from which city the journey to Glasgow by one of the "swifts", as these vessels were called (indicative of their speed), was made· in little more than nine hours! The early canal boats were drawn by two horses, with outriders in livery. In 1829 the steamer *Cyclops* appeared, sailing between Alloa and Port Dundas, followed in 1831 by *Lord Dundas*, and in 1832 by *Manchester*, plying between Port Dundas and Stirling. The *Gipsy*, a small undecked paddle steamer, was on the canal prior to her transfer in 1843 to Loch Katrine.

The right to ply passenger boats on the canal was leased in 1852 to Mr. Taylor, of Falkirk; and in 1860 the first passenger steamer made her appearance.

GEORGE AITKEN

S.S. *Rockvilla Castle*. This little steamer, dating from 1859, was better known along the banks of the canal as *The Swift*, and under this title appears in old prints, which show her, as having a cabin extending nearly the full length, and one mast very close to and immediately abaft the funnel. A contemporary writer in the *Evening Times* describes her thus: "A shapely clipper, about 50 feet long, or more, with a well-defined stem and stern. Midway, or nearer the stern, are situated her boiler and oscillating engine, and up through the saloon towers a substantial looking red funnel". Both passengers and cargo were carried, and *Rockvilla Castle* plied as far as Falkirk. She is thought to have done some sailing on the Union Canal, also, in her early days.

When only five years old she became the property of Mr. George Aitken, who was also her skipper, and whose family were, thereafter, associated with the ownership of the Forth and Clyde Canal steamers. It was a matter of regret when *Rockvilla Castle* was withdrawn from the route, and it was about 13 years before sailings were revived for excursions, but only as far as Craigmarloch.

JAMES AITKEN & CO. LTD.

S.S. *Fairy Queen* (I). The above company dated from 1893, when, under the management of Mr. James Aitken, son of the owner of *Rockvilla Castle*, a fresh start in passenger services on the canal was made. In June of that year the steamer *Fairy Queen* was placed on the route, and immediately became most popular with the travelling public. Two runs per day were made in each direction, the night being spent at Kirkintilloch; and she called at Rockvilla, Ruchill Bridge, Lambhill, Farm Bridge, Cadder, Torrance, Kirkintilloch, Twechar, Auchinstarry and Craigmarloch. Evening cruises from Kirkintilloch to Craigmarloch were also run on certain evenings, in connexion with the train from Glasgow, the return journey to Glasgow being made all the way by water.

Passengers only were carried (accommodation for 200 being provided) and her capacity was double that of her predecessor; but, though a splendid little steamer in every way, she was disposed of after only four years' service, her place being taken by a still larger vessel.

The first *Fairy Queen* had a promenade deck the full length, with an awning over the after part. The cabin was situated aft, and the dining saloon-forward. Her compound machinery was placed amidships, and her funnel was red with black top. This colouring also appeared on her successor, but at a later date the following colours were adopted, *viz.* funnels buff, and hulls blue with red waterline. The saloons were painted white, and deck-houses varnished teak. She was sold to Shannon Development Co. Ltd., Dublin.

S.S. *Fairy Queen* (II). This steamer was built by Messrs. Bow, McLachlan & Company at Paisley, to take the place of her namesake. She was of similar design, but larger, and had a deck-house on the promenade deck amidships, with a small top-deck on which the funnel was erected. After the appearance of *Gipsy Queen* in 1905, *Fairy Queen* was kept exclusively for private charter till she left the canal fleet, on being sold to R. & W. Hawthorn, Leslie & Co. Ltd., Newcastle-on-Tyne in 1912.

S.S. *May Queen*.   A further advance was made in the design of the canal steamers in the construction of *May Queen*, which had an upper deck extending the full width of the vessel, with an awning over the railed part and another awning over the after promenade deck. With a gross tonnage of 56 she was capable of carrying 231 passengers, and was a comfortable and popular vessel. She was sold in February, 1918 to Palmer's Shipbuilding & Iron Co. Ltd., Hebburn-on-Tyne; and later to Millom & Askam Hematite Iron Co. Ltd., Millom, Cumberland.

S.S. *Gipsy Queen*.   This steamer was larger than any of those previously mentioned, and was, in fact, of the greatest dimensions possible for sailing on the canal. She differed from the others in having three decks, with a consequent increase of height in the cabin and dining-saloon. As on the other steamers her dining-saloon was forward; and like them, too, she was a "one-class" ship. Her machinery, which was compound, received steam from one marine-type boiler having one furnace. She sailed in summer only, leaving Glasgow at 10.15 each forenoon for Craigmarloch, except on Saturdays, when the hour of departure was 2.15 p.m. Evening cruises also were run, principally by private parties which chartered the vessel. On being sold in May, 1940, she was scrapped at Dalmuir.

M.V. *Fairy Queen* (III).   This small motor ship was built by Messrs. H. McLean & Sons, Ltd., Govan, in 1923, and it was hoped that with a vessel of this type a greater speed would be obtainable than was possible with a steamer on the canal. She was smaller than any passenger vessel plying on the canal since the days of *The Swift* but had certain features in common with her larger sisters, notably a deck-house amidships and awning aft. The propelling machinery consisted of a set of Atlantic paraffin engines, developing 40 b.h.p., and she had no funnel. Accommodation for 100 passengers was provided. In 1931 she was sold to Mr. Boyle, Warrenpoint, Carlingford Lough.

* * * * * *

An opposition steamer to the established Aitken fleet appeared in 1904, *viz. Truro Belle*, which had a "Lochgoil" funnel, though for no known reason and sailed on the canal for only a season or two. There was no resumption of passenger sailings on the Forth and

Clyde Canal after the cessation of the Second World War; but shortly before the Canal was closed to navigation an interesting charter was arranged by Glasgow University Railway Society, of the Caledonian vessel *Ashton*, which on 12th October, 1962 sailed with passengers from Bowling to Kirkintilloch (during which she was delayed some hours at Blairdardie with a wire-rope round one of her propellers), returning the folowing day from Kirkintilloch to Bowling and Gourock.

FORTH & CLYDE CANAL SOCIETY

This society purchased from Clyde Port Authority *Ferry No. 2* and *Ferry No. 8* (*See* Chapter XV) with the intention of using them for pleasure trips on the Canal from Bowling and from Glasgow Road, Kirkintilloch. The former was sold without being restored, but the latter after very many hours of voluntary work was able to obtain a passenger certificate and has been in operation on public holidays and at weekends from The Stables to Cadder and Bishopbriggs, named *Ferry Queen*. In 1988, with superstructure reduced, she was transferred to sail between Bishopbriggs and Maryhill reverting next year to her former section of the canal.

CALEDONIAN ESTATES LTD.

At the same time as the foregoing were sold, Clyde Port Authority disposed also of the only other remaining passenger ferry, *No. 10*, to the above, who removed the machinery, fitted an outboard motor, and used her as a restaurant boat on the same stretch of the canal as that on which her sister plies, her name being changed to *Caledonian*.

SCOTLAND IN VIEW

Commander Le Pla, who did much to assist the Canal Society, has had built *The Lady Margaret*; which was brought by road from Market Harborough and launched (by crane) at Kirkintilloch on 18th February 1987. She is a restaurant boat on the stretch of Canal between Kirkintilloch and Maryhill, and aiming at the upper range of the market for such a craft.

SEAGULL TRUST

For disabled passengers, the above has acquired certain boats for use on the Canal, the *Yarrow Seagull* having been built mainly by apprentices at Yarrow's shipyard, and the *Govan Seagull* similarly at Govan, the former being based at Kikintilloch and the latter at Falkirk. In 1989 *Highland Seagull* was added. The Trust operates boats also on the Union Canal from Ratho including the *St. John Crusader* and *Jane Telford*, which had for company the *Pride of the Union* and *Countess of Edinburgh*, operating from the Bridge Inn, Ratho as restaurant boats. At Linlithgow, also on the Union Canal, is the excursion boat *Victoria*.

CALEDONIAN CANAL and LOCH NESS.

From the earliest years of steam navigation, the Caledonian Canal had a passenger steamer service (*see "W.H.S.*). This had lapsed with the departure in 1939 of the *Gondolier*; and it was not until 1948 that passenger sailings, this time restricted to the eastern end of the Canal and Loch Ness, were revived.

T.S.M.V. *Lenrodian*.   This Fairmile "B" type vessel, No. 525, built in 1942, was acquired by Mr. L. S. J. Wilkinson of Inverness in February, 1948, and next month was transferred to Lochness Cruises Ltd., by whom she was operated for two seasons from Muirtown Wharf, Inverness, along the Canal to Loch Ness, turning off Castle Urquhart, and with a whole day sail to Fort Augustus twice each week. Evening cruises also were given. After two seasons the services ceased, and the ship was advertised for sale in 1950. Her name was made up from the Christian names of the three shareholders in her owning company—Len Wilkinson, Rod. Smart and Ian MacDonald.

M.V. *Cramond Brig*.   After employment for the S.M.T. Company from South Queensferry and a spell on the Mill-port–Largs station, this motor vessel cruised from Muirtown in 1958.

M.V. *Scot II*.   Apart from the two seasons of excursions by *Lenrodian* and one by *Cramond Brig*, there had been no sailings on Loch Ness for over 20 years when the welcome announcement was made by British Waterways that they intended to operate cruises from Inverness in the summer of 1961. A regular programme was provided that year, and each year since, by *Scot II*. Built in 1931 as successor to another ice-breaking tug dating from 1876, *Scot II* was sent to Leith towards the end of 1960 and converted from steam to Diesel, being at the same time fitted out for passenger cruising. The funnel, originally buff with black top, now became white with yellow band and pale blue top, while the hull was black to main deck level, then off-white above, with a yellow line. She commenced for her owners—British Waterways—operating from Muirtown

Wharf, Inverness, in forenoon, afternoon and evening cruises, the shorter trips turning in Abriachan Bay, and the longer runs taking her to Drumnadrochit Bay. A charter by the Coastal Cruising Association on 7th May, 1966 took *Scot II* the whole length of the MacBrayne "swift steamer" stretch of the Canal, from Banavie to Fort Augustus and Inverness, and the same was done in the opposite direction on 2nd September, 1972.

M.V. *Jessie Ellen.* Built by Wm. Weatherhead & Son (1954) Ltd., Cockenzie, this vessel was designed for summer service on Loch Ness and winter service in the Orkneys. She had a passenger certificate for fifty-nine and commenced plying from Muirtown Wharf in 1961, her sailing bills being headed "Support private enterprise", as she was in direct competition with *Scot II.* Her owner, Mr. James Newlands, operated her on her original route till 1966. She spent the 1967 season based at Helensburgh; and apparently laid up in 1969 she was in 1970 acquired by Mr. Donald Kennedy for service on Loch Etive.

M.Vs. *Jacobite Princess, Jacobite Chieftain, Jacobite Clansman, Jacobite Lady.* These four passenger excursion vessels were placed on the Canal, two based at Inverness and two at Banavie for sailing therefrom and from Fort William, though the latter two seem to have ceased operating at the south end of the Canal after the 1976 season. The *Jacobite Chieftain* became the *Lomond Chieftain* on Loch Lomond and the *Jacobite Clansman* became the *Lochaber Lady* at Fort William, later the second *Lomond Queen* on Loch Lomond.

M.V. *Jacobite Queen* (II). The former Tyne ferry *Tyne Queen* was acquired late in 1988. After considerable alteration and improvement, on the lines of what was done to *Countess Fiona*, she called at Rothesay before proceeding to Inverness. She took the name previously borne by the first *Lomond Queen* while in this fleet.

M.Vs. *Abbey Princess* and *Caledonian Queen.* The above motor boats have given short cruises on Loch Ness, from their base at Fort Augustus.

M.V. *Neptune's Lady.* In 1988 this former Dutch vessel took up pleasure sailings between Banavie and Laggan Locks, operated by Neptune Cruises Ltd. of Onich. She was based at Fort Augustus in 1989.

CHAPTER XV

CLYDE CROSS-RIVER FERRIES

WRITING in the *Glasgow Herald* of 14th May, 1900, Mr. R. P. Lamond stated that originally the rights to all the ferries across the Clyde belonged to landowners or burghs, including Cardross, East and West Erskine, Renfrew and Whiteinch. The ferry rights were preserved for their owners under the various Clyde Navigation Acts, except Whiteinch. Govan Ferry, part of an old right-of-way known as the Kirk Road, was used by parishioners of the section of Govan Parish north of the river to reach the Parish Church on the south side. The rights to this ferry were purchased by the Clyde Navigation Trustees at Whitsunday, 1857 from Mr. and Mrs. Graham Gilbert of Yorkhill for an annual feuduty of £800, including 2000 square yards of ground, with the ferry house and pertinents adjoining the Govan Ferry and boats etc. This was confirmed by the Clyde Navigation Consolidation Act of 1858, which fixed dues within the limits between Mile Bridge or Kinninghouse Burn on the east and Marlinford on the west, which would include all the ferries between Whiteinch and Stobcross inclusive.

The rights of all the Clyde ferries vested in the Clyde Port Authority (formed on 1st January, 1966 to incorporate the Clyde Navigation Trust, Greenock Harbour Trust and Clyde Lighthouses Trust) passed to Strathclyde Region on its formation in May, 1975. The Clyde Navigation Trust had been formed in 1809 to manage the affairs of Glasgow Harbour.

Renfrew Ferry belonged to the Burgh of Renfrew from early times, and passed to the Clyde Navigation Trustees in 1911. The rights to Erskine (originally East) Ferry were acquired in 1904 from Lord Blantyre, then Laird of Erskine, along with those of West Ferry (near Langbank); but the latter was then no longer worked. The operation of Erskine (East) Ferry was in the hands of lessees till Whitsunday, 1907, when the Clyde Trust took over the working.

The various ferries above Govan were of fairly late origin, having come into being as required with the development of the harbour. All were originally operated by rowing-boats and were leased to a Mr. Adair. Some services, also were early discontinued, as for example that between York Street and West Street, which ceased on 8th March, 1913; and the Hydepark Street Ferry, which to the end was a rowing-boat, and ceased about 1890. There was also a ferry which provided a triangular service, calling at Highland Lane, Cessnock (Princes) Dock entrance and Kelvinhaugh. This was instituted by a rowing-boat, on 1st July, 1895, between Princes Dock and Highland Lane, a steam ferryboat being put on for the triangular run in 1897. It was discontinued on 3rd October, 1909.

Whiteinch Ferry was operated by a rowing-boat, later by a steam passenger boat, which was supplemented by a high-level vehicular ferryboat from 1900.

A ferry across the Kelvin at Partick was known as Meadowside Ferry, on which a rowing boat was placed on 2nd September, 1867. (The later Meadowside Ferry across the Clyde, also originally provided by a rowing-boat was at first called Govan West). No steamboat ever operated on the service across the Kelvin, which ceased on 13th September, 1890. Its place was taken by a pedestrian footbridge fixed to the side of the bridge over the Kelvin of the Stobcross (later North British) Railway, which served for many years, but was closed and removed before the opening on 12th March, 1968 of the Pointhouse Bridge for vehicles and pedestrians.

Reference should be made to Finnieston (otherwise Stobcross) Ferry, which was about 1936 removed from its old place at the foot of Finnieston Street to new landing stages farther up the Clyde, in a line with Elliot Street. This was rendered necessary on account of the projected Finnieston Bridge, which was intended to be built over the Clyde at or near the old ferry crossing, but which did not materialise.

Although the "Cluthas", introduced in 1884, made cross-river connexions, they were primarily concerned with traffic up and down the river. Readers are referred to *Clyde River Steamers of the last Fifty Years* by Andrew McQueen, for their history.

Apart from the Renfrew and Erskine Ferries, built in 1935-6, the Clyde Trust boats were distinguishable by their Indian-red hulls with white lining and lettering, the funnels being black except in the case of the high-level vehicular boats, which had yellow (formerly red) funnels with black tops. The *Renfrew* and *Erskine*, of 1935-6, had dark blue hulls with white lining and lettering, the funnels being yellow with black top; and the latter scheme was adopted by the Clyde Port Authority for the remaining ferries in 1966.

Govan Ferry (II). A hand-operated (rowed) ferry for vehicles and passengers was in use at Govan from 1734 followed by a second boat (hand-propelled—rope) in 1791, built by the Southfield Iron Company. This passed to the Clyde Navigation Trustees in May, 1857, and was superseded about ten years later by the first steam chain ferry on the Clyde.

D.T.J.S. *Ferry No. 1* (I).   The first steam ferry appeared on the Clyde in 1865, and was the fore-runner of the type that became so common-later—double-ended, and with a vertical boiler more or less amidships. As with the later boats, the exhaust was atmospheric, as the sailings of these vessels were so short that ample supplies of fresh water were always available. The first *Ferry No. 1*, however, was unusual in its method of propulsion. The engine drove a centrifugal pump, from which pipes led to the sides of the boat without protruding; and the vessel was moved by the reaction of the water forced out by the pump, direction (including steering) being effected by the use of valves controlled from the deck. The boat had four watertight compartments. The trial trip took place on 10th November, 1865, after which she entered service at Clyde Street.

D.T.J.S. *Ferry No. 2* (I).   Similar in design to the foregoing, this boat appeared two years later. She was for a time employed at York Street, but was withdrawn at the same time as her sistership, both being scrapped in 1891. There is some doubt as to whether this boat continued to be jet-propelled throughout its existence.

S.C.S. *Govan Ferry No. 1.*   Dating from 1867, this vessel was worked by means of a single chain only, on the same principle as the hand-operated ferry, but by steam power. The engine was originally of 10 horse-power, but in 1874 was increased to 15. The boat could carry three horses and carts in the carriageway in the centre and 50 passengers, or 200 passengers. In 1875 this boat became a stand-by, and received the designation "No. 1.". She was used at Erskine for a time, having sunk near the south bank in 1905.

D.S.S. *Ferry No. 3* (I).   Another passenger ferry appeared in 1869, similar in external appearance to Nos. 1 and 2, but propelled by a one-cylinder engine exhausting to atmosphere, driving through clutches a propeller at each end, and controlled from the deck. At each end also, was a horizontal steering-wheel. This boat was latterly at Kelvinhaugh, and survived till 1908.

D.S.S. *Ferry No. 4* (I).   An addition to the passenger ferry fleet was made in 1872, when *Ferry No. 4* appeared. This boat was used at York Street until the discontinuance of that service in 1913, and was thereafter retained for use at busy hours at Finnieston or Clyde Street, until withdrawn for scrapping. Though similar to her predecessors originally, *Ferry No. 4* had latterly a canvas shelter provided for the engineer, and still later was fitted with a plain stove-pipe funnel in place of the original one of the bell-mouthed type which was at one time a standard feature of the Clyde ferries. She was broken up in 1923.

D.C.S. *Govan Ferry No. 2*. This, the first double-chain ferry of the fleet, was designed by James Deas, Engineer to the Clyde Navigation Trustees, and entered service at Govan in 1875. She had two vertical boilers amidships, and on each side a space sufficiently wide to carry one row of vehicles, the total accommodation being for eight horses and carts and 140 passengers, or for 500 passengers alone. At each end were platforms which could be raised while the vessel was in motion, and lowered to assist in landing, and passenger gangways were provided—a refinement repeated in her immediate successor while at Govan, but otherwise absent from later chain ferries. She was superseded in regular service at Govan in 1903, and was for a time from 23rd October, 1904 employed at Erskine, though the Clyde Navigation Trust did not take over the working of that ferry till Whitsunday, 1907.

D.S.S. *Ferry No. 5* (I). In 1875, also, a further passenger ferry-boat was built. She was employed for a time at Finnieston, and was scrapped in 1910.

D.S.S. *Ferry No. 6* (I). Three years elapsed before another passenger ferry boat appeared, and she was for a time employed at Whiteinch, lasting till 1914.

D.S.S. *Ferry No. 7* (I). In 1882, two sister boats were built, both by W. S. Cumming at Blackhill, on the Monkland Canal. Of these, *Ferry No. 7*, employed at Finnieston and at Meadowside, was the first to be withdrawn, being broken up in 1914.

D.S.S. *Ferry No. 8* (I). The other product of 1882 had a much longer life than her sister and was latterly the only one remaining with an engine-room skylight. Like *Ferry No. 4*, she had latterly a plain stove-pipe funnel, and a shelter for the engineer. She could carry 94 passengers. In her earlier years she was on the Kelvin-haugh–Highland Lane–Prince's Dock triangular run; later on peak-hour services at Meadowside; and latterly she was similarly employed at Clyde Street, till withdrawn in January, 1950 and scrapped.

D.S.S. *Ferry No. 9*. A slight variation from the previous standard design occurred in the boats built from 1888 onwards, inasmuch as their engine-room skylights were on the top of a casing extending aft from the boiler, and forming at the rear a platform on which was placed the reversing lever, the steam control being situated on the skylight as before. This was to accommodate the height of the inverted diagonal machinery one cylinder being at 15° from vertical and the other at 45° to it, both driving one crank. Salvage and firefighting appliances were fitted to this ferry, as was also done in the case of the three following. Like the foregoing, _Ferry No. 9_ had latterly a shelter for the engineer, and was usually employed at Kelvinhaugh. She sank at Govan and was broken up in 1928.

D.S.S. _Ferry No. 10_ (I).   _Ferry No. 10_ was built by D. M. Cumming of Blackhill. She was for a time stationed at Whiteinch, then at Govan and finally at Kelvinhaugh. Her place in the fleet was taken by one of the new Diesel-engined boats in 1934, when she was broken up at Renfrew.

D.T.S.S. _Finnieston_ (I)/_Whiteinch/Vehicular Ferryboat No. 1_. A departure from previous practice occurred in 1890 when a vehicular ferry service was instituted at Finnieston with a boat of an entirely new design constructed by Messrs. W. Simons & Company of Renfrew. This steamer had a moveable elevated platform which could be raised or lowered to suit the tide, and on this platform the vehicles and passengers were carried. The platform was moved by steam mechanism, and was suspended from high girders along the sides of the hull. On the top of these was a bridge, from which the vessel was controlled, the steering being done by means of the twin screws, of which there was a pair at each end, so that the ferry could travel in either direction. Two sets of triple expansion machinery were provided, and two boilers, the latter having been renewed in 1927.

On the appearance of a new boat in 1900 this ferry was removed to Whiteinch, and her name was changed to suit the new surroundings. Later the name became _Vehicular Ferryboat No. 1_. She was sold in June, 1961 to Arnott, Young & Co. Ltd. for scrapping at Dalmuir, having been latterly in reserve.

D.S.S. _Ferry No. 1_ (II).   The original _Ferries Nos. 1_ and _2_ were worn out and withdrawn in 1891, their places being taken by two new boats bearing the same numbers. The second _Ferry No. 1_ was latterly at Govan, where a passenger ferryboat ran in addition to that for vehicles. She was broken up in 1934.

D.S.S. _Ferry No. 2_ (II).   _Ferry No. 2_ retained her original funnel which may be best described as a truncated cone with the wide end of the top. Originally the small passenger ferryboats were steered from aft, by a horizontal wheel, which involved having three members of crew, the master who was steersman, the engineer and a deckhand to secure the rope. In 1897 the system was altered to allow of steering from the forward end, so that the steersman could secure the rope and so dispense with one crew member.

The machinery consisted of two cylinders placed at 45 degrees to each other, the upper one being at 15 degrees to the centre line. Slide valves were used. Each three-bladed propeller had in its shaft a steel clutch, so that only the one at the after end was used. These two boats were fitted with Drysdale centrifugal pumps and fire-fighting equipment. *No. 2* was employed at Clyde Street until the appearance of the new *No. 7* in 1922, and thereafter was stationed at Finnieston for additional service at Clyde Street at busy hours. She was withdrawn along with her sister-ship in May, 1934.

D.T.S.S. *Finnieston* (II) */Vehicular Ferryboat No. 2.* The second ferry of the elevated platform type was built in 1900 and took the place of the previous vessel at Finnieston. This name was given to the new boat, but later changed as above. On the introduction of a high-level type of ferry at Govan in 1912, this steamer was transferred thither, and to Whiteinch in 1937. She was sold in 1966 for scrapping at Faslane.

D.C.S. *Govan Ferry No. 3.* To improve communication at Govan a new double-chain ferry was built in 1903, named as above, but losing her name on transfer in 1912 to Renfrew, where she remained till transferred to Erskine in 1935. She had two vertical boilers at one side, each having one funnel. The space in the middle of this ferryboat could accommodate eight motor-cars, and for passengers there was deck space at the sides, a part of which was covered in about 1934, electric lightning being at the same time installed. She was retained as a spare boat for use at Erskine till broken up at Renfrew in March, 1953.

D.S.S. *Ferry No. 11.* Two further passenger ferryboats were built in 1904 by D. M. Cumming at Blackhill, being numbered *11* and *12*. They were the first to have a deck-house amidships, giving length for the two-crank machinery, encasing the boiler and containing the engine controls, and also the first to have steering wheels of vertical pattern usual on board ships. These features were perpetuated in all the later boats. *Ferry No. 11* was the first of all the small ferryboats to have a shelter for passengers, fitted in April, 1945, and in 1949 applied to all the others except the old *No. 8*. At a later period all that remained were given wheel-houses to shelter the steersmen.

D.S.S. *Ferry No. 12*. This boat was usually to be found at Whiteinch, where—as at Govan—a separate passenger service was maintained in addition to that provided by the vehicular ferryboat. Both *Nos. 11* and *12* were scrapped in 1966.

For information additional to that in the earlier editions of this book acknowledgement is made to Mr. Iain Campbell of Rugby and to Mr. J. Craig Osborne of Knightswood, Glasgow, and, as before, to Mr. J. Campbell, Marine & Operations Manager, Clyde Port Authority for much useful information.

LORD BLANTYRE

A ferryboat named *Erskine*, operated by a hand-chain winch, capable of carrying four loaded carts on the Erskine (East) Ferry was the first vessel built in the shipyard at Bowling when the yard was established in May, 1851. She was superseded in 1859 by a single-chain steamboat of the same name, from the same yard, able to carry loads up to four tons. Both vessels belonged to Lord Blantyre, the proprietor of Erskine Estate, operated by lessees. It was reported in March, 1864 that when the steamboat was crossing the Clyde, the working chain broke, in consequence of the heavy current in the river: The boat swung round and sank. This mishap may have been the cause of the adoption of a double chain, in later boats such as the *Urania* about 1884, although a single-chain boat was later again used on the Erskine to Old Kilpatrick crossing.

The ownership of the ferry passed to the Clyde Navigation Trust in 1904, but operation remained with the lessee till Whitsunday, 1907. The first and second Govan and the first Renfrew steam ferries appear to have been used at different times, the last-named notably in 1905, after the first Govan one had sunk near the Erskine side.

D.C.S. *Erskine* (III). Similar to the *Renfrew Steam Ferry* of 1897, this boat dated from 1903 and, named as above, was normally employed at Erskine till superseded in 1935 by the two-funnelled boat previously at Renfrew and originally known as *Govan Ferry No. 3*. The *Erskine* was then sold for service at Kessock Ferry, Inverness, but sank while in tow off Campbeltown, on 28th February, 1936.

CLYDE NAVIGATION TRUST (contd.)

D.S.S. *Ferry No. 3* (II). This was a slight improvement in design from *Nos. 11* and *12*, the deckhouse being larger. This boat was fitted with salvage appliances and a powerful Merryweather fire pump. On occasion one of the ferryboats with this type of pump was able to empty one of the Clyde dry docks, using about 100 feet of hose, a very creditable performance for a vessel of her size. *Ferry No. 3* was for a time at Finnieston, latterly at Meadowside and closed the service there on 22nd January, 1966, by which time she had a new funnel of greater diameter than the old, and she carried the new colours of the Clyde Port Authority—blue hull with white band, and number at the middle of each side instead of at the ends, and funnel yellow with black top. She was the last survivor of the small steam ferryboats, and remained coalburning to the end.

RENFREW TOWN COUNCIL

One of the most-used crossings of the River Clyde (before it was deepened) was the Marlin Ford. At low water one could wade across and at high water a raft was used, tied by a rope to a tree on each bank. The right of ferry may have belonged to Renfrew from 1396 when it was created a Royal Burgh, and it was confirmed in the charter of 1614. The earliest known reference to a public ferry was in 1710, when the route was between King's Inch and Blawarthill. When the splendid mansionhouse of Elderslie was completed by Alexander Spiers in 1782 the old ferry road ran through his grounds. His son, having inherited the property, proposed to the Town Council five years later that the ferry be re-sited half a mile to the west, at the side of the Pudzeoch Canal (i.e. where it now is), and he bore the expense of building the landing places on both sides of the river, a ferry house with stabling on the south bank and a new road (that now known as Ferry Road).

Not only was the location changed, but a new boat was provided by subscription, capable of carrying a carriage and a pair of horses, which could be boated by one man in five minutes by using a rope fixed to each side of the river and running on four rollers, two at each end, one vertical and one horizontal.

The ferry rights were leased to various operators, James Elder from 1862, when the north slipway was reconstructed, followed by the introduction of the first powered craft on the route in 1868. The lease was latterly held by Peter Shaw; and the ferry rights passed to the Clyde Navigation Trustees in 1911.

S.C.S. *Renfrew Steam Ferry* (I). In 1911 the Clyde Navigation Trustees took over from the above the operation of Renfrew Ferry, and with it acquired the iron single-chain boat built for that station in 1868. This boat was distinguishable by a large wheel above deck level used for raising and lowering the end ramps but otherwise was somewhat similar to but smaller than the double-chain ferry built in 1897. She had the misfortune to sink near the south bank on 21st September, 1891. While she was out of service, passengers were carried in rowing-boats, but later by a passenger steam ferry borrowed from Clyde Navigation Trustees.

D.C.S. *Renfrew Steam Ferry* (II). In 1897 a new double-chain ferry was built for service at Renfrew, the old boat of 1868 being then laid up and kept in reserve till about 1912. The new boat like the old had the boiler at one side and the machinery at the other, the space between being available for vehicles, and passenger accommodation being provided round the sides.

From 1912 the service betweeen Renfrew and Yoker was given by the 1903 *Govan Ferry No. 3*, then un-named. Latterly the 1897 boat was kept in reserve, laid up at Renfrew, performing relief services at Renfrew or Erskine as required. She was sold in October, 1936 for service at Kessock, Inverness, but was dismantled on failure to negotiate the locks of the Caledonian Canal.

CLYDE NAVIGATION TRUST (contd.)

D.T.S.S. *Finnieston No. 1* / *Vehicular Ferryboat No. 3*. The third high-level ferryboat apppeared in 1908, and was considerably larger than the other two, with a gross tonnage of 379 and length of 104 feet. Her normal station was Finnieston, and she carried vehicles only, until 17th December, 1962, from which time she conveyed passengers also. On the closing of the Govan vehicular service in November, 1965 she was superseded at Finnieston by *Vehicular Ferryboat No. 4* (then transferred from Govan), and was sold in 1966 for scrapping at Faslane.

D.S.S. *Ferry No. 5* (II). For the passenger traffic at Finnieston this sister-ship to *No. 3* was built in 1912, remaining there till superseded in 1934 by one of the then new Diesel-engined boats. She thereafter was used for the rush-hour services at Meadowside or Kelvinhaugh. Like her sister she had a Merryweather fire pump. She was scrapped after withdrawal of the Meadowside service.

D.S.S. *Ferry No. 6* (II). Messrs. Harland & Wolff Ltd. were entrusted with the building of the next pair of passenger ferryboats, *Nos.* 6 and 7, which appeared in 1922, these being repeats of *Nos. 3* and 5, and like them fitted with Merryweather fire appliances. Both were launched on 7th November, 1922, and *No. 6* was employed principally at Kelvinhaugh.

D.S.S. *Ferry No. 7* (II). This boat was stationed at Clyde Street until the advent of the Diesel boats in 1934, when she became the extra boat for Clyde Street, and latterly was at Govan, which service she closed on 22nd January, 1966.

D.S.S. *Ferry No. 4* (II). The new *No. 4* was built in 1928, and was similar to the previous four small ferryboats, but with no hoop on the funnel. She took the place of *No. 9* in the fleet, and was usually stationed at Meadowside. During the night in April, 1965, *Ferry No. 4* sank at her moorings at Govan, but was raised, and served till scrapped in 1966.

D.S.M.V. *Ferry No. 1* (III). In 1934 three new passenger ferryboats were built, with internal combustion machinery, giving greater economy of working. The engine in each case was a Gleniffer four-cylinder Diesel, giving 80 b.h.p. at 900 revolutions per minute. Three to one reduction gearing was employed, and on trial a speed of 7·6 m.p.h. was attained. Externally the Diesel ferries were not unlike the later steamboats, being of dimensions similar to those of *No. 4* above described, and each could carry 140 passengers. *Ferry No. 1* was launched on 8th May, 1934 and was employed mainly at Kelvinhaugh. She was sold in February, 1968 and broken up at Bowling.

D.S.M.V. *Ferry No. 2* (III). All three of the original Diesel ferries were built by Barclay, Curle & Co. Ltd., and *No. 2* was launched on 15th May, 1934. She was normally at Clyde Street till its abandonment, and then became spare at Finnieston. She was one of the two ferryboats sold to the Forth & Clyde Canal Society (*see* Chapter XIV).

D.S.M.V. *Ferry No. 10* (II). This was the last of the three to appear, and was normally employed at Finnieston throughout her career. After withdrawal of the three remaining passenger ferryboats this one was sold to Caledonian Estates Ltd. for use as a restaurant boat operating from Glasgow Road Bridge, Kirkintilloch (*see* Chapter XIV).

D.C.S. *Renfrew* (I)/*Erskine* (V). In 1935 a chain ferry was designed by Mr. Daniel Fife, mechanical engineer of the Clyde Trust, for service at Renfrew. This boat incorporated many novel features, among them being covered accommodation with windows at each side for passengers, with promenade deck space on top. In the middle was accommodation for three lines of traffic, giving room for 12 motor-cars.

As in the case of the previous chain ferries, *Renfrew* had the boilers at one side and the machinery at the other, movable platforms being provided at each end of the vessel. The machinery was triple expansion placed longitudinally, differing thus from the older chain ferries.

After the appearance of the Diesel-electric ferry in 1952, the older *Renfrew* retired to obscurity as spare boat, but in 1962 was very much altered at the yard of James Lamont & Co. Ltd., Port Glasgow, by having the two Cochran boilers transferred to the same side as the engines, one at each end, each with its own funnel; and the passenger accommodation on the other side was narrowed, and the ramps shortened, so as to make the car deck capable of taking 20 cars instead of 12. Floats were built out at the sides to offset the extra weight of having boilers and engine at the same side of the boat, thus keeping her on an even keel. In this form she entered service at Erskine on 31st October, 1962, for which she was renamed *Erskine*. The opening of the Erskine Bridge on 2nd July, 1971 rendered the then occupant of the Erskine Ferry redundant; but she became spare for Renfrew, losing her name but carrying moveable boards marked "Renfrew".

She was sold in 1984 to Renfrew District Council and tastefully fitted .out as a museum of local history and industry with a span roof covering the vehicle deck. This floating museum formed the Council's contribution to the Glasgow Garden Festival in 1988 since which it has been berthed in Renfrew Harbour.

D.C.S. *Erskine* (IV). Another ferryboat similar to that constructed in the previous year was built by Fleming & Ferguson, Ltd., and being intended for service at Erskine, bore that name. She had less covered accommodation than *Renfrew* (I), and no passengers were carried on the upper decks. The machinery was compound and steam was supplied by two Cochran boilers, the uptakes from which were led into one funnel, as originally on the first *Renfrew*. During the Second War both *Erskine* and *Renfrew* had their names removed from their sides. From 1962 the *Erskine* of 1936 was spare and in August, 1971, while engaged in drilling operations off Irvine, was sunk but subsequently raised, being afterwards used as a platform during construction of Western Ferries' terminal at McInroy's Point.

When the Erskine vehicular ferryboats were being changed it was customary to provide a passenger service with one of the Clyde Port Authority launches, such as *Dunglass* or *Garmoyle*; but this was latterly not done, and even the vehicular service at Erskine was suspended during periods of overhaul of the Erskine and Renfrew regular boats.

D.T.S.M.V. *Vehicular Ferryboat No. 4.* This was the first Clyde ferryboat to be propelled by Diesel-electric machinery. She was of the high-level type, and employed at Govan except for a very short time at the end of her active career, when she operated at Finnieston. When the cruiser *Sussex* was set on fire on 18th September, 1940 by a German bomb at Yorkhill, the master of *Vehicular Ferryboat No. 4* was successful in manoeuvring his vessel alongside the burning cruiser, so that firefighting could be conducted from the deck of the ferryboat. This action averted an explosion of the cruiser's magazines.

No. 4 performerd the last vehicular crossing at Govan on 20th November, 1965, and took over the Finnieston service (then temporarily suspended) as from 29th October, till it was itself discontinued on 22nd January, 1966. She was used for experiments in Hymatic dredging and (in 1971) drilling off Ardeer. In 1975, *Vehicular Ferryboat No. 4*, after a period laid up at Renfrew, was sold and went round to Leith for work in association with the North Sea oil industry. It had been intended to re-name her *Cawsand*, but this did not take place; and, after a further period of idleness, she was scrapped.

D.S.M.V. *Ferry No. 8* (II). A further small passenger ferryboat similar to the three Diesel vessels of 1934 (but with passenger shelters from the outset) was added in 1951, being used initially at Govan but latterly at Kelvinhaugh. She was the successor of the old *No. 8*. The Diesel ferryboats were not fitted for firefighting, such duties being undertaken by the *St. Mungo*, specially built for that purpose. *Ferry No. 8* was sold to the Forth & Clyde Canal Society based at Glasgow Road Bridge, Kirkintilloch, now named *Ferry Queen*, but retaining *No. 8* on her bulwarks (*see* Chapter XIV).

D.C.M.V. *Renfrew* (II). The only Diesel-electric chain ferry on the Clyde entered service at Renfrew in June, 1952, with much greater capacity for vehicles than her predecessor. She had a funnel at each side, but later that beside the control-house was removed, to give better visibility, and then only a thin uptake remained there. The vehicular ferry service at Renfrew ceased on 30th May, 1984 amid scenes of nostalgia on board, and celebrated by a commemorative booklet and exhibition ashore. The *Renfrew* then withdrawn was sold to Euroyachts Ltd. for use as a floating restaurant, and after being laid up at Clyde Place Quay, moved to Govan during the Garden Festival in 1988, afterwards reverting to her former berth. With the vehicle deck roofed over, she was next spring converted into a floating theatre.

*   *   *   *   *   *

From the 1960s ferry services were gradually reduced. During work on the Clyde Tunnel at Whiteinch the vehicular ferry there was withdrawn, and the opening of the Tunnel brought about such a diminution in traffic that the passenger service there was discontinued from 14th December, 1963; the Govan vehicular service came to an end on 24th November, 1965, followed by the Govan and Meadowside passenger and Finnieston vehicle one on 22nd January, 1966. Clyde Street ceased on 28th January, 1967 on account of work in progress on the new Kingston Bridge; and on the opening of Erskine Bridge on 2nd July, 1971, Erskine Ferry ceased to operate.

The Finnieston passenger service ceased on 29th April, 1977, and next day that at Kelvinhaugh became continuous, 24 hours per day. It was, however, itself withdrawn at 10 p.m. on 3rd October, 1980 and so ended the harbour passenger ferries of Glasgow.

STRATHCLYDE REGIONAL COUNCIL

The Renfrew ferry operated profitably till 1972, when the loss of vehicle traffic to the Erskine Bridge and Whiteinch Tunnel reduced revenue so that a loss was being incurred. It was then decided that the Clyde Port Authority would continue the operation and Glasgow Corporation would meet the deficit, this responsibility being assumed by Strathclyde Regional Council from the re-organisation of local government in 1975. Operating costs continued to increase, while patronage diminished. At the end of 1982 the Council decided to terminate the vehicle service at the expiry of the D.o.T. certificate of the *Renfrew* in 1984, and itself to operate the passenger service with purpose-built vessels.

Messrs. A. Mylne & Co., Naval Architects, Rosneath were instructed by the Council to prepare plans and obtain tenders, the order for two vessels being placed in October, 1983 with Wm. McCrindle of Ardrossan, later McCrindle Shipbuilding Ltd. It was necessary to provide fender structures at each side of the river to assist in berthing, and these had to be built when the ferry was not operating, so that a period of a month was allowed from the cessation of the chain ferry till the introduction of the new boats:

during this time a temporary bus service was provided, using the circuitous route by Clyde Tunnel, Whiteinch.

T.S.M.V. *Renfrew Rose*. A target date of July, 1984 was decided for the introduction of the new service; and this was inaugurated by the first public sailing of the above, on 20th July, 1984. The names for the two vessels were chosen after a competition among local primary school children on both sides of the Clyde. The vessels are designed to operate on the existing 1:11 sloping ramp, and are provided with bow ramps for easy access of wheeled items such as prams and bicycles, and also for the transport of an ambulance in an emergency. The ferries can carry 50 passengers, most of them under cover in a comfortable heated cabin aft. A fuel transfer system is incorporated to ballast the vessel in the event of stranding on a falling tide seeming likely. The engine and ramp controls are from the wheelhouse.

T.S.M.V. *Yoker Swan*. Only one vessel normally operates at any one time, but the change over (usually weekly) takes place without the interruption that formerly occurred when chain ferries were being exchanged. The new vessels carry the Strathclyde Regional colours of orange and black, with white wheelhouse, and look very well. They are virtually a reduced version of the Caledonian MacBrayne "Small Island" class ships.

CHAPTER XVI

WESTERN FERRIES, LIMITED AND ASSSOCIATES

WITH the intention of providing more frequent services in the West of Scotland, and at lower cost than those existing, Western Ferries, Ltd. was formed in July, 1967, this to be achieved with simple, unsophisticated ships and terminals, combined with low crewing, on the lines of ferry operation in Norway.

T.S.M.V. *Sound of Islay.* The first member of the new fleet was launched at Port Glasgow on 27th February, 1968, for a twice-daily service between Kennacraig on West Loch Tarbert and Port Askaig, Islay, once daily to Gigha, which commenced in April, it being intended to be later extended to Jura. Carrying 20 cars and six lorries or a mixture, the ship had a service speed of 10·75 knots, horse-power being kept low to achieve low crew costs in accordance with the Company's policy. She was fitted with twin rudders controlled by hydraulic steering-gear, and has a bow thrust unit to assist in manoeuvring. Two small saloons were provided for passengers (80 in summer, 35 in winter) and it was interesting to note how much had been put into a small space, all forward, since the vessel's main purpose was to carry vehicles on her open flush deck aft. Later in 1968 proposals were made by the company to provide a larger vessel and to establish an "overland" route to Islay, *via* Jura, with a subsidy from public funds; but this was rejected by Mr. William Ross, Secretary of State for Scotland, who was opposed to fragmenting the service and considered that the proposals of David MacBrayne, Ltd. and Argyll County Council for improving the approach roads to Port Askaig on Islay, and between Feolin and Craighouse on Jura, would result in a much better service than these islands had had up to that time. In August the company stated that they would continue to operate without a subsidy, and that plans for a second ship were at an advanced stage. In September, 1969 it was announced that her owners were considering using her on a new ferry route on the Clyde, between Hunter's Quay (where they already owned the pier) and McInroy's Point, near the Cloch Lighthouse, if planning permission could be obtained: this service was later instituted, but not with this ship. She was registered initially at Glasgow, but re-registered at Campbeltown in 1970, from May, in which year till 1973 she was engaged in a summer run from Campbeltown to Red Bay,

from Campbeltown to Red Bay, Cushendall, County Antrim,
linking Kintyre with Ulster, with great expectations of increasing
tourism and commercial trafffic, which, however, did not materialise to an extent sufficient to justify the costs of running the
service. (She did this run also in winter, 1970-1, but for freight only,
not having a passenger certificate for this route in winter). In
November, 1971 it was announced that she would be available for
contract, in which, or on charter work, she became engaged from
early in 1972, including taking construction equipment from
Ardrossan to Campbeltown. A berth was made for her at Rothesay,
and in April she towed thither from Faslane a link-span that had
been intended for Colonsay. This enabled her to unload at any state
of the tide, and she conveyed many hoppers of granite chips from
Furnace, Loch Fyne to Rothesay. Her Irish sailings did not
commence till June, finishing in September. During October-
December, 1972, she was on charter to David MacBrayne, Ltd. for
the Portree and Small Isles. Her Irish runs were resumed in 1973,
but ceased in September, and have not since been operated. After a
trip to Orkney in July, 1974, she assisted on the Clyde-Argyll route
with lorries, from 30th being engaged regularly on the Ardyne run
from McInroy's Point, reverting to Kennacraig–Islay on the
departure of *Sound of Jura*. The terminal at Kennacraig was taken
over by Strathclyde Regional Council, and the land there bought by
Caledonian MacBrayne Ltd. with a view to their service being
transferred thither in 1978. Western Ferries' service to Islay was
suspended from 30th September, 1981 and the ship sold.

T.S.M.V. *Sound of Gigha.* For the short crossing betweeen
Port Askaig and Feolin, Jura the company bought the *Isle of Gigha*
from Eilean Sea Services—a vessel on the lines of a landing craft,
capable of bow-loading on beaches, dating from 1966, and the
prototype of the sort of craft envisaged when Western Ferries, Ltd.
was formed. Overhauled at Port Glasgow, she took up her reguular
run on 1st March, 1969, and has remained thereon, except during
periods when off for re-fit, when various chartered vessels have
been employed, including *Cara Lass* from the Gigha–Tayinloan
route, *Southern Star*, from Arrochar Boat-Hiring Company
(carrying passengers only), *Kilbrannan* from Caledonian Mac-
Brayne in 1972, carrying vehicles also, the next such vessel being
Caledonian MacBrayne's *Coll* in 1978, while in 1979 it was intended
to use the landing-craft-type *Spanish John* of Inverie Estates. In
1973 it was estimated that the Jura service was incurring an annual
loss of £8,000, not including depreciation; and in September, Islay
District Council arranged to contribute £1,250, with a similar
amount from Argyll County Council. The subsidy was substantially

increased and continued by Strathclyde Regional Council, which, however, would not provide any subsidy for the mainland to Islay service of Western Ferries.

T.S.M.V. *Sound of Jura.* In September, 1969 it was reported that an order had been placed in Norway for a second ship for the Kennacraig–Islay service, after the contract had been put out to tender to yards in Scotland and Norway, the successful tender, on price and delivery date, being from Hatlo Verksted, Ulsteinvik. She was to carry 35 vehicles and 200 passengers; and, fitted with twin rudders and bow thrust unit, would have a service speed of 14 knots, which would enable her to do three trips per day, or even four. She was the first drive-through seagoing vessel on the West Coast (though often used as a stern-loader only). Based on a Norwegian standard ferry design, modified for Scottish use, the ship had seating for 50 passengers in a carpeted observation lounge on the boat-deck and, like *Sound of Islay*, had vending machines for refreshments: also play-pens and a private room for mothers with young children. From September, 1970, she began calling (and bow-loading) at a link-span at the north end of Gigha, which was wrecked in a storm in January, 1972 and not replaced. It was assumed that Western Ferries would be the only operators to Islay, Gigha, Jura and Colonsay, as David MacBrayne, Ltd. had indicated withdrawal from 31st March. The proposed terminal at Scalasaig, Colonsay would not be ready before June; and, since the *Sound of Jura* had not a lift, crane loading would have been necessary there. It was then agreed that the MacBrayne services would continue till September, after which a further extension was made. In January, 1973, the *Sound of Jura* was fitted with an auto-pilot; and during overhaul in February next year her exhaust uptakes were painted blue, as on the *Sound of Islay*. In October and November, 1975, she made exceptional runs from Ardrossan to Portavadie with materials for the oil-rig construction site. No subsidy for the mainland-Islay service of Western Ferries being forthcoming either from Central or Local Government, the Company announced in July, 1976 that it could no longer run this ship in competition with the MacBrayne vessel then being subsidised to the extent of about £500,000 per year. The intention was to continue with *Sound of Islay* only, concentrating on freight; and the *Sound of Jura* was sold to the Mexican Government. She left Troon, after overhaul and under the name *Quintana Roo*, in September, 1976.

In September and October, 1972, negotiations were in progress for a take-over of Western Ferries, Ltd. by the Scottish Transport Group. Opposition to this was voiced in Islay and Jura, but on 7th

October, 1972 it was announced that the principal shareholders were likely to accept. On 1st November, however, a new bid for the company was announced, by Dornoch Shipping Co., Ltd., after a three-week campaign by Sir William Lithgow. This was accepted and the new arrangement took effect from 1st January, 1973. The operating company then became Western Ferries (Argyll) Ltd. After the withdrawal from the Company of Sir William Lithgow the operators became known as Western Ferries (Clyde) Limited.

D.S.M.V. *Sound of Shuna* and **D.S.M.V.** *Sound of Scarba.* In December, 1972, following the acquisition of the shares in the company by Dornoch Shipping, Sir William Lithgow, Chairman of Western Ferries, announced the purchase of two double-ended Swedish car ferries, subject to satisfactory survey and safe arrival on the Clyde. These were *Olandsund IV* and *Olandsund III*, with capacities of 27 and 22 cars respectively, to be towed across the North Sea early in the following year from the sound between the Swedish mainland and Oland Island in the Baltic, where they had become redundant following the opening of a bridge. Both were delayed at Stavanger by weather, then were towed to Inverness, proceeding under their own power by the Caledonian Canal to Corpach, and so to the Clyde by the Mull of Kintyre, *Olandsund IV* arriving at Hunter's Quay in March, 1973. Her sister was further delayed at Inverness by the temporary closure of the Caledonian Canal till April: she called at Kennacraig the following month and berthed at Kilmun. They were overhauled by Scott-Lithgow, Ltd. in their Cartsburn yard and dry-docked in the Garvel Graving Dock, Greenock. They emerged re-named respectively as above. *Sound of Shuna*, after trials in April, 1973 and tests of the link-spans in May, opened the service between McInroy's point and Hunter's Quay on Sunday, 3rd June, 1973, being joined by her sister on 14th July. A half-hourly service was then given, fares being competitive with those on the Gourock–Dunoon route. The new route was at first advertised as "Clyde Cross", but has since become known as the Clyde–Argyll ferry. A dolphin structure protected the link-span on the Renfrewshire coast, as did Hunter's Quay Pier on the north side, Kilmun being used for any spare vessel. The McInroy's Point span was wrecked by a severe gale on 27th September, 1973, and the service was suspended for nearly two weeks. In November, indication was given of inaugurating a service from McInroy's Point to Rothesay, but weather prevented the transfer of a link-span from Kennacraig to Rothesay. During overhaul in March, 1974 the red of the hull on *Sound of Scarba* was extended to the top of the bulwarks of the car-deck, making a useful distinguishing mark from the *Sound of Shuna*. The latter, on

Sunday, 18th July, 1976, went to Rothesay to take passengers from the disabled *Highland Seabird* to Dunoon and Greenock. She was also able to take passengers to Dunoon Pier from the *Waverley* when the latter grounded on the Gantocks on 1st July, 1977. The superstructure of *Sound of Shuna* was raised in 1982 to give greater headroom for vehicles.

D.S.M.V. *Sound of Sanda*. To provide a relief and extra vessel for the Clyde–Argyll route, the Company purchased the former Southern Railway Lymington–Yarmouth vehicle ferry *Lymington*, built by Wm. Denny & Bros., Ltd. at Dumbarton in 1938, one of the first in Britain with Voith-Schneider propulsion. After being berthed at Kilmun Pier for a time in April, 1974, she was overhauled and drydocked at Greenock, during which much replating was done and her life-boat superseded by two liferafts. She took up service in August. In common with the other members of this fleet, she has the name across the front of the bridge, in Scandinavian style, and carries the Company's colours—poppy-red hull, white superstructure, dark blue funnels, which in her case bear the emblem of a red circle with tangential lines above and below in opposite directions, ending each in an arrowhead, representing "roll-on, roll-off". On 1st May, 1988 she celebrated the 50th anniversary of entering service.

T.S.M.V. *Highland Seabird*. In April, 1976 the company indicated that it hoped to introduce a catamaran, which it was believed scored over other advanced craft, such as hydrofoils and hovercraft, for their reliability in heavy seas and ability to use existing piers. The twin-hulled vessel (the first in the Clyde service since the *Alliance* of 1857) was of welded aluminium construction and had a comfortable full-width carpeted lounge seating 160, with access to the open deck aft. Equipment included VHF and radio telephone, two radars, echo-sounders and gyro-compass, and a loud speaker system. She had a Class IIA passenger certificate for short international journeys. She had thus much more sophisticated equipment than indicated when the Company began. Chartered for a five-month proving period, she was based initially at Rothesay, operating to Dunoon, Helensburgh and Greenock (Customhouse Quay), intending to visit Glasgow Broomielaw at week-ends, and on Sundays, cruising as far as Tarbert Loch Fyne, this sometimes becoming a Round Bute cruise. The up-river trips were soon abandoned on account of the potential danger from floating timber. Before entering regular service she broke the Glasgow–Dunoon record time of 49 minutes by rail and steamer, set up by the *Duchess of Fife* over 50 years earlier, by establishing the new record of 42 minutes 38 seconds. By regular services connecting with trains at Greenock Central, the journeys from Dunoon and Rothesay to Glasgow could be completed in one and one-and-a-half hours respectively. In October, 1976, she was chartered by the Highlands & Islands Development board to visit various ports, giving short runs at each. Setting out from Greenock, she called at Brodick and Campbeltown, then round the Mull of Kintyre to Port Askaig, Colonsay and Oban, Fort William, Tobermory, Tarbert-Harris and Portree. Although more than 60,000 passengers were carried during the season, overhead expenses made the service uneconomic; and it had been the intention of the Norwegian owners to sell the craft to French owners for the Cartaret–Channel Islands run in the 1977 season. That, however, fell through, and Western Ferries were given the option to retain her for the ensuing year. After talks with the H.I.D.B. it was arranged that the *Highland Seabird* would be based at Oban: she would cruise on various West Highland routes, including that to Fort William (which had last had a steamer service, by *King George V*, in 1974), Tobermory, Iona and Crinan. The last-named had not had regular passenger steamer calls since the withdrawal of the through "Royal Route" service by the Crinan Canal at the end of the 1928 season. From October, 1977 to May, 1978 she was chartered to Howard Doris, Ltd., to convey workers to the oil platform then under construction at Loch Kishorn, being based at Strome Ferry. As a result of a successful year, Western Ferries were able, in October, 1977, to purchase the vessel outright. For the 1978 summer season the *Highland Seabird* added a long-distance excursion on Saturday and Sunday from Oban to Moville and Portrush, with coach connexions by Highland Omnibuses from Inverness and Fort William to Oban and from Portrush *via* Coleraine to Belfast and rail to Dublin; also from Oban to Cairnryan for the Townsend-Thoresen sailing to Larne, and vice versa. From 1979 she could call at certain states of the tide at the new jetty at Iona, and so avoid the necessity of being tendered to by the MacBrayne red boats or the *Morvern*. A public excursion from Campbeltown to Ayr was given on 18th September, 1978. During 1978 she made connexion to Iona and Staffa also *via* Criagnure and bus through Mull, and with landing at Staffa (weather permitting) by the dinghies of Staffa Marine. The Irish services were in 1979 restricted to Sundays only, and were not resumed in 1980; but in the latter year an interesting occurrence in the spring was the charter of the *Highland Seabird* by Sealink (U.K.), Ltd. for the Portsmouth–Ryde passenger service, following which Western Ferries operated a few cruises in the neighbourhood of the Isle of Wight.

After a period laid up on the ferry slipway at Old Kilpatrick, and later at Renfrew, the *Highland Seabird* was sold in March, 1985 to French owners; and so ended the experiment of using a catamaran in Clyde and West Highland waters.

P.M.V. *Farringford.* One of the few Diesel electric paddleships, this one was built for the Lymington–Yarmouth service of British Railways (Southern Region), by Messrs. Denny at Dumbarton. Used latterly on the Hull–New Holland crossing by British Railways (Eastern Region), she was purchased by Western Ferries for the McInroy's Point to Hunter's Quay service. She was not used by her new owners, but was scrapped in 1984.

D.S.M.V. *Sound of Seil.* Yet another former member of the Lymington fleet—*Freshwater*—was purchased and, re-named as above, after overhaul at Renfrew, entered service between McInroy's Point and Hunter's Quay in June, 1986, being employed along with *Sound of Shuna* on the principal rosters. Her design was a development from that of *Lymington*.

D.S.M.V. *Sound of Sleat.* For their next acquisition the Company went to Holland, purchasing the ferry vessel *De Hoorn*, previously engaged in service across the Maas, till superseded on the completion of a tunnel. This ship, capable of carrying 30 cars or equivalent, and with a speed of about 11 knots entered service at McInroy's Point in October, 1988, sharing the principal duties with *Sound of Shuna* and *Sound of Seil*. The other two ships are mainly engaged in charter work.

CHAPTER XVII

WAVERLEY STEAM NAVIGATION CO. LTD.
AND ASSOCIATES

P.S. *Waverley.* When it became known that the *Waverley* was to be withdrawn by Caledonian MacBrayne, Ltd. after the 1973 season, largely on account of the considerable expenditure then required on boiler re-tubing, the Paddle Steamer Preservation Society launched a campaign to save the ship, which was given to them for a nominal sum. Due to the great efforts of the members of the Society, including in particular Messrs. Terry Sylvester, Douglas McGowan, Peter Reid and George Train, it was found possible to raise funds and get assistance from many firms who supplied goods and services free or at nominal prices, so that after a year she was again operational. She was handed over to a limited company named as above and after considerable work had been done by voluntary effort and otherwise, she was able to have an inaugural voyage on 22nd May, 1975, followed by her first public sailing under her new owners on Saturday, 24th May, from Anderston Quay to Dunoon, Gourock, Tarbert and Ardrishaig. The funnel colours of the North British/London & North Eastern Railway—red with white band and black top—were restored and adopted by this Company, her saloons and deck shelters being white and paddle-boxes black with white panelling. Her master is Captain David Neill, who had had a boyhood's ambition to command a paddle steamer. During that summer the ship visited many Clyde coast piers, including Inveraray, Stranraer, Girvan, Campbeltown, but had some difficulties with the boiler, and with paddle floats. These troubles, however, were largely overcome by the next year. Subsidies were given by various local authorities and other public bodies, but in 1976 Strathclyde Regional Council decided to give their whole available subsidy to Caledonian MacBrayne, Ltd. for the *Queen Mary II* and *Maid of the Loch*; and sailings from Glasgow at week-ends were resumed in competition with those of *Waverley*. In June, 1976, inflatable dinghies were substituted for her port aft lifeboat, increasing her passenger complement. Her inaugural cruises in 1976 included calls at Blairmore, Kilmun, Millport and Ardrossan. 1977 was the first year in which the *Waverley* ventured beyond the Firth, spending some time in the spring on the Mersey, cruising from Liverpool to

various points, including calls at Llandudno, Fleetwood, etc.,
returning to the Clyde and making the first call by a Clyde
passenger steamer at Cairnryan, and reviving calls at Helensburgh.
In July, 1977 she was stranded on the Gantocks, but fortunately
without permanent damage. While she was absent for repairs, the
company chartered the *Queen of Scots* which, though much slower,
was able to carry out a modified cruise programme, bearing the
Company's funnel colours, till the return of the *Waverley* in
September. After appearing on the Clyde in the spring of 1978, the
Waverley went off south to visit or cruise from Newhaven,
Eastbourne, Hastings, Bournemouth, Southampton, Sandown and
Ryde; also Thames ports, including Tower Pier, London, Green-
wich and Clacton. Back on the Clyde the *Waverley* was one of the
ships which in 1978, staged a *Columba* Centenary Excursion,
leaving Glasgow (Stobcross Quay) at 7.11 a.m. on 24th June for
Ardrishaig, from which on the return trip to Tarbert she attempted
to beat the *Columba*'s best time. This she achieved, but from her
position with bow facing outwards, whereas the *Columba* berthed
bow-in. The *Waverley* made her first visit to Irvine on 22nd August,
1978, being the first Clyde steamer to carry passengers there since
about the 1880s. She was given the assistance of the tug *Garnock*.
In September, 1978, *Waverley* landed passengers at the old stone
pier at Lamlash by ferry, and the following spring she was again in
England and Wales, making many new calls, including Rochester,
Southend, Deal, Torquay, Plymouth, Weymouth, Avonmouth,
Ilfracombe, Barry, Penarth, and taking some stranded passengers
from Lundy. Regular calls were resumed at Helensburgh on
Saturdays. In 1979 her saloon entrances were re-modelled to help
to reduce congestion when crowded; and in September that year she
made another first call, at Ardyne, followed by a cruise up Loch
Striven, on charter to the P.S.P.S. The spring of 1980 found the
Waverley again in the South and Bristol Channel. After a season of
very bad weather on the Clyde, during which among other
interesting occasions she celebrated the centenary of the *Ivanhoe* by
sailing approximately on her route from Helensburgh to Arran, *via*
the Kyles, with bars closed in memory of the original temperance
principles and with, among the passengers, Mrs. Christopher
Jennings, a grand-daughter of Mr. Alexander Allan, one of the
promotors of the original *Ivanhoe* company, along with her
husband. An exhibition was mounted in the saloon, including the
bell of the *Ivanhoe* (lent by the Clyde River Steamer Club), models
and photographs. A new boiler was installed in the *Waverley* in the
spring of 1981, which has given greater economy in fuel consumption and greater reliability. She has continued to visit new ports,
including Garliestown, Douglas I.O.M., Dublin, Cork, et cetera, as

well as revisiting her old haunts: also each spring she has been at Oban for cruises to Fort William, Iona and round Staffa. In August, 1987 she had boiler trouble and was withdrawn, but was back as usual in 1988, and extended her operations to include Portree, Kyle of Lochalsh, Mallaig, Armadale and in 1989 Stornoway, Tarbert Harris and Lochmaddy.

T.S.M.V. _Shanklin/Prince Ivanhoe._ This former Southern Railway vessel, built at Dumbarton for the Portsmouth–Ryde route and excursions in the Isle of Wight area, sailed up the Clyde on 21st November, 1980 to the Waverley Terminal at Stobcross, having been bought by a consortium to co-operate with the _Waverley_, and to endeavour to provide funds to keep that ship running. With a large capacity—1000 passengers—and spacious saloons, this was a worthy addition to the Clyde passenger fleet; and the choice of a name to commemorate the _Ivanhoe_ in her centenary year was most appropriate, though it is unfortunate that, to avoid duplication of names on the British register, it was varied to _Prince Ivanhoe_.

The name of the owning company was changed to Firth of Clyde Steam Packet Company Limited, and the house-flag of the 1911 company of that name was re-introduced. After a visit to the Bristol Channel in the early part of 1981, the _Prince Ivanhoe_ performed some cruises on the Firth of Clyde, calling at most of the piers that could still be used, and seemed likely to have a successful career. Later that year, however, while engaged in cruising off the Gower Coast she struck a submerged object and had to be beached to avoid sinking. All the passengers and crew were successfully landed by boats, but the ship was found to be so badly damaged that she was abandoned, and the subsequent storms completed the breaking up of the vessel.

T.S.M.V. _Balmoral._ After a few years a successor to the _Prince Ivanhoe_ was found on the purchase of the former Southampton–Isle of Wight vessel _Balmoral_, dating from 1947 and so a contemporary of the _Waverley_. She had been built as a successor to the Southampton Company's famous paddle steamer _Balmoral_ of 1900, and in fact was, during construction, stated to be a rebuild of that ship, though this was not so: she was then completely new. A twin screw motor vessel, she was designed for passenger and vehicle traffic between Southampton and Cowes following the general design developed from _Medina_ of 1931 through _Vecta_ of 1938, having a car deck (open) at the stern. After various charters and changes of location she had become a floating restaurant at Dundee, moored at Craig Pier, scene of the operations of the Tay ferries until the opening of the Tay Road Bridge. After a time she had closed to the public, and, having been bought to act as a consort to the *Waverley*, she was taken into dry dock at Dundee and prepared for her voyage to the Clyde, which she performed under her own power under the command of Captain David Neill. After overhaul by Clyde Dock Engineering Ltd. at Govan, she joined the *Waverley* at Anderston Quay, but was not ready to sail; at Easter. Instead she proceeded to the Bristol Channel for the summer of 1986, but appeared on the Clyde in time for the Autumn Holiday sailing on the Saturday from Glasgow to Greenock, Helensburgh, Dunoon and Largs for a cruise to Millport for the Illuminations, still held on the last Saturday of September. On the Monday she performed a cruise Round Bute, then spent the winter at Anderston Quay. In the autumn of 1987 she performed similarly, then in 1988 visited new places, including Dundee, Perth, Arbroath and Montrose; also Inverness, Invergordon, Dornoch Firth, et cetera, followed by cruises in Northern Ireland and on the Clyde at the autumn holiday week-end. She is owned by Helseam Ltd.

T.S.M.V. *Southsea*. During the absence of *Waverley* this near-sister of the *Shanklin* was chartered from Sealink in September, 1987, performing many of the usual sailings including Round Bute; Glasgow–Helensburgh–Largs; Rothesay–Tighna-bruaich–Tarbert Lochfyne; Largs–Brodick. At the end of the charter *Southsea* returned to Portsmouth and next year performed cruises for her owners in the Isle of Wight area in addition to supplementing the catamaran service between Portsmouth and Ryde. She was laid up during the 1989 season.

GENERAL REMARKS

IN bringing our little history to a close, it is not inappropriate to draw our readers' attention to a few points of general interest pertaining to the subject.

In the spacious Victorian days, and for a number of years thereafter, even the casual observer could not fail to be impressed by the marked superiority of the Clyde's fleet of pleasure steamers compared with those of any other part of the United Kingdom. Things later became different, as there had been a steady levelling-up process at work for some years past; with the result that, apart from the number of ships employed, it was almost invidious to make any definite statement on the relative merits of the different areas throughout the Kingdom; and more recently services have dwindled to a greater extent in other areas. The growth of ownership of private motor cars has considerable bearing on this.

Reverting to the Clyde, it is interesting to note that (speaking generally) the tendency has been to lower the designed speeds of new vessels. The reason no doubt is simply an economic one, as experience in the past must have shown that the higher speeds, while technically perfectly feasible and safe, were too costly in proportion to the return. There has, too, been an encouragement to work on these lines by the reduction of competition—for the most part wholly wasteful—and the gradual fusion of private interests with the larger public companies and nationalised concerns. This tendency has also affected the number of vessels employed, one in many cases now performing the work done by two or three in pre-1914 days. From the passenger's point of view, these processes may not be all to the good; but today the primary consideration is to endeavour to run and maintain services that will at least cover their cost of operation, which in many cases is not now possible.

It is a significant fact that with the passing of the years the character of the ownership of many of the steamers has changed in a marked degree. Beginning with the private owner, who might or might not have commanded the vessel himself, one passes through the stages of private company-owned ships to that of the old Scottish Railway Companies' ownership; then to the railway grouping regime and thereafter to British Railways Board; and finally to the Scottish Transport Group, which controlled various omnibus operators but was independent of the Railways. From an essentially local and personal control the point was reached where the ultimate control was in London, distant and impersonal, though now in Edinburgh. Local management there is, of course, but financial control is ultimately with the Treasury. The enormous cost of new ships makes it imperative to utilise them to the full, with little time out of service.

Privatisation of the bus companies has taken place, and some form of this is envisaged in the long term for nationalised shipping. A resurgence of private ownership has occurred, with Western Ferries and the *Waverley* associates, the latter of which have as their object preservation rather than running an economic service.

It is right that the record of immunity from accident should again be applauded. A moment's thought of the numbers transported by the steamers and the corresponding fatalities (if any) compared with our road records is too obvious for comment. The worst enemy is fog; and a few minor collisions have occurred from this cause, fortunately without loss of life, but radar and other navigational devices have minimised the risks.

Few, if any, of the newer ships compare favourably in looks with their older colleagues, but their greater covered accommodation is much better from the passenger's point of view. A reason for the addition of a top-deck is to be found in the requirements of the later Department of Trade regulations as to the provisions of bulkheads, the presence of which make it impossible to have a large dining-saloon on the lower deck, as was formerly the usual practice. The dining-saloon in most of the later vessels was accordingly, situated on the main deck, so that additional accommodation on the promenade deck is required. For reasons of economy cafeterias have been adopted in most cases instead of the splendid dining saloons of former days.

The integration of two classes has resulted in accommodation much superior to that of the old steerage, but not with the appointments found in the first-class of the better steamers built before 1914, although the most recent major members of the car-carrying fleet show a marked improvement over their recent predecessors.

The steam engine, whether reciprocating or rotary, for long reigned supreme, the most notable departures from steam practice being the Diesel electric *Lochfyne, Lochnevis* and *Talisman*; and all the car ferries are propelled by internal combustion machinery. The oscillating engine vanished from the Clyde in 1936 with the departure of *Iona* and *Columba*.

Paddle design tended towards smaller wheels (to increase passenger and deck space) and hence relatively fast-running engines of light construction. This reduced the initial outlay, but resulted in higher upkeep costs. Three cranks came into favour, and are superior to two in most respects. The diagonal engine is represented now by the *Waverley* and *Maid of the Loch*.

Regarding turbine practice, the tendency was to revert to the triple-shaft direct drive, which arrangement was characteristic of the pioneer vessel *King Edward* and all the earlier cross-channel steamers with turbine machinery. The probability is that experience showed that the possible higher initial cost and weight of the geared installation was not offset by a corresponding economy of operation on the short runs, which are an inherent feature of Clyde passenger steamer operation. There are probably other considerations—possibly noise is one—which may have influenced owners in coming to this decision. No turbine ship has been built for Clyde service since 1936 and it is most unlikely that any will be. *Queen Mary* (non-operational) is the sole surviving representative of the Clyde turbine passenger steamer.

One reviewer of our book, *West Highland Steamers*, rightly drew attention to our omission of the fact that no turbine-driven ship had appeared in the MacBrayne fleet until the end of 1935. Actually at the time of writing and after publication of the first edition the transfer of *Queen Alexandra* and *King George V* had not taken place and the long careers of *Iona* and *Columba* had rendered such an acquisition unnecessary earlier. There had never been on the Clyde a passenger steamer with twin-screw steam reciprocating engines of such a type as bridged the gap for a number of years between the paddle and turbine-driven steamers in most cross-channel fleets, and of which a representative appeared on the Firth of Forth for a short time in pre-war days—*Roslin Castle* of the Galloway fleet; but during the 1947 season the *Robina* provided an example of this type on the Clyde. The single-screw passenger ship with reciprocating steam engine is represented by *Sir Walter Scott*, now a nonagenarian.

It is difficult to appreciate the vogue of twin-funnelled steamers with both "lums" forward of the paddle boxes other than the economic aspect already mentioned in connexion with *Columba*. There seems to be a lack of balance in the profile which is not pleasing to the eye. Examples of this from earlier times were *Eagle* (1864), *Brodick Castle* (1878), *Benmore* for a time and *Meg Merrilies* (1883) as built, while modern examples are *Jeanie Deans* (1931), *Jupiter* and *Juno* (1937), and *Waverley* (1947).

The cruiser stern has become fashionable and possess desirable utilitarian features, but aesthetically it can be regarded as nothing but a retrograde step. These, however, are really all matters of individual taste.

From time to time shiplovers write to the papers referring to the majestic spectacle of the large steam marine oscillating and reciprocating engines. These people go so far as to suggest that a complete engine-room should be preserved in one of our science museums, so arranged that the main engines can be put in motion. No doubt many readers would delight in such an exhibit, though with generally apathetic attitude displayed it is unlikely that such a scheme will ever materialise, in spite of the fact that our country led the world for years in the design and construction of marine machinery. One turbine of the *King Edward* was preserved (as a static exhibit) in the Kelvingrove Museum.

Certainly the large marine reciprocating engine—whether paddle or screw—is the steam engine in its noblest form and a magnificent sight to watch. The turbine and internal combustion engine can never make the same appeal, much as we appreciate the technical excellence of their principles of working and design. Fortunately it is still possible to enjoy the spectacle of a triple expansion diagonal engine in operation on the *Waverley*.

What has been written above regarding the Clyde steamers applies more or less to the other vessels dealt with in this book also; though few changes of note have taken place among them in recent years—the most striking difference being the cutting down of the services on the Scottish inland waters. To this many factors have contributed, chief among them being the coming of the motor-car and motor omnibus, and improvements in roads, which have given people other means of seeing the countryside, and have rendered obsolete most ships not specially adapted for the transport of vehicles.

Excursion services have been continued on Loch Lomond, Loch Katrine and Loch Etive and revived on Loch Awe and the Forth & Clyde and Caledonian Canals.

When the previous editions of this book were written, we doubted whether the new ships would endear themselves to the public at large in the way the old ones did, and have "lives" of 40-50 years. The younger generation had its mind so largely diverted towards the automobile and aeroplane that the same degree of early concentration on the ship could scarcely have been expected. The interest taken in steamers in Glasgow and the West of Scotland, however, is still great; and as the number of steamers on the Firth of Clyde declined, so did the interest increase; and the Clyde River Steamer Club, "launched" in 1932, now has a membership of over 600. Our question posed in 1937 is to a certain extent answered. The ships *have* endeared themselves, almost as the old ones did, and have had quite long careers, though none of the larger motorships has yet reached 40 years, the *Lochfyne* having been withdrawn just short of this. The *Sound of Sanda* ex *Lymington* has, however, reached her jubilee.

65.   Tr.S.S. "DUCHESS OF MONTROSE" (II) leaving Gourock:
T.S.M.V. "LOCHNEVIS" at the Pier   *G.E.L.*

66.   Tr.S.S. "DUCHESS OF HAMILTON" (II)
arriving at Largs, 12/6/67   *G.E.L.*

67.   P.S. "CALEDONIA" (II) leaving Tighnabruaich, 7/6/69

G.E.L.

68.   Tr.S.S. "QUEEN MARY" off Craigmore, 22/8/77

G.E.L.

69.   T.S.M.V. "COUNTESS OF BREADALBANE" (II) at Carrick Castle, 25/5/63

G.E.L.

70.   T.S.S. "MARCHIONESS OF GRAHAM" leaving Brodick

N. Shields

71.   P.S. "JUNO" (II) in Kyles of Bute, 5/1939

W. Forrester

72.   T.S.S. "KING GEORGE V" at Inveraray, 19/5/73

G.E.L.

73.   P.S. "WAVERLEY" (III) leaving Dunoon c. 1936

W. Forrester

74.   P.S. "JEANIE DEANS" (II) approaching Dunoon, 1935

per Phil. N. Thomas

75.   P.S. "PRINCE EDWARD" at Ardlui, c. 1947

D. Syme

76.   P.S. "MAID OF THE LOCH" at Rowardennan, 20/6/75

G.E.L.

77.   P.S. "MAID OF THE LOCH"
       approaching Rowardennan, 17/6/78   *G.E.L.*

G.E.L.

78.   T.S.M.Vs. "PORTREE" (II) and "BROADFORD" (II) at Colintraive, 31/5/86

79.   T.S.M.V. "MAID OF ASHTON" at Ardrishaig, 10/6/70

J. Aikman Smith

80.   T.S.M.V. "MAID OF CUMBRAE" leaving Gourock, 19/8/74

G.E.L.

81.　　　　T.S.M.V. "COWAL" (II) at Rothesay Pier, 17/8/74

82.　　　　T.S.M.V. "ARRAN" (V) arriving at Kilcreggan, 31/10/76

83.   T.S.M.V. "GLEN SANNOX" with Buachaille Fhinn
       in background, from Craigmore, 4/8/76   *G.E.L.*

84.   M.V. "KEPPEL" leaving Dunoon, 9/8/86

                                                      G.E.L.

T.S.M.V. "CALEDONIA" (III) entering Troon Harbour, 16/2/87

G.E.L.

85.

86.   T.S.M.V. "CLANSMAN" (IV) arriving at Brodick, 19/8/76

G.E.L.

87.   T.S.M.V. "LOCHFYNE" arriving at Innellan, 9/1969

J. Aikman Smith

G.E.L.

Tr.S.S. "SAINT COLUMBA" leaving Tarbert

88.

89.   T.S.M.V. "IONA" (VII) leaving Dunoon, 8/12/73

90.   T.S.M.V. "KILBRANNAN" leaving Lochranza, 15/7/72

91.   T.S.M.V. "RHUM" approaching Lochranza, 29/8/85

G.E.L.

92.   D.S.M.V. "SATURN" arriving at Wemyss Bay, 2/1/85

G.E.L.

93.

D.S.M.V. "JUPITER" (III) swinging, to back into Wemyss Bay, 11/11/81

G.E.L.

94.   D.S.M.V. "JUNO" (III) off Gourock, 9/1/85

G.E.L.

95.   D.S.M.V. "ISLE OF CUMBRAE" (II) leaving Largs, 4/6/77

G.E.L.

96. T.S.M.V. "ISLE OF ARRAN" (III)
arriving at Brodick, 23/9/87 *G.E.L.*

97. D.S.M.V. "LOCH STRIVEN" arriving at Largs, 28/10/87

G.E.L.

98.   D.S.M.V. "LOCH RANZA" arriving at Lochranza

G.E.L.

99.   T.S.M.V. "AILSA PRINCESS"
          backing out from Stranraer, 18/2/78   *G.E.L.*

100.   T.S.M.V. "GALLOWAY PRINCESS"
         arriving at Stranraer, 28/4/80   *G.E.L.*

101.   P.S. "WAVERLEY" at side berth, Helensburgh, 27/8/88

                                                G.E.L.

T.S.M.V. "QUEEN OF SCOTS" leaving Rothesay, 22/8/77

G.E.L.

102.

103.   T.S.M.V. "PRINCE IVANHOE" leaving Rothesay, 20/6/81

G.E.L.

104.   T.S.M.V. "SOUTHSEA"
        leaving Tarbert for cruise in Loch Fyne, 15/9/87   *G.E.L.*

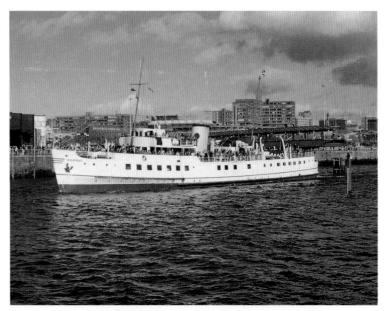

105.   T.S.M.V. "BALMORAL" having passed through Bell's Bridge
at Glasgow Garden Festival, leaving for Rothesay, 24/9/88   *G.E.L.*

106.   S.S. "LADY ROWENA" approaching Loch Awe Pier, 17/9/86

G.E.L.

T.S.M.V. "COUNTESS FIONA" leaving Luss, 26/7/86

G.E.L.

107.

108.   M.V. "ANNE OF ETIVE"
arriving at Taynuilt (Bonawe Ferry slip), 16/6/84   *G.E.L.*

109.   D.S.M.V. "SOUND OF SHUNA"
arriving at McInroy's Point, 17/9/88   *G.E.L.*

110.   D.S.M.V. "SOUND OF SEIL"
              arriving at McInroy's Point, 17/9/88   *G.E.L.*

111.   T.S.M.V. "HIGHLAND SEABIRD" off Craigmore, 4/8/76

                                                                     G.E.L.

112.   T.S.M.V. "THE SECOND SNARK"
at Tighnabruaich Pier, side berth, 15/8/84   *G.E.L.*

113.   T.S.M.V. "KENILWORTH" (II) arriving at Kilcreggan, 18/7/79

G.E.L.

114.   M.V. "ROBERT THE BRUCE" arriving at Central Station landing stage, Glasgow, 29/4/88

G.E.L.

115.   D.S.M.V. "FERRY QUEEN" ex "FERRY No. 8"
at The Stables, Glasgow Road Bridge, Kirkintilloch,
with M.V. "CALEDONIAN" ex "FERRY No. 10" beyond   *G.E.L.*

116.   T.S.M.V. "RENFREW ROSE" approaching Yoker, 20/7/84

G.E.L.

117.   T.S.M.V. "COLUMBA" (II) at Tarbert, Lochfyne, 2/4/88

G.E.L.

118.   T.S.M.V. "LORD OF THE ISLES" (III)
arriving at Tiree, 12/9/89

119.　　　　T.S.M.V. "PIONEER" at Kilcreggan, 21/10/79

120.　　　　D.S.M.V. "SOUND OF SLEAT"
leaving McInroy's Point 15/10/88

Latterly even the "Maids" were being regarded as uneconomic and it seemed that the Clyde and West Highland vessels of the future would be smaller car-ferries operating on the shortest practicable sea crossings, on the lines of the Norwegian ships as exemplified by Western Ferries' *Sound of Jura*, which successfully operated between Kennacraig (West Loch Tarbert) and Port Askaig (Islay), with still smaller vessels for feeder services and shorter crossings, such as the *Kyleakin* at Kyle of Lochalsh. The new "Loch" class with decks enclosed by ramps at each end have proved very useful not only at Rhubodach and Cumbrae but also at Lochranza–Claonaig and even larger vehicle-carriers have in recent years been built for the more exposed routes, the *Isle of Arran* at 3,296 tons gross being the largest so far engaged on any of the Firth of Clyde services. Hovercraft have been used experimentally on the Firth of Clyde, but so far have not proved capable of succeeding conventional ships on the regular runs. A catamaran operated successfully for a time, but was not economic.

The reduction in packet services has resulted in the use of the description "ferry" for Clyde and West Highland ships, and even for those on cross-channel routes. This does not please the traditionalists in the west of Scotland, where the term formerly was applied only to the cross-river and harbour ferries, and to small boats tendering to steamers at places which were without adequate piers. The *Maid of the Loch* on Loch Lomond was for a time shown in Lloyd's Register as a "ferry", even though the service on that loch calling at the various piers on both sides was typical of a packet route.

APPENDIX 1

FLEET LISTS

THE CALEDONIAN STEAM PACKET CO. LTD. 1888–1922

Dates Built Acqd. Displ.	Name	Type	Shipbuilders and Enginebuilders
1883 1888 7/1902	MEG MERRILIES	Iron P.S.	Barclay, Curle & Co. (1) Barclay, Curle & Co. (2) A. & J. Inglis
1886 1888 4/1911	MADGE WILDFIRE	Steel P.S.	S. McKnight & Co., Ayr (1) Hutson & Corbett (2) Rankin & Blackmore
17/5/89 1889 12/1933	CALEDONIA (I)	Steel P.S.	J. Reid & Co., Pt. Glasgow Rankin & Blackmore
1889 1889 1906	GALATEA	Steel P.S.	Caird & Co., Ltd.
15/4/90 1890 1935	MARCHIONESS OF BREADALBANE	Steel P.S.	J. Reid & Co. Rankin & Blackmore
1890 1890 4/1908	MARCHIONESS OF BUTE	Steel P.S.	J. Reid & Co. Rankin & Blackmore
1890 1890 29/11/15	DUCHESS OF HAMILTON (I)	Steel P.S.	W. Denny & Bros. Denny & Co.
27/4/91 1891 12/1923	MARCHIONESS OF LORNE (I)	Steel P.S.	Russel & Co. Rankin & Blackmore
20/4/95 1895 9/8/46	DUCHESS OF ROTHESAY	Steel P.S.	J. & G. Thomson, Ltd., Clydebank

THE FRITH OF CLYDE S.P. CO. LTD. 1880–5/1897

(Taken over by The Caledonian S.P. Co. Ltd.)

Dates Built Acqd. Displ.	Name	Type	Shipbuilders and Enginebuilders
1880 1880 2/1911	IVANHOE	Iron P.S.	D. & W. Henderson & Co.

	B.	D.	G.T.	N.H.P.	Machinery	Remarks
3′	21·4′	7·2′	244 279	205 220 81 R.H.P.	(1) S.D. 2-cyls. 43″ × 60″ (2) C.D. 2-cyls. 24″ & 43″ × 60″	N.B. 1888; 1893; made 1891, fitted 1897; 1898 and 1900 Cpd. 1898
0′	20·0′	7·1′	220	95 155	(1) D. 1-cyl. 49″ × 60″ (2) C.D. 2-cyls., (1 cr.) 27″ & 49″ × 60″	N.B. 1891 and 1903 Cpd. 1891
4′	22·0′	7·5′	244	188	C.D. 2-cyls. (1 cr.) 30″ & 54″ × 60″	N.B. 1903
1′	25·1′	7·8′	331	290	C.D. 2-cyls. 34″ & 64″ × 72″	
4′	22·1′	7·5′	246 338	188	C.D. 2-cyls. (1 cr.) 30″ & 54″ × 60″	N.B. 1901
4′	22·1′	7·5′	246	188	C.D. 2-cyls. (1 cr.) 30″ & 54″ × 60″	N.B. 1901
0′	30·1′	10·1′	553	266 233	C.D. 2-cyls. 34½″ & 60″ × 60″	N.B. 1906
0′	24·0′	8·3′	295	186	T.D. 4-cyls. (2 cr.) (2)17½″, 30″ & 49″ × 60″	N.B. 1897
′	26·1′	8·6′	338	206	C.D. 2-cyls. 27½″ & 58″ × 54″	N.B. 1914
′	22·2′	8·3′	282	231	S.D. O. 2-cyls. (1 cr.) 43″ × 66″	N.B. 1892 Also on charter 1915-20

THE CALEDONIAN STEAM PACKET CO. LTD.—(cont.)

Dates Built Acqd. Displ.	Name	Type	Shipbuilders and Enginebuilders
1902 1902 18/3/17	DUCHESS OF MONTROSE (I)	Steel P.S.	J. Brown & Co., Ltd.
9/5/03 1903 12/9/53	DUCHESS OF FIFE	Steel P.S.	Fairfield S.B. & E. Co., Ltd.
1906 1906 25/2/52	DUCHESS OF ARGYLL	Steel Tr.S.S.	Wm. Denny & Bros. Denny & Co.
1882 1922 1936	COUNTESS OF BREADALBANE (I)	Steel S.S.	Hanna & Donald, Paisley Hawthorns & Co., Leith

LOCH TAY STEAM BOAT COMPANY, LTD.

(Taken over by The Caledonian S.P. Co., Ltd. 1922)

Dates Built Acqd. Displ.	Name	Type	Shipbuilders and Enginebuilders
1882 1882 1929	LADY OF THE LAKE	Iron S.S.	Anderson & Lyall, Govan, at Kenmore D. Rowan & Son
1882 1882 1929	SYBILLA	Wood S.S.	D. Fenton, Perth, at Kenmore D. Rowan & Son
1882 1882 1907	MAGPIE	Wood S.S.	
9/6/83 1883 1923	CARLOTTA	Wood S.S.	A. G. Gifford & Co., Leith, at Acharn Ross & Duncan, Govan
19/6/07 1907 17/5/50	QUEEN OF THE LAKE	Steel T.S.S.	Ailsa Shipbuilding Co., Ltd. Ayr, at Kenmore

..	B.	D.	G.T.	N.H.P.	Machinery	Remarks
)·0′	25·1′	8·7′	321 399	206	T.D. 4-cyls. (2 cr.) (2) 16¾″, 35½″ & 53″ × 54″	
·3′	25·0′	8·5′	336 329	199	T.D. 4-cyls. (2 cr.) (2) 16½″, 35″ & 52″ × 54″	N.B. 1928
·0′	30·1′	10·1′	593	399 R.H.P.	3 steam turbines D.D.	
·9′	14·0′	7·0′	95	30 25	T. 3-cyls. 8¾″ 14½″ & 22″ × 15″	On Loch Awe N.E. 1898
·5′	12·8′	7·1′	68	21	C. 2-cyls. 12½″ & 22″ × 15″	
·2′	13·3′	6·6′	37	11	(1) S. 2-cyls. (2) C. 2-cyls. 9″ & 16″ × 12″	N.E. 1884
						Lighter
·0′	11·2′	6·8′	22 23	10	C. 2-cyls. 8″ & 15″ × 9″	
·1′	20·1′	9·3′	152	43 R.H.P.	C. 4-cyls. 10½″ & 23″ × 16″	

GLASGOW & SOUTH WESTERN RAILWAY COMPANY 1891-1922

Dates Built Acqd. Displ.	Name	Type	Shipbuilders and Enginebuilders
1861 1891 1893	SULTAN	Iron P.S.	Barclay, Curle & Co. J. Barr
1868 1891 9/3/97	SULTANA	Iron P.S.	Robertson & Co. W. King & Co.
1868 1891 5/1904	MARQUIS OF BUTE	Iron P.S.	Barclay, Curle & Co.
1875 1891 6/1907	VICEROY	Iron P.S.	D. & W. Henderson & Co. Hutson & Corbett
1880 1891 4/1901	CHANCELLOR	Steel P.S.	R. Chambers, Jr., Dumbarton (1) M. Paul, Dumbarton (2) Blackwood & Gordon
1880 1891 4/1893	SCOTIA	Iron P.S.	H. McIntyre & Co., Paisley W. King & Co.
10/3/92 1892 20/4/17	NEPTUNE	Steel P.S.	Napier, Shanks & Bell D. Rowan & Son
1892 1892 1925	GLEN SANNOX (I)	Steel P.S.	J. & G. Thomson, Ltd. Clydebank
1892 1892 12/1933	MERCURY (I)	Steel P.S.	Napier, Shanks & Bell D. Rowan & Son
6/5/93 1893 6/1920	MINERVA	Steel P.S.	J. & G. Thomson, Ltd. Clydebank
1893 1893 8/1939	GLEN ROSA	Steel P.S.	J. & G. Thomson, Ltd. Clydebank

	B.	D.	G.T.	N.H.P.	Machinery	Remarks
-0'	16·6'	7·2'	124	60	St. 1-cyl. 45″ × 42″ Ex "Wellington", b. 1853	N.B. 1877 Len. 1865 Original length 166'
1'	18·3'	7·3'	198 173	136	D. 1-cyl. 49″ × 54″	N.B. 1886
6'	18·1'	7·3'	196	85 R.H.P.	D. 1-cyl. 48″ × 60″	N.B. 1892
9'	20·1'	7·1'	236	99 R.H.P.	D. 1-cyl. (1) 51½″ × 60″ (2) 52″ × 60″	N.B. 1886 N.E. 1888 Len. 3/1891 N.B. 1897
7'	21·1'	8·2'	272	140 199 R.H.P. 149	(1) S.D. 2-cyls. 36″ × 60″ (2) C.D. 2-cyls. 26″ & 48″ × 60″	N.B. 1892 Cpd. 1892
2'	21·8'	8·3'	260	216	St. 2-cyls. 45″ × 48″	N.B. 1892
5'	26·0'	9·2'	378	248	C.D. 2-cyls. 33″ & 62″ × 60″	N.B. 1912
5'	30·1'	10·1'	610	353	C.D. 2-cyls. 34½″ & 74″ × 60″	
5'	26·0'	9·2'	378	248	C.D. 2-cyls. 33″ & 62″ × 60″	N.B. 1914
0'	25·0'	8·3'	306 315	185	C.D. 2-cyls. 26″ & 55″ × 54″	N.B. 1902
0'	25·0'	8·3'	306	185	C.D. 2-cyls. 26″ & 55″ × 54″	N.B. 1926 C.S.P. Co., Ltd. from 1938

GLASGOW & SOUTH WESTERN RAILWAY COMPANY 1891-1922—(contd.)

Dates Built Acqd. Displ.	Name	Type	Shipbuilders and Enginebuilders
1896 1896 12/1935	JUPITER (I)	Steel P.S.	J. & G. Thomson, Ltd. Clydebank
1898 1898 1932	JUNO (I)	Steel P.S.	Clydebank E. & S.B. Co., Ltd.
16/3/02 1902 18/11/17	MARS	Steel P.S.	J. Brown & Co., Ltd.
1902 1902 8/1930	TROON	Iron P.S.	J. P. Rennoldson, S. Shields
1897 1904 4/1908	VULCAN ex Britannia ex Kylemore	Steel P.S.	Russell & Co. Rankin & Blackmore
1906 1906 3/1937	ATALANTA	Steel Tr. S.S.	J. Brown & Co., Ltd.

DUKE OF PORTLAND—TROON HARBOUR—to G. & S.W.R. COMPANY 2/8/1901

Dates Built Acqd. Displ.	Name	Type	Shipbuilders and Enginebuilders
1866 1876 9/12/02	PORTLAND	Iron P.S.	W. Denny & Bros. Denny & Co.
1874 11/1881 12/1881	Reliance	Iron P.S.	
1857 1889 22/12/94	Vigilant	Wood P.S.	S. Shields
1879 31/7/95 9/12/02	TITCHFIELD ex Flying Scotchman	Iron P.S.	J. T. Eltringham J. P. Rennoldson & Sons

L.	B.	D.	G.T.	N.H.P.	Machinery	Remarks
30·5′	28·1′	9·0′	394	273	C.D. 2-cyls. 30½″ & 65″ × 60″	
45·0′	29·1′	9·7′	592	325	C.D. 2-cyls. 33″ & 71″ × 60″	
00·4′	26·1′	8·6′	317	172	C.D. 2-cyls. 28¼″ & 53″ × 54″	
00·0′	19·1′	9·6′	130	70 R.H.P.	L. 2-cyls. 28″ × 50″	Tug
00·5′	24·1′	7·7′	319	93 R.H.P.	C.D. 2-cyls. 23½″ & 47″ × 51″	
0·4′	30·1′	10·3′	486	200	3 Steam turbines D.D.	N.B. 1930
5·4′	19·1′	9·7′	122	80 R.H.P.	L. 2-cyls. 30″ × 48″	Reg. G. & S.W.R. 8/12/02
8·0′	16·2′	9·1′	89	50		
8·8′	18·2′	9·5′	111	70 R.H.P.	L. 1-cyl. 34¹/₈″ × 54″	Reg. G. & S.W.R. 8/12/02

AYR HARBOUR COMMISSIONERS to G. & S.W.R. COMPANY 25/3/1919

Dates Built Acqd. Displ.	Name	Type	Shipbuilders and Enginebuilders
1856 1856 1883	Ayr (I)	Iron P.S.	Glasgow
1878 1878 11/12/90	Ayr (II)	Iron P.S.	J. T. Eltringham, S. Shields J. P. Rennoldson
1885 1885 1/1/1950	KYLE	Iron & Steel T.S.S.	S. McKnight & Co., Ayr
1857 1890 1894	Flying Childers	Wood P.S.	S. Chisholm, N. Shields
1878 1894 1897	Ben Ledi	Iron P.S.	Hall, Russell & Co., Aberdeen
1897 1897 12/1930	AYR (III)	Iron P.S.	J. P. Rennoldson
1911 1911 1/1/50		Wood M.V.	Ayr Harbour Commissioners

HIGHLAND RAILWAY COMPANY (Scrabster Section) 1877-1882
HIGHLAND RAILWAY COMPANY (Strome Ferry Section) 1880-1882
LONDON, MIDLAND & SCOTTISH RAILWAY COMPANY (Kyle Section)

1877 1877 9/1882	JOHN O'GROAT	Iron S.S.	Gourlay Bros., Dundee

DINGWALL & SKYE RAILWAY COMPANY, 1870-1880
(Taken over by H.R. Company, 1880)

1857 5/1870 1871	JURA ex Admiral Cator	Iron S.S.	T. Wingate & Co.,
1850 6/1870 9/1870	OSCAR	Iron S.S.	Dumbarton

L.	B.	D.	G.T.	N.H.P.	Machinery	Remarks
3·4′	15·2′	7·4′	70	40		Tug
6·2′	18·6′	9·7′	111	50	S.L. 2-clys. 26½″ × 48″	Tug
6·0′	30·1′	12·5′	543	90		Bucket dredger
6·9′	17·0′	9·9′	102	40	S.L. 1-cyl.	Tug
0·0′	18·6′	10·2′	114	50	S.L. 2-cyls. 25″ × 48″	Tug
0·0′	19·2′	9·3′	124	50	S.L. 2-cyls. 25″ × 45″	Tug
4·0′	10·0′					Service launch
4·8′	24·8′	12·9′	384	115	C. 2-cyls. 28″, 52″ × 33″	Scabster-Orkney Mail Service
8·3′	22·1′	12·5′	330		S. 2-cyls.	
9·6′	23·2′	13·2′	341	75	S. 2-cyls.	

DINGWALL & SKYE RAILWAY COMPANY, 1870-1880—(cont.)

Dates Built Acqd. Displ.	Name	Type	Shipbuilders and Enginebuilders
1864 9/1872 6/1882	CARHAM	Iron P.S.	A. & J. Inglis, Pointhouse
1871 1873 1880	FERRET	Iron S.S.	J. & G. Thomson, Clydebank

LONDON MIDLAND & SCOTTISH RAILWAY COMPANY AND THE CALEDONIAN

1925 1925 16/7/54	GLEN SANNOX	Steel Tr. S.S.	WM. Denny & Bros., Ltd.
1904 1930 1950	WALNEY	Steel P.S.	J. P. Rennoldson & Co., South Shields
1930 1930 8/1965	DUCHESS OF MONTROSE (II)	Steel Tr.S.S.	Wm. Denny & Bros., Ltd.
1932 1932 12/1971	DUCHESS OF HAMILTON (II)	Steel Tr,S.S.	Harland & Wolff, Ltd., Govan Harland & Wolff, Ltd., Belfast
1933 1933 1/1/50	—	Wood M.V.	
1934 1934 25/12/40	MERCURY (II)	Steel P.S.	Fairfield S.B. & E. Co., Ltd.
1934 1934 1970	CALEDONIA (II)	Steel P.S.	Wm. Denny & Bros., Ltd.
1935 1935 17/2/55	MARCHIONESS OF LORNE (II)	Steel P.S.	Fairfield S.B. & E. Co., Ltd.
1935 1935 3/1953	WEE CUMBRAE	Steel T.S.M.V.	Wm. Denny & Bros., Ltd. Gleniffer Engines, Ltd.

L.	B.	D.	G.T.	N.H.P.	Machinery	Remarks
1·8'	20·0'	8·5'	158	60	S.O. 2-cyls. 42" × 48"	
0·9'	23·2'	12·7'	347	90	C. 2-cyls. 23", 40" × 33"	

STEAM PACKET COMPANY, LTD. 1923-1935

L.	B.	D.	G.T.	N.H.P.	Machinery	Remarks
9·9'	30·1'	10·1'	664	382	3 steam turbines D.D.	L.M.S.: to C.S.P. Co., Ltd., 1936
0·0'	21·1'	10·0'	204	66	S.L. 2-cyls. 30" × 54"	Tug: Troon. From Barrow Section, L.M.S.R. To Docks & Inland Waterways Executive. Scrapped 1951.
2·0'	32·0'	10·2'	806	420	3 steam turbines D.D. 2 WTB	C.S.P. Co., Ltd.
2·0'	32·1'	10·1'	795		3 steam turbines D.D. 1 DEB	C.S.P. Co., Ltd.
0·0'	8·5'			15 B.H.P.		L.M.S. Pilot boat for Ayr. To Docks and I.W. Executive.
3·8'	30·1'	9·5'	621	230	T.D. 3-cyls. 22½" 35" & 56" × 54"	L.M.S.: to C.S.P. Co., Ltd., 1938
3·6'	30·1'	9·4'	624	193	T.D. 3-cyls. 20" 31½" & 50" × 60"	C.S.P. Co., Ltd. N.B. 1955
9·5'	27·1'	7·5'	449	140	T.D. 3-cyls. 18½" 29" & 45" × 48"	C.S.P. Co., Ltd.
9·7'	12·5'	4·3'	37	48 B.H.P. each	2 Diesels each-4 cyls. $4^3/_8 \times 6"$	C.S.P. Co., Ltd.

L.M.S.R. GROUP—(contd.)
WILLIAMSON-BUCHANAN STEAMERS, LIMITED
BUCHANAN FLEET 1853-1919

Dates Built Acqd. Displ.	Name	Type	Shipbuilders and Enginebuilders
1852 1853 1862	EAGLE (I)	Iron P.S.	Denny, Dumbarton McNab & Clark, Greenock
1844 c. 1853 1861	CARDIFF CASTLE	Iron P.S.	Caird & Co.
1845 c. 1853 c. 1861	PETREL	Iron P.S.	Barr & McNab, Paisley
1864 1864 1894	EAGLE (II)	Iron P.S.	C. Connell & Co. (1) Anchor Line (2) W. King & Co.
1865 30/5/67 5/1879	ROTHESAY CASTLE	Iron P.S.	Henderson, Colbourn & Co., Renfrew J. Barr & Co.
1878 1878 2/1887	BRODICK CASTLE	Iron P.S.	H. McIntyre & Co., Paisley Anchor Line
1867 1879 1899	ELAINE	Iron P.S.	R. Duncan & Co. Rankin & Blackmore
1880 1880 1891	SCOTIA	Iron P.S.	H. McIntyre & Co., Paisley W. King & Co.
1842 2/1885 1891	BALMORAL ex Lady Brisbane	Iron P.S.	J. Barr, Paisley Barr & McNab, Paisley
1858 2/1885 1886	HERO	Iron P.S.	T. Wingate & Co.
1869 2/1885 1892	GUINEVERE	Iron P.S.	R. Duncan & Co. Rankin & Blackmore

	B.	D.	G.T.	N.H.P.	Machinery	Remarks
9′	16·5′	8·3′	92 N.T.	70 R.H.P.	S.O. 2-cyls.	
3′	19·0′	9·3′	96·57 N.T.	84	S.D. 2-cyls.	
6′	18·0′	8·4′	162	60	St. 1-cyl. 54″ × 51″	
0′ 5′)	20·5′	7·3′	208	96 R.H.P. 85 R.H.P.	(1) S.D. 2-cyls. 38¼″ × 66″ (2) D. 1-cyl. 50¼″ × 56″	Len. 1865 N.E. 1876 N.B. 1889
0′	19·3′	7·9′	203	80	St. 1-cyl. 51″ × 48″	N.B. 1870
6′	21·7′	7·5′	243	96 R.H.P.	S.D. 2-cyls. 38¼″ × 66″ (ex "Eagle", b1864)	
0′	17·1′	6·6′	128	70	S. O. 2-cyls. 28″ × 44″	N.B. 1880
2′	21·8′	8·3′	260	135 216	St. 2-cyls. 45″ × 48″	Forecastle added 1886
7′	18·2′	7·9′	127	70	St. 1-cyl. 47″ × 50″	N.B. 1883: From Keith & Campbell
9′	19·1′	7·1′	157	80	St. 1-cyl. 48″ × 42″	N.B. 1868: From Keith & Campbell
5′	19·1′	6·8′	169	90	S.O. 2-cyls. 36″ × 48″	From Keith & Campbell

BUCHANAN FLEET—(cont.)

Dates Built Acqd. Displ.	Name	Type	Shipbuilders and Enginebuilders
1864 2/1885 1894	SHANDON ex Chancellor	Iron P.S.	Blackwood & Gordon
1853 2/1885 2/3/86	VESTA	Iron P.S.	J. Barr, Glasgow
1864 2/1885 1902	VIVID	Iron P.S.	Barclay, Curle & Co.
1876 2/1885 15/10/91	BENMORE	Iron P.S.	T. B. Seath & Co. W. King & Co.
14/5/92 1892 4/1933	ISLE OF ARRAN (II)	Steel P.S.	T. B. Seath & Co. W. King & Co.
1877 1894 7/1912	ISLE OF BUTE ex Guy Mannering ex Sheila	Iron P.S.	Caird & Co.
1884 1904 1920	ISLE OF CUMBRAE (I) ex Duchess of York ex Jeanie Deans	Iron and Steel P.S.	Barclay, Curle, & Co.
14/4/10 1910 9/8/46	EAGLE III	Steel P.S.	Napier & Miller, Ltd. A. & J. Inglis, Ltd.
1886 1913 3/1927	ISLE OF SKYE ex Madge Wildfire	Steel P.S.	S. McKnight & Co. Rankin & Blackmore

L.	B.	D.	G.T.	N.H.P.	Machinery	Remarks
3·2′	18·7′	7·0′	171	80	S.D. 2-cyls. 32″ × 51″	From Keith & Campbell N.B. 1885
2·3′	16·5′	6·8′	124	70	St. 1-cyl. 42″ × 42″	N.B. 1875: From Keith & Campbell
3·3′ 7·3′	18·2′	7·8′	157 164	80 R.H.P.	St. 1-cyl. 48″ × 48″	Len. 1877: From Keith & Campbell N.B. 1887
4·2′	19·1′	7·3′	198 235	85	D. 1-cyl. 50″ × 56″	From Keith & Campbell N.B. 1887 and 1890
)·0′	24·1′	7·4′	313	161	D. 1-cyl. 52″ × 60″	W. & J. C. & J. D. Buchanan W. Buchanan ('94) Buchanan Strs., Ltd. W. B. Strs., Ltd. ('19): N.B. 1911
5·5′	20·0′	7·7′	248	163	D. 1-cyl. 50″ × 72″	W. Buchanan Buchanan Strs., Ltd. N.B. 1891
•·0′	20·1′	7·6′	258	163	D. 1-cyl. 50″ × 72″	Buchanan Strs., Ltd. N.B. 1901:
·0′	25·1′	8·1′	432 441	176	D. 1-cyl. 52″ × 72″	Buchanan Strs., Ltd. W. B. Strs., Ltd. ('19) C.S.P. Co., Ltd., 1935-6 W. B. Strs., (1936) Ltd. C.S.P. Co., Ltd., 1943-6
0′	20·0′	7·1′	211	155	C.D. 2-cyls. (1 cr.) 27″ & 49″ × 60″	N.E. & B. 1891: N.B. 1903 Buchanan Strs., Ltd. W. B. Strs., Ltd. ('19)

WILLIAMSON FLEET 1862-1919
TURBINE STEAMER SYNDICATE 1901-1902
TURBINE STEAMERS LTD. 1902-1919

Dates Built Acqd. Displ.	Name	Type	Shipbuilders and Enginebuilders
1861 1862 9/1891 1892 1894	SULTAN/ARDMORE	Iron P.S.	Barclay, Curle & Co. J. Barr
1868 1868 9/1891 1896 7/1899	SULTANA	Iron P.S.	Robertson & Co. W. King & Co.
1875 1875 9/1891	VICEROY	Iron P.S.	D. & W. Henderson & Co. (1) D. & W. Henderson & Co. (2) Hutson & Corbett
1868 4/4/89 9/1891 5/1904 7/1904	MARQUIS OF BUTE	Iron P.S.	Barclay, Curle & Co.
1876 15/10/91 1923	BENMORE	Iron P.S.	T. B. Seath & Co. W. King & Co.
9/4/95 1895 8/8/96	GLENMORE	Steel P.S.	Russell & Co. Rankin & Blackmore
1897 1897 1908	STRATHMORE	Steel P.S.	Russell & Co. Rankin & Blackmore
1897 1897 1897 1904 1904 1908 21/8/40	KYLEMORE /BRITANNIA /VULCAN /KYLEMORE	Steel P.S.	Russell & Co. Rankin & Blackmore

L.	B.	D.	G.T.	N.H.P.	Machinery	Remarks
6·0' 6·0' '65)	16·6'	7·2	124	60	St. 1-cyl. 45″ × 42″ (b. 1853, ex "Wellington")	A. Williamson Len. 1865: N.B. 1877 John Williamson (1892) Ren. ('93)
8·1'	18·3'	7·3'	177	80	D. 1-cyl. 49″ × 54″	A. Williamson N.B. 1986: John Williamson (1886)
4·7' 3·9' 91)	20·1'	7·1'	218 236	194 150 322	(1) D. 1-cyl. 51½″ × 60″ (2) D. 1-cyl. 52″ × 60″	A. Williamson: N.B. 1886 N.E. 1888 Len 3/1891
5·6'	18·1'	7·3'	173	85 R.H.P.	D. 1-cyl. 48″ × 60″	A. Williamson John Williamson (1904)
·2'	19·1'	7·3'	235	85 R.H.P.	D. 1-cyl. 50″ × 56″	John Williamson W. B. Strs., Ltd.: N.B. 1903
·3'	21·1'	7·2'	210	81 R.H.P.	C.D. 2-cyls. 22″ & 44″ × 51″	John Williamson
·5'	24·1'	7·7'	316	93 R.H.P.	C.D. 2-cyls. 23½″ & 47″ × 51″	John Williamson
·5'	24·1'	7·7'	319	93 R.H.P.	C.D. 2-cyls. 23½″ & 47″ × 51″	Renamed 1897, 1904 and 1908 respectively John Williamson W. B. Steamers C.S.P. Co., Ltd. W. B. Strs. (1936), Ltd.

WILLIAMSON FLEET 1862-1919—(contd.)

Dates Built Acqd. Displ.	Name	Type	Shipbuilders and Enginebuilders
1866 6/4/97 11/1897	ATHOLE	Iron P.S.	Barclay, Curle & Co.
1898 1900 1901	ALERT	Steel S.S.	Paisley
1901 1901 6/6/52	KING EDWARD	Steel Tr.S.S. (Orig. 5 screws)	Wm. Denny & Bros. Parsons Marine Steam Turbine Co., Ltd., Newcastle
1902 1902 12/1911	QUEEN ALEXANDRA (I)	Steel Tr.S.S. (Orig. 5 screws)	Wm. Denny & Bros. Parsons Marine Steam Turbine Co., Ltd., Newcastle
9/4/12 1912 3/10/35	QUEEN ALEXANDRA (II)	Steel Tr.S.S.	Wm. Denny & Bros. Denny & Co.
1912 1912 9/8/46	QUEEN-EMPRESS	Steel P.S.	Murdoch & Murray Rankin & Blackmore
1879 4/1912 1913	EDINBURGH CASTLE	Iron P.S.	R. Duncan, Port Glasgow Rankin & Blackmore
25/4/91 4/1912 10/1928	LORD OF THE ISLES (II)	Steel P.S.	D. & W. Henderson & Co.
1880 6/1914 9/1920	IVANHOE	Iron P.S.	D. & W. Henderson & Co.

.	B.	D.	G.T.	N.H.P.	Machinery	Remarks
2·1′	18·5′	7·8′	165	80	St. 1-cyl. 48″ × 48″	John Williamson
·3′	17·1′	7·5′	78	17		
·5′	30·1′	10·0′	551	399	3 steam turbines D.D.	Turbine Steamer Syndicate Turbine Strs., Ltd. ('02) W.B. Strs., Ltd. (30/11/26) C.S.P. Co., Ltd., (1935) W. B. Strs. (1936) Ltd. C.S.P. Co., Ltd., (22/2/43)
·0′	32·1′	11·0′	665	450	3 steam turbines D.D.	Turbine Steamers Ltd.
·3′	32·1′	11·0′	785 792	400	3 steam turbines D.D.	Turbine Steamers Ltd.
·0′	25·6′	8·4′	411	178	C.D. 2-cyls. 27½″ & 54″ × 54″	John Williamson W. B. Strs., Ltd. C.S.P. Co., Ltd. W. B. Strs. (1936) Ltd. C.S.P. Co., Ltd., (1943-46)
·3′	19·9′	7·6′	234 261	83	D. 1-cyl. 50″ × 66″	N.B. 1893 From Lochgoil and Inver- aray Steamboat Co. Ltd. Turbine Steamers, Ltd.
·0′	25·6′	9·1′	466	280	S.D.O. 2-cyls. (1 cr.) 48″ × 66″	N.B. 1908 From Lochgoil and Inver- aray Steamboat Co. Ltd. Turbine Steamers, Ltd.

·3′	22·2′	8·3′	282	231	S.D.O.
					2-cyls. (1 cr.)
					43″ × 66″
						From the Firth of Clyde
						  S.P. Co. Ltd. (from
						  2/1911)
						Turbine Steamers, Ltd.

WILLIAMSON-BUCHANAN STEAMERS, LTD. 1919-1935

TURBINE STEAMERS, LTD. 1919-1935

Dates Built Acqd. Displ.	Name	Type	Shipbuilders and Enginebuilders
29/4/26 1926 3/10/35	KING GEORGE V	Steel T.S.S.	Wm. Denny & Bros. Ltd. Parsons Marine Steam Turbine Co., Ltd.
1933 1933 1978	QUEEN MARY /QUEEN MARY (II) /QUEEN MARY	Steel Tr.S.S.	Wm. Denny & Bros. Ltd.

L. M. S. R. GROUP—(contd.)

LONDON MIDLAND & SCOTTISH RAILWAY COMPANY,
THE CALEDONIAN STEAM PACKET CO., LTD.
AND WILLIAMSON-BUCHANAN STEAMERS (1936) LTD.

	Name	Type	Shipbuilders and Enginebuilders
1936 1936 12/1958	MARCHIONESS OF GRAHAM	Steel T.S.S.	Fairfield S.B. & E. Co., Ltd.
1936 1936 5/1971	COUNTESS OF BREADALBANE (II)	Steel T.S.M.V.	Wm. Denny & Bros., Ltd. Gleniffer Engines, Ltd.
1936 1936 11/1951	ARRAN MAIL	Steel T.S.M.V.	Wm. Denny & Bros., Ltd. Gleniffer Engines, Ltd.
1937 1937 4/1961	JUPITER (II)	Steel P.S.	Fairfield S.B. & E. Co., Ltd.
1937 1937 19/3/41	JUNO (II)	Steel P.S.	Fairfield S.B. & E. Co., Ltd.
1938 1938 7/1965	ASHTON	Steel T.S.M.V.	Wm. Denny & Bros., Ltd. Gleniffer Engines, Ltd.

..	B.	D.	G.T.	N.H.P.	Machinery	Remarks
·6′	32·1′	10·6′	789	388 3,500 S.H.P.	7 steam turbines /6 steam turbines (1935) S.R.G.	Turbine Steamers, Ltd. N.B. 1929 and 1935
2·5′	35·1′	10·1′	870 821 1014	350	3 steam turbines D.D.	W. B. Steamers, Ltd. C.S.P. Co., Ltd. W. B. Strs. (1936), Ltd. C.S.P. Co., Ltd. from 1943 Renamed 1935 and 1976 N.B. '57
)·2′	30·1′	10·1′	585	267	4 steam turbines S.R.G.	C.S.P. Co., Ltd.
·9′	18·1′	7·2′	106	26 N.H.P. 144 B.H.P.	Oil engines 4 S.C.S.A. 12-cyls. 4¾ × 6″	C.S.P. Co., Ltd. Loch Awe: to Clyde 1952 N.E. 1956
·1′	20·1′	7·7′	137	240 B.H.P.	Oil engines 4 S.C.S.A. 12-cyls. 6″ × 7″	C.S.P. Co., Ltd.
·6′	30·1′	9·7′	642	288	T.D. 3-cyls. 25″, 39″ & 61″ × 60″	C.S.P. Co., Ltd.
·6′	30·1′	9·7′	642	288	T.D. 3-cyls. 25″, 39″ & 61″ × 60″	C.S.P. Co., Ltd.
·0′	13·5′	5·1′	38	96 B.H.P.	Oil engines 4 S.C.S.A. 8-cyls. 4¾″ × 6″	C.S.P. Co., Ltd.

L. M. S. R. GROUP—(contd.)

Dates Built Acqd. Displ.	Name	Type	Shipbuilders and Enginebuilders
1938 1938 1965	LEVEN	Steel T.S.M.V.	Wm. Denny & Bros., Ltd. Gleniffer Engines, Ltd.
4/3/38 1938 1/1/50	CARRICK	Steel T.S.S.	Wm. Simons & Co., Ltd. Renfrew

KYLE–KYLEAKIN FERRY VESSELS—For a time operated by lessees of H.R. and L.M

Taken over by L.M.S.R., 1/1/1945

Dates Built Acqd. Displ.	Name	Type	Shipbuilders and Enginebuilders
1914 1914	—	Wood M.V.	
1916 1918 1918	—	M.V. Wood	
1917 1918 1938	Kyle	Wood M.V.	Bergius Co., Glasgow
1922 1945 8/1950	SKYE	Wood M.V.	J. Miller & Sons, St. Monance
1930 1945 1951	KYLEAKIN (I)	Wood M.V.	Goole Bergius Co.
1936 1945 1954	MOIL	Wood M.V.	H. McLean & Son, Ltd., Renfre Gleniffer Eng. Co.
1942 1945 1954	CUILLIN	Steel M.V.	Wm. Denny & Bros. Ltd. Gleniffer Eng. Co.

..	B.	D.	G.T.	N.H.P.	Machinery	Remarks
0·0'	13·5'	5·1'	38	96 B.H.P.	Oil engines 4 S.C.S.A. 8-cyls. 4¾" × 6"	C.S.P. Co., Ltd.
6·1'	40·1'	15·2'	846		T. 6-cyls. 12" 19" & 32" × 24"	L.M.S./B.T.C. Bucket dredger: Ayr: to Docks & I.W. Executive

ompanies

			6 N.T.	15 B.H.P.	4 S.A. 2-cyls. Kelvin Paraffin	To D. MacBrayne, Ltd.
0'	10·25'		8	15 B.H.P.	4 S.A. 2-cyls. Kelvin Paraffin	L.M.S./B.T.C. Kyle Ferry: to A. McNeil, Greenock
			7 N.T.	36 B.H.P.	4 S.A. 4-cyls. Kelvin-Ricardo petrol	L.M.S./B.T.C. Kyle Ferry
0'	17·7'		15	36 B.H.P.	4 S.A. 3-cyls. Gleniffer Diesel	L.M.S./B.T.C. Kyle Ferry: to B.T.C. (Docks), Grangemouth
0'	17·5'		24	36 B.H.P.	4 S.A. 3-cyls. Gleniffer Diesel Gear 2:1	L.M.S./B.T.C. Kyle Ferry: to Newry

L. & N. E. R. GROUP
NORTH BRITISH STEAM PACKET COMPANY 1866-1902 (Clyde Section)
NORTH BRITISH RAILWAY COMPANY 1902-1922
LONDON & NORTH EASTERN RAILWAY COMPANY (Scottish Area) 1923- 31/12/47

Dates Built Acqd. Displ.	Name	Type	Shipbuilders and Enginebuilders
1866 1866 4/1868	MEG MERRILIES (1)	Iron P.S.	A. & J. Inglis
1866 1866 1888	DANDIE DINMONT (I)	Iron P.S.	A. & J. Inglis
1864 1869 9/1872	CARHAM	Iron P.S.	A. & J. Inglis
1872 1872 1891	GARELOCH	Iron P.S.	H. Murray & Co., Port Glasgow D. Rowan, Glasgow
1877 1882 1894	SHEILA /GUY MANNERING	Iron P.S.	Caird & Co.
1883 1883 1883	MEG MERRILIES (II)	Iron P.S.	Barclay, Curle & Co.
1884 1884 1896	JEANIE DEANS (I)	Iron and Steel P.S.	Barclay, Curle & Co.
1885 1885 1901	DIANA VERNON	Iron P.S.	Barclay, Curle & Co.
1888 1888 1949	LUCY ASHTON	Steel P.S.	T. B. Seath & Co., Rutherglen (1) Hutson & Corbett (2) A. & J. Inglis, Ltd.
1858 1888 1896	PRINCE OF WALES	For particulars, see Fleet List of	
1862 1888 1896	PRINCE CONSORT	For particulars, see Fleet List of	

	B.	D.	G.T.	N.H.P.	Machinery	Remarks
1′	23·1′	7·1′	213	110	S.D.O. 2-cyls. 40″ × 60″	
2′	22·1′	6·9′	215	110	S.D.O. 2-cyls. 40″ × 60″	N.B. 1870 and 1881
8′	20·0′	8·5′	159	60	S.O. 2-cyls. 42″ × 28″	
0′	18·2′	6·8′	172	85 R.H.P.	S.O. 2-cyls. 35″ × 54″	N.B. 1890
5′	20·0′	7·7′	225 256	120	D. 1-cyl. 50″ × 72″	Ren. '83 N.B. 1891
3′	21·4′	7·2′	244	220	S.D. 2-cyls. 43″ × 60″	
3′	20·1′	7·6′	234 268	166	D. 1-cyl. 50″ × 72″	
5′	18·1′	7·1′	154 193	103	D. 1-cyl. 43″ × 60″	N.B. 1890
0′	21·1′	7·2′	271 224	150 174	(1) D. 1-cyl. 52″ × 60″ (2) C.D. 2-cyls. 28″ & 52″ × 60″	N.E. & B. 1902 N.B. 1923
:h Lomond Steamers						On Loch Lomond
:h Lomond Steamers						On Loch Lomond

L. & N. E. R. GROUP—(contd.)

Dates Built Acqd. Displ.	Name	Type	Shipbuilders and Enginebuilders
1883 1888 1896	THE QUEEN	For particulars, see Fleet List of	
1888 1888 1896	EMPRESS	For particulars, see Fleet List of	
1891 1891 1903	LADY ROWENA	Steel P.S.	S. McKnight & Co., Ayr Hutson & Corbett
24/6/91 1891 1906	LADY CLARE	Steel P.S.	J. McArthur & Co., Paisley Hutson & Corbett
1895 1895 1909	REDGAUNTLET	Steel P.S.	Barclay, Curle & Co., Ltd.
1895 1895 1928	DANDIE DINMONT (II)	Steel P.S.	A. & J. Inglis
1896 1896 1934	TALISMAN (I)	Steel P.S.	A. & J. Inglis
22/2/98 1898 1938	KENILWORTH	Steel P.S.	A. & J. Inglis
1899 1899 29/5/40	WAVERLEY (III)	Steel P.S.	A. & J. Inglis
5/5/06 1906 4/1941	MARMION	Steel P.S.	A. & J. Inglis Ltd.
23/12/15 1915 6/11/16	FAIR MAID	Steel P.S.	A. & J. Inglis Ltd.

..	B.	D.	G.T.	N.H.P.	Machinery	Remarks
					ᴏch Lomond Steamers	On Loch Lomond
					ᴏch Lomond Steamers	On Loch Lomond
)·5′	21·1′	7·2′	314 332	166	D. 1-cyl. 50″ × 72″	N.B. 1901
)·5′	19·3′	6·5′	257	115 180	D. 1-cyl. 44″ × 60″	
5·0′	22·1′	7·4′	277 384	183	D. 1-cyl. 53″ × 72″	
5·2′ ⋅6′ 2)	22·1′	7·2′	218 343	144	D. 1-cyl. 48″ × 66″	Len. 1912 N.B. 1912 and 1918
5·0′	23·0′	7·5′	234 279 293	176	D. 1-cyl. 52″ × 72″	N.B. 1910
5·0′	23·1′	7·6′	333 390	176	D. 1-cyl. 52″ × 72″	N.B. 1915
5·0′	26·1′	8·4′	449 405 537	304	C.D. 2-cyls. 37″ & 67″ × 66″	N.B. 1920
⋅0′	24·0′	8·3′	403 414 409	212	C.D. 2-cyls. 31″ & 56″ × 66″	N.B. 1932
5·0′	28·0′	8·4′	—	304	C.D. 2-cyls. 37″ & 67″ × 66″	

LONDON & NORTH EASTERN RAILWAY COMPANY (Scottish Area) 1923—

Dates Built Acqd. Displ.	Name	Type	Shipbuilders and Enginebuilders
1931 1931 10/1965	JEANIE DEANS (II)	Steel P.S.	Fairfield S.B. & E. Co., Ltd.
1935 1935 1967	TALISMAN (II)	Steel P.M.V.	A. & J. Inglis, Ltd. (1) English Electric Co., Ltd. Stafford (2) British Polar Engines Ltd.
1946 1947 8/8/1974	WAVERLEY (IV)	Steel P.S.	A. & J. Inglis Rankin & Blackmore, Ltd.

LOCH LOMOND STEAMERS
DAVID NAPIER
NAPIER & McMURRICH } 1817-1844

1816 1816 1827	MARION	Wood P.S.	A. McLachlan, Dumbarton David Napier
1820 1827 1837	EUPHROSYNE ex Post Boy	Wood P.S.	Wm. Denny, Dumbarton David Napier, Glasgow
1835 1835 /1837	BALLOCH ex Robert Napier	Wood P.S.	John Wood Robert Napier
1836 1836 7/3/46	LOCHLOMOND	Iron P.S.	David Napier, Glasgow

THE LOCHLOMOND STEAM BOAT COMPANY 1825-1829. To JOHN McMURRICH

1825 1825 11/1834	THE LADY OF THE LAKE	Wood P.S.	Wm. Denny R. Napier

B.	D.	G.T.	N.H.P.	Machinery	Remarks
5′ 30·1′	8·7′	635 814	338	T.D. 3-cyls. 26″, 41½″ & 66″ × 60″	To C.S.P. 5/11/51
0′ 27·7′	8·9′	450	312	(1) 4 Vertical 4-stroke solid injection S.C.S.A. oil engines 32-cyls. 10″ × 12″, coupled to D.C. generators: double-armature motor on paddle shaft, working at 50 R.P.M. (2) 4-oil engines, 4 S.A., each 8 cyls., 180 × 300 mm. and elect. drive	To C.S.P. 5/11/51 N.E. 1954
6′ 30·2′	8·6′	693		T.D. 3-cyls. 24, 39″ & 62″ × 66″	To C.S.P. 5/11/51
0′ 13·0′	2·8′	57	20	L	On Clyde in 1816. Sent to Loch Lomond 1817
0′ 13·0′		65	26 20	S.L.	
6′ 11·2′	7·3′	39·21′ N.T.30	28		
0′ 15·2′ 0′ 15·1′	8·5′ 7·7′	82 77	40		On Loch from 1838. Transferred to new company 1845
329 and to DAVID NAPIER 6/1829					
2′ 15·9′	7·6′	62⁹/₂₄	51	S.L. 1-cyl.	Not rigged; standing bowsprit, square stern

LOCH LOMOND STEAMERS—(contd.)
THOMAS BARCLAY (LEWIS McLELLAN)

Dates Built Acqd. Displ.	Name	Type	Shipbuilders and Enginebuilders
1838 1838 1838	QUEEN OF SCOTS	Wood P.S.	Smith & Rodger

NEW LOCHLOMOND STEAM BOAT COMPANY 1845-1845. JOHN BELL 2/4/1844—

1843 1844 1853	WATERWITCH (I)	Iron P.S.	Caird & Co., Greenock

G. & J. BURNS

1844 1846 1850	PILOT	Iron P.S.	Barr & McNab

LOCHLOMOND STEAM BOAT COMPANY 1845-1888
(Taken over by North British Steam Packet Company 1888)

5/1847 1847 10/1847	MARCHIONESS OF BREADALBANE	Iron P.S.	Wm. Denny & Bros.
	ANN		
	WATERWITCH (II)		
1850 1850 1862	PRINCE ALBERT	Iron P.S.	Wm. Denny & Bros. Caird & Co., Greenock
26/5/52 1852 9/1868	QUEEN VICTORIA	Iron P.S.	A. Denny & Bro. Caird & Co., Greenock (Fitted by M. Paul, Dumbarto
1858 1858 1901	PRINCE OF WALES	Iron P.S.	Laurence Hill & Co., Port Glasgow Scott & Sinclair, Glasgow

.	B.	D.	G.T.	N.H.P.	Machinery	Remarks
·5′	15·7′	7·2′	$95^{84}/_{94}$			Clincher built; 2 m
345						
·0′	16·3′	5·5′		50	S.D. 2-cyls. 22″ × 48″ inclined 20°	McBrayne & McIndoe Saloon on Deck John Bell 2/4/44—14/5/45 Transferred to third L.L.S.B. Co. N.B. 1850
·4′	15·8′	7·9′	192	210	St. 1-cyl.	On the loch for a short time in 1850
·1′	17·7′	7·0′	130	64	S.O. 2-cyls. 32″ × 39″	
						Scow
						Lighter (on Loch Katrine)
2′	17·1′	7·0′	109	60	S.D. 2-cyls. 30″ × 48″	
7′	15·1′	7·3′	93	30	S.D. 2-cyls. 22″ × 48″	Engine made 1843 and boiler made 1850, both ex "Waterwitch" (I)
8′	18·6′	7·7′	142	75 R.H.P.	S.D. 2-cyls. 34″ × 42″	N.B. 1877 Saloon 12/1864

LOCH LOMOND STEAMERS—(contd.)

Dates Built Acqd. Displ.	Name	Type	Shipbuilders and Enginebuilders
18/3/1862 1862 1899	PRINCE CONSORT	Iron P.S.	Caird & Co. Greenock
1866 1866 1881	PRINCESS OF WALES	Iron P.S.	Aitken & Mansel, Glasgow J. Aitken & Co., Glasgow
1883 1883 1911	THE QUEEN	Steel P.S.	Caird & Co. Greenock
6/11/88 1888 1933	EMPRESS	Steel P.S.	Napier, Shanks & Bell, Yoker D. Rowan & Son

LOCH LONG STEAM BOAT COMPANY

	Name	Type	Shipbuilders and Enginebuilders
1864 1864 1881	CHANCELLOR (II)	Iron P.S.	Blackwood & Gordon
1880 1880 1885	CHANCELLOR (III)	Steel P.S.	R. Chambers, Jr., Dumbarton M. Paul, Dumbarton

DUMBARTON & BALLOCH JOINT LINE COMMITTEE 1896-1933
L. M. & S. and L. & N. E. RAILWAY COMPANIES, 1933—31/12/47

	Name	Type	Shipbuilders and Enginebuilders
1898 1898 1942	PRINCE GEORGE	Steel P.S.	A. & J. Inglis
1898 1898 1953	PRINCESS MAY	Steel P.S.	A. & J. Inglis
1911 1911 3/1955	PRINCE EDWARD	Steel P.S.	A. & J. Inglis
1905 1914 1939	PRINCESS PATRICIA ex Shakespeare	Steel P.S.	J. I. Thornycroft, Woolston Scott's S.B. & E. Co., Ltd., Greenock

.	B.	D.	G.T.	N.H.P.	Machinery	Remarks
·3′	18·1′	6·5′	169	80 R.H.P.	S.D. 2-cyls. 32″ × 44″	
·6′	16·7′	6·8′	118	80 R.H.P.	S.O. 2-cyls. 30″ × 42″	
·1′	20·3′	6·5′	233 205	86 R.H.P.	S.D. 2-cyls. 36″ × 48″	
·0′	20·1′	6·3′	229	86 R.H.P. 138 N.H.P.	S.D. 2-cyls. 36″ × 48″	N.B. 1915
2′	18·7′	7·0′	171	80 R.H.P.	S.D. 2-cyls. 32″ × 51″	N.B. 1873
7′	21·1′	8·2′	233	140	S.D. 2-cyls. 36″ × 60″	
5′	21·6′	6·0′	256	130	S.D. 2-cyls. 34″ × 48″	
5′	21·0′	6·0′	256	130	S.D. 2-cyls. 34″ × 48″	
0′	22·1′	6·0′	304	133	C.D. 2-cyls. 26″ & 48″ × 48″	
3′	18·0′	6·8′	127	53 R.H.P.	C.D. 2-cyls. 16″ & 31″ × 36″	Ren '15

DUMBARTON & BALLOCH JOINT LINE COMMITTEE 1896-1933
L. M. & S. and L. & N. E. RAILWAY COMPANIES, 1933—31/12/47—(contd.)

Dates Built Acqd. Displ.	Name	Type	Shipbuilders and Enginebuilders
1905 1914 1929	QUEEN MARY ex Earl Godwin	Steel P.S.	Napier & Miller, Ltd. Scott's S.B. & E. Co., Ltd., Greenock

RAILWAY EXECUTIVE (SCOTTISH REGION) ETC. AND THE CALEDONIAN STE

1947 5/1950 1951	CORUISK (I) ex Silver Grid	Wood T.S.M.V.	Yorkshire Yacht Building Co., Bridlington F. Perkins, Peterborough
1951 7/1951 4/1958	LOCHALSH (I) /LOCHALSH II (I) (2/57)	Steel T.S.M.V.	W. Denny & Bros. Ltd., Dumbarton Gleniffer Eng. Co.
1951 1951 1965	PORTREE (I) /PORTREE II	Steel T.S.M.V.	W. Denny & Bros. Ltd., Dumbarton Gleniffer Eng. Co.
3/3/53 1953 3/1982	MAID OF THE LOCH	Steel P.S.	A. & J. Inglis, Ltd., Glasgow (1474P) (erected at Balloch) Rankin & Blackmore, Ltd.
17/2/53 5/1953 2/1973	MAID OF ASHTON	Steel T.S.M.V.	Yarrow & Co., Ltd. British Polar Engines, Ltd.
4/3/53 6/1953 4/1974	MAID OF ARGYLL	Steel T.S.M.V.	A. & J. Inglis, Ltd., Glasgow (1490P) British Polar Engines, Ltd.
2/4/53 1953 4/1973	MAID OF SKELMORLIE	Steel T.S.M.V.	A. & J. Inglis, Ltd., Glasgow (1491P) British Polar Engines, Ltd.

	B.	D.	G.T.	N.H.P.	Machinery	Remarks
0′	18·5′	6·8′	116	53 R.H.P.	C.D. 2-cyls. 16″ & 31″ × 36″	Ren '15

KET COMPANY, LTD. 1/1/48—3/12/68

	B.	D.	G.T.	N.H.P.	Machinery	Remarks
1′	10·5′		19	36 100 S.H.P.	4 S.A. 12-cyls. $4^3/_8″ × 5″$	
2′	17·5′	5·0′	23·78	6 36 B.H.P.	3-cyls. $4^3/_8″ × 6″$	To C.S.P. Co. 5/1957
5′	17·05′		53·03	160 B.H.P.	8-cyls. 6″ × 7″	To C.S.P. Co. 5/1957 Ren. 4/1965
0′	28·1′	7·1′	555 295 N.T.	1060 I.H.P. 57	C.D. 2-cyls. 24″ & 48″ × 51″	To C.S.P. Co. 5/1957
3′	28·2′	8·9′	508 233 N.T.	650 B.H.P. at 425 R.P.M.	2 × 2 S.A., each 6-cyls. $9^7/_8″ × 16½″$	C.S.P. Co.
3′	28·2′	8·9′	508	40 M.N. 105 H.P.	2 × 2 S.A., each 6-cyls. $9^7/_8″ × 16½″$	C.S.P. Co.
3′	28·2′	8·9′	508	40 M.N. 105 H.P.	2 × 2 S.A., each 6-cyls. $9^7/_8″ × 16½″$	C.S.P. Co.

RAILWAY EXECUTIVE (SCOTTISH REGION) ETC. & THE CALEDONIAN STEAM

Dates Built Acqd. Displ.	Name	Type	Shipbuilders and Enginebuilders
13/5/53 7/1953 8/1978	MAID OF CUMBRAE	Steel T.S.M.V.	Ardrossan Dockyard, Ltd. (419) British Polar Engines, Ltd.
22/9/53 12/1953 8/11/1969 1/1970 1980	ARRAN (V)	Steel T.S.M.V.	Wm. Denny & Bros. Ltd. British Polar Engines, Ltd.

RAILWAY EXECUTIVE (Scottish Region) ETC. and THE CALEDONIAN STEAM PA THE CALEDONIAN STEAM PACKET COMPANY, LTD. (Scottish Transport Group)

Dates Built Acqd. Displ.	Name	Type	Shipbuilders and Enginebuilders
12/1953 1954 1967	BROADFORD (I) /BROADFORD II	Steel T.S.M.V.	Wm. Denny & Bros. Ltd. Gleniffer Eng. Co., Ltd.
20/1/54 1954 1979	COWAL (II)	Steel T.S.M.V.	Ailsa S.B. Co., Ltd., Troon (48 British Polar Engines, Ltd.
28/9/54 11/1954 5//11/79	BUTE (VI)	Steel T.S.M.V.	Ailsa S.B. Co., Ltd., Troon (48 British Polar Engines, Ltd.
30/5/57 6/1957 24/7/89	GLEN SANNOX (III)	Steel T.S.M.V.	Ailsa S.B. Co., Ltd., Troon (1) Sulzer Bros., Winterthur (2) Wichmanm Motorenfabrik, fitted by Hall Russell & Co., Aberdeen
2/1957 4/1957 1971	LOCHALSH (II) /LOCHALSH II (II)	Steel T.S.M.V.	Gleniffer Eng. Co., Ltd.

...T COMPANY, LTD. 1/1/48—3/12/68—(contd.)

.	B.	D.	G.T.	N.H.P.	Machinery	Remarks
·3′	28·2′	8·9′	508	40 M.N. 105 H.P.	2 × 2 S.A., each 6-cyls. $9^7/_8'' \times 16\frac{1}{2}''$	C.S.P. Co. Converted to car ferry, stern and side loading, 3/1972
·8′	35·1′	7·3′	568	393	2 × 2 S.A., each 6-cyls. $13^3/_8'' \times 22^7/_{16}''$	C.S.P. Co. To David MacBrayne Ltd., 8/11/69 then back to C.S.P. Co., Ltd., 1/19/70; remained on charter to David MacBrayne Ltd.; converted to stern-loading 3/1973

...MPANY, LTD. 1/1/48—3/12/68
69

.	B.	D.	G.T.	N.H.P.	Machinery	Remarks
·5′	21·0′	5·7′	57	29	8-cyls. $6'' \times 7''$	To C.S.P. Co. 5/1957 Ren. 1967
·8′	35·1′	7·3′	569	393	2 × 2 S.A., each 6-cyls. $13^3/_8'' \times 22^7/_{16}''$	C.S.P. Co.
8′	35·1′	7·3′	568 199·09 N.T.	393	2 × 2 S.A., each 6-cyls. $13^3/_8'' \times 22^7/_{16}''$	C.S.P. Co.
9′	44·1′	9·4′	1107	2400 B.H.P. 864	(1) 2 × 2 S.A., each 8-cyls. 420 mm. × 500 mm. (2) 2 × 2 S.A., each 8-cyls., 450 mm. × 500 mm.	C.S.P. Co. Converted to stern loading, but retaining lift for side-loading 1970, then thw.forward from 10/1972. N.E. 1977
·0′	21·5′	6·0′	60		2 × 2 S.A.	C.S.P. Co. Ren. 1970 Transferred to David MacBrayne, Ltd. and re-named SCALPAY (II)

RAILWAY EXECUTIVE (Scottish Region) and THE CALEDONIAN STEAM PACKET

Dates Built Acqd. Displ.	Name	Type	Shipbuilders and Enginebuilders
9/6/60 1960 20/11/86	KYLEAKIN (II) /KYLEAKIN II /LARGS	Steel T.S.M.V.	Ailsa S.B. Co., Ltd., Troon Gleniffer Eng. Co., Ltd.
1965 7/1965 11/1986	PORTREE (II)	Steel T.S.M.V.	Jas. Lamont & Co., Ltd.
1966 10/1966 11/1986	BROADFORD (II)	Steel T.S.M.V.	Jas. Lamont & Co., Ltd.
1961 5/1967	ROSE /KEPPEL	Steel M.V.	White's Shipyard, Southampton Lister Blackstone, Dursley
1969 7/1969 1986	CORUISK (II)	Steel T.S.M.V.	Ailsa S.B. Co., Ltd., Troon
1966 12/1969	STENA BALTICA /CALEDONIA (III)	Steel T.S.M.V.	A/S Langesunds Mek. Verk. MAN Augsburg
1970 1970	HM2–011	Sidewall Hovercraft	Hovermarine
7/1970 1970	KYLEAKIN (III)	Steel D.S.M.V.	Newport S.B. & E. Co., Ltd. Newport, Mon. Gardner & Sons Ltd.
1971 1971	LOCHALSH (III)	Steel D.S.M.V.	Newport, Mon. Gardner & Sons Ltd.

BUTE FERRY COMPANY LTD.

(Controlled by The Caledonian S.P. Co. Ltd. from 24/12/1969)

1926 1946 8/1951	BRANDANE ex Dorbet II	Wood M.V.	Fraserburgh

ANY, LTD. From 1/1/69—(Contd.)

.	B.	D.	G.T.	N.H.P.	Machinery	Remarks
·5′	21′	6′	60		2 × 2 S.A.	C.S.P. Co. Ren. 6/70 Converted to bow-loading
						C.S.P. Co. To Rhubodach Ferry 1970: N.E. '70
			64			C.S.P. Co. To Rhubodach Ferry 1971
			214			C.S.P. Co. One dir. prop.
0′			60			C.S.P. Co.
·0′	40·0′	10′4½″	1157	2670 B.H.P.	2 4 S.A. each 9-cyls. 300 mm. × 450 mm.	Ren. 4/4/70. Engine made '64, fitted '66
·0′						
·0′	42·3	4′1¼″			2 oil eng. 4 S.A. each 8-cyls. 5½″ × 7¾″	
·0′	42·3	4′1¼″			2 oil eng. 4 S.A. each 8-cyls. 5½″ + 7¾″	
9′	13·0	7·3′	28	60 B.H.P.		

BUTE FERRRY COMPANY LTD.—(contd.)

Dates Built Acqd. Displ.	Name	Type	Shipbuilders and Enginebuilders
— 12/1946 4/1949	BUTEMAN	Wood M.V.	Cowes
1912 6/1948 30/8/1951	GOLDEN LILY	Wood M.V.	Lowestoft
1903 1/1949 30/8/51	JESS-IAN	Wood M.V.	Fraserburgh
— 2/1950 196–	EILEAN MOR /EILEAN MHOR	Wood T.S.M.V.	Canada
— 10/1950 1957	EILEAN FRAOICH	Wood T.S.M.V.	Canada
— — 1962	SEATON CASTLE	Wood M.V.	
— — 1963	ENDEAVOUR	Wood M.V.	
— — —	EILEAN FRAOICH II	Wood M.V.	
— — —	EILEAN DEARG	Wood M.V.	
1963 5/1963 1971	EILEAN BUIDHE	Wood T.S.M.V. /T.J.S.	Dickie of Tarbert
— 6/1965 1971	EILEAN DHU	Wood T.S.M.V.	
1957 4/1967 8/1971	DHUIRNISH	Wood M.V.	Jas. Noble (Fraserburgh) Ltd.

L.	B.	D.	G.T.	N.H.P.	Machinery	Remarks
8·0′	14·0	5·5′	38	100 B.H.P.		
0·2′	19·1	9·0′	57	70 B.H.P.		
0·0′	20·0	6·7′	54	50		
2·5′	18·0	5·7′	28	180 B.H.P.		Named 1951: re-named 1964
7·4′	14·0	5·8′	27	3		Named 25/1/52
						Cabin Cruiser
						N.E. 1964
						To Roy Ritchie Engines to *Gourockian*
·6′	17·2′	4·4′	29	9	Oil eng.	To Robert Beattie

DAVID MACBRAYNE, LTD.

In service on Clyde since 1935*

Dates Built Acqd. Displ.	Name	Type	Shipbuilders and Enginebuilders
1864 1864 1836	IONA (III)	Iron P.S.	J. & G. Thomson, Govan
1878 1878 1936	COLUMBA (I)	Steel P.S.	J. & G. Thomson, Clydebank
1905 1907 5/1947	COMET (III) ex Win	Steel T.S.M.V.	A. W. Robertson & Co., London Gardner, Manchester
1910 1910 1938	MOUNTAINEER (III)	Steel P.S.	A. & J. Inglis, Ltd.
1931 1931 3/1970	LOCHFYNE	Steel T.S.M.V.	Wm. Denny & Bros., Ltd. (1) Davey, Paxman & Co. (Colchester), Ltd. (2) British Polar Engines Ltd. and Metropolition Vickers Ltd.
1934 1934 1970	LOCHNEVIS	Steel T.S.M.V.	Wm. Denny & Bros., Ltd. Dumbarton (1) Davey, Paxman & Co. (Colchester), Ltd. and G.E.C. (2) National Gas & Oil Eng. Co. Ltd. Ashton-upon-Lyne
1912 1935 12/1958	SAINT COLUMBA ex Queen Alexandra	Steel Tr.S.S.	Wm. Denny & Bros., Ltd. Denny & Co.

* For others please see "W.H.S."

..	B.	D.	G.T.	N.H.P.	Machinery	Remarks
5·5′	25·6′	9·0′	396	280	S.O. 2-cyls. 50½″ × 51″	N.B. 1891
1·4′	27·1′	9·4′	602	351 N.H.P. 2200 I.H.P.	S.O. 2-cyls. 53″ × 66″	N.B. 1900 50 lb.
5·0′	14·1′	5·1′	43	144 B.H.P.	Two 4-cyls. Paraffin motors	N.E. 1927
)·0′	20·1′	7·7′	235	86	C.D. 2-cyls. 20½″ & 38½″ × 48″	
9·9′	30·1′	7·9′	748	Dsls. 2,000 I.H.P. Mtrs. 1,340 S.H.P.	(1) Two 5-cyl. 4-stroke Diesels, $15^7/_8$″ × 20″: 330 R.P.M. 2 D.C. generators, 520 v., 540 kws.: 2 D.C. motors 438 R.P.M. (2) Two 2 S.A., each 4-cyls. 340 mm. × 570 mm. connected to elec. motors and screw shafts	N.E. 6/53
5·0′	31·0′	10·5′	568	Dsls. 1,300 B.H.P. Mtrs. 1050 S.H.P.	(1) Two sets of 6-cyl. 4-stroke Diesels, 13″ × 16″: 500 R.P.M. Motors, 2 D.C. 400 R.P.M. Generators: 2 D.C. 500 v., 420 kws. (2) Two oil engines, 4 S.A. each 6-cyls. 305 × 381 mm.	N.E. '57
·3′	32·1′	11·0′	827	3,000 S.H.P.	3 steam turbines D.D.	

DAVID MACBRAYNE, LTD.—(Contd.)

Dates Built Acqd. Displ.	Name	Type	Shipbuilders and Enginebuilders
1926 1935 3/4/75	KING GEORGE V	Steel T.S.S.	Wm. Denny & Bros., Ltd. Parsons Marine Steam Turbine Co. Ltd.
1939 1939 3/1970	LOCHIEL (IV)	Steel T.S.M.V.	Wm. Denny & Bros., Ltd. Dumbarton Davey, Paxman & Co. (Colchester) Ltd.
5/1914 12/6/46 1948	ROBINA	Steel T.S.S.	Ardrossan, D.D. & S.B. Co., Ltd. McKie & Baxter, Glasgow
20/11/63 4/1964 11/1985	HEBRIDES (II)	Steel T.S.M.V.	Hall, Russell & Co., Ltd. Aberdeen Crossley Bros., Ltd., Manchester
15/1/64 6/1964 14/8/84	CLANSMAN (IV)	Steel T.S.M.V.	Hall, Russell & Co., Ltd. Aberdeen Crossley Bros., Ltd., Manchester

NOTE—A list of the Hutcheson/MacBrayne and Caledonian MacBrayne steamers from 185 Son & Ferguson, Limited in 1987.

.	B.	D.	G.T.	N.H.P.	Machinery	Remarks
0·6′	32·1′	10·6′	797 801 815	3,500 S.H.P.	6 steam turbines S.R.G.	N.B. 1929 and 1935 To Caledonian MacBrayne, Ltd. as at 3/4/.75 1/1/1973, later to Caledonian MacBrayne Holdings, Ltd.
3·6′	32·0′	10·0′	580	70	4 S.C.S.A., 8-cyls. 9½″ × 17″	
9·6′	26·1′	8·8′	306	114 M.N.	T. 6-cyls. 10½″, 17″ & 28″ × 18″	On charter from Coast Lines Limited
)·0′ 5·0 L.	46·3′	13·0′	2,104 1420†		2 oil engs. each 8-cyls. 10½″ × 13½″bow-thrust propeller	Charter transferred to Caledonian MacBrayne, Ltd.; 1/1976 to Caledonian MacBrayne Holdings Ltd., and ownership transferred from Secretary of State to David MacBrayne, Ltd., and 1980 to Caledonian MacBrayne Ltd.
)·0 ·0′	46·3′	13·0′	2,104 1,420†		As for HEBRIDES above.	Len. 73′ to 266′; super- structure raised to permit drive-through, with bow and stern loading. G.T., excluding car deck then 1707, and dimensions 75·60 × 13·26 × 3·97m. Ownership transferred from Secretary of State to David MacBrayne Ltd., 10/1973 and to Caledonian MacBrayne Holdings, Ltd., 4/1974: operated by Caledonian MacBrayne, Ltd. and ownership also to them by 1980.

:mber, 1986 will be found in *West Highland Steamers* (Fourth Edition), published by Brown,

DAVID MACBRAYNE, LTD.—(Contd.)

Dates Built Acqd. Displ.	Name	Type	Shipbuilders and Enginebuilders
12/3/64 30/7/64 14/10/88	COLUMBA (II)	Steel T.S.M.V.	Hall Russell, & Co., Ltd., Aberdeen Crossley Bros., Ltd., Manchester
22/1/70 5/1970	IONA (VII)	Steel T.S.M.V.	Ailsa S.B. Co., Ltd., Troon English Diesels Ltd. (Paxman Engine Division)

CALEDONIAN MACBRAYNE SERVICES

Dates	Name	Type	Shipbuilders and Enginebuilders
19/5/72 1972	KILBRANNAN	Steel T.S.M.V.	James Lamont & Co, Ltd. Port Glasgow English Electric Diesels, Ltd., (Kelvin), Glasgow
18/12/72 1973	MORVERN	Steel T.S.M.V.	James Lamont & Co, Ltd. Port Glasgow English Electric Diesels, Ltd., (Kelvin), Glasgow

CALEDONIAN MACBRAYNE, LTD. From 1/1/73

Dates	Name	Type	Shipbuilders and Enginebuilders
1904 3/1973 1975	TIGER	Wood M.V.	
22/3/73 1973	BRUERNISH	Steel T.S.M.V.	James Lamont & Co, Ltd. Port Glasgow English Electric Diesels, Ltd., (Kelvin), Glasgow
23/5/73 6/1973	RHUM	Steel T.S.M.V.	James Lamont & Co, Ltd. Port Glasgow English Electric Diesels, Ltd., (Kelvin), Glasgow

.	B.	D.	G.T.	N.H.P.	Machinery	Remarks
)·0' 5·0' L.	46·3'	13·0'	2,104 1,420†		As for HEBRIDES above	Transfers as for HEBRIDES above
)·0'	44·0'	11·6'	1,192	1,600 B.H.P.	Vee oil, 4 S.A., each 12-cyls 5½″ × 6½″	To Caledonian MacBrayne, Ltd. as at 1/1/1973, later to Caledonian MacBrayne Holdings, Ltd. and to Caledonian MacBrayne, Ltd. 2/1974
·0'	21·0'	6·9'	65	300 B.H.P.	(2) 4 S.A., each 6-cyls. 5″ × 5⁵/₈ rev. red. gear	Launched for David MacBrayne Ltd.
·0'	21·0'	6·9'	64	300 B.H.P.	(2) 4 S.A., each 6-cyls. 5″ × 5⁵/₈ rev. red. gear	
						Ferry at Iona
·0'	21·0'	6·9'	69 71	300 B.H.P.	2 × 4 S.A., each 6-cyls. 5″ × 5⁵/₈ rev. red. gear	
0'	21·0'	6·9'	69	300 B.H.P.	2 × 4 S.A., each 6-cyls. 5″ × 5⁵/₈ rev. red. gear	

† (Excluding car deck)

CALEDONIAN MACBRAYNE LIMITED,—(Cont.)

Dates Built Acqd. Displ.	Name	Type	Shipbuilders and Enginebuilders
2/8/73 18/9/73	COLL (II)	Steel T.S.M.V.	James Lamont & Co, Ltd. Port Glasgow English Electric Diesels, Ltd., (Kelvin), Glasgow
27/11/73 3/1974	JUPITER (III)	Steel D.S.M.V.	James Lamont & Co, Ltd. Port Glasgow Mirrlees Blackstone, Ltd., Stockport
1/4/74 1974	PIONEER (III)	Steel T.S.M.V.	Robb Caledon, Ltd., Leith Mirrlees Blackstone, Ltd., Stamford
19/4/74 8/1974	SUILVEN	Steel T.S.M.V.	Moss Rosenberg Vaerft A/S, near Oslo Wichman Motorenfabrik
16/9/74 11/1974	JUNO (III)	Steel D.S.M.V.	As JUPITER, *supra*
11/12/74 3/1975	[CANNA]/EIGG (II)	Steel T.S.M.V.	As BRUERNISH, *supra*
1923 28/3/75 11/3/85	KILDONAN (II) ex Silver Darling ex Falcon	Wood M.V.	— Bergius Co., Ltd., Glasgow
1934 20/5/75	STAFFA (VII) ex Silver Spray	Wood M.V.	Munro, Blairmore Gardner
31/10/75 23/3/76	[EIGG]/[RAASAY]/ CANNA	Steel T.S.M.V.	As BRUERNISH, *supra*
23/3/76 4/1976	[VATERSAY]/[PABBAY]/ RAASAY	Steel T.S.M.V.	As BRUERNISH, *supra*

L.	B.	D.	G.T.	N.H.P.	Machinery	Remarks
·0'	21·0'	6·9'	69	300 B.H.P.	2 × 4 S.A., each 6-cyls. 5″ × 5⁵/₈ rev. red. gear	
7·9'	43·9'	12·9'	849		2 × 4 S.A., each 8-cyls. 8¾″ × 11½″	2 dir. props.
0·2'	44·2'	13·2	1071	3,400 B.H.P.	2 × 4 S.A., each 16-cyls. 222 × 292 mm. S.R.G.	Cont.-pitch props. Thw. fwd.
5·7'	50·8'	12·5'	1908	3,500	2 × 2 S.A., each 7-cyls. 300×450 mm.	Cont.-pitch props. 2thw. fwd.
7·9'	43·9'	12·9'	854		As JUPITER	2 dir. props.
·0'	21·0'	6·9'	69	300 B.H.P.	2 × 4 S.A., each 6-cyls. 5″ × 5³/₈″ rev. red. geared	
						Ferry at Eigg
·0'	9·0'	2·5'				Ferry at Iona/Eigg
·0'	21·0'	6·9'	69	300 B.H.P.	As BRUERNISH	
·0'	21·0'	6·9'	69	300 B.H.P.	As BRUERNISH	

CALEDONIAN MACBRAYNE LIMITED—(Contd.)

Dates Built Acqd. Displ.	Name	Type	Shipbuilders and Enginebuilders
22/12/76 3/1977	ISLE OF CUMBRAE (II)	Steel D.S.M.V.	Ailsa S.B. Co., Ltd., Troon L. Gardner & Sons, Ltd.
30/6/77 27/1/78	SATURN	Steel D.S.M.V.	Ailsa S.B. Co., Ltd., Troon Mirrless Blackstone, Ltd., Stockport

13/8/78
12/1978
	CLAYMORE (III)	Steel
		T.S.M.V.
			Robb Caledon S.B., Ltd., Leith
			    Mirrlees Blackstone, Ltd.,
			    Stamford

11/6/79 1979	LOCHMOR (II)	Steel T.S.M.V.	Ailsa S.B. Co., Ltd., Troon A/B. Volvo Penta, Gothenburg

2/12/83
1984
	ISLE OF ARRAN (III)	Steel
		T.S.M.V.
			Ferguson Ailsa Ltd.
			    Port Glasgow
			Mirrlees Blackstone
			    (Stockport) Ltd.

4/7/85
2/12/85
	HEBRIDEAN ISLES	Steel
		T.S.M.V.
			Ferguson Ailsa Ltd.
			    Port Glasgow
			Mirrlees Blackstone
			    (Stockport) Ltd.

8/5/86 7/1986	LOCH STRIVEN	Steel D.S.M.V.	R. Dunston (Hessle) Ltd. A/B Volvo Penta
22/5/86 7/1986	LOCH LINNHE	Steel D.S.M.V.	R. Dunston (Hessle) Ltd. A/B Volvo Penta
19/8/86 1986	LOCH RIDDON	Steel D.S.M.V.	R. Dunston (Hessle) Ltd. A/B Volvo Penta
17/12/86 1987	LOCH RANZA	Steel D.S.M.V.	R. Dunston (Hessle) Ltd. A/B Volvo Penta
8/10/87 4/1988	ISLE OF MULL	Steel T.S.M.V.	Appledore Ferguson Shipbuilders Ltd., Pt. Glas. Mirrlees Blackstone
7/3/89 5/1989	LORD OF THE ISLES (III)	Steel T.S.M.V.	Ferguson Shipbuilders Ltd., Port. Glasgow Mirrlees Blackstone

L.	B.	D.	G.T.	N.H.P.	Machinery	Remarks
2·0 m.	10·0 m.	2·39 m.	201		2 × 4 S.A., each 8-cyls. 140 × 197 mm.	2 dir. props
6·5 m.	13·4 m.	4·0 m.	851	4,880 B.H.P.	2 × 2 S.A., each 8-cyls. 222 × 292 mm.	2 dir. props.
08′ m.	15·5′ m.	4·8′ m.	1631	3,400 B.H.P.	2 × 4 S.A., each 16-cyls. 222 × 292 mm. geared to 2 sc. shafts	2 cont.-pitch props. Thw. fwd.
8·3′ m.	7·6′ m.	2·8′ m.	198	520 B.H.P.	2 × 4 S.A., each 6-cyls. 130 × 150 mm. rev. red.-geared	
7·0′	52·0′	10·0′	3,296	4,690 B.H.P.	2 × 4 S.A., each 8-cyls. 275 × 305 mm. props. fwd.	With clutches, flex. Couplings & SRG 2 cont.-pitch
79·0′	52·0′	10·0′	3,040	4,690 B.H.P.	2 × 4 S.A., each 8-cyls. 275 × 305 mm. props. fwd.	With clutches, flex. Couplings & SRG 2 cont.-pitch
6·5′	32·8′	8·5′	206	660 B.H.P.	(4) 4 S.A., each 6-cyls.	Fluid coupling geared
6·5′	32·8′	8·5′	206	660 B.H.P.	(4) 4 S.A., each 6-cyls.	Fluid coupling geared
6·5′	32·8′	8·5′	206	660 B.H.P.	(4) 4 S.A., each 6-cyls.	Fluid coupling geared
6·5′	32·8′	8·5′	206	660 B.H.P.	(4) 4 S.A., each 6-cyls.	Fluid coupling geared
0·0′ 7·1′	51·8′	10·0′	4,331 4,719	4,620 B.H.P.	2 × 4 S.A., each 6-cyls. 275 × 305 mm.	Flex. coup., 2 SRG, 2 cont. pitch props. 2 Thw. fwd. Len. 11/1988
6·0′	51·8′	10·0′	3,504	2,896 B.H.P.	2 × 4 S.A., each 6-cyls. 275 × 305 mm.	2 cont. pitch props. Plain red. gear. Twin Becker rudders

CLYDE & CAMPBELTOWN SHIPPING CO. LTD.
etc.

SEALINK BRITISH FERRIES
(Stranraer Section)

BRITISH TRANSPORT SHIP MANAGEMENT (SCOTLAND) LIMITED. later **SEALIN**
Previously CALEDONIAN STEAM PACKET COMPANY (Irish Services) LIMITED, CL**Y**
(A)   J. HILL & COMPANY – J. RODGER – J. D. RODGER, 1871-1915

Dates Built Acqd. Displ.	Name	Type	Shipbuilders and Enginebuilders
1871 8/1871 c. 1876	SUCCESS (I)	Wood	Robt. McLea, Rothesay
8/1876 1876 1882	SUCCESS (II)	Iron S.S.	Murdoch & Murray, Port Glasg**o** Kesson & Campbell
22/2/79 1879 18/12/90	BUTE (I)	Iron S.S.	Scott & McGill, Bowling W. King & Co.
1863 14/3/82 16/3/94	CUMBRAE ex Marquis of Lorne ex Victory	Iron P.S.	Barclay Curle & Co. J. Barr, Glasgow
1867 1/3/83 2/7/84	DUNOON CASTLE /ARRAN (I)	Iron P.S.	T. Wingate & Co., Glasgow
17/4/90 5/1890 17/7/91	BUTE No. 2	Iron T.S.S.	Scott & Co., Bowling W. Kemp
12/1/92 1892 4/1899	BUTE (III)	Steel S.S.	J. Fullerton & Co., Paisley Cameron, Mills & Co.
21/1/98 1898 1935	BUTE 4	Steel S.S.	J. Fullerton & Co., Paisley Cameron, Mills & Co.
1879 11/1912 8/1917	BARMORE /ARRAN (II)	Iron S.S.	J. Fullerton & Co. W. King & Co., Paisley

(B)   JURA STEAMBOAT COMPANY
LOCHFYNE & GLASGOW STEAM PACKET COMPANY, LTD. 1882-1913
MINARD CASTLE SHIPPING COMPANY, LTD. 2/1913-1922

1869 1876 3/4/13	JURA	Iron S.S.	Dumbarton

COTLAND) LTD.
& CAMPBELTOWN SHIPPING CO., LTD.

L.	B.	D.	G.T.	N.H.P.	Machinery	Remarks
						Jas. Hill, Duncan Hill Jas. Hill, Jr.
6·6'	17·7'	8·0'	69	20	S. 2-cyls. 10″ × 12″	
5·1'	19·0'	9·2'	143	35	C. 2-cyls. 16″ & 28″ × 22″	
6·7'	17·6'	6·8'	126	75 R.H.P.	St. 1-cyl. 54″ × 42″	N.B. '67 and '79 Ren. 20/7/82
1·7'	18·2'	7·5'	171	90 85	St. 1-cyl. 50″ × 45″	N.B. '83 Ren. 30/7/83
6·4'	22·0'	8·7'	159·86 170 231·15 4/9/91	38	C. 4-cyls. 12″ & 23″ × 18″	
0·0'	20·0'	9·0'	158	43 R.H.P.	C. 2-cyls. 16″ & 32″ × 26″	
5·0'	21·1'	9·0'	174	43 R.H.P.	C. 2-cyls. 16″ & 32″ × 24″	N.B. '19
0·3'	18·0'	9·0'	126	45 R.H.P.	C. 2-cyls. 18″ & 32″ × 22″	N.B. 1/1881 Ren. 1913 and 5/1909
2·0'	17·3'	7·9'	69	16		

(B) LOCHFYNE & GLASGOW STEAM PACKET COMPANY, LTD.—(cont.)

Dates Built Acqd. Displ.	Name	Type	Shipbuilders and Enginebuilders
19/6/82 7/1882 11/1926	MINARD CASTLE	Steel S.S.	J. Fullerton & Co. W. Kemp
1868 7/1899 23/7/00	SULTANA	Iron P.S.	W. Robertson & Co. W. King & Co.

(C) CLYDE CARGO STEAMERS, LTD. 1915-1937

1903 23/4/18 4/1931	LAPWING /COWAL (I)	Steel S.S.	Scott & Co., Bowling Hutson & Sons, Ltd.
1901 1924 5/1926	JANE	Steel S.S.	Ardrossan D.D. & S.B. Co., Ltd. Fisher & Co., Paisley
1909 c. 3/1925 1925	LINTIE	Steel S.S.	Geo. Brown & Co., Greenock Gauldie, Gillespie & Co., Glasgow
1/12/25 1/1926 4/1955	MINARD	Steel S.S.	Scott & Sons, Bowling Aitchison Blair, Ltd., Clydebank
26/1/26 1926 31/12/32	ARRAN (III)	Steel S.S.	Ayrshire Dkyd. Co., Ltd., Irvine Aitchison Blair, Ltd.
1928 1928 4/1955	ARDYNE	Steel S.S.	Scott & Sons, Bowling Aitchison Blair, Ltd.
31/7/33 1933 2/1958	ARRAN (IV) /KILDONAN (I)	Steel S.S.	Ardrossan Dkyd., Ltd. Aitchison Blair, Ltd.

.	B.	D.	G.T.	N.H.P.	Machinery	Remarks
·2′	22·0′	10·4′	223	80	C. 2-cyls.	N.B. '89
			246	R.H.P.	23″, 42″ × 30″	
·1′	18·3′	7·3′	173	136	D. 1-cyl.	N.B. '86
					49″ × 54″	
·2′	21·2′	9·4′	211	64	C. 2-cyls.	J. D. Rodger till 3/7/23
			284	R.H.P.	19″ & 36″ × 27″	Ren. 25/1/26
8′	19·1′	7·5′	104	24	C. 2-cyls.	
				R.H.P.	12″ & 24″ × 18″	
·1′	20·6′	8·8′	172	30	C. 2-cyls.	
			174	R.H.P.	11″ & 24″ × 16″	
		167				
·1′	25·1′	9·7′	241	53	C. 2-cyls.	
				R.H.P.	17½″ & 36″ × 24″	
7′	21·1′	8·3′	132	34	C. 2-cyls.	
				R.H.P.	14″ & 29″ × 21″	
·1′	25·1′	9·2′	242	53	C. 2-cyls.	
				R.H.P.	17½ & 36″ × 24″	
4′	23·1′	8·6′	208		C. 2-cyls.	
					15″ & 32″ × 24″	Ren. 30/4/53

(D) CAMPBELTOWN & GLASGOW STEAM PACKET JOINT STOCK COMPANY 1
CAMPBELTOWN & GLASGOW STEAM PACKET JOINT STOCK COMPANY, LTD.
(Absorbed by Clyde Cargo Steamers, Ltd. 3—4/3/1937)

Dates Built Acqd. Displ.	Name	Type	Shipbuilders and Enginebuilders
1822 1826 30/5/45	DUKE OF LANCASTER	Wood P.S.	Mottershead & Hayes, Liverpoo
1835 1835 1848	ST. KIARAN	Wood P.S.	R. Duncan, Greenock J. & W. Napier
1842 1842 20/10/66	DUKE OF CORNWALL	Iron P.S.	Caird & Co., Greenock J. & W. Napier
1848 1848 4/1868	CELT	Iron P.S.	W. Denny, Dumbarton T. Wingate & Co.
1857 1857 15/8/68	DRUID	Iron P.S.	Barclay, Curle & Co.
1867 4/1867 1884	GAEL	Iron P.S.	Robertson & Co., Greenock Rankin & Blackmore
10/6/68 1868 18/9/07	KINTYRE	Iron S.S.	Robertson & Co. (1) Blackwood & Gordon (2) Kincaid, Donald & Co., Greenock
30/5/78 1878 5/1926	KINLOCH	Iron S.S.	A. & J. Inglis
17/5/85 1878 7/1943	DAVAAR	Steel S.S.	London & Glasgow Co., Ltd., Govan
16/3/26 1926 19/6/42	DALRIADA (I)	Steel S.S.	R. Duncan & Co., Ltd., Port Glasgow D. Rowan & Co., Ltd.

33
937

L.	B.	D.	G.T.	N.H.P.	Machinery	Remarks
3·5′	17·0′	9·5′	91 N.T.	50	S.L. 2-cyls.	From Jas. Winder & others, Liverpool
5·8′	19·1′	11·9′	128·7 N.T.	110		
2·9′	18·2′	9·5′	189 211	90	St. 1-cyl. 45″ × 45″	N.B. 1847 Regd. 25/8/42
5·9′	20·9′ 20·3′	10·3′	273 252	140	1-cyl. 62″ × 56″	Regd. 21/6/48
)·1′	20·6′	9·7′	229	150	S. 2-cyls. 44″ × 52″	To Robertson & Co., Greenock
1·0′	23·2′	10·6′	347 403	160 150	S.O. 2-cyls. 45″ × 63″	N.B. '79
4·7′	22·9′	11·5′	299 314	90 90 R.H.P.	(1) S. 2-cyls. 36″ × 30″ (2) C. 2-cyls. 26″ & 48″ × 30″	N.E. '82 N.B. '82 and '93
5·0′	24·1′	12·7′	425 428 480 427	135 158	C.2-cyls. 29″ & 54″ × 42″	N.B. '90 and '14
7·8′	27·0′	12·9′	543 516 568 535	182	C.2-cyls. 29″ & 58″ × 42″	N.B. '03
)·0′	34·7′	14·8′	758	348	T.4-cyls. 22″, 35½″ & (2) 40″ × 33″	

(E) CLYDE & CAMPBELTOWN SHIPPING CO., LTD. 3/1937

Dates Built Acqd. Displ.	Name	Type	Shipbuilders and Enginebuilders
1904 6/1939 4/1949	MARIE	Steel S.S.	W. Chalmers & Co., Rutherglen Ross & Duncan

1939
1945
1946
	EMPIRE TULIP
	    ex Pallas
		Steel
		M.V.
			N.V. Delfzilvil Gebr. Sailtes,
			Delfzil
			Appingedammer Brows Motorer
			    fb N.V.

(F) CALEDONIAN STEAM PACKET COMPANY (Irish Services) LTD.
(Stranraer Section)
(i) Directors of the Portpatrick or Carrickfergus & Larne Railways, 1861-63

1862 1/10/62 c. 1/1864	BRITON	Iron P.S.	Tod & McGregor, Glasgow

(ii) Caledonian Railway Company (Stranraer Section)

1859 1865 1869	FANNIE	Iron P.S.	Caird & Co.
1857 1866 1869	ALICE	Iron P.S.	Caird & Co.

(iii) Larne & Stranraer Steamboat Company Ltd. 1871-1890
Portpatrick & Wigtonshire Railways Joint Committee, 1890—31st December, 1922
London, Midland & Scottish Railway Company (Stranraer Section), 1st January, 1923-
British Railways Scottish Region (Stranraer Section), 1st January, 1948-1961
Caledonian Steam Packet Company (Irish Services) Ltd. 1961-31/12/1966
British Railways Board, Scottish Region (Stranraer Section) managed by The Caled⊄
(Scotland) Ltd. from 1/1/1969 till name changed in March, 1980 to Sealink (Scotland) Lt

1872 1872 1890	PRINCESS LOUISE	Iron P.S.	Tod & McGregor
1875 1875 1904	PRINCESS BEATRICE	Iron P.S.	Harland & Wolff, Belfast (1) Harland & Wolff, Belfast (2) D. Rowan & Co.

..	B.	D.	G.T.	N.H.P.	Machinery	Remarks
2·8′	19·8′	8·1′	105	36 R.H.P.	C.2-cyls. 13″ & 28″ × 18″	N.B. 6/1925
5·4′	23·5′	7·3′	288	195 B.H.P.	2 S.C.S.A., 4-cyls. 9⁷/₁₆ × 14³/₁₆	On charter (from M.O.T.- Ross & Marshall, Ltd., Managers)
·1′	24·1′	11·7′	486	150	2-cyls. 48″ × 60″	
·6′	30·8′	14·3′	699	250	S.O. 2-cyls. 60″ × 66″	
·5′	26·2′	13·3′	654			
·6′	26·2′	13·3′	635	250	S.O. 2-cyls. 60″ × 72″	

ecember, 1947

am Packet Company I.S. Ltd. from 1/1/1967 and by British Transport Ship Management
1 1/1/1987 SEALINK BRITISH FERRIES (Stranraer Section)

·4′	24·1′	12·4′	497	200	St. 2-cyls. 54″ × 60″	N.B. '78
·6′	24·0′	12·6′	556	200 325	(1) S.D. 2-cyls. 54″ × 60″ (2) C.D. 2-cyls. 39″ & 71″ × 60″	N.E. & B. '83

STRANRAER SECTION—(cont.)

Dates Built Acqd. Displ.	Name	Type	Shipbuilders and Enginebuilders
25/1/90 1890 1910	PRINCESS VICTORIA (I)	Steel P.S.	Wm. Denny & Bros. Denny & Co.
1892 1892 1914	PRINCESS MAY	Steel P.S.	Wm. Denny & Bros. Denny & Co.
1904 1904 1932	PRINCESS MAUD (I)	Steel Tr.S.S.	Wm. Denny & Bros. Parsons' Marine Steam Turbine Co., Ltd.
2/2/12 1912 1934	PRINCESS VICTORIA (II)	Steel Tr.S.S.	Wm. Denny & Bros. Denny & Co.
1931 1931 1962	PRINCESS MARGARET	Steel T.S.S.	Wm. Denny & Bros. Ltd.
12/1933 1/1934 1965	PRINCESS MAUD (II)	Steel T.S.S.	Wm. Denny & Bros., Ltd.
21/4/39 1939 21/5/40	PRINCESS VICTORIA (III)	Steel T.S.M.V.	Wm. Denny & Bros., Ltd. Sulzer Bros. Ltd., Winterthur
27/3/46 1947 31/1/53	PRINCESS VICTORIA (IV)	Steel T.S.M.V.	Wm. Denny & Bros. Ltd.
5/4/61 9/1961 4/1984	CALEDONIAN PRINCESS	Steel T.S.S.	Wm. Denny & Bros., Ltd.
1964 1965 1965	LOHENGRIN	Steel M.V.	Bremen
1965 1966 1971	STENA NORDICA	Steel T.S.M.V.	At. et Ch. de la Seine Maritime Klöckner-Humboldt Deutzmot
1967 12/1967 1986	ANTRIM PRINCESS	Steel T.S.M.V.	Hawthorn Leslie (S.B.) Ltd. At. & Ch. de Nantes (Bretagne Loire)

.	B.	D.	G.T.	N.H.P.	Machinery	Remarks
·5′	35·6′	13·4′	1096	624	C.D. 2-cyls. 51″ & 96″ × 66″	
·5′	35·6′	13·4′	1123 1128	650 548 4,800 I.H.P.	C.D. 2-cyls. 52″ & 90″ × 66″	
6′	40·1′	15·8′	1655		3 turbs. D.D.	
6′	40·2′	15·8′	1687 1732		3 turbs. D.D.	
2′	47·1′	15·9′	2523 2552	1,375	4 turbs. S.R.G.	
2′	49·1′	15·9′	2886 2883	1,375	4 turbs. S.R.G.	
8′	48·1′	13·0′	2197	5,000 S.H.P.	2 S.C.S.A., 14-cyls. $18^7/_8″ × 27^9/_{16}″$	
8′	48·1′	13·0′	2694	5,000 S.H.P.	2 S.C.S.A., 14-cyls. $18^7/_8″ × 27^9/_{16}″$	
5′	55·0′	17·5′	3650	11,500 S.H.P.	2 steam turbs. D.R.G. Directional propeller forward	
9′	42·4′	11·8′	710		Oil engs.	Chartered from Wallenius, Bremen G.m.b.H.
3′	53·2′	12·8′	2607	600 B.H.P.	2 × 4 S.A., each 12-cyls. 400 × 500 mm.	Chartered from Stena Line, Gothenburg
5′	42·4′	33·5′	3,630	7,180 B.H.P.	2 × 4 S.A., each 16-cyls. 400 460 mm.	Cont. pitch props. Thw. fwd.

(BRITISH RAILWAYS BOARD—SEALINK (U.K.) LTD.
Managed by
BRITISH TRANSPORT SHIP MANAGEMENT (SCOTLAND) LTD. } From 1/9/71
of which name changed in March, 1980 to   to 31/12/80
SEALINK (SCOTLAND), LTD.
SEALINK BRITISH FERRIES (Stranraer)

Dates Built Acqd. Displ.	Name	Type	Shipbuilders and Enginebuilders
28/11/70 1971	AILSA PRINCESS /EARL HAROLD	Steel T.S.M.V.	Cantiere Navale Breda, S.p.A., Marghera, Venice Crossley-Paxman
27/2/71 1971	DALRIADA (II) ex Stena Trailer	Steel T.S.M.V.	Broderne Lotha A/S Flyttedokk Haugesund, Norway Normo Crippen A/S
1970 12/1974	ULIDIA ex Stena Carrier	Steel T.S.M.V.	Kristiansands M/V A/S Normo Gruppen A/S., Bergen
1978 10/8/78	DARNIA Launched as Stena Topper	Steel T.S.M.V.	Osterreichische Schiffswerfter A Korneuburg, near Vienna Köln-Humboldt-Deutz
24/5/79 4/1980	GALLOWAY PRINCESS	Steel T.S.M.V.	Harland & Wolff, Ltd. Belfast Crossley Premier Engines, Ltd. (Pielstick, U.K.)
24/5/79 4/1980	ST. DAVID	Steel T.S.M.V.	Harland & Wolff, Ltd. Belfast Crossley Premier Engines, Ltd. (Pielstick, U.K.)

	B.	D.	G.T.	N.H.P.	Machinery	Remarks
5′	55·0′	34·5′	3630	7,180 B.H.P.	2 × 4 S.A., each 16-cyls. 400 × 460 mm.	Cont. pitch props. Thw. fwd. Returned on charter intermittently
0′	52·5′	35·1′	4590		2 × 4 S.A., each 8-cyls. & 9-cyls. 250mm × 300mm. one of each geared to each screw shaft.	2 cont. pitch props. Thw. fwd.
0′	52·5′	38·1′	1581	4590 B.H.P.	4 oil, two geared to each shaft (i) 2 S.A., each 8-cyls. (ii) 4 S.A., each 9-cyls., 250 × 300 mm.	In name of Barclay's Export & Finance, Ltd. 2 cont.-pitch props. Thw. fwd.
5	17·6 m. ·	11·74 m.	4150	10000 B.H.P.	2 Vee oil, 4 S.A., each 12-cyls. 370 × 400 mm.	In name of Barclay's Mercantile Industrial Finance Ltd. Sub-chartered from James Fisher & Sons, Ltd. Later became owners.
7 4′	21·0 m.	11·8 m.	6268	16000 B.H.P.	2 Vee oil, 4 S.A., each 16-cyls. 400 × 460 mm. Geared	In name of Midland Montague Leasing, Ltd. chartered to Sealink, U.K., Ltd. 2 cont.-pitch props., thw. fwd.
7 4	21·0 m.	11·8 m.	6268	16000 B.H.P.	2 Vee oil, 4 S.A., each 16-cyls. 400 × 460 mm. Geared	2 cont.-pitch props., thw. fwd.

GLASGOW, AYRSHIRE & CAMPBELTOWN STEAMBOAT CO. LTD.
(Duncan T. Clark, Manager)

Dates Built Acqd. Displ.	Name	Type	Shipbuilders and Enginebuilders
1891 1895 8/1900	CULZEAN CASTLE ex Windsor Castle /CARRICK CASTLE (II)	Steel P.S.	Southampton Naval Works

GIRVAN—AILSA CRAIG STEAMERS, WM. GIRVAN & SON, ARCHIBALD S. GIR'

Dates Built Acqd. Displ.	Name	Type	Shipbuilders and Enginebuilders
1874 1906 c. 1912	NIMROD	Wood S.S.	Culzean
1906 1906 1924	AILSA (I)	Steel S.S.	Ailsa Shipbuilding Co., Ltd., Troon Colin Houston & Co.
1924 1924 1932	AILSA II /LADY AILSA (I)	Steel S.S.	Ailsa Shipbuilding Co., Ltd., A A. Hall & Co., Aberdeen
1934 1934	LADY AILSA (II)	Wood M.V.	H. McLean & Sons, Ltd., Gova

ROBERT L. GREIG

Dates Built Acqd. Displ.	Name	Type	Shipbuilders and Enginebuilders
1894 1912 1914	KATE	Wood S.S.	Bristol
1934 1934 1937	CARRICK LASS	Wood M.V.	H. McLean & Sons, Ltd., Gov.

CALEDONIAN CANAL AND LOCH NESS

Dates Built Acqd. Displ.	Name	Type	Shipbuilders and Enginebuilders
1942 2/1948 1950	LENRODIAN ex No. 525	Wood T.S.M.V.	Curtis
1921 1958 c1959	CRAMOND BRIG		Sandhaven
1931 1931	SCOT II	Steel S.S./M.V.	Leith
1961 1961 1970	JESSIE ELLEN	Wood M.V.	Wm. Weatherhead & Son (195 Ltd., Cockenzie Gardner

	B.	D.	G.T.	N.H.P.	Machinery	Remarks
6′	28·3′	10·3′	599	384	T.D. 3-cycls., 26″, 42″ & 65″ × 60″, geared to paddle-shaft	Ren. 1899
5						
0′	8·3′	4·7′	7	7		Regd. Ayr 1885
0′	15·1′	7·4′	60	20	C. 2-cyls. 10½″ & 21″ × 16″	
7″	22·4′	8·3′	120	40	T. 3-cyls. 9″, 16″ & 24″ × 18″	
2′	15·1′	6·3′	28	105 B.H.P.	Paraffin motor	
4′	10·3′	5·4′	18	11		
5′	16·0′	7·3′	38	120	Paraffin motor	
0′	18·0′			225	(1) (2) Gray Diesels Fairmile "B"	Lochness Cruises Ltd.
′	14·1′	5·6′	34	9		
′	15·1′	7·5′	59	36		Tug converted for passenger cruising from 1961. N.E. '60
′	14·0′	6′11½″				

LOCH AWE

Dates Built Acqd. Displ.	Name	Type	Shipbuilders and Enginebuilders
1861 1861 c. 1862	EVA	S.S.	Swan, Kelvindock, Maryhill

D. HUTCHESON & CO., DAVID MACBRAYNE, and DAVID MACBRAYNE, LTD.

1863 1863 1882	QUEEN OF THE LAKE	Iron S.S.	— Loch Awe
1876 1876 1925	LOCHAWE	Iron S.S.	A. & J. Inglis, Pointhouse, at Loch Awe Muir & Caldwell

THOMAS CAMERON, Port Sonachan

— —	SONACHAN	Wood S.S.	
1883 1883 —	KILCHURN CASTLE	Iron S.S.	
1895 1895 1918	CALEDONIA	Steel T.S.S.	Bow, McLachlan & Co., Paisley

CARGO STEAMERS, owned successively by THOMAS DOW, DAVID WILSON and C

— 1901	MARGERY	S.S.	
1881 1881 1935	EAGLE	Iron S.S.	Leith
1901 1901 1935	BEN CRUACHAN /GLENORCHY	S.S. /M.V.	Rodger, Port Glasgow

	B.	D.	G.T.	N.H.P.	Machinery	Remarks
·9′	14·9′	6·5′				
·0′	15·4′	5·7′	51	15		
·2′	16·8′	8·8′	97	100 I.H.P.		
						Launch
·0′	14·5′	8·0′			C. 4-cyls. 10″ & 20″ × 17″	
FFS						
						Converted to motor vessel and re-named 1921

DUNCAN FRASER
LOCHAWE HOTEL CO., LTD.

Dates Built Acqd. Displ.	Name	Type	Shipbuilders and Enginebuilders
1822 1882 1922	COUNTESS OF BREADALBANE (I)	Steel S.S.	Hannah & Donald, Paisley (1) (2) & (3) Hawthorns & Co., Lei●
— — c. 1900	MONA	S.S.	
— c. 1900 1936	GROWLEY (I)	S.S.	
1936 1936 c. 1939	GROWLEY (II)	M.V.	

J. H. LYNN, DALMALLY

1940 1952 1955	LADY OF LORN		

DALRIADA STEAM PACKET COMPANY CO., LTD. — AVERIL and HARRY WAT●

pre 1914 1985	SILVER HERON	Wood M.V.	—
1927 9/1984	LADY ROWENA ex Water Lily	Wood S.S.	C. H. Breaker, Bowness-on-Windermere Langley Engineering, Storringt●

LOCH ECK

c. 1820 c. 1820 c. 1828	AGLAIA	Iron P.S.	
c. 1828 c. 1828 —	—	Iron P.S.	

.	B.	D.	G.T.	N.H.P.	Machinery	Remarks
•·9′	14·0′	7·0′	95	30	(1) S. 2-cyls. (2) C. 2-cyls. (3) T. 3-cyls. 8¾, 14½″ & 22″ × 15″	N.E. 1884 and 1898 To Caledonian S.P. Co., Ltd. *See* their list.
						Launch
						Launch
						Launch
						35 passengers
					(Petrol) Morris-Vedette	Cabin Cruiser N.E. (made '36)
·0′	8·0′	2·5′ (draught)		15 I.H.P.	C. 2-cyls. 3¾″ & 6″ × 4½″	N.E. 1986 Sisson replica engine, non-condensing
						D. Napier
						D. Napier

LOCH ECK—(cont.)

Dates Built Acqd. Displ.	Name	Type	Shipbuilders and Enginebuilders
1878 1878 1926	FAIRY QUEEN	Iron S.S.	T. B. Seath & Co. A. Campbell & Son

LOCH KATRINE

1843 1843 1843	GIPSY	Iron P.S.	Stirling
1845 1846 1855	ROB ROY (I)	Iron P.S.	Wm. Denny Wingate & Co.
21/7/55 1855 c.1911	ROB ROY (II)	Iron S.S.	Alex. Denny, Dumbarton (assembled at Stronachlachar)
1900 1900	SIR WALTER SCOTT	Steel S.S.	Wm. Denny & Bros. M. Paul & Co., Dumbarton

LOCH ETIVE

1877 1877 1879	BEN STARAV ex Morvane	Iron S.S.	Laird Bros., Birkenhead
1880 1880 c.1886	GLENETIVE	Iron S.S.	T. B. Seath & Co., Rutherglen
1885 1885 1913	OSSIAN	Iron S.S.	T. B. Seath & Co., Rutherglen

L.	B.	D.	G.T.	N.H.P.	Machinery	Remarks
9·5′	12·1′	3·6′	43	20		Glasgow & Inveraray S.P. Co., Ltd. /Lochgoil & Inveraray S.P. Co., Ltd. (1909)
0·0′			30	15		Loch Catrine Steam-Boat Co.
4·5′	17·5′		77	16	S. 2-cyls.	Saloon 38′ long Loch Catrine Steamboat Co. Loch Katrine Steamboat Co., Ltd.
0·6′	19·1′	8·9′	115	20	T. 3-cyls. 8½, 13″ & 19¾″ × 12″. 160 lb.	Loch Katrine Steamboat Co., Ltd. /Corporation of Glasgow /Lower Clyde Water Board N.B. '56
·0′ L.	12·0′		22 yacht register		S.D. 2-cyls.	Mr. Campbell
·0′	12·0′	4·1′	44	20		James Murray, Taynuilt
5·5′	16·0′	5·6′	97	25	C. 2-cyls. 12½″ & 24″ × 18″	James Murray, Taynuilt /John Currie, Ballachulish /Mr. Margt. Macpherson. Corpach

LOCH ETIVE—(Contd.)

Dates Built Acqd. Displ.	Name	Type	Shipbuilders and Enginebuilders
— 1922 1922	JANO	Wood M.V.	Tighnabruaich
1923 1923 10/9/41	LOCH ETIVE QUEEN	Wood M.V.	Dumbarton
1911 1924 10/1940	RENA ex Southamnpton Belle ex George Wishart the Martyr	Steel M.V.	John Cran & Co., Leith Wm. Beardmore & Co., Ltd., Dalmuir
1924 c. 1934	EUGLENA	Wood M.V.	Kilcreggan
1939 1939 1964	DARTHULA II	Steel M.V.	Dickie Bros., Tarbert
— — —	EULA	Wood M.V.	
194– 1964 1967	SHEARWATER /ETIVE SHEARWATER ex Pembroke Shearwater	Wood T.S.M.V.	
1924 12/6/65 21/4/66	CATERINA	Wood M.V.	Geo. Brown & Co. Greenock Atlantic, Wishaw
1960 1970 1974	JESSIE ELLEN	Wood M.V.	WM. Weatherhead & Sons (1954 Ltd., Cockenzie
1975 1975	ANNE OF ETIVE	Fibre Glass M.V.	

L.	B.	D.	G.T.	N.H.P.	Machinery	Remarks
						Scott & Smith, Taynuilt
0·0′	10·0′	4·5′	12	33 B.H.P.		D. R. Mackay, Taynuilt
2·1′	11·5′	5·3′	22	94 B.H.P.	Oil engine, 4-cyls. 8″ × 12″	D. R. Mackay, Taynuilt
9·5′	7·5′	3·2′	5	14		Alex. Black
5·2′	15·1′	5·6′	46	60		Alex. Black / J. H. Lynn (1955) / Loch Etive Tours, Ltd. (1962)
						Donald Kennedy
			58			Loch Etive Cruises, Ltd. Ren. '64
5·0′			72		Two oil engs., each 4-cyls.	Loch Etive Cruises, Ltd.
8·0′	14·0′	6·9′		84 B.H.P.		Donald Kennedy 9 knots
						Donald Kennedy

LOCH SHIEL

{ LORD HOWARD OF GLOSSOP
  LOCH SHIEL STEAMBOAT SERVICE CO., LTD.

Dates Built Acqd. Displ.	Name	Type	Shipbuilders and Enginebuilders
1899 1899 3/1902	CLANRANALD	Steel S.S.	T. B. Seath & Co., Rutherglen J. Fisher & Co., Paisley
1900 1900 1954	CLANRANALD II	Steel S.S. /T.S.M.V.	T. B. Seath & Co., Rutherglen (1) J. Fisher & Co. (2) L. Gardner & Sons, Ltd.
1894 1894 1951-2	LADY OF THE LAKE	S.S. /M.V.	Dartmouth

DUNCAN HENDERSON

	ROSE ISLE	Wood M.V.	
	GARRY		

NOTE—For the MacBrayne vessels MAUD, LOCHSHIEL, LOCHAILORT and GARRY o

LOCH EARN
PETER CRERAR—W. ALEXANDER & SONS, LTD.

1922 1922 1937	QUEEN OF LOCH EARN	Wood T.S.M.V.	Forbes Bros., Fraserburgh Rolls Royce, Ltd.

LOCH MAREE
DAVID MACBRAYNE—for MABEL see 'W.H.S.'

LOCH TREIG

	LOCH TREIG	S.S.	H. Robb, Leith

.	B.	D.	G.T.	N.H.P.	Machinery	Remarks
2·0′	13·0′	7·0′	37	16 95 I.H.P.	C. 2-cyls. 9½″ & 20″ × 12″	
·0′	14·0′	6·7′	50	90 B.H.P.	(1) steam (2) motor	N.E. 1926
·0′	8·0′				(1) Q. 4-cyls. (2)	N.B. 1914; N.E. 1936
						From David MacBrayne. Ltd. *See* "W.H.S."
Shiel *see* 'W.H.S.'						
0′	9·0′				2 sets of petrol engines, each 12-cyls.	
0′	12·0′					Lighter

LOCH RANNOCH
GEN. ALASTAIR MACDONALD

Dates Built Acqd. Displ.	Name	Type	Shipbuilders and Enginebuilders
1881 1881 6/8/22	GITANA	Iron S.S.	T. B. Seath & Co.

CAPTAIN WENTWORTH OF DULL

| | FIREFLY | | |

LOCH OSSIAN
SIR JOHN MAXWELL STIRLING MAXWELL

| 1904 1904 193– | CAILLEACH | S.S. | |

LOCH AKRAIG
CAMERON OF LOCHIEL

| 186– 186– 193– | THE RIFLE | Iron S.S. | |

LOCH ERICHT

— 1910 1919	HERON	S.S.	
— — 193–	SHIELDRAKE	S.S. M.V.	
192– 192– —	GRAMPIAN ENTERPRISE	Wood M.V.	

LOCH MORAR

| — — — | — | S.S. | |
| — 1947 — | GOBHAR | Wood M.V. | — |

L.	B.	D.	G.T.	N.H.P.	Machinery	Remarks
·0′	12·1′	4·0′	54	25		
						Trulmbank Hotel (Ex Admiralty pinnace).
						Grampian Elec. Supply Co., Ltd.

LOCH MORAR—(contd.)

Dates Built Acqd. Displ.	Name	Type	Shipbuilders and Enginebuilders
— 1949 —	SILVER SPRAY	Wood M.V.	J. & G. Forbes, Sandhaven
— — —	CHIEFTAIN	Wood M.V.	

LOCH AILORT

— 1967	JACOBITE	Wood M.V.	

LAKE OF MENTEITH

	MARY (?)		
20/6/02 1902 c. 1914	THE MACGREGOR	M.V.	

FORTH & CLYDE CANAL
A. TAYLOR—GEORGE AITKEN 1860-1880

1859 1859 1880	ROCKVILLA CASTLE	Iron S.S.	T. Wingate & Co.

JAMES AITKEN & COMPANY, LTD. 1893-1940

1893 1893 1897	FAIRY QUEEN (I)	Steel S.S.	Ayrshire Dkyd. Co., Ltd., Irvine
1897 1897 1912	FAIRY QUEEN (II)	Steel S.S.	Bow, McLachlan & Co., Paisley
1903 1903 1918	MAY QUEEN	Steel S.S.	P. McGregor & Sons, Kirkintilloch

L.	B.	D.	G.T.	N.H.P.	Machinery	Remarks
					Paraffin motor	To McKellaig, Morar Hotel
2·0′	11·4′			20	Kelvin Diesel P. 4 R.	Ex lifeboat of P. & O. *Mooltan* Bruce Watt, Mallaig
					Oscillating 3-cyls. 1 cr. and 1 eccentric	
3·3′	14·0′	7·2′	45	20	C. 2-cyls.	
5·0′	14·1′	6·8′	50	10	C. 2-cyls.	
7·2′	15·1′	7·0′	56	22	C. 2-cyls. 8″ & 16″ × 12″	

JAMES AITKEN & COMPANY, LTD. 1893-1940—(contd.)

Dates Built Acqd. Displ.	Name	Type	Shipbuilders and Enginebuilders
1905 1905 1940	GIPSY QUEEN	Steel S.S.	Bow, McLachlan & Co., Paisley
1923 1923 1931	FAIRY QUEEN (III)	Steel M.V.	Hugh McLean & Sons, Ltd., Govan Atlantic Eng. Co.

FORTH & CLYDE CANAL SOCIETY

1934 1982 1984	FERRY NO. 2	Steel D.S.M.V.	From Clyde Port Authority, qv.
1951 1982	FERRY NO. 8 /FERRY QUEEN	Steel D.S.M.V.	From Clyde Port Authority, qv.

CALEDONIAN ESTATES LTD.

1934 1982	FERRY NO. 10 /CALEDONIAN	Steel M.V. (outboard)	From Clyde Port Authority, qv.

SCOTLAND IN VIEW

18/2/87 1987	THE LADY MARGARET	Steel M.V.	Market Harborough

SEAGULL TRUST

1984 1984	YARROW SEAGULL	Steel M.V.	Yarrow Shipbuilders Ltd.
1985 1985	GOVAN SEAGULL	Steel M.V.	Govan Shipbuilders Ltd.

L.	B.	D.	G.T.	N.H.P.	Machinery	Remarks
7·3′	17·1′	3·7′	75	11	C. 2-cyls. 8″ & 16″ × 12″	
				40 B.H.P.	Paraffin motors	
					Outboard motor	
	50·0′	10·0′				

VARIOUS PRIVATE OWNERS

As most of the ships referred to in Chapter XII appear elsewhere under other ownership, they have, in order to save space, not been included here again.

Dates Built Acqd. Displ.	Name	Type	Shipbuilders and Enginebuilders

MAC SHIPPING CO. LTD—WIMAISIA SHIPPING CO. LTD.

Dates Built Acqd. Displ.	Name	Type	Shipbuilders and Enginebuilders
1936 4/1948 10/1948	WIMAISIA ex Duchess of Abercorn	Steel T.S.M.V.	Harland & Wolff, Ltd., Belfast
1930 4/1948 12/1955	TARANSAY	Steel M.V.	Hall, Russell & Co., Ltd., Aberdeen (1) L. Gardner & Son, Ltd. (2) Gleniffer Engines Ltd.

JOHN HALL (CRUISES) LTD.

194– 6/1948 4/1954	ULSTER LADY ex Tay Lady ex Royal Tay Lady	Wood T.S.M.V.	Brook Marine Motorcraft Ltd. for Fairmile Marine Co., Ltd.

CLYDE PORT AUTHORITY FERRIES

GOVAN FERRY PROPRIETORS (To Clyde Navigation Trust 15/5/1857)

1734 1734 c. 1795	GOVAN FERRY (I)	Hand- propelled (row)	
1791 1791 c. 1867	GOVAN FERRY (II)	Iron Hand- propelled (rope)	Southfield Iron Co., Pointhouse
1865 1865 1891	FERRY No. 1 (I)	Iron D.T.J.S.	R. Hedderwick & Co., Govan Jas. Howden & Co., Glasgow
1867 1867 1891	FERRY No. 2 (I)	Iron D.T.J.S.	R. Hedderwick & Co., Govan Jas. Howden & Co., Glasgow
1867 1867 c. 1912	GOVAN STEAM FERRY /GOVAN FERRY No. 1	Iron S.C.S.	Wm. Simons & Co., Renfrew

L.	B.	D.	G.T.	N.H.P.	Machinery	Remarks
19·7'	27·1'	11·2'	309	219	2×2 S.A., each 8-cyls. $8^{11}/_{16} \times 14^{9}/_{16}''$ to elec. drive	
					(1) Oil eng., 8-cyls. Ex yacht. $9\frac{1}{2}'' \times 10\frac{3}{4}''$ (2) 4 S.A., 12-cyls. $6'' \times 7''$	On Clyde during 1948 only.
06·8'	17·8'	9·7'	124	10		On Clyde during 1950 only.
					None	
0·0'	12·0'			4	High pressure jet	
7·0'	12·0'			4	High pressure jet	
5·0'	29·0'	3·0'		10 15	D. 1-cyl.	N.E. 1874 Govan/Erskine

CLYDE PORT AUTHORITY FERRIES—(Contd.)

Dates Built Acqd. Displ.	Name	Type	Shipbuilders and Enginebuilders
1869 1869 1908	FERRY No. 3 (I)	Iron D.S.S.	C.N. Trust
1872 1872 1923	FERRY No. 4 (I)	Iron D.S.S.	C.N. Trust
1875 1875 c. 1912	GOVAN FERRY No. 2	Iron D.C.S.	T. Wingate & Co.
1875 1875 1910	FERRY No. 5 (I)	Iron D.S.S.	C.N. Trust
1878 1878 1914	FERRY No. 6 (I)	Iron D.S.S.	Wm. S. Cumming, Blackhill Hanna, Donald & Wilson
1882 1882 1914	FERRY No. 7 (I)	Iron D.S.S.	Wm. S. Cumming
1882 1882 1/1950	FERRY No. 8 (I)	Iron D.S.S.	Wm. S. Cumming
1888 1888 1928	FERRY No. 9	Steel D.S.S.	Wm. S. Cumming
1889 1889 1934	FERRY No. 10 (I)	Steel D.S.S.	D. M. Cumming, Blackhill
1890 1890 6/1961	FINNIESTON (I) /WHITEINCH /VEHICULAR FERRY- BOAT No. 1	Steel D.T.S.S.	W. Simons & Co., Renfrew
1891 1891 1934	FERRY No. 1 (II)	Steel D.S.S.	D. M. Cumming Kesson & Campbell
1891 1891 1934	FERRY No. 2 (II)	Steel D.S.S.	D. M. Cumming Kesson & Campbell

L.	B.	D.	G.T.	N.H.P.	Machinery	Remarks
					1-cyl.	
9·5′	12·5′	4·0′		6½	S. 2-cyls. 6¼″ × 10″	80 lb. pressure
0·0′	35·0′	3·8′			S.D. Inverted; 2-cyls. 11″ × 18″	2 boilers, 8′ × 3′ 6″
6·0′	12·5′	3·9′			D. 2-cyls.	
9·3′	12·6′	3·9′			D. 2-cyls.	
9·3′	12·5′	⁻3·9′			D. 2-cyls.	94 passengers
9·3′	12·5′	4·2′			Inverted diagonal 2-cyls.	
1·0′	12·5′	4·2′			Inverted diagonal 2-cyls.	
0·0′	43·0′	9·6′	236	30 R.H.P.	T. 6-cyls. 9″ 14½″ & 24″ × 18″	N.B. 1927 Ren. 1900 and c.1912
1·0′	12·5′	4·2′			Inverted diagonal 2-cyls. 6½″ × 10″	108 passengers
1·0′	12·5′	4·2′			Inverted diagonal 2-cyls. 6½″ × 10″	108 passengers

CLYDE PORT AUTHORITY FERRIES—(Contd.)

Dates Built Acqd. Displ.	Name	Type	Shipbuilders and Enginebuilders
1900 1900 1966	FINNIESTON (II) /VEHICULAR FERRY-BOAT No. 2	Steel D.T.S.S.	Fleming & Ferguson, Paisley
1903 1903 3/1953	GOVAN FERRY No. 3 —	Steel D.C.S.	Ritchie, Graham & Milne Campbell & Calderwood

PROPRIETORS OF ERSKINE ESTATE, from before 1793
LORD BLANTYRE AND HIS LESSEES

Ferry rights to C.N.T. 1904: operated from 15th May, 1907

1851 1856 c. 1858	Erskine (I)	Hand winch chain	Bowling
1858 1858 18--	Erskine (II)	Iron-S.C.S.	Scott & McGill, Bowling
18-- c. 1884 18--	URANIA	Iron-D.C.S.	
1903 1903 1936	ERSKINE (III)	Steel D.C.S.	John Reid & Co., Whiteinch Lees, Anderson & Co.

CLYDE NAVIGATION TRUST—(Contd.)

1904 1904 1964	FERRY No. 11	Steel D.S.S.	D. M. Cumming Smith, Allen & Co.
1904 1904 1964	FERRY No. 12	Steel D.S.S.	D. M. Cumming Smith, Allen & Co.
1908 1908 1967	FERRY No. 3 (II)	Steel D.S.S.	Ardrossan D.D. & S.B. Co., Ltd. McKie & Baxter
1908 1908 1966	FINNIESTON No. 1 /VEHICULAR FERRYBOAT No. 3	Steel D.T.S.S.	Ferguson Bros., Port Glasgow

..	B.	D.	G.T.	N.H.P.	Machinery	Remarks
·0′	43·2′	10·2′	264	61 R.H.P.	T. 6-cyls. 10″, 15½″ & 24″ × 18″	N.B. 1919 and 1937 Withdrawn 21/10/66 Ren. 1912
·0′	41·0′	4·5′			C. 2-cyls.	Name removed 1912 when transferred to Renfrew N.B. 1928
·0′	18·0′					
				10		
·0′	38·5′	4·5′			C. 2-cyls.	
·3′	13·5′	4·9′			Vertical 2-cyls.	Withdrawn 26/2/64
·3′	13·5′	4·9′			Vertical 2-cyls.	Withdrawn 26/2/64
·3′	13·5′	4·9′			Vertical 2-cyls.	Withdrawn 28/1/67
·0′	45·1′	10·5′	379	89 R.H.P.	T. 6-cyls. 12″, 18½″ & 29″ × 20″	N.B. 1918 and 1937 Withdrawn 22/1/66 Ren. 1912

CLYDE NAVIGATION TRUST—(contd.)

Dates Built Acqd. Displ.	Name	Type	Shipbuilders and Enginebuilders
RENFREW TOWN COUNCIL (Renfrew Ferry takenover 1911)			
1868 1868 1912	RENFREW STEAM FERRY (I)	Iron S.C.S.	T. Wingate & Co. Whiteinch
1897 1897 10/1936	RENFREW STEAM FERRY (II)	Steel D.C.S.	S. McKnight & Co., Ayr Lees, Anderson & Co.
CLYDE NAVIGATION TRUST—(contd.)			
1912 1912 1965	FERRY No. 5 (II)	Steel D.S.S.	Ritchie, Graham & Milne. Whiteinch Clyde Trust
1922 1922 1964	FERRY No. 6 (II)	Steel D.S.S.	Harland & Wolff, Ltd., Govan Clyde Trust
1922 1922 1966	FERRY No. 7 (II)	Steel D.S.S.	Harland & Wolff, Ltd., Govan Clyde Trust
1928 1928 1966	FERRY No. 4 (II)	Steel D.S.S.	Geo. Brown & Co., Greenock Clyde Trust
1934 1934 2/1968	FERRY No. 1 (III)	Steel D.S.M.V.	Barclay, Curle & Co., Ltd. Gleniffer Engines, Ltd.
1934 1934 1981	FERRY No. 2 (III)	Steel D.S.M.V.	Barclay, Curle & Co., Ltd. Gleniffer Engines, Ltd.
1934 1934 1981	FERRY No. 10 (II)	Steel D.S.M.V.	Barclay, Curle & Co., Ltd. Gleniffer Engines, Ltd.
1935 1935 1984	RENFREW (I) /ERSKINE (V)	Steel D.C.S.	Fleming & Ferguson, Ltd.
1936 1936 8/1971	ERSKINE (IV) /—	Steel D.C.S.	Fleming & Ferguson, Ltd.

..	B.	D.	G.T.	N.H.P.	Machinery	Remarks
·0′	38·8′	4·3′			D. 2-cyls. 12″ × 16″	
·3′	13·5′	4·9′			Vertical 2-cyls.	Withdrawn 5/11/65
·3′	13·5′	4·9′			Vertical 2-cyls. 8″ × 9″. 120 lb.	Withdrawn 28/9/64
·3′	13·5′	4·9′			Vertical 2-cyls. 8″ × 9″. 120 lb.	Withdrawn 22/1/66
·3′	13·5′	4·9′			Vertical 2-cyls.	
·3′	13·8′	4·9′		80 B.H.P.	D.A. Diesel engine, 4-cyls. 3 to 1 gearing	Speed 7·6 M.P.H.
·3′	13·8′	4·9′		80 B.H.P.	D.A. Diesel engine, 4-cyls. 3 to 1 gearing	Speed 7·6 M.P.H.
·3′	13·8′	4·9′		80 B.H.P.	D.A. Diesel engine, 4-cyls. 3 to 1 gearing	Speed 7·6 M.P.H.
·0′ ·4′ erall)	48·0′ 61·0′	5·8′ (5·0′ at (centre)			C. 2-cyls.	Converted to oil fuel and altered '62 From 1971 spare at Renfrew
0′	48·0′	5·8′	160		C. 2-cyls. 10″ & 16″ × 16″	2 vertical boilers by Cochrane & Co.

CLYDE NAVIGATION TRUST—(Contd.)—CLYDE PORT AUTHORITY

Dates Built Acqd. Displ.	Name	Type	Shipbuilders and Enginebuilders
1938 1938 1975	VEHICULAR FERRY-BOAT No: 4	Steel D.T.S.M.V.	Ferguson Bros. (Port Glasgow) Ltd. Davey Paxman & Co. (Colchester) Ltd., & G.E.C.
1951 1951 1981	FERRY No. 8 (II)	Steel D.S.M.V.	H. McLean & Sons, Ltd. Renfrew Gleniffer Engines, Ltd.
1952 1952 1984	RENFREW (II)	Steel D.C. D.sl. Elec.	Fleming & Ferguson, Ltd., Paisley

STRATHCLYDE REGIONAL COUNCIL

Dates Built Acqd. Displ.	Name	Type	Shipbuilders and Enginebuilders
1984 7/1984	RENFREW ROSE	Steel T.S.M.V.	McCrindle Shipbuilding Ltd., Ardrossan Kelvin Diesels
1984 7/1984	YOKER SWAN	Steel T.S.M.V.	McCrindle Shipbuilding Ltd., Ardrossan Kelvin Diesels

L.	B.	D.	G.T.	N.H.P.	Machinery	Remarks
2·4′	44·1′	10·5′		500 B.H.P.	4 S.A., 12-cyls. 9½″ × 12″, driving 160 k.W. generators	
7·3′	15·2′	4·5′	35	80 B.H.P.	4 S.A., 4-cyls. 6″ × 7″,	
2·0′	49·3′ (at centre)	5·8′		120 B.H.P.	4 S.C.S.A., 4-cyls. D.C. 3. 4 self-contained generator sets	Registered as RENFREW FERRY
12 n.	5·5 m.		65	180 B.H.P.		Renfrew Ferry
12 n.	5·5 m.		65	180 B.H.P.		Renfrew Ferry

WAVERLEY STEAM NAVIGATION CO., LTD.

Dates Built Acqd. Displ.	Name	Type	Shipbuilders and Enginebuilders
1947 1974	WAVERLEY	Steel P.S.	A. & J. Inglis, Ltd. Rankin & Blackmore, Ltd.

FIRTH OF CLYDE STEAM PACKET CO., LTD.

1951 11/1980 1981	SHANKLIN /PRINCE IVANHOE	Steel T.S.M.V.	Wm. Denny & Bros., Ltd. Wm. Denny (Sulzer)

HELSEAM LTD.

27/6/49 3/1985	BALMORAL	Steel T.S.M.V.	J. I. Thornycroft & Co., Ltd., Southampton

WESTERN FERRIES, LTD.
WESTERN FERRIES (ARGYLL) LTD.
WESTERN FERRIES (CLYDE) LTD.

27/2/68 1968 1981	SOUND OF ISLAY	Steel T.S.M.V.	Ferguson Bros. (Pt. Gls.), Ltd. Bergius Kelvin Co. Ltd.
1966 1/1969	SOUND OF GIGHA ex Isle of Gigha	Steel T.S.M.V.	— Bideford, N. Devon (1) Thorneycroft (2) A/B Scania, Vabis, Sodertal
18/4/69 1969 9/1976	SOUND OF JURA	Steel T.S.M.V.	Hatlo Werksted A/S, Ulsteinvik, Norway Lister Blackstone Marine, Ltd., Dursley
1962 12/1972	SOUND OF SHUNA ex Olandsund IV	Steel D.S.M.V.	A/B Asi Verken, Amal, Swede (1) Albin Motor, Kristinehamn (2) A/B Scania, Vabis, Soderta
1960 12/1972	SOUND OF SCARBA ex Olandsund III	Steel D.S.M.V.	A/B Asi Verken, Amal, Swede A/B Scania Vabis Sodertalje
1/1/38 3/1974	SOUND OF SANDA ex Lymington	Steel D.S.M.V.	Wm. Denny & Bros. Ltd. W. H. Allen, Sons & Co. Ltd., Bedford

* Interchangeable engines

.	B.	D.	G.T.	N.H.P.	Machinery	Remarks
·6′	30·3′	8·6′	693	2100 B.H.P.	T.D. 3-cyls. 24″, 39″ & 62″ × 66″	N.B. 1981
·0′	46·0′	10·5′	986	1900 B.H.P.	2 oil, 2S.A., each 8-cyls. 320 × 380 mm.	14 kn.
·2′	30·0′	11·1′	688		2 × 2 S.A. each 6-cyls. 320 × 425 mm.	
·1′	30·0′	7·5′	276 280	640 S.H.P.	2 × 4 S.A., each 8-cyls. 370 × 500 mm, (6½″ × 7¼″) S.R.Rev.G.	10¾ kn.
)5	5·88 m.	1·524 m.	65		(1) (2) As SOUND OF SCARBA*	From Eilean Sea Services, Ltd. Regd. Cambeltown
9′	36·1′	13·2′	558	2,000 B.H.P.	2 × 4 S.A., each 8-cyls. 8¼″ × 11¾″	Regd. Cambeltown 14 kn. Cont.-pitch props. Thw. fwd.
4′	29·5′	11·5′	244	600 B.H.P.	(1) 4 × 4 S.A., each 6-cyls. 120 × 145 mm. geared to three screw shafts (2) As S. OF SCARBA*	From R/A Olandsund, Kalmar, Sweden Dornoch Shipping Co. 2 Dir Props.
6	13·5 m.		175		(1) 4 × 4 S.A., each 6-cyls. (2) 127 × 135 mm.*	From R/A Olandsund, Kalmar, Sweden Dornoch Shipping Co. 2 Dir. Props.
0′	36·8′	5·7′	275	400 B.H.P.	2 × 4 S.A., each 6-cyls. 230 × 300 mm.	Cont. pitch props. one fwd., one aft.
2′	26·1′	8·0′				

WESTERN FERRIES LTD., etc.—(contd.)

Dates Built Acqd. Displ.	Name	Type	Shipbuilders and Enginebuilders
1976 1976 1985	HIGHLAND SEABIRD	Aluminium T.S.M.V. Catamaran	Westermoen Hydrofoils A/S, Mandal Mercedes M.T.U.
21/3/47 1982 3/1984	FARRINGFORD	Steel P.M.V.	Wm. Denny & Bros. Ltd. English Elec. Co., Ltd. Stamford
1959 1985	SOUND OF SEIL ex Freshwater	Steel D.S.M.V.	Ailsa S.B. Co., Ltd., Troon Crossley Bros., Ltd., Manchester
1961 7/1988	SOUND OF SLEAT ex De Hoorn	Steel D.S.M.V.	Shipyard "De Merwede", Holland Stork Werkspoor

L.	B.	D.	G.T.	N.H.P.	Machinery	Remarks
9·0' 5·0'	29·0'		202	2200		Cruising speed 27kn Owned from 7/10/1977
2·0'	28·1'	8·6'	489		4 S.A., 12-cyls. 10″ × 12″	Diesel electric. Regd. Glasgow 3/84.
5·0'	30·0'	10·0'	363	640 B.H.P.	2 × 2 S.A., each 8-cyls. 7″ × 9″	Cont. Pitch prop one fwd. one aft.
9·9' m.	15·3' m.	4·85' m.		1000 B.H.P.	2 × 4 S.A., each 8-cyls.	

APPENDIX II

FLEETS
(as at 31st December, 1989)

CALEDONIAN MACBRAYNE, LTD.
M.V. *Keppel*
D.S.M.V. *Kyleakin*
D.S.M.V. *Lochalsh*
T.S.M.V. *Iona*
T.S.M.V. *Kilbrannan*
T.S.M.V. *Morvern*
T.S.M.V. *Bruernish*
T.S.M.V. *Rhum*
T.S.M.V. *Coll*
D.S.M.V. *Jupiter*
D.S.M.V. *Juno*
T.S.M.V. *Pioneer*
T.S.M.V. *Suilven*
T.S.M.V. *Eigg*
T.S.M.V. *Canna*
T.S.M.V. *Raasay*
D.S.M.V. *Isle of Cumbrae*
D.S.M.V. *Saturn*
T.S.M.V. *Claymore*
T.S.M.V. *Lochmor*
T.S.M.V. *Isle of Arran*
T.S.M.V. *Hebridean Isles*
D.S.M.V. *Loch Striven*
D.S.M.V. *Loch Linnhe*
D.S.M.V. *Loch Riddon*
D.S.M.V. *Loch Ranza*
T.S.M.V. *Isle of Mull*
T.S.M.V. *Lord of the Isles*
Small ferryboats *Ulva* and *Dart Princess*

SEALINK BRITISH FERRIES—STRANRAER
T.S.M.V. *Darnia*
T.S.M.V. *Galloway Princess*
T.S.M.V. *St. David*

WESTERN FERRIES (CLYDE) LTD.
T.S.M.V. *Sound of Gigha*
D.S.M.V. *Sound of Shuna*
D.S.M.V. *Sound of Scarba*
D.S.M.V. *Sound of Sanda*
D.S.M.V. *Sound of Seil*
D.S.M.V. *Sound of Sleat*

WAVERLEY STEAM NAVIGATION CO., LTD. and ASSOCIATES.
    P.S. *Waverley*
    T.S.M.V. *Balmoral*

MAID OF THE LOCH LTD. (Loch Lomond)
    P.S. *Maid of the Loch* (laid up)
    T.S.M.V. *Countess Fiona*

DALRIADA STEAM PACKET CO., LTD. (Loch Awe)
    M.V. *Silver Heron*
    S.S. *Lady Rowena*

DONALD KENNEDY (Loch Etive)
    T.S.M.V. *Anne of Etive*

STRATHCLYDE REGIONAL COUNCIL (Loch Katrine)
    S.S. *Sir Walter Scott*

STRATHCLYDE REGIONAL COUNCIL (Renfrew Ferry)
    T.S.M.V. *Renfrew Rose*
    T.S.M.V. *Yoker Swan*

FORTH & CLYDE CANAL SOCIETY
    D.S.M.V. *Ferry Queen*

SCOTLAND IN VIEW
    M.V. *The Lady Margaret*

CLYDE MARINE MOTORING LTD.
    T.S.M.V. *The Second Snark*
    T.S.M.V. *Rover*
    T.S.M.V. *Kenilworth*
    M.V. *Sir William Wallace*
    M.V. *Robert the Bruce*
    and several other craft.

BIBLIOGRAPHY

About Clyde Steamers and Clyde Skippers, "Senex Afloat" (Gillespie Bros., Ltd., Glasgow, 1886).

An t-Aiseag an Iar (The Passage West), DOMHNALL E. MEEK (Clò-beag, Glasgow, 1977).

A Bed of Nails (History of P. MacCallum & Sons Ltd.), JOHN R. HUME and MICHAEL S. MOSS, (Lang & Fulton, Greenock, 1981).

British Paddle Steamers, GEOFFREY BODY (David & Charles, 1971).

British Pleasure Steamers, 1920-1939, GEOFFREY GRIMSHAW (Richard Tilling, 1945).

British Railways Shipping and Allied Fleets. W. PAUL CLEGG & JOHN S. STYRING (David & Charles, 1971).

British Railways Steamers of the Clyde, JOHN THOMAS (Ian Allan, Ltd., 1948).

Chamber of Commerce Papers, Parliamentary Returns.

Caledonian Princess, JOHN F. HENDY, (Published by the Author, 1981).

Caledonian Railway Centenary, Stephenson Locomotive Society

Caledonian Railway, O. S. NOCK (Ian Allan, Ltd., 1961).

Caledonian Steam Packet Company Ltd., The Sixtieth Anniversary of, Rev. WILLIAM C. GALBRAITH (Clyde River Steamer Club, 1949).

The Caledonian Steam Packet Company Ltd., IAIN C. MAC ARTHUR (Clyde River Steamer Club, 1972).

Campbeltown & Glasgow Steam Packet Joint Stock Company, Limited, Centenary History—(Campbeltown Courier, 1927).

Classic Scottish Paddle Stamers, A. J. S. PATERSON (David & Charles, Newton Abbot, 1982).

The Clyde, JOHN RIDDELL (The Fairlie Press, 1988).

The Clyde Passenger Steamer, 1812-1901, JAMES WILLIAMSON (James Maclehose & Sons, Glasgow, 1904: reprint by Mainmast Books, Saxmundham, 1988).

Clyde Piers, IAN McCRORIE and JOY MONTEITH (Inverclyde District Libraries, 1982).

Clyde Navigation, JOHN F. RIDDELL (John Donald, Edinburgh, 1979).

Clyde Pleasure Steamers, IAN McCRORIE (Orr, Pollock & Co., Ltd., Greenock, 1986).

315

Clyde River Steamer Club Souvenir Booklets.
  Paisley, 1966.
  Millport, 1974.
  Gareloch, 1972.
  75 Years of Clyde Turbine Steamers, 1976.
  Lochgoil Route, 1979.
Clyde Shipwrecks, PETER MOIR and IAN CRAWFORD (Moir Crawford, Wemyss Bay, 1988).
Clyde to the Hebrides, Sketches by the Way (Wilson & McCormick, Glasgow c.1855).
Clyde River Steamers of the Last Fifty Years, ANDREW MCQUEEN (Gowans & Gray, Glasgow 1923).
Clyde Steamers of Yesteryear, MACARTHUR, MCCRORIE and MACHAFFIE, (Motherwell, 1966).
The Clyde Steamers, DESMOND BANKS (The Albyn Press, Ltd., Edinburgh, 1947).
Clyde Steamers and Loch Lomond Fleets in and after 1936, PETER MILNE (Ian Allan, Ltd., 1955).
Clyde Steamers at a Glance, JOHN MARSHALL (The Albyn Press, 1948).
To the Coast—100 years of the Caledonian S.P. Co., IAN MCCRORIE (The Fairlie Press, 1989).
Colour on the Clyde, A. CAMERON SOMMERVILLE (Bute Newspapers Ltd., Rothesay).
Craigendoran Steamers, ALAN BROWN (Aggregate Publications, Johnstone, 1979).
The Craigendoran Story, GEORGE M. STROMIER (Clyde River Steamer Club, 1983)
Columba Centenary, (Clyde River Steamer Club 1978).
Cross Channel and Coastal Paddle Steamers, FRANK BURTT (Richard Tilling, 1934).
Days at the Coast, HUGH MACDONALD (Robert Lindsay, Glasgow, c. 1873).
Echoes of Old Clyde Paddle Wheels, ANDREW MCQUEEN (Gowans & Gray, 1924).
The Forth & Clyde Canal—a Kirkintilloch View, DON. MARTIN (Strathkelvin District Libraries and Museums, Bishopbriggs, 1985).
From the Clyde to the Hebrides—Sketches by the way, (Wilson & McCormick, Glasgow, c. 1880).
The Floating Post Offices of the Clyde, JAMES A. MACKAY (Dumfries, 1979).
The Forth and Clyde Canal, JOHN HUME , for travelling exhibition from the Collins Exhibition Hall, University of Strathclyde.

The Gipsy o' Kirky, A. I. BOWMAN (Strathkelvin District Libraries and Museums, Bishopbriggs, 1987).

Glasgow Harbour Report Book, (Strathclyde Regional Archives).

Glasgow & South-Western Railway, 1850-1923, Stephenson Locomotive Society, 1950.

Glen Sannox, IAN MCCRORIE (Caledonian MacBrayne Ltd., 1979).

Glen Sannox, 30 Years of, WALTER J. H. BOWIE and J. AIKMAN SMITH (Caledonian MacBrayne Ltd., 1987).

The Golden Years of the Clyde Steamers, ALAN J. S. PATERSON (David & Charles, 1969).

Half of Glasgow's Gone, MICHAEL DICK, (Brown, Son & Ferguson, Ltd., 1986).

Hebridean and Clyde Ferries, IAN MCCRORIE, (Caledonian MacBrayne Ltd., Gourock, 1985).

The Highlands and Islands, J. E. BOWMAN (Allan Sutton, Gloucester; Hippocrene Books Inc., New York).

History of Steam Navigation, JOHN KENNEDY (Chas. Birchall, Liverpool, 1906).

The History and Development of Machinery for Paddle Steamers, G. E. BARR (Paper No. 1,150 of the Institute of Engineers and Shipbuilders in Scotland, Glasgow, 1951).

History of Paddle-wheel Steam Navigation, HENRY SANDHAM (Institution of Mechanical Engineers Procedings, March, 1885).

Jeanie Deans, FRASER G. MACHAFFIE (Clyde River Steamer Club, 1977).

King Edward, Turbine S.S. Notes for International Conference of Naval Architects and Marine Engineers, 1951.

The Little Railways of South West Scotland, DAVID L. SMITH (David & Charles, 1969).

Lloyd's Register of British & Foreign Shipping.

Loch Lomond Steamboat Companies, DONALD MACLEOD (Bennett & Thomson, Dumbarton, 1888).

Lucy Ashton Diamond Jubilee, REV. WILLIAM C. GALBRAITH (Clyde River Steamer Club, 1948).

Lymington, Sound of Success, ALAN BROWN (Allan T. Condie Publications, Nuneaton, 1988).

Maid of the Loch, ROBERT CLEARY (Caledonian MacBrayne Ltd., Gourock, 1979).

Mercantile Navy List.

Paddle Steamers in Camera, ALAN T. CONDIE (Allan T. Condie Publications, Nuneaton, 1987).

Passenger Steamers of the River Fal, ALAN KITTRIDGE (Twelveheads Press, Truro).

Pleasure Steamers of Old Yorkshire, ARTHUR GODFREY (A. Godfrey, Filey, Yorks).

Queen Mary, RICHARD ORR, (Caledonian MacBrayne, Ltd., Gourock 1976).

Railway and Other Steamers, DUCKWORTH and LANGMUIR (T. Stephenson & Sons Ltd., 2nd Edition, 1968).

The Renfrew Ferry, J. WALLS and G. HAMILTON (Renfrew Historical Society, 1984)

River Ferries, NANCY MARTIN (Terence Dalton Ltd., Lavenham, Suffolk, 1980)

Rollo's Tour in Europe, JACOB ABBOT (Sheldon & Co., New York, 1864).

Rothesay Harbour, 1752–1975, IAN MACLAGAN, (Volume XIX of the Transactions of the Buteshire Natural History Society, Rothesay).

The Royal Route; Glasgow and the Highlands, D. MACBRAYNE 1879-1939; issued most years except the two war periods).

Ship Registers.

Ships of the Fleet, IAN MCCRORIE (Caledonian MacBrayne, Ltd., 1977).

The Short Sea Route, FRASER G. MACHAFFIE (T. Stephenson & Sons, Ltd., Prescot, 1975)

Sixty Years of the Lucy Ashton, WM. C. GALBRAITH (Clyde River Steamer Club, 1948).

The Native Steamboat Companion, QUENTIN DALRYMPLE (Edinburgh, 1845).

The North British Railway, C. HAMILTON ELLIS (Ian Allan Ltd., 1955).

Shanklin, Ill-fated Prince, ALAN BROWN (Waverley Excursions Ltd. 1985).

Song of the Clyde, FRED M. WALKER (Patrick Stephens Ltd., Cambridge, 1984).

South Coast Pleasure Steamers, E. C. B. THORNTON (T. Stephenson & Sons, Ltd.).

Southsea, 40th Anniversary, JOHN HENDY (Published by the Author, 1987).

The Steamboat Companion, (James Lumsden & Sons, Glasgow, 1820)

Steamers of the Clyde and Western Isles, MACARTHUR, MCCRORIE & MACHAFFIE, 1964 and 1965.

Steamers of the Clyde, GEORGE M. STROMIER and JOHN NICHOLSON (Scottish Field).

Steamers of the Forth, IAN BRODIE (David & Charles, Newton Abbot, 1976).

Steamers of the Highlands and Islands, IAN MCCRORIE (Orr, Pollock & Co., Ltd, Greenock, 1987).

Steamers of North Wales, F. C. THORNLEY (T. Stephenson & Sons Ltd., 1954).

Steamers of the Thames and Medway, FRANK BURTT (Richard Tilling, 1949).

Steamships of Europe, ALISTER DEAYTON (Conway Maritime Press, 1989).

A Summer in Scotland, JACOB ABBOT (New York, 1848 and 1854, and James McGlashan, Dublin, 1849).

Swifts & Queens, A. I. BOWMAN (Strathkelvin District Libraries & Museums, Bishopbriggs, 1984)

Thames Coast Pleasure Steamers, E. C. B. THORNTON (T. Stephenson & Sons, Prescot, 1968).

The Victorian Summer of the Clyde Steamers, ALAN J. S. PATERSON (David & Charles, 1972).

Talisman, Diesel Electric Paddle Boat, G. A. INGLIS, B.Sc. (Institution of Engineers & Shipbuilders, 1936).

Talisman, the Solitary Crusader, ALAN BROWN (Aggregate Publications, Johnstone, 1980).

Waverley, 5th Edition, FRASER G. MACHAFFIE (Waverley Excursions Ltd., Glasgow, 1986).

West Coast Steamers, 3rd Edition, DUCKWORTH & LANGMUIR (T. Stephenson & Sons, Ltd., 1966).

West Country Passenger Steamers, 2nd Edition, GRAHAME FARR (T. Stephenson & Sons, Ltd., 1967).

West Highland Steamers, 4th Edition, DUCKWORTH & LANGMUIR (Brown, Son & Ferguson Ltd., 1987)

Wotherspoon Collection "In the Track of the Comet", Mitchell Library, Glasgow.

PERIODICALS:—

The American Neptune
Bulletin
Buteman
The Caledonian Journal (Caledonian Railway Association)
Clyde River Steamer Club Magazine (Clyde Steamers) and Review
Cruising Monthly
Engineering
The Engineer
Fairplay
Greenock Telegraph
Glasgow Herald
Evening Times
Evening News
Evening Citizen
Chamber of Comerce Journal
Lloyd's List
Marine News

Mitchell's Steam Shipping Journal
Motor Ship
Nautical Magazine
North British Daily Mail
Oban Times
Paddle Wheels
Railway Magazine
Railway and Travel Monthly
Scotsman
Sea Breezes
The Shipbuilder
Shipbuilding and Shipping Record
Shipping World
Syren and Shipping
Ship Ahoy
Ships Illustrated
Ships Monthly
Transport History
West Highland Steamer Club Reviews and Newsletters

INDEX

328   CLYDE RIVER & OTHER STEAMERS